Big Hunger

Food, Health, and the Environment

Series Editor: Robert Gottlieb, Henry R. Luce Professor of Urban and Environmental Policy, Occidental College

Big Hunger

The Unholy Alliance between Corporate America
and Anti-Hunger Groups

Andrew Fisher
Foreword by Saru Jayaraman

The MIT Press
Cambridge, Massachusetts
London, England

This book was set in ITC Stone Sans Std and ITC Stone Serif Std by Toppan Best-set Premedia Limited. Printed and bound in the United States of America.

Library of Congress Cataloging-in-Publication Data

Names: Fisher, Andy, 1963- author.
Title: Big hunger : the unholy alliance between corporate America and anti-hunger groups / Andrew Fisher ; foreword by Saru Jayaraman.
Other titles: Food, health, and the environment.
Description: Cambridge, MA : The MIT Press, [2017] | Series: Food, health, and the environment | Includes bibliographical references and index.
Identifiers: LCCN 2016040544 | ISBN 9780262036085 (hardcover : alk. paper)
Subjects: | MESH: Nutrition Policy | Malnutrition--prevention & control | United States
Classification: LCC RA645.N87 | NLM QU 145.7 AA1 | DDC 362.1963/9--dc23
    LC record available at https://lccn.loc.gov/2016040544

10 9 8 7 6 5 4 3 2 1

For Orion, may you always have such a fierce sense of justice.
For Kassady, may your love for the natural world and its inhabitants lead your path.

Contents

Series Foreword

Big Hunger is the twelfth book in the Food, Health, and the Environment series. The series explores the global and local dimensions of food systems and the issues of access; social, environmental, and food justice; and community well-being. Books in the series focus on how and where food is grown, manufactured, distributed, sold, and consumed. They address questions of power and control, social movements and organizing strategies, and the health, environmental, social and economic factors embedded in food-system choices and outcomes. As this book demonstrates, the focus is not only on food security and well-being but also on economic, political, and cultural factors and regional, state, national, and international policy decisions. Food, Health, and the Environment books therefore provide a window into the public debates, alternative and existing discourses, and multidisciplinary perspectives that have made food systems and their connections to health and the environment critically important subjects of study and for social and policy change.

Robert Gottlieb, Occidental College
Series Editor (gottlieb@oxy.edu)

Foreword

This book could not be coming out at a more important moment in our history. We as a nation are facing the greatest income inequality since the Gilded Age. The lowest-wage sectors of our economy are the fastest growing, with incredibly dangerous portent for the viability of our gross domestic product. Where I live in the San Francisco Bay Area, and in metropolitan regions across the country, gentrification is both increasing housing costs and displacing thousands of working-class communities, and bringing their survival into question. And, as Andy Fisher points out, food insecurity remains a persistent facet of the economic landscape, as the rates of hunger were just dropping to pre-recession levels in 2015.

At the same time, social movement organizations working to raise the minimum wage, fight displacement, and generally curb income inequality are reaching a zenith. The Fight for $15 has spawned a wave of ambitious minimum wage increases nationwide, the likes of which have not been seen in decades. Alongside millions of workers, hundreds of "high road" employers have come out publicly in support of policies like raising the minimum wage. The possibilities for a true social movement to end hunger in the United States—one that addresses the root causes of hunger—are more visible and viable than they ever were.

Unfortunately, as Andy points out, the "hunger industrial complex" is not sufficiently focused on income inequality or any other analysis of the root causes of hunger. All too often it is focused on sustaining and growing itself as a sector, and in doing so it not only assumes that hunger is inevitable and even increasing, but it also *depends* on hunger remaining a fact of American society. So how can it call itself an "anti-hunger sector"? This is the national paradox Andy refers to—if the goal of an anti-hunger sector is to eliminate hunger—and not just manage it—then the sector should be willing to focus on putting itself out of business.

For me, as the leader of a social movement organization dedicated to improving wages and working conditions in the restaurant industry, the questions this book raises are incredibly vital. In my mind, the epitome of this national paradox is the restaurant industry, in which large and small restaurant corporations and franchise operators spend millions of dollars on "charity" for anti-hunger programs *while simultaneously paying the lowest wages of any sector in the United States, and sending millions of its employees to food banks to feed their families.* In my last two books I tell stories of restaurant workers working at an array of restaurants—fine dining, fast food, coffee shops—having to go to food banks to feed their families. All too ironically, many of these workers' employers are well-known nationally for their championship of the anti-hunger cause.

There certainly are exceptions to this rule. Several notable restaurant employers championing hunger do pay their workers well and support minimum wage increases. But it is notable that the chain restaurants contribute in great volumes—and with great fanfare—to food banks and anti-hunger organizations, and at the same time spend millions to lobby against minimum wage increases for the very same population of people using food banks. At one point I shared information about an Applebee's franchisor in Texas whose daughter raised a great deal of money for a charity she set up for her father's employees while her father continued to pay his workers a minimum of $2.13 an hour, the subminimum wage for tipped workers. I do not blame the franchisor alone—$2.13 is all that Applebee's corporation requires franchisors to pay, and in fact, Applebee's lobbies with vitriol, on its own and through the National Restaurant Association, against any kind of minimum wage increase. *Why not demand that these multimillion dollar corporations simply pay their workers more?* We certainly would save millions in overhead for anti-hunger organizations that raise money from restaurant corporations that should be paying their own workers a livable wage.

This book raises fundamental questions about the assumptions undergirding the current focus of the anti-hunger sector, with implications for the viability of our democracy and our economy. First, an anti-hunger sector that is focused on raising funds from corporations and the American public to sustain and grow itself *assumes that poverty is a necessary, ever-present, even growing evil.* The very idea that hunger can be solved by simply increasing the flow of charitable food assumes that there will always be a substantial population of people who cannot be self-sufficient. History tells us this is not true—in any number of other nations and even in other moments in history in America, people have not suffered the levels of income inequality and lack of self-sufficiency that a growing number of Americans face. Further, if we presume that there will be persistent and growing poverty, what does that say about the long-term viability of our residents' ability to consume and support the economy—or even to support the very corporations willing to provide charity, but unwilling to raise their workers' wages?

Second, an "anti-hunger" sector that believes that the best way to address hunger is by "feeding the need" assumes that a growing underclass of people cannot or perhaps need not be self-sufficient. It assumes that there must be an underclass that is dependent on the largesse of their superiors, rather than being able to earn enough money from working full-time to support their families. It is important to note that an increasing number of clients of food banks and food pantries are working people, often with multiple jobs. They clearly seek self-sufficiency, and a solution that focuses on increasing charity rather than increasing income denies them the ability to be so.

Third, and perhaps most disturbing, the notion that hunger will be solved by charities receiving funds from large corporations that simultaneously lobby to keep minimum wages as low as possible fundamentally removes all accountability and responsibility from these corporations to actually pay their employees livable wages that allow them to support their families. The notion that these corporations are to be lauded for providing funds for charities that serve much of the same population they employ promotes the idea that these corporations are supporting charities with largesse, on a whim, and removes all public accountability for their role in the economy.

On the other hand, there are some shining examples in the anti-hunger movement that do as Andy suggests, and partner with groups like mine and others fighting for higher wages and better working conditions for low-income people. If more agencies within the anti-hunger sector were to follow suit, the results could be truly transformational. The possibilities are dazzling. An anti-hunger sector that worked collaboratively with labor on raising wages could effectively reduce the number of clients on its rolls and reduce the need for greater funding. Instead, these organizations could harness their power, stature, and resources to support movements for change that would both increase their clients' self-sufficiency and provide food and other necessities needed to live until support was no longer needed. They could look at broader systemic issues faced by their clients, including housing and transportation, and partner with organizations working on these issues to move policy that addressed their clients' needs. By partnering with these and many other types of organizations, the "anti-hunger sector" would be more effectively able to call itself an "anti-hunger movement."

Saru Jayaraman
Director, Food Labor Research Center, University of California, Berkeley
Co-Founder, Restaurant Opportunities Centers United

Acknowledgments

This book draws from the writings of Janet Poppendieck, Mark Winne, Graham Riches, and Nick Saul. Sharon Thornberry played a key role as a sounding board throughout the project. In particular, pertaining to the beginning of the research process, I owe a debt of gratitude to Ellen Parker for her generosity, wisdom, and insights. Mark Winne was, as he has always been, extraordinarily thoughtful and supportive, and he helped me to think through the structure and purpose of the book. Wayne Roberts, in his affable Canadian way, was able to provide insights into the American political system, which few of us Americans possess.

Robert Gottlieb was instrumental in making this book happen. As the editor for MIT Press's Food, Health, and the Environment series, he was key in gaining the press's approval to publish this volume from a first-time author. He reviewed and commented on the book, chapter by chapter, and provided countless instances of advice and encouragement when I got stuck or frustrated. Bob has been a steady friend and mentor over the course of some 25 years as well.

Numerous persons reviewed sections or chapters, providing invaluable feedback. These individuals include Katherine Alaimo, Anne Barnhill, Andrew Kang Bartlett, Mariana Chilton, Alison Cohen, Monica Cuneo, Robert Egger, Mara Einstein, Kate Fitzgerald, Thomas Forster, Kim Hanson, Janie Hipp, Betty Izumi, Becca Jablonski, Sonya Jones, Marion Kalb, Joann Lo, George Manalo Le Clair, Kevin Morgan, Robert Ojeda, Ellen Parker, Janet Poppendieck, Jess Powers, Wayne Roberts, Nick Saul, Kathryn Scharf, Frank Tamborello, Julia Tedesco, Sharon Thornberry, and Mark Winne.

Scott Richardson was instrumental in helping me find information and understand the arcane world of USDA Foods. Jerry Hagstrom was kind enough to grant me an extra-long free trial period of his inside-the-Beltway, food and agriculture–oriented Hagstrom Report. Daniel Bowman Simon provided me with countless articles and tidbits of information. Numerous others shared articles and pointed me toward individuals to interview.

Saru Jayaraman was kind enough to take the time to write a compelling foreword.

I was the beneficiary of the generosity of more than a hundred friends, colleagues, and neighbors who supported me through a crowdfunding campaign. Their generosity not only helped make the book a reality, but also made me feel accountable to them to continue the research and writing when my focus on the project wandered. Thanks in particular to Margie Roswell, Gus Schumacher, the late Tom Ferraro, Nancy and Barney Straus, and Chris Schwier.

This book truly would not have happened without Luci's moral, financial, and emotional support, which allowed me to pursue my dream. Her encouragement and advice were instrumental to the completion of this book.

And thank you to all the folks at MIT Press who labored to get this book to press, including Beth Clevenger, Marcy Ross, Anthony Zennino, Susan Mai, Susan Clark, Miranda Martin, and Mary Bagg. Their contributions helped to make *Big Hunger* a much more powerful, well-written, well-distributed, and impactful document.

If I missed anyone, I apologize for the oversight. Your omission does not diminish your valued contribution.

Introduction: Lost Opportunities and Collateral Damage

Rust Is Not an Emergency

In 1958 Youngstown, Ohio was a thriving city, its vibrant economy fueled by steel. Located halfway between Chicago and New York City—and between Cleveland and Pittsburgh as well—it occupied a central place in America's industrial heartland. Youngstown's population hit its apex of 167,000 residents by the late 1950s, and at that time became the fourth-largest steel-producing region in the United States.[1]

The demand for steel with its multiple uses—for the country's 19th-century westward expansion, for World War I, and for the burgeoning auto industry as well—had contributed heavily to America's prosperity, and Youngstown's in particular. The city had survived the Great Depression better than most. A magazine promotion in 1931 described Youngstown as the "City of Homes," fifth in the nation in home ownership.[2] The union members employed in the area's steel mills, and later on in the nation's largest auto assembly plant at nearby Lordstown, continued to enjoy the trappings of middle-class life.

In 1958 my parents and three siblings moved from New York to Youngstown. Five years later I came along, and when I was five years old, the city suffered devastating civil disturbances, like so many other urban locales around the country, protesting the racism and unequal conditions that plagued the African American community. By the end of the 1960s, the city's population had declined 16 percent to 140,000, as the white population fled to the suburbs.

Youngstown had its challenges in the 1960s and 1970s, including a high degree of racial segregation. Growing up in this period I experienced Youngstown, if not as a culturally progressive community, at least as a modestly prosperous one. Downtown bustled with people shopping at department stores or working in the five-story office buildings. The public golf course, where I spent my summers playing barefoot and shirtless, hummed with steel and autoworkers on their days off, or those who worked the night shifts.

Black Monday interrupted Youngstown's prosperity in 1977, when Youngstown Sheet and Tube closed its local plant after having been bought out by a larger firm. By 1980, the bottom fell out, as U.S. Steel, Republic Steel, and other mills closed up their ancient, inefficient plants after struggling to compete with Japan's modern mills and lower labor costs. The steel giants had chosen not to invest in modernizing the Youngstown-based mills, and the workers suffered as a result. Youngstown reportedly lost 40,000 manufacturing jobs, 400 satellite businesses, and from one-third to three-quarters of school tax revenues during this period.[3] Unemployment soared and stayed unusually high for more than a decade.

This scene was replicated across the region, in places like Detroit, Cleveland, Dayton, Gary, and Flint, where Michael Moore chronicled the decline of his hometown in *Roger and Me*. Sixty-five miles southeast of Youngstown, in Pittsburgh, Pennsylvania, the United Steelworkers (USW) locals worked closely with the Hunger Action Coalition to create a rapidly growing network of food pantries to support the newly struggling unemployed steelworkers (and others whose businesses were affected by the loss of income in the region). These local economic collapses, combined with the devastating recession of the early 1980s and Reagan-era rollbacks in human services, gave birth to the "emergency food system."[4] The emergency in this case referred not to a natural disaster but to the ravages resulting from changes in economic and political policies that moved the country toward austerity and globalization. As the 1980s rolled on, the Hunger Action Coalition became closely aligned with labor unions and saw itself as part of a broader progressive movement.[5]

I went off to college in 1981, coming back to northeast Ohio only for vacation. My mom had moved to the suburbs of Cleveland after remarrying, but my brother had returned to Youngstown in the mid-1980s to practice medicine. Every year for the next two decades or so, I would visit my hometown and watch it become a shell of what it once was. The local shopping plaza first lost its department store, then its movie theater, then its supermarket, bank, and even its discount stores. In their place now sits a Walmart Supercenter.

Today Youngstown seems to top all the negative indices. Some have called it the most vanishing city in America. The Brookings Institute noted that it has the most concentrated poverty in the United States, with almost 50 percent of its population in poverty in 2011.[6] MSN ranked Youngstown as the most miserable metropolitan area in 2013, due to its income levels, violent crime rates, poor rates of educational attainment, high unemployment, and population shrinkage.[7] By 2014 the population had declined to 65,000, a 60 percent drop in a bit more than 50 years.[8] Entire neighborhoods were boarded up, as the city shrunk to a fraction of what it once was. Even the private prison that created some 400 jobs lost its federal contract and laid off half of its staff in 2015.[9]

Not coincidentally, the decline of Youngstown since the early 1980s has been paralleled by the institutionalization of the emergency food sector—the vast array of food banks, pantries, and soup kitchens in the United States that now serve 46 million people each year. What was once a response to an emergency caused by a crisis of capitalism is now a national institution, existing far beyond its original temporary intentions.

From one perspective, the 200 plus food banks and the approximately 60,000 food pantries and soup kitchens that distribute $5 billion worth of food every year in virtually every corner of America are a tribute to the astonishing ingenuity and dedication of the American spirit. Food charity has become one of the largest focal points of civil society in America, embedded in churches, schools, and volunteer associations, with tens of millions of donors and volunteers. Charitable food receives a billion dollars or more in government support through tax credits to donors, cash, and USDA commodities. Companies large and small donate billions of dollars' worth of food and cash to the effort as well, while encouraging their employees to volunteer by packing boxes and sorting food.

Tens of thousands of Youngstown area residents remain dependent on the charity of the emergency food system that was geared to benefit their parents and grandparents. The Second Harvest Food Bank of the Mahoning Valley (serving a three-county area around Youngstown) boasts that it served 7,916,667 meals in 2014.[10] It can be argued that the emergency food system and the food stamp program, now known as the Supplemental Nutrition Assistance Program (SNAP),[11] are both doing their jobs in helping reduce poverty and hunger in depressed communities such as Youngstown.

On the other hand, the continued expansion of the charitable food system marks a national paradox. The emergency that launched this effort has long passed. In its place has come a period of long decline with a new reality of shrinking cities, budgets, and entrenched poverty. The industrial heartland comprising Youngstown, Gary, Flint, Toledo, and similar cities is now known as the "Rust Belt."[12] But rust is not an emergency. Rust does not happen in one day, but over a long period of time.

Reversing rust requires different strategies, ones that bring living-wage jobs back to the region. Food charity was once an admirable stopgap for a man-made economic disaster, but has since become little more than a Band-Aid on a gaping wound. Yet anti-hunger groups continue to dedicate enormous amounts of resources to protecting and expanding food charity in isolation from necessary longer-term approaches. Not only does this compartmentalization fail to address hunger's root causes, it limits our collective sense of what social change is possible. It shortchanges the longer-term upstream solutions, diverting public attention and resources from them. By not coupling short-term hunger relief with structural reform, anti-hunger leaders have reinforced the false notion that hunger can be solved through charity, while diminishing our collective ability to make the deeper reforms. But anti-hunger advocates are not alone in this decoupling of human services from social change. Their narrow emphasis has followed the broad nonprofit trends of specialization and professionalization over the past few decades.

Nevertheless, the laser focus of anti-hunger advocates has had its benefits. By concentrating their efforts on those issues where they enjoy the greatest power and expertise, anti-hunger leaders have by some measures been extraordinarily effective. For example, federal food programs have remained intact against the onslaught of small government ideology, whereas other programs targeted for the poor have been eliminated or slashed (such as welfare).

Overall, however, the disconnect between upstream and downstream approaches has resulted in lost opportunities and collateral damage. For instance, the reluctance of anti-hunger advocates to publicly address long-term solutions has made it seem like they believe charity and public benefit programs to be the primary answer to food insecurity. As a result, significant parts of the public have come to believe that the answer to hunger is increased dependence on government nutrition programs and charity. This in turn reinforces the stigma that the poor face as being reliant on public or private handouts. Precious resources, public awareness, and political action will have been diverted to programs that by definition cannot solve the underlying problems. These programs place the emphasis to solve the hunger problem on the voluntary efforts of the private sector and non-profits, and on the narrow role of the government to fund food assistance programs. Advocates have failed to hold the business community accountable for its anti-worker practices, such as offshoring jobs, cutting benefits, and resisting minimum wage increases.

This strategy may have been a blind spot in the vision of anti-hunger leaders, or simply a tactical division of labor. Or both. The fact is that the anti-hunger sector has done little to support the return of well-paying manufacturing jobs to Youngstown and similar cities, or to fight against legislation that reduced the power of labor unions, such as right-to-work statutes. Few if any anti-hunger leaders marched in Seattle against the World Trade Organization in 1999, or fought against free trade agreements, such as NAFTA or the Trans Pacific Partnership in 2015. As will be seen later in chapter 6, only a small fraction of anti-hunger groups even actively supported increases in the minimum wage.

Working toward Community Food Security

In 1990, I moved to a place that couldn't be more different than Youngstown: Los Angeles. I came to pursue Latin American studies and later Urban Planning at UCLA. In the wake of the 1992 civil disturbances after the acquittal of the police officers that beat Rodney King, five fellow graduate students and I, under the tutelage of Professor Robert Gottlieb, decided to examine why the food system seemed broken in South Central Los Angeles, and how it could be a force for community development. Our report, perhaps the first-ever community food assessment, was completed as a pro bono consulting project for the Southern California Interfaith Hunger Coalition (IHC), the leading anti-hunger group in Los Angeles at the time.

Back in the late 1970s, IHC had launched the first farmers markets in Los Angeles as a means to increase access to healthy food in low-income neighborhoods while supporting small farmers. In the 1980s, IHC had dropped this path to focus on protecting nutrition programs in the wake of Reagan-era cutbacks. But by 1993, IHC's associate director Carolyn Olney embraced a new vision for her organization, one that was grounded in urban ecology, health, and connections with family farming. She turned out to be ahead of her time.

A few years later, UCLA's Gottlieb, the Hartford Food System director Mark Winne, and myself launched a national coalition to unite the anti-hunger sector with others in agriculture, gardening and community development. We called it the Community Food Security Coalition (CFSC). At its heart was the new concept of "community food security." This loosely defined idea helped both the small farm sector and urban consumers, especially in low-income communities, recognize that the mainstream food system marginalized their interests alike. Community food security provided a framework for connecting these disparate elements politically and programmatically. It was an idea that played a pivotal role in building today's food movement.

CFSC was embraced by the leading edge of the anti-hunger movement, as a few dozen food banks and advocacy organizations became members over the years. Over time, support for community food security would gain a toehold if not a foothold in the anti-hunger arena. Yet, at the same time, the field was narrowing its agenda and goals in the face of policymakers and portions of the electorate who were increasingly hostile to government social programs. As the bipartisan consensus around reducing hunger, framed by the partnership between Senators George McGovern (D-SD) and Robert Dole (R-KS), began to dissolve the anti-hunger field retrenched. For its part, the anti-hunger lobby and its network, seeing the challenge to federal food programs, refocused their energies on protecting them at all costs.

In doing so, the anti-hunger movement was defining a narrow role for the government (its redistributive function), while largely ignoring the government's role in setting the terms of how the marketplace worked (the types of jobs available, how much they paid, and of how workers could organize to protect their interests). It was ignoring the lessons from Youngstown's decline.

The anti-hunger sector was also slow to take into account the changing nature of hunger in America, in which individuals employed in low paying and/or part time jobs were increasingly populating the food stamp rolls and relying on food pantries to make ends meet. Stagnant wages, the decline of employees represented by labor unions, and the growing predominance of service sector jobs have been key factors in this trend.

Instead, the anti-hunger movement chose to build an alliance with corporate America. The business community provided the movement with money, political capital, and food donations in exchange for positive publicity and a de facto (although at times explicit) commitment not to oppose corporate interests. Hunger became a cause célèbre for numerous corporations, and anti-hunger advocates embraced that partnership under the guise of hunger's universal immorality: "we're all in this together."

In both allying themselves with corporate America and not pursuing labor-related issues, anti-hunger advocates tacitly exonerated businesses from their role in fostering income inequality and, in various cases, of engaging in practices that perpetuated hunger among their own workers or subcontractors. One effect of this alliance has been to obfuscate the role of Big Business in causing food insecurity and, in the case of the SNAP program, reinforcing its role in generating wealth for the food industry.

To give credit where credit is due, this alliance has ameliorated hunger through contributing to the political survival of the SNAP program during various Farm Bill cycles and by enabling the emergency food system to reach many more people in need with more food. Yet, the anti-hunger sector's overarching strategy has not been successful in reducing food insecurity, much less income inequality over the past 20 years.

Since 1995, when the federal government began to keep statistics, food insecurity has remained largely unchanged from 12 percent in 1995 to 12.7 percent of the population in 2015. Similarly, it has not eased the depth of food insecurity, with 4 percent of the people experiencing very low food security in 1995 and 5 percent in 2015 (see appendix 2).[13] While the rise and fall of these rates are linked to economic cycles, it remains striking nonetheless that there has been no overall downward movement in these indicators over the past 20 years. These stagnating indicators can be compared to progress in reducing hunger globally during roughly the same timeframe. The United Nations reports that the percentage of undernourished people in lesser-developed nations fell by almost half from 23 percent in 1990–1992 to 13 percent in 2014–2016.[14]

The logical response is to ask what can be done differently, to seek out innovation and change. The world around the anti-hunger community is changing and it must evolve as well. The bipartisan consensus around federal nutrition programs in Congress has largely evaporated. Reducing economic inequality has become an imperative, backed by such powerful figures as the Democratic presidential primary candidate Bernie Sanders, President Barack Obama, and Pope Francis. The links between obesity, diabetes, and food insecurity require a new coordinated approach that connects dietary behavioral change with income boosts. The food movement is demanding and gaining substantive changes to the way our food is produced, processed, and sold based on sustainability concerns, including climate change. The labor movement is experiencing a small but important renaissance in efforts to increase the minimum wage to more livable levels.

Much of the anti-hunger community has embraced change in the form of adding health and sustainability concerns to their portfolios. For example, food banks are increasingly offering more produce, and at times paying local farms to grow it for them. Many groups have embraced incentives that allow SNAP users to double their money when buying fruits and vegetables at farmers markets. However, going upstream to address the root causes of hunger, to join forces with the progressive community in reforming the economic and social structures that have led to poverty and food insecurity continues to prove challenging, especially for emergency food groups. Some, such as Hunger Action Network of New York State and Illinois Hunger Coalition, have been able to make that leap. Most have not.

Those who do not, whose solutions only address the symptoms of the problem and not the problem itself are kicking the can down the road. They are fostering the institutionalization of the problem. This business-as-usual approach speaks of an anti-hunger industrial complex, in which anti-hunger work has become big business, and big business profits from anti-hunger efforts. It is not unlike President Eisenhower's farewell address of 1961 in which he warned of the military industrial complex, as entrenched economic interests linked to the government were threatening progress toward peace.[15]

Chapter Summaries

This book is an indictment of the business-as-usual practices endemic in the anti-hunger industrial complex. It draws upon my 20-plus years of experience in the field as a researcher, policy advocate, coalition builder, executive director, organizer, and thought leader. It incorporates interviews from hundreds of anti-hunger, public health, food movement, and economic development leaders, and draws as well from my careful analysis of hundreds of printed and electronic materials, journal articles, books, and reports.

Big Hunger: The Unholy Alliance between Corporate America and Anti-Hunger Groups is not a book about hunger and its impacts on individuals and communities. Much has been written on that subject. It is instead an analysis of the actions and communications of groups and individuals involved in the anti-hunger field, of how our American society organizes to define and address a wicked social problem.[16]

As I critique the way our country addresses hunger in this book, I attempt to point out efforts in a new direction. There is an urgent need to redefine the anti-hunger field away from business as usual, to take it back, or, using the lexicon of the popular protests, to *occupy* it. I strive to lay out a vision for what anti-hunger work could be, based on the examples of cutting-edge initiatives in the United States and abroad. I also include numerous recommendations, both long and short-term that can help steer us in the right direction.

Specifically, *Big Hunger* comprises this introduction, eight main chapters, and a ninth as a conclusion. The first part of the book lays out the problems with the private sector response to the hunger problem. Chapter 1, "Occupy Hunger," explores the meaning of the social construct "hunger," in the United States. It examines the strengths and weaknesses of hunger as a problem statement, asking who benefits from the usage of this highly emotional yet imprecise term. It also considers alternative frameworks, such as food security and the right to food.

Chapter 2, "The Charity Trap," delves into the history and structure of the emergency food system to understand its scope, strengths, and numerous weaknesses. The chapter explains the collateral damage food charity causes to individuals and society, while seeking to shed light on the rationale behind its continued expansion. It closes with a vision for reforming food charity.

The amount of money that corporations give to anti-hunger causes, and for what reasons, is the focus of chapter 3, "The Politics of Corporate Giving." It examines the rationales behind these gifts, as well as the implications that such philanthropy imposes on the hunger movement and low-income individuals. It discusses in particular the concept of cause marketing and Walmart's $2 billion commitment to anti-hunger efforts.

The next part of the book lays out a vision for the anti-hunger field, grounded in public health, economic democracy and economic justice. Chapter 4, "SNAP's Identity Crisis," delves into the conflict around excluding sugar-sweetened beverages from the SNAP programs. It explains the nutritional science behind that proposition, as well the anti-hunger community's adamant opposition to changes in the SNAP eligibility list. It puts forth recommendations in which SNAP recipients can maintain a degree of consumer choice while enhancing the nutritional purpose of the program.

Chapter 5, "Economic Democracy through Federal Food Programs," poses a simple question with complex answers: What if the $100 billion in federal food program expenditures were directed to support not just Big Food and Big Ag companies, but a more democratic array of producers, retailers, and processors? How could this huge sum of money be used to catalyze a more economically democratic food system? The chapter offers examples from the SNAP program, school meals, and USDA commodity purchases to show possible directions in each area toward this goal.

The question of why anti-hunger advocates have focused almost exclusively on building federal food programs while giving short shrift to supporting increases in the minimum wage is the focus of chapter 6, "Who's at the Table Shapes What's on the Agenda." It links this choice to the lack of the participation of the poor in the decision-making structures of anti-hunger groups and closes with very specific recommendations on how the anti-hunger field could better focus on economic justice and enhance grassroots leadership.

In the final part, chapters 7 ("Innovation within the Anti-Hunger Movement") and 8 ("Innovative Models from Outside the Anti-Hunger Field") provide case studies of organizations and initiatives that can serve as inspiration for the rest of the field. The conclusion of *Big Hunger* describes the elements of a new vision for anti-hunger work and provides a series of overarching recommendations for how that vision can be accomplished in the short, medium, and long term.

1 Occupy Hunger

Walk for Hunger

Boston's spring rains finally gave way to sunny skies and mild temperatures on Sunday May 5, 2013, for the Walk for Hunger, Project Bread's 45th annual fundraising event. Starting at the Boston Common, the nation's oldest park, approximately 30,000 persons participated that day. Such a turnout, in that particular year, was a testament to the Walk for Hunger as a Boston "institution": the ubiquitous "Boston Strong" stickers and t-shirts were the only things reminding the walkers that less than three weeks had passed since the Boston Marathon bombing, in which 3 persons were killed and 264 persons injured.[1]

Launched in 1969, the Walk for Hunger has evolved into a Boston institution. Some 30,000 to 40,000 walkers participate every year, raising three to four million dollars from half a million individual pledges.[2] In a town known for its parochialism and racial divisions, the Walk is universally beloved. Multigenerational and multiracial, the Walk features teams of participants coming from schools, workplaces, and clubs across the metropolitan area. Project Bread's executive director Ellen Parker asserts that she has never met anyone from Boston who does not know about the Walk.[3]

The Walk is as much about the community of participants as it is the greater cause of hunger. It's about such people as Monica, an African American woman in her 30s who is employed by Bain Capital, and has raised over $10,000 for Project Bread. She participates because the walk makes her feel like she is part of something bigger.

The Walk is about a senior citizen from a South Boston working-class neighborhood with a handwritten sign pinned to the back of her green track suit celebrating that this is her 40th walk. It's about the young African American man who cheered her on with a high five for her commitment to the cause. It's about a 78-year-old Quaker woman, who declares with a patrician accent that this, her tenth walk, will likely be her last because of her deteriorating physical condition. She appreciates Project Bread's focus on sustainable food systems.

The indisputable rock star of the walkers is Gabriel, a Colombian-born bartender at a local men's club. A sprite of a man with a thin well-trimmed gray beard, Gabriel has, over the years, raised more than $450,000 for Project Bread. His secret: a few months before the Walk he stops shaving; when his wealthy clients see the stubble emerge on his face, they know to add a sizable donation to their tab.

Project Bread staff emphasize that the Walk is an exercise in democracy. Project Bread does not collect a registration fee or impose a fundraising requirement to participate. The public has assumed ownership of the Walk. Some people will take it upon themselves to cover the route the prior weekend if they're going to be out of town the weekend of the Walk. Every year, a handful of folks complete the route backward because they believe that the event should be called a walk *against* hunger, not a walk *for* hunger. One staff member hypothesizes that if Project Bread didn't organize the Walk, it would still happen spontaneously, albeit less safely.

The Walk for Hunger serves as a testament to the power of the social problem of hunger to mobilize and engage persons from wide-ranging walks of life. People care about hunger like they do about few other social issues. Janet Poppendieck, a sociology professor at Hunter College in New York City and a leading scholar on hunger writes, "As a social problem, hunger in America has demonstrated an unusual capacity to command public attention and concern. It has shown an ability to mobilize substantial resources of money, prestige, volunteer time, skilled advocacy, and public policy."[4] And when it appears that the government wants to sweep the existence of hunger under the rug, the public reacts strongly.

Hunger Becomes Food Insecurity

In November 2006, the MSNBC television personality Keith Olbermann dubbed a USDA Economic Research Service employee, Mark Nord, the "worst person in the world," a dubious award that Olbermann bestows on a daily basis, although not usually on a bureaucrat.[5] Mr. Nord's crime was to lead the effort to change the terminology used by the Department of Agriculture to measure food deprivation, eliminating "hunger" from the official lexicon and replacing it with "very low food security." This move unleashed a firestorm within the media and advocacy groups. Lisa Stark reported for ABC News that "only in Washington could there be a debate about the meaning of the word 'hunger.'"[6] Jim Weill, the executive director of the Food Research and Action Center, the primary lobbying group for federal food programs, affirmed that this change in the lexicon didn't affect reality: "We have got 35 million people according to this report who, no matter what name you put on it, are facing a daily struggle against hunger."[7]

These critics inferred that the conservative Bush administration wanted to minimize the scope of the hunger problem by changing the terminology. Deborah Leff of the Public Welfare Foundation, a left-leaning, DC-based funder, acknowledged the power of "hunger" to mobilize the public, saying: "When they hear 'very low food security' it sounds like bureaucratic jargon. It doesn't sound like people who can't get enough to eat."[8] The social scientist David Himmelgreen agreed, noting that the removal of "hunger" from the national dialogue would likely lead to less political support for developing programs that meet low-income Americans' food needs.[9] Years later, because of this episode, Susannah Morgan, the executive director of the Oregon Food Bank still thinks of "food security" as a "government weasel word."[10]

In large measure, the problem with the term "food security," according to many anti-hunger advocates, is that it fails to convey the universally emotive power of "hunger." Food security does not capture the sense of social isolation or marginalization that hunger implies. Sharon Thornberry of the Oregon Food Bank has passionately declared, "Hunger is violent. You feel violated when you're hungry and your kids are hungry."[11] The term "food security," while scientifically more precise than "hunger," remains a cold-blooded phrase lacking soul and spirit for a problem that hits the core of our humanity.

Advocates and scientists generally agree that the concept of "food insecurity" more accurately describes the context of food deprivation in the American context.[12] It is a condition characterized by such experiences as missing occasional meals, relying on inexpensive filling foods, reducing the quantity of foods consumed, and feeling anxious about future meals.

The USDA has, in conjunction with the Census Bureau, used a food security questionnaire to interview thousands of households annually since 1995.[13]

Food security came into favor not just because it was perceived as being more accurate, but also because it was easier to assess. Scientists found over the course of the 1980s and 1990s that "measuring the extent of hunger is exceedingly difficult. No easily defined line of causality exists between hunger, biochemical indices of malnutrition, poor health, and disease. Chronic hunger over a substantial time period may lead to undernutrition and disease, but the health effects of episodic hunger remain uncertain."[14] Similarly, researchers discovered that economic proxies such as poverty and unemployment were imprecise measurements.[15] A special committee of the National Academy of Sciences recommended eliminating usage of the term "hunger" in official measurements in favor of "food insecurity" because the behavioral changes marked by food insecurity were preferable as a framework for understanding food deprivation.[16] The subsequent media firestorm unleashed by this change in language not only highlighted the tension between science and politics in such a delicate matter, but it also served as an indictment of mistrust in the Bush administration's stance on domestic hunger as well as a marker of the public's commitment to hunger (at least among certain sectors of the public).

Public Commitment to Anti-Hunger Efforts

These examples shine a light on the public's extraordinary commitment to addressing domestic hunger. This dedication stretches into virtually every American household, as 79 percent of Americans, according to one poll, have contributed to the "fight against hunger."[17] The public's participation in food drives and anti-hunger fundraising initiatives seems almost universal. So many Americans care about hunger that it is one of the few issues that unite us across the ideological spectrum. Nonetheless, the vitriolic comments left in online articles have made clear that there exists a small but vocal undercurrent of opinion in today's America that sees hunger as a natural—even desirable—consequence among the poor. Whether the tone of the national debate on this topic is becoming more mean-spirited, or these beliefs have always been present among a subset of the population but are just becoming more evident through the Internet, remains unknown.

There are Americans, citizens and politicians alike, who begrudge others they deem lazy or immoral the comforts and trappings of middle-class life; they label these allegedly shiftless souls the undeserving poor, for their unworthiness of assistance. But it is quite rare to hear in today's America— even among those most sold on the Horatio Alger mythology of pulling oneself up by the bootstraps—that someone deserves to be hungry. Because food is so basic to life, to assert such a position is tantamount to challenging that person's right to life. As a civilized nation, Americans generally do not embrace a social Darwinist philosophy that restricts survival only to the "fittest." A Malthusian approach has thankfully not reached our shores such that we see starvation as a way of culling the weak. American civilization, through an implicit social contract, holds all human life to be intrinsically worthy, and grants even those whose lifestyles, values, and behaviors we condemn (with the exception of those executed for heinous crimes) the right to a healthy and productive life. Freedom from hunger remains enshrined in the Declaration of Independence as intrinsic to the "pursuit of life, liberty, and the pursuit of happiness."

In addition, our nation's material abundance amplifies the moral repugnance of food deprivation. Hunger is simply unnecessary in the United States in the early 21st century. Our society has evolved to the point at which we can expect to have everyone's most basic needs met. When some people's needs remain unfulfilled, we collectively recognize the inherent unfairness of this situation. Allowing people to suffer—and thus to waste their potential as humans or be hampered from fully contributing to society—goes against American values, whether secular or religious. Hunger violates our sense of fairness, while tugging at our heartstrings.

In addition to these bedrock values of compassion and the sanctity of life, other beliefs and experiences shape our concerns about hunger. Some persons hold a personal connection to the topic, being or having been poor at some point in their lives. Some, such as Monica from Bain Capital, have friends or family who struggle with putting food on the table. For others, supporting anti-hunger efforts creates a tangible and concrete way for them to give back to their community, or to even build community across social classes.[18] Some people arrive at the hunger problem through their faith.

Jeremy Everett, the director of the Texas Hunger Initiative, notes that all major religions acknowledge a moral imperative to feed the hungry.[19]

Religious Perspectives

In the Judeo-Christian tradition, both the Old and New Testaments contain frequent mentions of hunger. Andrew Kang Bartlett, the associate for National Hunger Concerns of the Presbyterian Church, comments that in the book of Exodus, "The first challenge to the people escaping Egypt is food. Moses tells them that God will provide Manna for them, and he tells them that if they hoard it (i.e., if [they] don't have faith in God's generosity and don't share with [their] neighbor) it will rot. This is very powerful imagery."[20] The book of Isaiah (chapter 58) encourages people to be charitable out of their own goodwill rather than to curry God's or other people's favor. In Leviticus and Deuteronomy, farmers are mandated not to harvest the corners of their fields such that the poor may glean them.

Similarly, hunger forms an integral part of the New Testament. All four gospels tell the story of Jesus feeding the multitudes through the miracle in which he makes five loaves of bread and two fishes multiply to feed 5,000 people. Both the Last Supper and the Eucharist, in which wine and bread become the flesh and blood of Jesus, further underscore the importance of food within the Bible. Bartlett comments, "As one of the sacraments, food is sacred and linked to Jesus. If our food is sacred, it leads us to ask questions about it. Where does it come from? How were the workers who raised it treated? How was the land treated? We start to ask how can we love our neighbors through the food chain. Food has a real community building aspect to it."[21]

Reverend David Beckmann, the executive director of Bread for the World and the recipient of the 2010 World Food Prize, is a leading figure in mobilizing the Christian community to take political action to end hunger and poverty. He maintains, "No one thinks that you can be close to God and not care about poor people."[22] The Bible does not present, however, a unified approach to the way we should care about poor people. Instead, biblical parables contain kernels of wisdom that have led to both social justice and charity-based approaches to dealing with hunger.

Christianity has led many believers to focus on social justice–oriented solutions. Some of the Protestant denominations operate their own anti-poverty and anti-hunger focused entities. These bodies, such as the Presbyterian Hunger Program (PHP) and the Evangelical Lutheran Church in America's World Hunger Program, educate their adherents, and fund movement building and social justice–oriented work both inside and outside their denominations. Within the Catholic Church, the Catholic Worker Movement, founded during the depths of the Great Depression, has played a lead role in articulating the need for social justice in addressing poverty.[23]

At the local level, numerous interfaith and ecumenical organizations advocate on such issues as federal food programs, health care, and anti-poverty programs, among other priorities. Bread for the World, one of the nation's largest interfaith-oriented nonprofits, mobilizes 5,000 congregations and parishes to take action on behalf of the poor and hungry across the globe. Bread does not shy away from economic justice issues that other national anti-hunger groups may avoid. Beckmann writes: "I have come to see this generation's struggle against hunger and poverty as a great exodus in our own time. It is like the Lord's deliverance of the Hebrew people from slavery in Egypt on a much larger scale, and God did not send Moses to Pharaoh's court to take up a collection of canned goods and blankets. God sent Moses to Pharaoh with a political challenge: to let Hebrew slaves go free."[24]

On the other hand, charity has arguably dominated the modern-day Christian response to hunger. An estimated two-thirds of the nation's 61,000 emergency food outlets affiliated with the Feeding America network of food banks are linked to a house of worship.[25] The root of the word charity comes from the Latin term "caritas," which means expressing one's love for God through love for one's neighbor and oneself. Over time, caritas has largely lost this meaning in the vernacular. It has come to signify "almsgiving," or providing food and material objects to people in need.[26] Free food programs such as food pantries and soup kitchens comprise one of the most visible expressions of charity/almsgiving. To its credit, this modern manifestation of charity can provide the added benefit of opening the door for individuals to become more socially and politically aware, leading them to engage in practices that address the root causes of hunger.

The roots of charity in the Judaic tradition provide a counterpoint to Christianity's caritas framework. The Hebrew word for charity, *tzedekah*, provides a different twist on an age-old concept. "It is derived from the

Hebrew root Tzadei-Dalet-Qof, meaning righteousness, justice or fairness. In Judaism, giving to the poor is not viewed as a generous, magnanimous act. It is simply an act of justice and righteousness, the performance of a duty, giving the poor their due."[27] The Sephardic Jewish philosopher Maimonides wrote in the 12th century about the different levels of the righteousness of charity. He asserted that charity—being similar to the concept in Islam, becomes increasingly more virtuous the less the giver and receiver know about each other. Ideally, charity should be anonymous such that the receiver does not feel shame, and the giver no increased pride or social standing from his act of generosity. The highest level of *tzedekah* is considered to occur when the giver enables the receiver, through a gift, loan, partnership, or employment, to be self-reliant so he no longer depends on charity.[28]

In Islam, compulsory charity, transliterated as *zakah* or *zakat*, underlies the Third Pillar of Islam. As in Christianity, Islamic charity purifies the heart from greed and brings the donor closer to God. Islam holds that people enjoy the wealth of the Earth in trust for Allah, and that in order to purify their wealth every capable adult Muslim must donate 2.5 percent of his or her assets to support charitable acts. Donations must be distributed to people of the following categories or for the following purposes: the destitute, the indebted, stranded travelers, new Muslims, to free slaves, to projects that help Muslims, and to pay workers who collected and distribute *zakat*.[29] *Sadaqah* is the term used to describe voluntary almsgiving apart from the mandatory contribution of *zakat*. The best *sadaqah* is one that helps donors continuously such as schools or clinics or funding business start-ups.[30]

What Is Hunger?

Despite the fact that hunger is such a universal concern for the American public and so integrated into its multiple religious traditions, its meaning has become somewhat murky. For some, it brings to mind starving African children with swollen bellies. For others, it conjures images of the homeless person standing at a freeway ramp begging spare change.

Hunger has multiple layers of meaning. It can describe the growling stomach caused by skipping breakfast. It can refer to chronic food deprivation, with its related health impacts. It can mean, for one person or for many in a community, lacking enough food to lead a healthy and active life. In sum, hunger is a personal experience, a medical condition, and a societal problem. Because of its multifaceted, often subtle and personal nature, it can be challenging to define and measure.

In medical terms, hunger is defined as "a sensation resulting from lack of food, characterized by dull or acute pain (in) the lower part of the chest ... usually accompanied by weakness and an overwhelming desire to eat. Hunger pains coincide with powerful contractions of the stomach."[31] Clinically, signs of severe hunger can be seen among children in low-weight-for-height or low-height-for-age.[32] The effects of hunger in the United States tend to be more subtle and difficult to measure, and include headaches, dizziness, fatigue, irritability, frequent colds and infections, and difficulty concentrating.[33]

The Committee on National Statistics of the National Academy of Sciences (the same committee that recommended "food insecurity" replace "hunger" in the USDA lexicon) combined the societal, physiological, and experiential elements of hunger in its 2006 definition: "[hunger] should refer to a potential consequence of food insecurity that, because of prolonged, involuntary lack of food, results in discomfort, illness, weakness, or pain that goes beyond the usual uneasy sensation."[34] This definition excluded deprivation by fasting or dieting in its emphasis on the involuntary nature of such a lack of food. In doing so, it focused on the structural constraints, such as poverty, that limit access to food.

Perpetuating Hunger

Even though the American public overwhelmingly considers hunger to be morally repugnant, the problem has remained largely static. Entrenched levels of hunger cannot be attributed to a lack of public concern, as hunger has been on the public agenda, off and on, since the beginning of the Great Depression.[35] "Fighting hunger" has become a national pastime, even reflected by a college football bowl game of the same name.

Although the public comes together in its gut-level aversion to the existence of hunger, it remains divided over the solutions to hunger's root causes. For example, the public has not reached consensus over increasing the minimum wage or even expanding nutrition programs. Hunger as a societal problem exists within this purgatory of united emotions and divided politics. Captured in this limbo, hunger and its solutions attract much attention and resources, but efforts to address hunger's causes remain limited.

The identification of hunger as an issue in its own right, decoupled from broader societal problems and systemic solutions, lends itself to the illusion of success. We seemingly make progress in reducing hunger on a daily basis, with a meal, a food package, or a new allocation of food stamps, only to have it come back the next day or the next month. A parallel can be drawn to peacekeeping efforts in areas of conflict. Peacekeepers know that a truce, meaning an absence of hostilities, is not peace. The underlying conflict has not been resolved, and the conditions for violence are still in place. Similarly, a bag of groceries handed to a person suffering from hunger does not make them food secure, because the underlying conditions that led to their hunger remain. Just as peace is more than absence of violence, or health just an absence of disease, food security is ultimately more than a bag of groceries or a full belly.

As a result, the very focus on hunger as a social problem acts as a barrier to its own elimination. *Hunger* has become a double-edged sword: enormously successful as a strategy to motivate people to action, but defined in such a way as to perpetuate the problem through shallow strategies.

Individuals may experience being hungry, but *hunger* as a societal problem is an artificial concept. Individuals do not lack food in isolation from other causes or conditions. Instead, hunger exists because individuals do not have the resources to acquire sufficient food, whether through paid employment, government transfers, or other means.[36] The availability of these resources is shaped by broader economic and social factors such as unemployment rates, wage levels, and government benefits, as well as by the presence of prejudices such as racism or sexism. It is affected by where a person lives and by his or her access to affordable and nutritious food. The cost of living as well as the possession of such skills as food preparation and budgeting also influence whether an individual or household enjoys access to adequate food. The choice to untangle this complex web and isolate "hunger" as a problem worthy of attention has become inherently political as it has been made consciously or unconsciously by multiple organizations and individuals over the years.

At the very best, the concept of "hunger" can be an extremely powerful agent for social change, as seen by the Walk for Hunger and the opposition to the USDA's changing terminology. Its emotive power and easily understood nature can mobilize the public and policymakers toward action. In the 1960s, concerns about hunger were linked to anti-poverty strategies, and embedded within the civil rights movement. For example, the Black Panthers ran some of the first school breakfast programs in the country, in part as a community organizing strategy.[37]

At worst, "hunger" provides a watered-down or sanitized framing of a challenging and contentious set of social and economic problems. Though it addresses the symptoms of poverty, the hunger-problem statement fails to establish the necessary justification to build the financial, human, or social capital needed to eliminate the problem on a more permanent basis. One example of this phenomenon concerns the unrelenting focus on federal food programs, such as SNAP. The author and Hunger Free America executive director Joel Berg writes in "All You Can Eat" that hunger is eminently solvable in America. When asked how this would happen, Berg replied that the federal government would simply allocate enough funding to federal food programs: "You do it year after year."[38] Nonetheless, Berg's solutions don't address the much deeper and entrenched set of issues that lead to hunger in the first place. He presents a strategy that ignores among many things, the government's role in shaping the rules surrounding employment, as the primary source of income for most non-elderly persons.

J. C. Dwyer, the senior director of policy and communications at Feeding Texas, alludes to the problematic use of the term "hunger," with an echo of Winston Churchill's famous phrase about democracy, by calling it "the worst possible word except for all of the others."[39] Dwyer is not alone among anti-hunger advocates in his mixed reaction to this term. Some use it avidly. Others avoid it studiously. And many others couch their references to hunger by talking about people "at risk of hunger," "going hungry," "struggling with hunger," or "struggling to put food on the table." They do so in an effort to be more accurate, as they recognize that hunger in America tends to be more episodic than an on-going condition.

The weaknesses of the hunger concept as commonly understood today, can be placed into three broad categories, each described below. First, it is imprecise, hard to measure, and emotionally exploitative. Second, the concept of hunger diverts attention from a broader set of strategies, weakening a more political and dynamic approach to the problem. Third, by focusing on the symptoms of a more deeply rooted problem, it sets up shallow strategies that only perpetuate the problem.

Imprecise Definitions Lead to Emotional Exploitation

The author and long-time community food security activist Mark Winne believes it is misleading to talk about "hunger in America" because the public has two conceptions of hunger: one for the third world and one for the United States.[40] Since hunger in the United States doesn't jibe with a mental image of children with swollen bellies, the public underestimates its prevalence. Hunger remains largely hidden because its physical manifestations do not conform to the public's expectations. It is perceived as outside "our community," a problem that "others" suffer. Mike Moran of the Oregon Food Bank clarifies this point: "People don't think of the kid in a free lunch program who might have had a playdate with their kids [as being hungry]."[41]

And yet, hunger's power resides in its ability to forge an "emotional connection," as Oregon Food Bank's Susannah Morgan notes, echoing her colleague Sharon Thornberry's thoughts on the potential to feel violated when you or your kids are hungry.[42] Hunger's capacity to engage the emotions, however, has a darker side. Anti-hunger appeals can be emotionally exploitative, especially in their portrayal of vulnerable individuals, such as children or the elderly. Pictures of sad children abound on the websites and fundraising appeals of missions and food banks, as these organizations seek to instill guilt on the public to donate money or food.[43]

Like pictures of doe-eyed children, the phrase "fighting hunger" can be found in almost any public communication of anti-hunger organizations or funders, from the smallest pantry to the Walmart Foundation. It has become trite. The term "fighting" conjures images of an enemy, of an individual or institution that must be overcome for all persons to have enough to eat. It bespeaks the American tendency to couch social change in militaristic phrases, such as "the war on drugs" or "the war on poverty."

Oregon Food Bank's Mike Moran dislikes the violent connotations of this term: "I bristle at the war metaphor. It inherently creates a dichotomy of a zero sum game. As soon as we create the impression of winners and losers, that leads to a fear among the wealthy that someone is going to take away their part of the pie in the anti-hunger battle."[44] Mariana Chilton, a professor of public health at Drexel University who works closely with low-income women in Philadelphia through the Witnesses to Hunger program, agrees: "I can't stand the term 'fighting hunger.' It's old and tired and unclear. I think of oppression when I think of the term 'fighting hunger.' Fighting hunger to me is just about raising money to fill the big warehouses [food banks] with sugary pop."[45] An anonymous Southern food banker echoed this sense of the self-serving nature of the term. "I don't have a problem with the term 'fight.' But I don't like gerunds [verbs that end in "ing"] because they let people off the hook. They mean the problem is never ending."

Responses Too Focused on Symptoms

The nature of hunger is such that it requires an immediate response. In her book *Sweet Charity*, Poppendieck raises an issue emblematic of this response by quoting Harry Hopkins, one of the architects of the New Deal: "People don't eat in the long run. They eat every day."[46] The conventional anti-hunger narrative has established food as the solution to hunger. There exists a certain beautiful simplicity to this approach that appeals to our pragmatism, yet it addresses only the symptom rather than the root cause of the problem. Going beyond poverty, scholars have identified the causes of hunger as linked to misogyny, racism, domestic violence, and a high cost of living (such as a lack of affordable housing), as well as to broader issues related to a lack of human rights, even powerlessness and a scarcity of democracy.[47] The Nobel Prize–winning economist Amartya Sen has shown that no famine has ever occurred in a nation with a functioning democracy.[48]

By focusing on the symptoms instead of these root causes, anti-hunger work creates surface-level strategies that manage the problem in the short term, but do little to create long-lasting solutions. Providing a box of free food or even food stamps may keep families fed, but hardly changes the circumstances that led them to need help in the first place. It doesn't build self-reliance or address other external factors, such as the lack of affordable healthy food in many neighborhoods, that impede families from becoming more food secure. This approach treats hunger as if it were a disease, and food the medicine. The hunger problem, especially as we have addressed it for the past 30 years, leads to pyrrhic victories: daily battles won, but battles that undermine the success of the long-term struggle.

These daily fixes block more systemic solutions. Poppendieck asserts that by defining the problem as hunger, we direct attention away from poverty. The "repeated focus on hunger," she says, contributes "to a distortion that reduces our ability to confront and solve the underlying problem."[49]

Engenders Charity, Not Income Redistribution

On a very basic level, the anti-hunger movement can be divided into two broad overlapping categories: groups that promote income redistribution through the vehicle of federal food programs and other public policies, and those that promote charitable food distribution. The latter approach has been ascendant since the 1980s, and has dramatically influenced public understanding of the hunger problem. Over time, the anti-hunger field has become increasingly defined by charitable food distribution, whose resources exponentially outstrip those of advocacy groups (although more and more food banks do undertake public policy advocacy). While charity softens the edges of society, it is not a solution to problems as complex as those that underlie hunger. The charitable approach lends itself to, in the words of Robert Egger, the founder of DC Central Kitchen, the "redemption of the giver, not the liberation of the receiver."[50]

Chilton notes that she has visited nearly every food pantry in Philadelphia, and finds a racist and classist bias inherent in the charitable food system. This charitable approach to hunger doesn't rock the boat. In Egger's words, "Hunger is safe." Winne believes it an issue "we can drain the politics out of."[51] Charity depoliticizes hunger, rendering it an issue for personal, not public, action. Graham Riches, a Canadian scholar who has written extensively on the relationship between hunger, food banks, and the right to food, states that the privatization of hunger through charity (the charitable food system) undercuts the ability of government to intervene in favor of hungry people.[52] It allows the right wing to claim that a partnership between the private sector and nonprofit organizations, rather than the government, can best solve the hunger problem. Given that this remains blatantly untrue, charity has become hunger's worst enemy. Or in the words of the comic strip character Pogo, "We have met the enemy and he is us."

Shooting Oneself in the Foot with Pragmatism

Given these flaws, we are left to wonder why funders, advocates, and poli-cymakers have not been more critical of the anti-hunger approach over the years. Why has hunger become such a popular issue in the United States, while in most other industrialized nations, the framework for addressing what the British call "food poverty" remains less focused on food and more on poverty reduction? Perhaps the peculiarities of the American context have lent themselves to fostering a focus on anti-hunger work above other issues. One such American eccentricity is our moralizing on the decisions made by the poor.

Undeserving Poor

In idyllic La Jolla, California, Jason Greenslate spends his days surfing the waves, playing guitar, chasing women, and using food stamps to buy sushi and lobster for his buddies. A 2013 Fox News documentary, "The Great Food Stamp Binge," holds up Jason as the poster child of the lazy undeserv-ing poor, and of why the SNAP program needs work requirements.[53]

In 1993, some 120 miles to the north in the liberal enclave of Santa Monica, a business association strategically placed four dolphin-shaped statues in highly trafficked areas of the city; each "dolphin" had a slit in the back where passersby could drop contributions. The statues were built to funnel donations *away* from the city's substantial homeless population and *to* community agencies that provide social services to this population. As of 2015, $235,000 has been donated to various charities through the dolphin program.[54] The CEO of the business association, Kathleen Rawson, has commented, "The dolphin program is a responsible alternative to direct giving."[55] The underlying assumption is that the homeless would not put spare change to good use but instead waste it on booze, street drugs, and cigarettes. While substance abuse among the homeless is a real problem, the dolphin program epitomizes a paternalistic approach to the poor.

The way in which Santa Monica's business association typifies the home-less and Fox News' portrayal of Jason Greenslate are emblematic of the con-cept of the undeserving poor. They are considered to be poor because of their own alleged personal flaws: laziness, shiftlessness, immorality, sub-stance abuse, or poor life choices. This concept of the deserving and unde-serving poor can be traced back to our Calvinist heritage. Colonists would differentiate between those who merited assistance and those who did not. "Because Calvinism taught that idleness was a sin, colonists provided aid only to the deserving poor, those whose destitution resulted from age, illness, physical or mental disability, widowhood, abandonment, or other unpreventable circumstances and no fault of their own. ... The able-bodied who, by all appearances, lived immoral lives and chose not to work frequently were indentured, run out of town, whipped, or thrown into jail. 'For those who indulge themselves in idleness, the express command of God unto us is, that we should let them starve,' said the influential Puritan minister Cotton Mather."[56]

Deserving Poor

By contrast society considers the deserving poor to be those who are impoverished through no fault of their own: children, the disabled, the mentally ill, senior citizens, and perhaps veterans. Surprisingly, women do not fit into this "deserving poor" category. Women are one of the most vulnerable populations to food insecurity, especially single woman–led households with kids. As of 2014, households with children led by single women were more than twice as likely to be considered food insecure (35 percent) than average (14 percent).[57]

This statistic illustrates the relative powerlessness of single women within society, especially single women of color or those from low-income backgrounds. There exists within certain sectors of American society a belief that single women's poverty is of their own making, a product of their own moral deficiencies. Yet, researchers have found in many cases that their food insecurity is linked to an epidemic of domestic violence in impoverished neighborhoods. Chilton has identified the centrality of violence to food insecurity as a factor to contributing to victims' anxiety, difficulty in concentrating, depression, and an inability to maintain healthy relationships, all of which could contribute to productive employment.[58]

Caveats against Categorizing

One problem with sorting the poor into worthy and unworthy categories is that it ignores the structural determinants of poverty. It assumes that people are poor because of their own failings, not because social mobility is limited by external factors. This lack of empathy that the American public feels for the poor has been partially shaped by our collective prejudice. To some degree, what has made the poor appear undeserving is that they are often "the other," of a different race, ethnicity, or national origin. Racism and bigotry feed our tolerance for deprivation among others. Outsiders to the dominant culture suffer from the reduced sense of obligation that mainstream society feels toward them. Outsiders may coexist in the same country, but they are perceived to be of a different community. It's no secret that throughout American history religious or ethnic groups, one after another, have been condemned for their alleged immoral behavior or unscrupulous attitudes.

This categorization of the poor into the deserving and the undeserving irks anti-hunger advocates to their core. They believe that society's failure to provide adequate and equal opportunities for all contributes significantly to the reason why some people are poor. Yet, despite their rejection of the differentiation of poor people into undeserving and deserving categories, anti-hunger advocates shoot themselves in the foot every day, reinforcing this distinction through their pragmatism.

One example of their practicality has been the decision to focus attention onto hunger and away from poverty. Few knowledgeable persons dispute that hunger is a symptom of poverty. By redefining the poverty problem as hunger, advocates have obfuscated the root causes of hunger and the steps needed to address it. The journalist Nick Kotz reports that in 1967 a bipartisan group of advocates and Congressional members strategized on how to gain public support for addressing the horrendous conditions of poverty prevalent in the country. Kotz writes: "They reasoned that 'hunger' made a higher moral claim than any of the other problems of poverty. Federally supported housing and jobs programs could wait; but no one should go hungry in affluent America."[59] In effect, they chose to make hunger the poster child for poverty: the heartrending moral imperative in a gritty landscape marked by the undeserving poor's ideological landmines. In other words, hunger was the lowest common denominator in American politics.

This reasoned and reasonable bargain, of choosing the politically downhill route rather than the uphill slog of transforming public opinion, continues to this day. If anything, the ruts on the moral imperative trail are deeper than ever. Today's anti-hunger advocates concur that "poverty" remains a challenging framework for political action. Jessica Chanay, formerly of Partners for a Hunger-Free Oregon states, "Poverty has a lot of baggage. It evokes a negative image that is continually reinforced through media spin and political rhetoric. The baggage makes it difficult to work toward more positive outcomes because we're trying to change both systems and beliefs."[60]

Doubling Down on Childhood Hunger

Politics can lead us down paths that we prefer not to trod, or ones that may not be in our long-term interests. We hope that the road chosen will eventually take us to our destination, not to a strategic dead-end. But when after decades of wandering through the proverbial desert we keep going in circles, it might just be time to look for a new guide. Instead of sending out the scouts to identify new paths to their destination, anti-hunger advocates have doubled down on their moral imperative bet. It wasn't enough that hunger had become the poster child of poverty. Advocates went even further and made children the poster child of hunger. In other words, they sold the "undeserving poor" down the river to try to save the so-called deserving poor.

Children are the ultimate demographic of the deserving poor. Chuck Scofield, chief development officer for the anti-hunger group Share Our Strength, confirms this understanding, "Kids are the most voiceless and least responsible for their situation."[61] They can't control the circumstances of their birth or the identity of their parents. They haven't made the life mistakes that would deem them unworthy of assistance, according to proponents of the concept of the undeserving poor.

As it has become increasingly challenging to convince the public and Congress to care about food insecurity, anti-hunger advocates have cherry-picked the most valuable weapon in their arsenal: childhood hunger. Laura Golino de Lovato, former development director for the Oregon Food Bank, notes: "Childhood hunger is an issue that really resonates with people on an emotional level, and it's appealing to funders. But a focus on child hunger excludes others who are hungry, including the child's family."[62]

It is indisputable that child hunger is real, significant, and dangerous. Forty seven percent of individuals receiving food stamps are children. Nationally, 29 percent of kids are SNAP recipients.[63] Even at mild levels, food insecurity in children can have significant health impacts. Studies have shown that food insecurity can impede brain development in children, be irreversible, and impact educational performance.[64] The toxic stress that hunger causes in households can also act as an obstacle to bonding between mother and child, further retarding brain development.[65] Multiple episodes of hunger in children can lead to ill health later in life, even 10 to 15 years down the road.[66] In 2015, the American Academy of Pediatrics issued a landmark policy statement, documenting the pernicious effects of childhood hunger and urging pediatricians to screen all children for food insecurity.[67] These facts make the discussion of whether advocates should concentrate on childhood hunger all the more difficult.

The focus on childhood hunger includes but transcends the use of pictures of kids in fundraising appeals. Efforts to ameliorate food insecurity among kids have exploded in recent years, especially in the charitable food distribution sector. For example, Kids' Cafés serve snacks and meals in the after-school hours in 1,500 sites to 122,000 children each year. In 2010, 400 school pantries served 70,000 kids. The Child Hunger Corps, funded by ConAgra Foods, supports food banks in the development of child hunger initiatives. And backpack programs, intended to compensate for the lack of school meals on weekends, provide 230,000 students with a knapsack full of single-serving containers of food to take home.[68]

Children are, of course, part of families, and providing food to kids specifically for their consumption can set up difficult household dynamics. Some food banks have recognized the limitations of the backpack program and moved to school-based food pantries instead. Despite the limitations of backpack programs, they continue in part because they remain extremely fundable.[69] Thornberry, of the Oregon Food Bank, contends: "Backpack programs are so popular because what's better than feeding kids? Seniors are probably thinking of their grandkids when they're volunteering to fill the backpacks. Feeding children is seductive and makes people feel warm, fuzzy and self-righteous. It is a great way to assuage guilt without making any real effort at change."[70]

And fundable they are. Support for child nutrition programs sits at the top of corporate philanthropic anti-hunger priority lists, in part because of the noncontroversial nature of the programs and their value for enhancing corporate reputations. For example, Walmart Foundation announced on June 20, 2013, that it would be granting $14 million to support child nutrition efforts, while ConAgra Foods Foundation, which focuses almost exclusively on childhood hunger issues, committed $10 million to Feeding

America for childhood hunger–related programs.[71] The Kellogg Company donated $1 million in 2013 and 2014 to three nonprofits to improve school breakfast programs.[72]

In addition to the child-oriented programs, the focus on childhood hunger can be seen in the language advocates use to educate the public about food insecurity. Through their own reports, websites, and the media they call attention to the plight of hungry children, often to the exclusion of other needy people. For example, national anti-hunger advocates have chosen to issue entire reports and press releases dedicated to the analysis of how potential SNAP cutbacks in the 2012/2013 Farm Bill affect children.[73] The Food Research and Action Center's (FRAC) communiqué of August 13, 2013, epitomizes how advocates highlight only the deserving poor: "Nearly half of SNAP enrollees are children, and the program helps feed roughly one in three children in America. Additionally, almost 75 percent of SNAP participants are in households with children, seniors, or a disabled individual."[74] A review of 198 food bank websites (out of 202 food banks then affiliated with Feeding America) found that five of every six of these organizations contained an image of children on their home pages and/or language about childhood hunger and related programs.[75]

Perhaps the most significant example of the growing resonance of childhood hunger has been the launch of the No Kid Hungry campaign by the fundraising powerhouse Share Our Strength (SOS). Known for being an early adopter of cause marketing through its partnership with American Express's Charge Against Hunger campaign, SOS was historically a significant funder of the charitable food system. No Kid Hungry seeks to end childhood hunger through advocacy, partnerships, funding, public education, and capacity building. According to SOS founder and executive director, Billy Shore, the No Kid Hungry campaign was inspired by a quote from Jonathan Kozol—"pick battles big enough to matter, small enough to win"—to set a goal that was bold but achievable. The campaign didn't change the organization's priorities, but instead focused their activities into a coherent message. Shore expects that childhood hunger will be more likely to gain bipartisan support given that children are the "least responsible for their situation" (i.e., the deserving poor). He hopes that the movement can leverage this success to show America's political parties that they can work together on bigger issues. In other words, Shore thinks that childhood hunger is the lowest common denominator between political parties—a moral imperative that will force them to transcend the partisan bickering that dominates Congress these days.[76]

The fact that anti-hunger groups feel the need to concentrate on the plight of children in order to be effective demonstrates just how entrenched the dichotomy between the undeserving and deserving poor is. While anti-hunger advocates implement strategies based on their likelihood of success, there remains an element of opportunism in this choice. Few publicly ask such questions as: What does this focus on kids cost the broader "fight against hunger" and how does it affect the plight of the "undeserving poor?" What is the collateral damage of this increasingly narrow focus— from poverty to hunger and then to childhood hunger—and what is its impact on the underlying hunger problem? Are we digging ourselves into a deeper conceptual rut that will be increasingly more difficult to get out of, one that will continue to plague anti-poverty activists for generations to come? If we don't start to challenge this societal bias, how will we ever overcome it?

Who Benefits from the Hunger Concept?

In *Sweet Charity* Poppendieck discusses how useful hunger has been to many different interest groups. She concludes (partially tongue-in-cheek) that because hunger meets so many people's needs, if it didn't exist we would have to invent it.[77] One facet of its utility has been the alliance created between parts of the business community and parts of the anti-hunger sector. This anti-hunger industrial complex keeps attention focused on the hunger problem without pursuing the necessary steps to truly end it. Such a focus on meeting basic human needs while reinforcing the status quo of growing economic inequality is what Peter Buffett, the son of the billionaire investor Warren Buffett, calls a "perpetual poverty machine."[78]

Business

Hunger opens the door for corporate philanthropy, and corporations have pounced on this opening with their giving programs. The hunger frame provides companies multiple benefits with few downsides. Hunger relief requires little explanation, enjoys universal moral appeal, and does not generate controversy. Anti-hunger work as currently constituted rarely challenges corporate business practices. In other words, it allows corporations to appear to be solution providers rather than problem creators on the cheap. One way to better understand this phenomenon is by looking at the separate but related field of obesity.

In an insightful *Huffington Post* article of 2013, the registered dietitian Andy Bellatti writes that the public health sector's focus on obesity acts as an obstacle to progress in improving public health. He contends: "Such a clinical and quantitative frame gives very little thought to—and leaves no room for a conversation about—socio-political and environmental factors that pose a threat to our health (including, but not limited to food industry lobbying, Big Food predatory marketing, and misguided agricultural subsidies). ... It is precisely the neutral and apolitical focus on weight that has contributed to our current public health mess. When health is only discussed through a lens of weight, it is easy for the food industry to consider itself part of the dutiful troops, whether it's with 'commitments to physical activity' or reduced-calorie, minimally nutritious processed foods that feature artificial sweeteners and 'fat replacers' made from genetically modified corn."[79]

Substitute "hunger" for "weight," change the subject of the sentence above from "health" to "social justice," and the message takes on a similar significance: when *social justice* is only discussed through a lens of *hunger*, it is easy for the food industry to consider itself part of the dutiful troops, whether it's with commitments of employee volunteer time, donations of cash, trucks, or of mislabeled, expired, or misshapen food items. The hunger frame does not take on industry for its poverty-scale wages, abusive labor practices, heavy marketing of inexpensive and unhealthful foods, supermarket redlining of impoverished neighborhoods, and poor track record on food safety. It gives them a pass, and on top of that enables them to repair their oft-damaged reputations through accepting their philanthropic donations. Mark Winne sums it up quite nicely: "Hunger is good for business in America."[80]

Advocates and Organizations

Anti-hunger advocates and groups often use the buzzword "hunger" to convey a dire yet imprecise situation in a manner that will elicit the action they desire. In other words, the emotional reaction caused by "hunger" motivates and mobilizes people to take action, such as writing a letter to a Congress member or volunteering at the local food pantry. It does so better than any other term. "Food security" is bloodless and too convoluted. "Poverty" is a broken brand.

"Hunger" also makes for an easy fundraising pitch, given people's visceral reactions. Erik Talkin, the iconoclastic executive director of the Food Bank of Santa Barbara County (CA) agrees with this analysis: "Hunger is a $25 word. I tried selling 'healthy' in direct mail and it didn't work. The fear that *I could be hungry* can be a major motivator for people to care." The perpetual poverty machine even extends beyond charity. When Talkin attended his first national anti-hunger policy conference in 2013, he found it all about the "ecosystem of federal food programs" that manages hunger as a symptom but does not eliminate its root causes. He concludes, "There's huge pressure on keeping the hunger maintenance industry going."[81]

Taking Back Hunger

There is seemingly no good answer to the hunger terminology dilemma. On one hand, the concept of hunger as a social problem in 21st-century America has created a public mindset that has unintentionally perpetuated the problem. It has set up solutions that mitigate the problem in the short-run and ultimately weaken its resolution in the long-term. The movement needs a new conceptual framework that will facilitate reaching its goals more easily.

On the other hand, hunger's universality, history, and emotional appeal provide real and irreplaceable value. Few terms can resonate so powerfully in the English language. Mariana Chilton sums up this conundrum, "I hate the term, but we're stuck with it."[82]

Instead, a third alternative would be to give hunger an extreme makeover, to pun on the reality television show that fixes up people's homes. Or better yet, in social movement rhetoric, we could occupy it: take it back from the charitable industrial complex and reshape it toward more progressive ends. The first place to consider in the occupation of hunger and anti-hunger work is the concept of the right to food.

The Right to Food: Definition and Challenges
The 1948 Universal Declaration of Human Rights (UDHR) spells out numerous human, civil, and political rights, many of which resemble the U.S. Constitution and Declaration of Independence. In addition, the UDHR

promulgates basic economic rights beyond the American legal framework. Article 25 states, "Everyone has the right to a standard of living adequate for the health and well-being of himself and of his family, including food, clothing, housing and medical care and necessary social services, and the right to security in the event of unemployment, sickness, disability, widowhood, old age or other lack of livelihood in circumstances beyond his control."[83]

These rights are further outlined in the International Covenant on Economic, Social, and Cultural Rights (ICESR), the protocol for the implementation of the UDHR. The United States has signed on to the ICESR, but has not ratified this agreement. This seeming technicality indicates that the government agrees with the covenant's tenets, but does not want to be held accountable for their implementation into law.[84] Ratification of the ICESR could provide an important platform for substantive changes to domestic social policy. According to Graham Riches and Tiina Silvasti, the right to food implies "a framework of national law which moves beyond policy guidelines to legislative action. It also implies the development and adoption of coordinated national plans, strategies and tools to advance and ensure the development of 'joined-up' food policy including the setting of targets, benchmarks and indicators, monitoring, justiciable remedies and all actions necessary to secure a just and sustainable food system."[85]

The UDHR defines the right to food as "the right to have regular, permanent, and unrestricted access, either directly or by means of financial purchases, to quantitatively and qualitatively adequate and sufficient food corresponding to the cultural traditions of the people to which the consumer belongs, and which ensures a physical and mental, individual and collective, fulfilling and dignified life free of fear."[86]

Governments must uphold four basic legal mandates regarding the right to food: *respect, protect, fulfill,* and in the ultimate instance *provide.*

To *respect* the right to food means that the government should not interfere with a person's ability to acquire food by evicting them from their land unduly, for example, or taxing them excessively. Similarly individuals should be able to work and earn money to purchase food.[87]

To *protect* the right to food is to make sure that others do not interfere with access to food. This includes protecting people from theft.[88]

To *fulfill* the right to food means the state must engage in activities that strengthen people's access to and use of resources that ensure their livelihood, such as establishing minimum wages.[89]

To *provide* food to the public signifies that the government has the obligation to make available food to those who for reasons beyond their control cannot provide for themselves. Feeding programs such as SNAP would fit into this category.[90]

The right to food does *not* guarantee a right to be fed, only that each individual has the right to feed him or herself. It does not obligate the government to feed the public, but to create the conditions by which individuals can feed themselves.[91] Only for the most vulnerable, unable to feed themselves, does the government have an obligation to provide them with adequate food. Conversely, the existence of a strong charitable food system, making up for the public sector's policy failures, is anathema to the right to food. The concept of human rights establishes that individuals have an inherent dignity, which cannot be met through charity. Charity is a gift, not something to which people are entitled. "Dignity does not come from being fed."[92]

The dignity that comes from this basic human right highlights that right to food is not just a legal entitlement as much as it is a political and moral claim. The rights of disenfranchised populations, such as women and persons of color, are at the center of this concept because they tend to suffer from food insecurity more than whites and men. The gender wage gap in which women earn only between 75 and 90 percent of what men earn is a prime example of discrimination against women as economic agents, resulting in less economic independence and greater exposure to domestic violence.[93] These kinds of broad societal considerations and the potential transformations that they engender are what make the right to food such a powerful tool for fostering equity and ultimately greater political empowerment.

Despite these political advantages, few anti-hunger groups in the United States, with notable exceptions, utilize a human rights discourse. George Manalo Le Clair, executive director of California Food Policy Advocates, explains why his organization no longer presses the case for the right to food in California. "We found over time that the right to food language works better in an international context than in a domestic context.

Legislators in Sacramento believe that a right equals a mandate which equals money."[94]

Rights, like poverty, remain a difficult sell in today's political climate; the government's mandate to protect and empower citizens is under fierce challenge. Some common misperceptions feed into the difficulty in marketing the right-to-food framework as well. Many falsely believe that if the right to food is ratified, the government would be responsible to solve all social ills related to poverty and deprivation.[95]

Because the rights framework has proven so politically problematic in the short term, anti-hunger groups have instead chosen to employ language based on the moral imperative of ending hunger. They focus on food as a human need rather than as a human right. Anti-hunger groups have found that this approach generally works well in raising awareness and mobilizing the public toward modest goals.

The right-to-food framework provides an interesting lens through which the advocacy activities of the anti-hunger field can be viewed. The sector's efforts have by and large been focused on the fourth mandate: to *provide* for food. Federal food programs and support for the charitable food system fit squarely within the role of the government to assist those who cannot help themselves.

The role of the state in *fulfilling* the right to food, for example, through supporting individuals' livelihoods through fiscal and labor policies, has lacked support among all but the most progressive of the anti-hunger groups. For the complete spectrum of anti-hunger organizations to fully embrace the right to food would require many of them to take on a much broader policy agenda than they have to date.

The Right to Food: Benefits

Despite these challenges, the right to food framework provides a significant improvement over the current needs-based, moral imperative–oriented messaging. These benefits include the following aspects:

Accountability   The right to food establishes a mechanism to hold the government accountable for making progress toward food security. Currently, the U.S. government collects data on food insecurity, but has no legal mandate to implement policies or programs to reduce food insecurity. There is no connection between the measurement of the food insecurity problem and the implementation of an action plan to reduce it.[96] The right to food would provide citizens and their representatives a way to hold the government accountable for policies that block food security.

Political Voice   One of the biggest missed opportunities of the anti-hunger movement is that it has not been able to convert the tens of millions of persons that are food insecure, receiving food stamps, or relying on food pantries into a powerful grassroots movement. Poppendieck holds that patrons of the emergency food system have become portrayed as victims and as such have become profoundly depoliticized. They are dejected objects waiting in lines whose images are used to raise money, rather than the empowered poor people of the late 1960s who marched on Washington, DC, and conducted a sit-in at the USDA. They look more like "objects of compassion than potential allies."[97] The right to food helps to shift this dynamic by imbuing individuals not only with that right but also with the legal framework to hold the government accountable for its obligation. It gives people the voice and power that they don't have when perceived as "beggars," "clients," "recipients," or the "needy."

A Tool in the Equity Toolbox   The right to food provides a broad framework for addressing social inequities that negatively impact the right to food among the disadvantaged, such as women and persons of color. It does so in a way far beyond what a needs-based anti-hunger framework can provide. As such, it is an important element of a social movement that builds the voice and political power of these populations.

Reshape the Food System   When a government establishes the right that adequate nutritious food should be available at all times, it opens the door into broader considerations of agriculture and the food system. For example, it invites an examination of policies related to the long-term sustainability of food production, such as farmland preservation, soil conservation, farmer training, the profitability of agriculture, climate change, and the availability of adequate water for irrigation. It opens the door for questions about the structure of the food retailing sector, food safety, and the healthfulness of the food that is being produced. In short, it leads to a more robust policy framework that formalizes a connection between consumer and producer, a national food policy.

Limitations of the Right to Food   In addition to the challenges of communicating economic rights in a political environment that seeks to reduce or eliminate existing government entitlements, the right to food presents one other key limitation. Its focus on the government as the sole guarantor of rights misses key opportunities for ensuring the public's food security. The right to food assumes that the government will rein in abuses impeding individuals' right to food by the marketplace. It ignores the fact that citizen pressure—outside of the government sphere, through organized campaigns and initiatives—have improved livelihoods for millions. For example, boycotts and consumer education have shifted corporate practices without government regulation. Similarly, union organizing has been another important activity in this realm (although the government does formulate the rules by which unions and corporations engage in these struggles).

It is unlikely that, in the short or medium term, the United States will ratify the right to food, but it remains an important educational and organizing tool. Just as the hunger concept has led the public down a dead end, the right to food can serve to recast the public's understanding of the broader suite of issues located at the intersection of poverty, hunger, health, and food.

The right to food can also help make the case for a more robust government role in addressing the problems found at this intersection. It serves a partial solution to the challenges presented by the hunger problem statement, but must be accompanied by a mechanism for anti-hunger groups to hold the corporate sector accountable for its actions as they relate to the public's food security.

Summary

The right to food provides important insights into understanding the deficiencies of the hunger concept while laying out the elements of a new framework. Yet it is not practical to expect groups to merely swap one phrase for the other, as the federal government did in substituting the term "food security" for "hunger." The hunger concept is too intrinsically valuable to surrender. Instead it must be crafted anew.

Perhaps the best way to move forward is by working backward, by redefining *the solution to hunger* as a way of remaking the nature of *hunger*. After all, many of the problems with the hunger concept relate to the ineffective solutions it promotes. Janet Poppendieck has written that the solutions to hunger presented in the 1930s, 1960s, and 1980s shaped the public's understanding of the problem. In the 1930s, the presence of surplus commodities helped frame hunger as a matter of want among waste. In the 1960s, policy and juridical solutions led to an understanding of the issue as a matter of civil rights and failed government programs. And in the 1980s, the growth of the charitable food distribution became inextricably linked to the perception of hunger as an issue to be solved in part by the private sector.[98]

To occupy *hunger*, we must first remake the *anti-hunger field*. Any such redefinition of the anti-hunger field must include a holistic framework for understanding the relationship of health, hunger, economic development, and agriculture and how they intersect at the community level. It should focus on and seek to resolve the root causes of hunger, with a broader vision for social change, and foster the necessary alliances to reach that goal. It must build the political power and voice of the poor, while engaging them to a greater degree in this struggle. While not all anti-hunger groups or initiatives will focus on all of these goals, their work should be designed so as not to impede progress on the other goals. For example, an effort that seeks to increase the income of the poor, such as through SNAP, should not do so at the cost to their health.

These goals of economic justice, healthy individuals, and a democratic food system create a three-legged stool on which an integrated and successful anti-hunger field sits. Remove any of the legs and the stool will topple over, weakening the ability of the initiative to fully address food insecurity. Each of these three goals brings a unique perspective to this issue.

2 The Charity Trap

The Greater Boston Food Bank

From the second floor observation deck of the Greater Boston Food Bank (GBFB), you can see the machinery of the warehouse hum along. Forklifts move pallets, placing them on industrial strength shelving 35-feet high. Vans and trucks from food pantries across the region pull into the loading docks where their boxes of food await them in a neatly ordered stack. Built in 2009 at a construction cost of $35 million, the GBFB is likely the most expensive building of its kind in the nation. Its 117,000 square feet of space (about the size of an average Home Depot store), holds refrigerators two stories tall and freezers that can accommodate a forklift.[1]

The GBFB is an intimidating, sterile building whose massive warehouse and multistory, starkly furnished atrium remind visitors of a highly efficient food distribution corporation rather than a social services agency feeding the poorest of the poor. That image of an efficient business is exactly what the organization hopes to portray. In a story in the *Boston Globe*, the Food Bank's vice president of acquisition comments on how much she "loves bringing food industry executives in for a tour, because many are surprised at how advanced the operations are—how much the warehouse resembles their own."[2]

The size and sophistication of the GBFB's facility highlights the single-minded purpose of the organization to distribute as much food as possible throughout eastern Massachusetts. By any measure, its food distribution efforts have been stunningly successful. From 1990 to 2015, GBFB increased the amount of food it distributes ten-fold, to 54 million pounds through 547 agencies to more than half a million people.[3] The group plans to increase its distribution to provide every person in need in eastern Massachusetts with one meal per day, or a third of their food needs.[4]

The GBFB operates one of most successful and sophisticated charitable food distribution organizations in the United States. Its singular focus on food distribution is emblematic of the conventional mindset among food banks nationally. In the early 1980s, charitable food distribution began to adopt a more institutionalized approach, using a model that has now become a seemingly permanent feature of the anti-hunger landscape. Some 37 million people receive charitable food assistance[5] from roughly 61,000 soup kitchens and food pantries in the Feeding America network at some time during a year.[6] In the ten-year span from 2002 to 2012, Feeding America–affiliated food banks distributed 22 billion pounds of food, and raised $5 billion in cash.[7] They provide more than 3 billion meals per year.[8]

These meals have become an important part of the survival strategies of many low-income households. Food banks help persons living on the edge to make ends meet, supplementing inadequate paychecks or federal benefits. They serve persons otherwise ineligible for federal programs, such as undocumented immigrants. They allow families to divert scarce cash to keep their homes warm and lit, buy medicine, and put gas in the family car. Food banks are fundamentally a humanitarian institution. They distribute existing resources to help the vulnerable avert the suffering that comes from inadequate nutrition.

We saw in the introduction, however, with the example of Youngstown, that food distribution does not suffice to meet the needs of those who drop in and out of poverty, as is common in the 2010s.[9] It is an approach better suited for a situation in which individuals need a helping hand once or twice, not on a recurring basis. Our changing economy, disinvestment in human capital, and a shredded safety net have combined to marginalize wide swaths of the population. Poverty has become mainstream, but charitable food distribution, the safety net underneath the safety net, is poorly prepared to cushion the blow of this new reality.

Most Americans accept without question the good that food banks do, without delving below the surface. The sheer simplicity and directness of their feeding efforts appeal to the public. The public accepts the emergency food system because it seems to make sense. They believe in charity as the right and moral thing to do, especially in an era of declining support for government initiatives. In addition, food banks allow the public to wash their hands of the knotty hunger problem through a donation of time, money, or food. Charitable food is straightforward, tangible, and easily understandable. These qualities may make charity attractive, but they don't necessarily make it effective.

Perhaps there is insufficient questioning of the charitable food system because, as Ellen Parker, the executive director of Project Bread notes, the emergency food system doesn't have an academic home.[10] For example, if individuals want to get jobs in public health, they become trained in the principles and practices of public health in an academic setting. Public health programs are evaluated rigorously and findings published in peer-reviewed journals. Funders require evidence that strategies will have a good chance of success before committing resources. The same goes for other fields, such as social work, housing (linked to urban planning), and nutrition. However, no one earns a college degree in the emergency food system or even anti-hunger work. This lack of an academic discipline means that the assumptions of charitable food distribution—and more broadly, anti-hunger work—typically go unquestioned. The field of charitable food distribution has little incentive, much less a requirement, for rigorous analysis.

History and Structure of the Charitable Food System

Feeding programs that offer a place where the poor can come together, have a meal, and enjoy companionship have been in existence for centuries. Soup kitchens began in England in the 1700s and became popular in the United States with the onset of the Great Depression. Food pantries can be traced back to the Depression, when individuals would queue up to receive free bread and other foods to take home. In time, these breadlines have turned into more formalized entities, typically linked to churches or other places of worship.

The great innovation in charitable food distribution, however, occurred in the latter half of the 20th century. In 1967, in Phoenix, John van Hengel created the modern food bank as a distribution center for free food. Struggling with the aftermath of a divorce and health problems, he discovered that grocery stores were discarding edible food. Moved by a documentary on hunger in Africa, he asked a grocery store manager if he could have the edible unused items. He started collecting food from multiple grocery stores and eventually from manufacturers, while distributing the food to low-income persons. His efforts turned into St. Mary's Food Bank Alliance.

Food Banks as Connectors

At a basic level, food banks are both a warehouse and trucking business (as in Boston's example)—connectors between those who have extra food and those who need it. They provide a convenient mechanism for manufacturers and retailers to donate their products safely and efficiently, without having to deal with requests from multiple parties. They facilitate companies receiving a single tax deduction for their goods rather than having to deal with multiple receipts. They serve as an intermediary between food donors, including the federal government's commodity distribution program, and the agencies that work on the frontlines of hunger relief. Food banks obtain their food from a variety of sources, depending on their geographic location and the nature of food processing and farming nearby. These sources include foods purchased by the federal government to bolster the farm economy; donations of products that are unsellable by supermarkets; surplus from food manufacturers; excess, blemished, or undersized produce; prepared food recovered from caterers or restaurants, and canned food drives.

By 1977 a national organization called Second Harvest had been established in Chicago to guide the replication of food banks based on the St. Mary's model in communities across the country. The emergency food system grew dramatically in the early 1980s in the wake of a deep recession and cutbacks to safety net programs by the Reagan administration. In 1979 there were 13 food banks. By 1989, there were 180.[11]

Feeding America, the rebranded identity for Second Harvest, continues to serve as the hub for the 202 food banks in its national network, some of which serve additional smaller food banks in their service area (in addition, dozens of food banks exist outside of the Feeding America network). Feeding America contracts with these organizations, establishing standards by which they must operate, including food handling procedures and the distribution of a minimum number of pounds per person in poverty in each geographic area. Feeding America also raises funds from corporate and other donors, some of which it redistributes to its affiliates to run certain programs or to purchase equipment, such as refrigerated trucks. It gains access to donations of food from manufacturers, and makes them available to food banks through a computerized bidding system. It provides technical assistance to food banks on a wide variety of organizational matters, lobbies at the federal level on select issues, conducts research into hunger in America, and develops public education campaigns. Food banks pay a membership fee to Feeding America based on the size of their organization.

While all food banks have as their core purpose the distribution of charitable food, they are not all cut from the same cloth. Although Feeding America and the federal government impose certain standards on them, there exists tremendous variation from organization to organization in its food sourcing, political stances, and programming. Each food bank's size, geographic service area, leadership, and history shape its character.

At the "retail level," food pantries and soup kitchens set their own rules and policies, such as the quantity and type of food they distribute, and the frequency with which recipients may rely on their services. Pantries and soup kitchens must follow a cascade of regulations that emanate from the federal and state governments if they are to distribute federal commodities. Likewise, food banks impose additional rules on the pantries to ensure fairness, safe food handling standards, means testing (i.e., documenting wage-based need), and refraining from requiring individuals to worship in order to receive food. Pantries typically pay food banks a shared maintenance fee to cover the costs of the food, no more than 18 cents per pound.[12]

Intersection of Waste and Want

The charitable food system exists at the intersection of waste and want. Driven by inefficiencies in the supply chain, it was invented as a morally preferable alternative to throwing away "perfectly good food." Although increased food insecurity was the background situation that fostered the dramatic growth of the charitable food system, to a large degree the existence of waste in the food chain led to the establishment of the charitable distribution system. (The current focus on minimizing food waste to reduce climate-changing gases is an offshoot of this phenomenon.) *Supply creates demand*: Julia Tedesco, co-executive director of Foodlink in Rochester, New York, reinforces this point, noting that even if Foodlink were to close its doors, some other group would take its place, simply because surplus food exists in the region.[13]

The amount of surplus food that manufacturers and retailers generate has shrunk in recent times. Retailers have developed more sophisticated computerized inventory systems that allow them to better control the flow of products. Manufacturers have adopted more efficient processes, and now sell surplus or damaged foods to such outlets as dollar stores.[14] Despite this shrinking donation base, food banks have continued their inexorable growth, filling the gap by purchasing food. The Rhode Island Food Bank, for example, now buys 40 percent of the food it distributes.[15] Demand for free food always seems to exceed the currently available (and exhaustible) supply.[16] Mark Winne, in *Closing the Food Gap*, contends that increasing the supply of food through the emergency food system is akin to trying to reduce traffic congestion by building bigger highways: just as wider freeways encourage more people to drive, a greater supply of free food encourages increased demand.[17]

As long as food bankers focus on trying to meet demand, or in their lingo, "feed the need," the emergency food system remains self-perpetuating. Supply and demand interact in a self-reinforcing loop that makes it virtually impossible to find an exit from this ever-accelerating treadmill. How did we wind up here? Neither van Hengel nor the pioneers of the emergency food system from the early 1980s planned that we should be in this position in the second decade of the 21st century. In fact, the very intent of the emergency food system, as it grew to nationwide proportions, was temporary in nature, hence the moniker "emergency food system."[18] It was intended to relieve suffering from a human-made social disaster. As Janet Poppendieck noted regarding the term "hunger," the emergency food system grew out of control, in part because it met the needs of so many. The collateral damage caused by the rapid growth and institutionalization of this system is described in the next two sections of this chapter.

The Toll on Recipients

Undignified. Racist. Classist. Toxic. Stigmatizing. A slow death of the soul. Humiliating.[19] Observers have used these phrases to describe the experience of being a client at a food pantry. A study of food pantry clients in San Francisco confirms the emotional toll that food pantries exact. Selena, a 26-year-old Latina, has commented on the food pantry she frequents: "I think it makes me feel helpless. … It makes me feel helpless, like oh my god, really? Does it have to come down to this?"[20] Her statement and those of others interviewed in this study found that food pantries are a last resort. My own experiences as a food pantry volunteer and recipient confirm the collateral damage pantries can cause to the psyche.

Volunteering

During the summer of 2013, I volunteered at a food pantry (call it St. Mary's) a few miles from my house in Portland. According to colleagues at the Oregon Food Bank, St Mary's is one of the best pantries in the metropolitan area. It occupies the basement of a church, and mimics a grocery store's layout, allowing clients to "shop for" their own food based upon their family size and available products. Shopping pantries provide their clients with a more dignified experience than traditional pantries, which hand out boxes of food that may contain items the recipients don't like, don't know how to cook, or are not appropriate for their health status or culture.

On my first day, a friendly teenager completing community service gives me a basic orientation. She explains my role as a cross between personal shopper and security guard. I am supposed to help people understand what foods they can select, as well as to ensure that they don't take too much of any item, especially the higher value items such as frozen meat and chicken. Following the rules ensures that all clients will receive roughly equitable amounts of food (although the last persons get the most limited choices).

During a four-hour shift, I help about 10 or 15 persons "shop." Even though I am casually dressed, I feel like I am wearing my race and class privilege on my sleeve. This privilege smacks me square in the face when I escort a middle-aged African American couple around the pantry. They look dejected and tired from their two-hour wait. I introduce myself to them, ask them how they are doing, and start to tell them what they can pick out: "a can of tuna and three cans of beans …" The instructions ingrained in my brain, I step away from the cart to give them some space, yet watch them to make sure they don't take more than their allotment. I realize that this couple, down on their luck, is just trying to get a bit of food to keep them going until next week. And here I am making sure they don't slip a few extra potatoes into their cart. I feel like an oppressor, and an unduly suspicious one at that. We both had been ensnared in charity's web. I can't imagine the couple left feeling liberated and uplifted. I end the shift feeling despondent and ashamed.

Undercover Pantry Recipient

After experiencing the food pantry as a volunteer, a few weeks later I decide to check out the other side of the transaction. I choose a food pantry—I'll call it "First Lutheran"—located in a church in a lower-income community of north Portland. I go "undercover," using my own name but pretending to meet income qualifications.[21] Like St. Mary's, First Lutheran is also a shopping pantry. While waiting for the doors to open, I listen to the chitchat of the women in line. It becomes clear that many, if not most of them, have been there before. A study from the Oregon Food Bank verifies this. While only 19 percent of clients relied on emergency food only once or twice per year, roughly one-third received more than 12 food boxes per year.[22]

A few minutes before the doors open, I notice "Frank," a colleague from the former Portland Food Policy Council. Concerned that Frank will blow my cover, I motion for him to come talk to me privately on the side of the church. Before I can explain that I am here as part of my book research, he misinterprets my desire for a confidential conversation. He says, "It's okay if you need a little help. I need some help. I had some guests staying at my house and they ate all of my food for the week." As a periodic client of First Lutheran, Frank was trying to help me out by minimizing the stigma associated with relying on emergency food.

The doors open and the 50 people milling about pile into the church and take their seats on folding chairs. We wait for a middle-aged white man to randomly hand out the numbers that will indicate not only how long we have to wait, but also what food will be left for us. I feel lucky to draw number 16. After a brief intake and a half hour wait, my number is called, and a volunteer leads me to the basement. Just as I had done as a volunteer at St Mary's, a young Latina walks me through the pantry to help me pick out my food. The atmosphere is cordial and polite, but I feel a clear power imbalance between the volunteers and myself. I am admonished to bring cloth bags next time because the paper bags that I brought this time often break. The tacit assumption is, of course, that I will be back. I feel pitied and put in my place.

The Haul

At home, I unpack my bags. The quantity is far more than I expected (after five days my "three day supply" was only half depleted). The quality is decidedly mixed. On the plus side, there's a two pound bag of red beans, six eggs, a container of organic tofu, a box of mushroom lentil soup and another of butternut squash soup, a cantaloupe, a few pounds of carrots, some grapefruit juice, a $10 can of chestnut cream imported from France, and a half gallon of organic almond milk. On the down side, I picked up a couple jars of highly processed peanut butter, four cans of potatoes and carrots, six soft potatoes, three cans of thoroughly mediocre spaghetti sauce, a box of stale donut holes, and four ears of shriveled corn. An unlabeled plastic bag containing eight rectangular frozen fish patties of unknown species and ingredients (I found out later that they were Alaskan cod) wins the scary food contest of the day. I throw a couple in the toaster oven to check them out. They are the poor man's version of the Filet-o-Fish. I feel fed but not nourished. I ate a lot of bitterness that week.

Collateral Damage

This resentment is a symptom of what Robert Lupton, a veteran of four decades of faith-based charity work in Atlanta, calls toxic charity. He believes that compassion can be "a powerful force, a stamp of the divine nature within our spirits." Yet when it takes place outside of its optimal context, he says, beyond natural disasters or true emergencies, "when relief does not transition to development in a timely way, compassion becomes toxic."[23]

Roger Sandberg of the international relief organization Medair echoes this sentiment, defining three stops in responding to the needs of the most vulnerable. *Relief* work takes place during and immediately after an emergency. *Rehabilitation* builds the ability of communities to respond to future crises. *Development* work is longer term and seeks to better the standard of living over the course of many years or decades. Sandberg maintains that the relief phase should last months, rehabilitation years, and development decades.[24]

Lupton sees food in the United States as being a long-term need, not a disaster requiring humanitarian intervention. He asserts: "And when we respond to a chronic need as though it were a crisis, we can predict toxic results: dependency, deception and disempowerment." Food pantries have been one of the worst cases of toxic charity. According to one woman he encounters in a meeting, food pantries thrive "Because it's easier! ... It costs less in time and money to run a food pantry and that's what the churches want. ... Churches want their members to feel good about serving the poor, but no one really wants to become involved in messy relationships."[25]

Interestingly, embracing those messy relationships were the key to the transformation of The Stop from a dingy Toronto food pantry into a thriving community food center over the course of a decade (profiled in chapter 7). Nick Saul, the former executive director of The Stop, holds that the secret to the center's success was to redirect its efforts away from a transaction-based orientation and toward a relationship-based focus.[26] This stands in direct contrast to the volume-based model of food charity embodied by the Greater Boston Food Bank and its cohorts, whose focus on efficiency Lupton criticizes as "overlooking the cost to human dignity."[27] This lack of dignity also plays out in the types of food that the charitable food system distributes.

Food Quality

In early 2012, the media broke the story that the meat industry was routinely adding ammonia-doused meat trimmings, nicknamed "pink slime," to ground beef. Pink slime, known as lean finely textured beef (LFTB), was used as an inexpensive filler as well as to reduce the fat content of ground beef. Found in 70 percent of ground beef sold in supermarkets prior to the 2012 controversy, LFTB was made by "gathering waste trimmings, simmering them at low heat so the fat separates easily from the muscle, and spinning the trimmings using a centrifuge to complete the separation. Next the meat is sent through pipes where it is sprayed with ammonia gas to kill bacteria."[28] LFTB had been declared safe for public consumption by the Food and Drug Administration (FDA).

When the controversy broke, Michael Peck, the new director of Nutrition Services at Boston Public Schools (BPS), actively sought out information about whether the tons of ground meat in his possession contained LFTB. He had been hired to help clean up BPS after it was discovered that the district was serving expired food to its students because of poor inventory control and menu-planning practices. He wanted to be proactive and get out in front of the issue. USDA, which had provided the meat through its commodity distribution program, was unable to verify whether the beef possessed by the BPS was pink slime–free (highlighting the complexity of the supply chain and the extent to which meat is often an untraceable commodity). Public pressure was mounting across the country to refrain from serving school meals made from containing pink slime. Following BPS protocols, Peck offered the questionable beef to other school districts. Unsurprisingly, no takers stepped forward. The next step in district protocols was to offer the food for donation to an appropriate agency. He contacted Greater Boston Food Bank, informing them that the meat might have LFTB in it. GBFB agreed to take meat off Peck's hands.[29]

The student population of BPS is almost universally from low-income households, with three-quarters qualifying for free or reduced-price school lunch.[30] Many of their families undoubtedly rely on food pantries to help make ends meet. By GBFB distributing what Boston Public Schools would not, food that was unfit to serve at school lunch became acceptable to eat at family dinner. This raises questions of how different institutions that serve the same population have different standards, and how the Greater Boston Food Bank, which administered $14 million in state funds in 2014, is less transparent and accountable to public opinion than the school system.[31]

Nonetheless, many food bankers have become acutely aware that the quality of the food they distribute is mixed at best. They have heard numerous criticisms over the years, and many are increasingly receptive to concerns about the healthfulness of their food. A study of 137 food banks in the Feeding America network found conflicting results in this area. It concludes that the organizational culture of food banks is "evolving toward a more systematic and thoughtful consideration of nutritional quality," but the "food bank culture has some way to go to be able to fully support the implementation of a comprehensive nutrition policy."[32]

Efforts toward Improvement

Many food banks have made progress in increasing their distribution of healthy food, especially fresh produce. Yet food banks have found it much more challenging to reduce or eliminate the amount of unhealthful products in their distribution stream. For example, the Community Food Bank of Fresno (California) accepts entire truckloads of candy, because they believe "it's just part of getting calories into kids."[33] This takes place in a county where about 40 percent of the population was obese in 2011, as compared to the national average of 24 percent in 2010.[34] They do so in part because the more junk food they accept from Feeding America's procurement system, the more food they are entitled to receive later on. In the neighboring county to the southeast, Foodlink for Tulare County has taken a diametrically opposite approach. It has stopped accepting sugary snacks and drinks. The price it has had to pay for this transgression against the interests of food manufacturers and retailers has been challenging, according to their executive director Sandy Beals. "Some donors who liked the tax write-off and good PR associated with donating to a food bank were upset, and withdrew financial support. That's hard for a food bank that's had to lay off staff and can often barely afford to pay its electric bill. But I've never had one instance of regret. … I can see the difference in people's health by eating healthy food rather than junk. We don't serve corporations, we don't serve food manufacturers. We serve people who are hungry and who need healthy food."[35]

Most food banks are severely constrained in their ability to distribute healthier food by the lack of physical, human, and policy infrastructure. Nutrition policies have not been developed across the board. For example, 60 percent of food banks have policies related to fresh fruits and vegetables, while only 22 percent do on sugar-sweetened beverages.[36] Even in places that do have such policies, food bankers report challenges in fully implementing them. Most food banks are flying blind when it comes to assessing nutrition quality. Only one in six employ a nutrition rating system, and only two in five have access to a nutritionist on staff or within their network.[37] Their ability to distribute fresh produce and other perishables is limited by a lack of capacity of their pantry partners to accept and store these products.

Driving the improvement in food quality have been two overarching themes. First, the obesity and diabetes epidemics, disproportionately affecting persons of color and the poor, have led food bankers and their funders to consider how the charitable food system might potentially ameliorate these conditions. For example, Mazon: the Jewish Response to Hunger, has partnered with Kaiser Permanente to fund 12 food banks in Kaiser service areas to develop formal written nutrition policies and implement a nutrition rating system.[38] Feeding America has connected with the pharmaceutical company Bristol Myers Squibb and three food banks in Ohio, Texas, and California to "create and pilot bi-directional food bank-health center partnerships that will provide diabetes screening, care coordination, nutrition and disease education, and healthy foods." And in the fall of 2013, Feeding America created the Healthy Food Bank Hub website dedicated to promoting healthy food distribution and nutrition education, which highlights that two-thirds of the foods distributed within the Feeding America network are healthy.[39] According to the long-time nutrition activist Helen Costello of the Food Bank of New Hampshire, the website is the product of a serious attempt to improve the quality of food distributed within the emergency food system.[40]

Second, as food bankers purchase an increasing percentage of their food, they are able to better control their distribution stream. Across the board, food banks are buying higher quality and healthier food than they would typically receive as donations. The Farm to Family program in California represents one successful example of this trend. Managed by the California Association of Food Banks (CAFB), Farm to Family distributed about 125 million pounds of produce in 2012 in the form of 52 different commodities. CAFB works with packinghouses in the state to accept produce that doesn't meet marketing codes because it is too small or cosmetically imperfect, or when there is overstock.[41] CAFB has also developed a nutrition education toolkit that it provides to the food banks to help encourage clients to utilize the fruits and vegetables. Other similar programs exist in produce-rich states such as Florida, Texas, Arizona, and Michigan.

Limitations on Improvement

Conversely, food banks' structure and relationship with food donors limits their ability to reduce the amount of unhealthy food they distribute. According to a study by Campbell, Ross, and Webb, food bank staffers perceive that, out of all their stakeholders, food donors are the most resistant to the creation of nutrition policies. Donors want free waste removal, convenience, a tax deduction, and the halo effect that accompanies hunger relief efforts. Donors do not want to be judged about the quality of the food they provide. Food bankers fear that if they decline a product the donor will not deliver other desirable items.[42] For example, the Greater Boston Food Bank continues to accept Pepsi and Coke products because it doesn't want to discourage these bottlers from delivering orange juice (Coke manufactures Minute Maid and Pepsi owns Tropicana).[43] It remains unclear whether this fear is justified. Both the Food Bank of Central New York and the Second Harvest Food Bank of Santa Cruz County have banned soda without major repercussions. Some food banks refuse to take entire truckloads of soda, but will accept them as part of a mixed load. Other food banks will pour the soda down the drain and redeem the bottles for cash. Feeding

America does not track food bank practices with regards to sugar-sweetened beverages.[44]

Reducing the quantity of "bad food" from food banks' distribution stream creates a conflict between balancing the needs of the donor and the needs of the recipient. Since the ability to "feed the need" is dependent upon the goodwill of donors, food banks are likely to take the necessary steps to preserve those relationships that keep the flow of food coming. Simply, the donors hold the cards, or are at least perceived to.

Soda and other unhealthy foods are not the only food quality issue that the charitable food system faces. Food pantries distribute a lot of poor quality food: expired dairy products, stale bread, dented cans, failed manufacturing experiments, moldy fruit, and wilting vegetables. The very structure of the charitable food system lends itself to the distribution of poor quality foods. Manufacturers and retailers typically donate what they cannot sell, because of its inferior quality or condition. This mediocre quality can affect negatively both the dignity of recipients as well as their health. In their book *The Stop*, Nick Saul and Andrea Curtis document how they sought to improve the quality of food distributed through the Toronto-based food pantry as a means to create a more dignified experience for the "members" that patronized it.[45]

Saul's fellow Torontonian Debbie Field, executive director of Foodshare, agrees with this analysis. She believes that when food banks distribute "dead" food to the poor they are revealing their patronizing attitude, often linked to racism and classism, toward their clients. She quotes one food pantry client who saw parallels between the way food bankers perceived their clients and the bad food that they give away. This client mocked food bankers as believing that they were handing out "garbage food for garbage people."[46]

Shortening the Line, or Finding the Exit Signs

In Greek mythology, Sisyphus was condemned to Hades to roll a massive boulder up a hill. Just as the boulder reached the top, he would have to watch it roll down the hill to the bottom. And back down the hill he would go to try it again and again, for eternity. Food bankers resemble Sisyphus, perpetually trying to meet an ever-increasing demand, but never really succeeding. Every time the boulder rolls back down the hill, they bulk up with more trucks, better software, and more donors. But the hill is enchanted such that every time they implement some strategy, their goal gets further and further away.

As Mark Winne has noted, not only does greater supply create a greater demand, but it also legitimizes cutbacks in federal food assistance programs, such as the Supplemental Nutrition Assistance Program (SNAP). The larger the emergency food system becomes, the more it allows conservatives to claim that charity can replace the role of the government in meeting the needs of the hungry. For many years, it has been commonplace to hear assertions that charity can make up for any cutbacks to federal food programs. The yarn spun by these forces for the privatization of anti-hunger efforts is more values-oriented than evidence-based.

Food bankers understand that the amount of food they provide makes up a tiny percentage of the total food purchased by low-income populations. They know that maintaining and even growing federal food programs is essential to keeping a lid on food insecurity. And yet food banks find themselves trapped in a system partially of their own making. As conservative political forces impose austerity measures on the public through cuts in federal expenditures and enact policies that favor greater economic inequality, the nonprofit sector has stepped up to fill the void. No good deed goes unpunished. The more charity succeeds, the more it undercuts the public perception of the role of government as the protector of the vulnerable. This in turn feeds the flames of further reductions in the government's role, threatening to overwhelm the already-frayed-at-the edges charitable food sector. In essence, the charitable food system is too small to replace the federal government's role (even if that were desirable), but large enough to be considered by some as a credible alternative. It's a no-win situation. The only solution for food bankers is to stop trying to "feed the need" and instead to "shorten the line."

Federal Policy Advocacy

Arguably, the biggest potential bang for the buck is found through federal policy advocacy. The federal government's resources far outstrip those that the private sector can provide, and even modest positive or negative changes to federal policy, such as SNAP, the minimum wage, and earned income tax credits, can have far bigger impacts than any other action. Food banks have the moral responsibility to undertake policy advocacy to shorten the line, as their resources and community outreach potential are far greater than other anti-hunger groups in general.

Not every food bank employs staffers dedicated to public policy advocacy, however, and those that do typically employ only an individual or two. Oregon Food Bank houses the largest policy department of any food bank in the nation with eight full-time staff members, and it spends only 3.6 percent of the organization's budget on policy advocacy.[47] By comparison, the Greater Boston Food Bank did not have any dedicated policy staff as of spring 2013.[48]

Many food banks rely on their state associations to conduct policy advocacy for them. This allows them to take more liberal policy positions than they could by themselves.[49] J. C. Dwyer agrees: "I think state associations (and broad collaboratives in general) can be a way to take bolder stances [or] talk about bigger issues more safely than stepping forward as a single organization."[50] Dwyer's opinion rings true in Ohio, where the state food bank association supported a constitutional amendment to increase the minimum wage and index it to inflation. According to Lisa Hamler Fugitt, state associations have been partly able to take more progressive positions because their boards of directors include representatives of the member food banks rather than the businessmen and women that tend to populate individual food bank boards.[51] This inoculates state associations from the political pressure that their member food banks experience from their communities, boards, and donors.

Nonetheless, more food banks are undertaking policy advocacy than ever before. The Jewish anti-hunger funder Mazon, for example, has made advocacy efforts a precondition of their grant making. Feeding America has increased its policy advocacy department to eight persons in 2015.[52]

The policy advocacy of Feeding America and its food bank affiliates, however, can be very narrow and skeletal. Two of Feeding America's top policy priorities—increased funding for TEFAP (The Emergency Food Assistance Program, the government program that provides hundreds of millions of dollars' worth of commodities and funding for the emergency food system), and the renewal of charitable giving tax incentives—further institutionalize the charitable food sector. Gloria McAdam, the former executive director of Foodshare in Hartford, Connecticut, notes: "It is easy for food banks to work on TEFAP, and it is self-serving. One of my frustrations is that we need to do more than that gimme gimme kind of ask. We have to be solving the problem."[53]

Similarly, on the very day that the House of Representatives voted for the first time in history to pass a farm bill that excluded food stamps, Feeding America sent out a legislative update to its food bank members about its "current advocacy focus." The main message of this update was not even about the SNAP program. Instead it encouraged food bankers to contact their Congress members to increase the supply of government commodities for food banks, and to protect charitable tax incentives.[54]

Feeding America has also avoided forays into issues other than federal food programs that would have an impact on food security. While medical bills drive many families into poverty and hunger (a report by Oregon Food Bank found that 40 percent of food pantry clients had medical debt), Feeding America never joined the primary coalition supporting the Affordable Care Act's passage.[55]

Nutrition policy often serves as a safety zone within food banks. Boards and donors can easily understand the linkages between a food bank's mission and federal food programs such as SNAP and WIC. While conservative stakeholders can be opposed to the role of government in meeting the needs of the poor, by and large nutrition programs are nonthreatening to food bank supporters. As Michael Flood, the executive director of the Los Angeles Regional Food Bank notes, "By staying in the nutrition area you're safe—with regard to donors' perceptions of your policy work."[56]

Policy work in a food bank resembles an archery target with concentric rings. TEFAP and state programs that fund the charitable food system sit in the highest-value bullseye ring. Very few food bankers would argue with advocating for a government program that provides them with commodities and cash to help distribute those products. Moving outward to the next ring sit federal and state nutrition programs. These are generally but not universally accepted as a legitimate activity by all food banks. Moving out further lies the Earned Income Tax Credit, which provides working families with cash back on their tax returns. It is highly prized by liberals and conservatives alike for incentivizing work. Continuing outward lies the ring of non-nutrition-related policies that affect low-income households' income or expenditures, such as the minimum wage and other employment issues, affordable housing, child care, public transportation, and affordable health care. These are all core issues for low-income and working class families, but on the periphery of what most food banks undertake. Even further out lie the state and federal tax policies that ensure an adequate funding stream for government provision of services.

Out in the periphery, light years from the bullseye and so controversial that most food bankers consider this topic to be radioactive, lies immigration reform. Anti-hunger groups have historically advocated for the rights of immigrants, as they have fought over the years for the right of immigrants to participate in the SNAP program and, in the case of California, to create a state-administered program for immigrants that don't qualify for SNAP.[57] Yet few if any food banks have taken a position on this issue, despite the fact that immigration reform can reduce poverty by enabling 20 million undocumented immigrants (including children) to qualify for federal benefits and, for those of working age, the ability to access better-paying jobs.[58] As Andrew Wainer of Bread for the World Institute asserts, "Unauthorized legal status isn't the only barrier to economic advancement, but it poses a significant obstacle. That's why legalization for certain unauthorized immigrations would facilitate their ability to find better jobs and pursue further education, helping them get out of poverty. The 1986 Immigration Reform and Control Act legalized the status of nearly 2.7 million immigrants. Following legalization, social scientists across the political spectrum documented wage increases in the range of 6 to 13 percent, with some finding larger gains."[59]

The occasional reactionary nature of donors underscores the challenge of taking a position on a controversial topic outside of the "nutrition safety zone." Laura Golino de Lovato, the development director at Oregon Food Bank (OFB), tells of an incident in which an individual from the eastern (and red) side of the state sent them a check for $10,000 along with a note stipulating that none of the donation was to be used to feed "illegal immigrants."[60] While OFB returned the check, politely stating that they were unable to meet that condition, it does show how the broad political leanings of donors can inhibit food banks from taking progressive stances on issues such as immigration reform.

Constraints

Four basic factors keep the majority of food banks in the "feed the need" model. These include the nature of their leadership and organizational culture, the interests of donors, how they communicate the problem, and the ways in which they measure their success.

1: Leadership and Organizational Culture

There's a commonly heard explanation for why food banks tend to take such moderate policy positions. Food bank staff members tend to be relatively liberal, and want to address the underlying causes of hunger through programs and policy advocacy. Their boards, however, are reluctant to support such efforts, because they conflict with the vested interests of those who employ the board members. As a result, staffers must toe the line, keeping their focus within the "nutrition safety zone."

An examination of food bank websites finds a high degree of affiliation with large corporations among the board members. Of the 202 food banks in the Feeding America network, 154 (or 76 percent) listed the affiliations of the board members on their websites or provided this information after a phone call. Of the 2,817 board members listed with these 154 food banks, 715 (or 25 percent) worked for a Fortune 1000 company, or for a privately owned or foreign-owned company of similar size.[61] Table 2.1 shows the most common employers of these individuals.

As might be expected, the greatest concentration of these large corporate-employed board members (one-third of the 715), work for food-related companies, such as grocers, manufacturers, and food service providers.

The other 75 percent of the board members who don't work for Fortune 1000 firms (or their equivalent), are employed at other businesses or a nonprofit, are self-employed, retired, or simply listed as community volunteers. Only two of the 2,817 board members work for a labor union, both of them at the Food Bank of Eastern Michigan (the state being heavily unionized).

Similarly, the participation of food pantry or soup kitchen clients on food bank boards of directors falls outside of the norm. Most food banks are large institutions that do not prioritize accountability to their clients when looking for new board members. For example, low-income individuals don't meet the needs of food banks that use their boards as fundraising entities, whose responsibilities are bluntly phrased as "give, get, or get off." One East Coast food bank requires its board members to raise or donate $25,000 annually.

Table 2.1
Corporate Employees on Food Bank Boards

Corporation	Number of Food Banks	Type of Business
Kroger	32	Grocery
Walmart	31	Grocery/Retail
Bank of America	22	Financial Services
Wells Fargo	22	Financial Services
Ernst and Young	10	Accounting Services
Kraft	10	Food Manufacturing
Blue Cross	10	Insurance
JP Morgan Chase	10	Financial Services
Royal Ahold	9	Grocery
H-E-B	8	Grocery
Sodexo	7	Food Service
Sun Trust	7	Financial Services
UPS	7	Shipping
Albertsons	6	Grocery
Nationwide	6	Insurance
PNC Bank	6	Financial Services
Safeway	6	Grocery
Supervalu	6	Grocery
Target	6	Grocery/Retail
Delhaize	5	Grocery
US Foodservice	5	Food Service

As sophisticated organizations with multimillion dollar budgets and significant infrastructure, food banks seek highly competent board members with the requisite experience to provide effective governance. Given their close relationships with the food industry, it should come as no surprise that they look to colleagues from these firms to serve on their boards. Likewise, as food banks have much in common with the grocery business, for example in their warehousing, inventory control, and distribution functions, board members employed in this sector can help food banks leverage needed technical support and resources to professionalize their operations.

Board members from the grocery industry can also carry over their company's financial interests into their volunteer position in food banks.

The profitability of the supermarket industry remains highly dependent on keeping a lid on labor costs. The industry's representatives on food bank boards have in some cases opposed them from undertaking public policy advocacy to raise the minimum wage.[62] That does not mean that all employees of major corporations who sit on food bank boards have right-wing political beliefs. Nor do corporate food bank board members hold their positions as representatives of their employers. Most do not typically check in with their bosses, except perhaps on rare occasions, to discuss how they should vote on organizational matters. Yet it is highly unlikely that, in their volunteer roles, they will contravene their company's interests. Kevin Bott, the former chief information officer of Ryder Inc., explains: "Senior management of top companies is already heavily Republican. Middle management might be more liberal, but they will not do anything to embarrass their employer, or that will cause them problems at work, if it (their vote on a controversial matter) were to go public."[63]

Food bank leaders differ on the actual influence that corporate employees have on their boards. Joyce Rothermel, the former CEO of the Greater Pittsburgh Community Food Bank (GPCFB), notes that she wanted the food bank to support a living wage ordinance, but she refrained from bringing it to her board because she knew they would shoot it down. In the end, the most the GPCFB could accomplish in this area was to establish an internal wage policy. Similarly, the food bank did not publicly associate itself with the Occupy protests in Pittsburgh, despite Rothermel's Catholic social justice roots. These protests were targeted in part at BNY Mellon, a major donor to the food bank and the employer of a member of the GPCFB's board of directors.[64]

Gloria McAdam, in liberal Hartford, Connecticut, agrees: "It's an easy sell to this board to be doing SNAP outreach and advocacy on SNAP. But it is more challenging to convince them that we should work on health care and minimum wage. They [her board members] are business people with their own business objectives, and they don't see these things so well in that regard." As a result, she has done little work on these issues, and has avoided conflict with her board. But she imagines that "if I were too out there on living wages, I would get backlash. Walmart is now the biggest donor to food banks." Instead, she buries what little economic justice work the food bank undertakes as a participant in various coalitions.[65]

Down in conservative Louisiana, Natalie Jayroe, the head of the food bank in New Orleans, asserts that the corporate employees on her board are not any different from any other board member in terms of their political beliefs. "Nor have I ever had any corporation on my board that threatened to cut off food if we took a certain political position." She believes that "there are very few boards that would give food bankers leeway to fight for a living wage."[66]

In Los Angeles, Michael Flood, the CEO of the LA Regional Food Bank, believes that whether a food bank board member hails from a big corporation is irrelevant for the political stances of food banks from blue states. He sees the lack of focus on the root causes of hunger as more a matter of self-censorship, of how far the food bank is willing to go politically, without jeopardizing its credibility or respectability.[67]

It's difficult to determine the impact that employees of multinational corporations on food bank boards have had on these organizations' public policy advocacy choices. But food banks' undeniably corporate-heavy boards do indicate the extent to which these organizations have strayed from their social justice roots. They have become "mainstream, respectable, and rich," according to McAdam, and intend to keep their privileges.[68] Some food bankers contend that their middle-of-the-road political position combined with their connections to the poor enables them to maintain high levels of credibility with the media and policymakers, which they can use to the benefit of their clients.

Accountability Nonetheless, the composition of food bank boards brings up the broader issue of accountability. Most food banks are not membership organizations, and as such do not have a formal accountability mechanism beyond the legal requirements demanded of nonprofit organizations. The representatives of food pantries and the clients that frequent them may be combined on advisory committees, which shape programmatic work but have little formal authority. Instead, the formal authority rests with the board of directors, typically comprising a diffuse set of civic and business leaders. These connections perpetuate the food bank and its interests by building a strong base of financial support throughout the community. But this structure leaves an accountability vacuum, which in practical terms means that the contributions of the donors, both of food and cash, assume a greater importance than the social or political values that lie behind the food bank's decision making.

Accommodating the interests of corporate donors translates into very real costs similar to that of the use of hunger terminology: watered-down politics, partial downstream solutions, and built-in conflicts of interest. This accommodation impedes food banks from transcending their service orientation to address the root causes of hunger, tying their feet to the business as usual treadmill.

Corporate Culture   Corporate boards, donors, and CEOs have brought to food banks practices from their own organizations. Slowly over time these practices have changed the organizational culture of food banks such that they become more like their corporate partners. This should not be construed as an entirely negative phenomenon. Kate MacKenzie, the director of policy and government relations at City Harvest in New York City and a long time community food activist, believes it crucial to import "good business practices from the private sector."[69]

Corporate culture has manifested itself within food banks in both obvious and subtle ways. CEO salaries in some food banks have replicated corporate practices of paying top staffers substantially more than others in the organization. A quick examination of the tax returns of the nation's largest food banks found that the salaries of various food bank CEOs exceeded $300,000. These are astonishing salaries, indicators of the degree to which food banks have become "mainstream, respectable, and rich." One way in which food banks justify these salaries is by inflating their annual revenues to include their food distributions as income. For example, Feeding America lists its annual revenue on its 2014 tax returns as $2.06 billion, of which $1.942 billion is in the form of noncash donations (food and in-kind volunteer time). Its cash budget is only about 5 percent of its stated budget at $118 million.[70]

The organizational culture of food banks mimics that of its corporate partners far beyond the pay levels of its executives. One program director describes a culture of fear within the ranks of staff at his food bank. He reports that, in order to keep their jobs, staff become very skilled at specific tasks, but hesitate to attempt anything new or different. This fear of innovation leads them to be very focused on a narrow set of indicators, such as pounds distributed or people served. Their fear is driven by program evaluations that seek to identify deficiencies rather than drive improvement through constructive criticism. The rise to power of individuals with financial backgrounds also reinforces this focus on efforts that

Table 2.2
Highly Paid Food Bank Staff

Name	Organization	Position	Year	Salary (w/o benefits)
Robert Aiken	Feeding America	CEO	2015	606,521
Jan Pruitt	North Texas Food Bank	CEO	2013	516,871
Matthew Knott	Feeding America	President	2015	377,619
Jilly Stephens	City Harvest	CEO	2015	328,413
Catherine D'Amato	Greater Boston Food Bank	CEO	2015	324,896
William Thomas	Feeding America	Chief Supply Chain Officer	2015	296,676
Paul Ash	San Francisco Food Bank	CEO	2014	294,061
Margarette Purvis	Food Bank of NYC	CEO	2015	293,044
Paul Henrys	Feeding America	CFO	2015	285,876
Maura Daly	Feeding America	Chief External Affairs Officer	2015	277,415
Johanna Vetter	Feeding America	CMO	2015	273,121
Kate Maehr	Greater Chicago Food Depository	CEO	2014	272,223
Kathryn Jackson	Food Bank of Santa Clara County	CEO	2014	270,560
Deborah Flateman	Maryland Food Bank	CEO	2014	263,671

Source: Form 990 (filed by tax-exempt organizations) accessed from http://www.guidestar.org.

yield quantitative measurements to the detriment of relationship-oriented, more qualitative initiatives such as community organizing. Just as corporations can have a single-minded focus on exceeding quarterly earnings reports to please Wall Street, food banks concentrate on meeting annual poundage targets, losing sight of longer-term goals.

In addition to the influence of donors and board members, this food banker contends that Feeding America has played a strong role in accelerating the adoption of corporate principles in the emergency food system. First, Feeding America gives each food bank a rating based on how efficiently they distribute food. This score reinforces the primacy of the "feed the need" approach and the use of quantitative measurements of success. In choosing "Food Bank of the Year" awards, Feeding America utilizes a number of criteria such as how many pounds per person in poverty the food bank provides, how efficiently it does so, the number of volunteer hours it mobilizes, and the amount of funds it raises from the community.[71] It does not recognize efforts to reduce demand on the food bank nor reduce poverty in the region.

2: Donors

During the Great Depression, in an effort to keep farm prices high, surplus food was dumped while many went hungry. This waste amid want challenged the public's support for capitalism. A system that killed baby pigs and poured milk down the sewer was seen as uncaring and not in the public's interests.[72] Now, more than 80 years later, capitalism has learned its lesson well, integrating the charitable food system into its business planning. The emergency food system bolsters industry, both inside and outside the food system, in direct and indirect ways.

Manufacturers and retailers receive an enhanced tax deduction for the food they donate to charitable outlets. Internal Revenue Code 170e3 allows corporations to deduct from their taxes the cost to produce the food plus half the difference between the cost and the full fair market value (up to twice the cost of the item).[73] This policy allows companies to capture part of their overhead on top of production costs or purchase price. The Congressional Budget Office has projected the cost of this deduction to the government's coffers at $189.6 million per year, (based on a tax year average from 2013 to 2022).[74]

Various states also provide tax benefits for fresh produce donations. In California, a state law allows growers to take a tax credit in the amount of 10 percent of the food's production costs. The state estimates that this provision will cost it $400,000 in lost revenue by fiscal year 2013–2014.[75]

Federal and state governments not only buttress the donation of excess food to charitable outlets, they also purchase significant quantities for distribution through food pantries and soup kitchens. The largest of these programs is TEFAP. In fiscal year 2012 TEFAP provided more than $610 million worth of food and cash to the charitable food system, or about 17 percent of the total food distributed by food banks.[76]

In addition to the federal dollars that subsidize the charitable food system, states also chip in tens of millions of dollars annually, largely for food purchases, transportation, and equipment. As of 2009, 37 states provided some form of tax credits or earmarked support, either through administrative channels or authorized through legislation, to food banks and food pantries. These programs vary from the sale of themed license plates in Florida, to partnerships with deer hunters and meat lockers in Iowa, to programs that fund tens of millions of dollars' worth of food in New York, Pennsylvania, and Massachusetts.[77]

Public policy incentivizes the participation of the agri-food industry in the charitable food system with roughly three-quarters of a billion dollars of contracts and tax write-offs.[78] This public-private partnership underscores the importance of taxpayer support in subsidizing the charitable food system. State and federal programs pay for a significant portion of the food handled by food banks, roughly between one-quarter and one-third of their total poundage.[79] Tax deductions incentivize retailers and manufacturers to donate an even greater amount of food.[80] Together these multiple laws and programs create an integrated framework as the public policy underpinnings of the charitable food system.

3: Defining Success

In December 2011 my son Orion, in third grade at the time, came home excited about the Christmas food drive in his class. "There's a contest for who can raise the most money and donate the most pounds of food for Oregon Food Bank. I want our class to win," he said, as he started scouring the kitchen for the heaviest food items he could find. My wife stopped him from stripping our cupboard bare. A week later, as I was headed out the door on a shopping trip, he pleaded with me to buy some more heavy food, as his classroom's donation barrel wasn't very full. At the store, I looked for nutritious food that was heavy and inexpensive.

As I was shopping, I realized that the food drive at Orion's school was a microcosm of how food banks operate: they measure their success in the millions of pounds of food that they distribute. Orion's class does not stand alone in framing anti-hunger efforts to a sporting contest. Food banks in Alabama utilize the rivalry between Auburn University and the University of Alabama as part of a contest to determine which university can donate more food. The "20th Beat 'Bama Food Drive" sought to exceed the 275,000 pounds donated by Auburn in 2012.[81]

While virtually every food bank conducts canned food drives, they do so knowing that the costs can outweigh the benefits. The drives fulfill an important purpose in maintaining awareness of the hunger problem as well as in building brand awareness for food banks. They are an inefficient use of resources, however, collecting a limited amount of food for the volunteer time that they require.

These canned food drives create an illusion that food banks put a dent in hunger. Likewise, every food bank annual report or website that heralds the millions of pounds the organization distributes every year leads our country a step deeper into a labyrinth from which escape becomes an increasingly distant dream. The more society celebrates its charitable food achievements, the further it defines those achievements as the solution to hunger rather than as an unfortunate activity it feels morally obligated to undertake because of our societal failure to prevent hunger in the first place.[82]

Just as the school offered Orion's class a prize for collecting the most pounds of food, the Greater Boston Food Bank provides its CEO an annual bonus based on the number of pounds it distributes, among other factors.[83] These two incentives further engrain in the public's mind and in food banks' organizational structure a one-sided and simplistic approach to dealing with the problem of food insecurity.

There is a truism in management: you get what you measure. The way organizations define success shapes what gets done. Individuals and their organizations want and need to be successful in order to keep their jobs and please their stakeholders. Measure success in terms of pounds distributed and people served and that's what will be produced in spades. This measurement produces an unfortunate opportunity cost. A focus on pounds distributed and people served limits the organization's "bandwidth" to attempt projects of a more preventative nature. If staff members are kept busy meeting poundage goals, they will have less time and energy to fundraise for and implement upstream initiatives, such as policy advocacy.

At a basic level, "pounds" and "people" are the obvious measurements by which to evaluate the work of food banks. They are tangible and easily attributed to the work of the organization. Broader indicators such as reductions in food insecurity depend on other factors, such as the unemployment rate, that tend to exist beyond the control of any single nonprofit organization. Food banks can contribute to that broader societal change, but proving causality is quite difficult. For this reason, Judy Alley, the executive director of Sno-Cap food pantry, characterized by Oregon Food Bank staff as another one of the top-tier food pantries in the Portland metro area, strongly believes in focusing on these very concrete indicators: "I refuse to measure anything except pounds and people. Relationships built, skills learned, I wouldn't be honest if I tried to measure those. Nor it is honest to say, give me a can of corn and I can change a life with that."[84] In other words, food may not be *the* solution to ending hunger, but it is a very beneficial thing that food pantries offer.

The focus on pounds moved and people served does have a straightforward simplicity that is measurable and tangible. It is, however, limited as evaluation practice. In the evaluation field, practitioners make a very clear distinction between outputs and outcomes. "Outputs" are the products that occur because of an organization's activities, such as the number of pounds distributed. "Outcomes" are the changes in the environment, behavior, or knowledge that happen because of those activities. Outcomes, or results, are paramount in the human services field. Programs live or die based upon whether they show adequate results. For example, success in an AIDS reduction program is measured by a drop in the rate of HIV in the population, not by the number of condoms distributed or bus shelter ads purchased (these are outputs). The condoms and the ads may have led to the decrease in HIV, but they are not the disease reduction itself. They are a means toward an end.

When food banks boast about the amount of food they distribute or the number of people they serve and claim that they are reducing hunger, they are treating outputs as outcomes. Feeding a person is not an outcome. An outcome might be if that person were to no longer self-report as food insecure. Implicit in this output-outcome confusion is the assumption that the food they distribute reduces hunger for a certain number of days. Yet this assumption is based on an limited understanding of hunger as a problem that repeats itself day in, day out, rather than as a symptom of deeper issues.

Human service programs are designed to solve a problem among a certain population within a specific timeframe. No service provider wants to be mentoring at-risk "youth" forever. It is absurd to think that individuals would participate in the same job training programs for decades until they reach retirement age. At some point they gain the skills and experiences they need to be successful.

Yet the "feed the need" model operates under this assumption of eternal service. Measuring pounds and people doesn't provide food banks with an exit strategy from what should be a temporary service. Instead, it provides them with a framework for continuing their work forever.

The focus on pounds and people is not only driven by canned food drives and CEO incentives, but also by our society's passion for growth. Food bank board members hailing from the business sector have pushed food banks toward growth as an unquestioned good. These boards know that growth is de rigueur in the for-profit sector, so they assume that it should be the case in the nonprofit sector, especially when there is such pent up demand for free food. If growth is good for food banks, then the conditions that foster growth must be perversely considered positive as well. Robert Egger acerbically drives home this point: "The recession was the best thing that happened to the anti-hunger movement."[85] Not only did food banks get more funding and attention to cope with the increased demand caused by the economic downturn, but, as their distribution totals soared, they were able to claim greater success.[86] Conversely, during economic good times, many hunger relief agencies suffer from reductions in their food and cash donations, as hunger goes off-radar for the general public.

The incentives and regulations that Feeding America place on its affiliates also push them heavily in a growth-oriented direction. It has established what it calls the "One Goal," a target of increasing the amount of food distributed nationally from 2.63 billion meals to 3.63 billion meals from 2010 to 2018. Each food bank receives its own individual targets within this broader national framework (to their credit, Feeding America does allow food banks to count applications for enrollment in the food stamp program completed in their service area toward their target numbers). Food banks that do not meet their targets would not lose their membership in the Feeding America network, but could potentially lose eligibility for grants and other rewards given out through national competitions.[87]

4: Buildings as Stakeholders

Foodlink's old warehouse is a five-story stone structure in a down-and-out weed-strewn industrial neighborhood of Rochester, New York. The street is lined with crumbling buildings and pothole-filled streets. The neighborhood looks like a forgotten part of the city, except perhaps by the drug dealers who used to do business in the parking lot. It is generous to say that the building has seen better days. Dark and dingy, with a freight elevator that needs to be gently coaxed into operation, it's the kind of place where one would expect to see a rat the size of a housecat scurry by. After years of operation, Foodlink's long-time executive director Tom Ferraro finally moved the organization out of the building. He could no longer ask his employees to come to work there. It was killing their morale.

Five miles away on the western edge of the city, along a frontage road, sits Foodlink's new site. It's located in a no-man's land, near other light industrial and warehouse-type operations. The building is clean, humble in appearance, and sprawls across one story. It has carpeted offices, a large meeting space, and a kitchen for nutrition education classes. It feels to be on a human scale, a welcoming environment. Employees like coming to work here. A big section of the warehouse sits empty, set aside to catalyze a new catering business that will source locally grown foods for many of the city's social service agency and institutional food programs. Because of the depressed real estate market in Rochester, Foodlink was given partial ownership without having to raise millions of dollars to acquire the property.

The organization has a unique philosophy related to the stewardship of its assets, encouraging their use in off-hours. Ferraro explains, "Is it appropriate to (only) use these millions and millions of dollars of food related assets five days a week, eight hours a day, to only impact on the 'symptom' of hunger? Or do we feel obligated to make them available to the wider food and agricultural community, in an effort to create wealth and opportunities, especially jobs? These food-related assets and their excess capacity is what we believe must be used for a 'greater good' in an effort to impact on a community's overall food security."[88]

While Foodlink's move was a wise move both for the organization and the community, food bank capital campaigns can further institutionalize the organization as a permanent feature of the community's landscape. Key stakeholders, such as foundations and the business community, not only dedicate millions for new buildings but also become more bought into the expansion of the charitable food distribution model. In doing so, they become less likely to support alternatives to the emergency food system.

Capital campaigns also create an expectation that the newly constructed, and probably much larger, warehouse must be filled. Efficiency demands it. Why build the space if not to fill it up with food? As a result, food banks redouble their efforts to fill up the new and larger warehouse. They get bigger and better freezers and refrigerators. They acquire loading docks that back right into freezers, so frozen foods never have to leave a climate controlled environment. They buy new inventory management software to help find all that new food and deliver it more speedily to their clients. The expansion creates new demands on staff, and may lead to the need to hire additional warehouse workers. It creates the need to strengthen efforts to source additional food, and perhaps an augmented food procurement budget. It fosters expectations among the board and donors that the organization will greatly increase its distribution now that it has larger facilities. Supply, this time in the form of square footage, has once again generated demand, and the vicious cycle spirals onward. Buildings become stakeholders.

Let's return to Boston, where the Massachusetts governor at the time, Deval Patrick, once commented about the size of Greater Boston Food Bank's new 117,000 square-foot building to the Food Bank's CEO, Catherine D'Amato. She responded, "It's a big building because it's a big problem."[89] Yet the size and cost of this warehouse makes it challenging for the food bank to consider alternative methods of addressing food insecurity. To not utilize it to capacity or near-capacity would be an embarrassment to the organization and to the individuals who put the squeeze on their friends and colleagues to donate. In other words, the size of the new GBFB's building puts pressure on the organization to keep it full. The building creates only one course of action for GBFB: unfettered growth. The size of the building further pushes Massachusetts toward the wrong approach in addressing food insecurity. To play on Catherine D'Amato's answer to Governor Patrick, *the big building is a big problem.*

A Vision for Charitable Food

We have allowed an unplanned system to play an integral role in the way our country confronts a protracted and tragic social problem. Sharon Thornberry, speaking at an Oregon Food Justice fundraiser, puts this quite simply: "We did not create this system deliberately. It's not what we would create if we were to sit down to design a system to deal with hunger."[90] The charitable food sector has snowballed out of control. It has grown from what was supposed to be a temporary stopgap into a seemingly permanent feature of our country's landscape, in part because numerous entrenched interests backstop it. Food charity has turned into big business, and an integral part of the business strategy of many corporations. Nonetheless, there exists a growing cadre of organizations interested in finding and scaling up new solutions. Indeed, the time has come that our society engage in a serious dialogue about whether there might be better ways to tackle food insecurity than through charity.

Criticisms of the food bank system are often met with a strenuous and emotional counter-argument that closing the food banks would cause untold suffering among the poor. It is immoral for society to let people starve in the face of abundance. That is undoubtedly a bottom line of our social contract. Conversely, society should not keep the poor in the current system that feeds their bodies without nourishing their souls, depriving them of their dignity while providing them with corporate leftovers. Neither option is very humanitarian. Charitable food distribution needs to be dramatically transformed, if not entirely discontinued. Similarly, the charitable food sector must shrink, perhaps significantly.

We need a slow and steady transition to a society in which the emergency food system looks quite different. It took 30-plus years to get to this point, and transformative change to get off the charity treadmill will take another generation. It's a long time, but the sooner we get started the sooner we'll get there. But, where is *there*?

Painted in broad strokes, community should become front-and-center in the emergency food system. Food and community in all of its aspects—geographic, spiritual, cultural, and social—are truly inseparable. Linked, they contain enormous resonance and power for changing society. Food banks should utilize food to build social capital through a community development approach; they can be actively engaged as partners in improving the food environment of communities with low-income residents. Food banks can assist low-income communities in food-related community economic development strategies to help them create jobs and build wealth; they should become an important support partner by providing food to social service agencies, which would benefit from the food banks' logistics and brokering expertise. Food banks can minimize the amount and frequency of food that they distribute to individuals, except in true emergencies, such as natural disasters. Food should be provided to individuals perhaps only in concert with a comprehensive social service support system to help the unfortunate acquire the skills, resources, and opportunities they need to escape poverty and food insecurity.

Of equal importance, food banks should become more politically engaged, hosting community organizing campaigns to develop grassroots leadership as a voice for reducing social and economic inequality. Food is the great connector. Food banks exist at the center of many linkages between disciplines, geographies, and social classes in a way that few other institutions in this country do. They would be remiss not to utilize their extensive networks to build the political will to reduce not just food insecurity but also to nurture a more resilient and equitable society.

Getting to this place will require changing the political discourse and the way in which we deal with poverty in America. The political dynamics are already in flux. Interest in food system issues has grown unabated since the late 2000s. Efforts to reduce childhood obesity, such as Michelle Obama's Let's Move Initiative, have led to significant changes in access to healthy affordable food in schools and communities. Faced with a multigenerational decline, labor organizing is experiencing a renaissance in the service sector. There exists a growing understanding that economic inequality drags down the nation's fortunes. Some food banks have jumped into the fray on some of these issues, especially those related to health and food systems. Nevertheless, most need to suit up and get off the sidelines. Leadership needs to be provided by Feeding America, and if not forthcoming, by a growing community of progressive food banks. Food banks can help move in the right direction by spending more time and money on activities that "shorten the line" instead of "feeding the need."

Specifically, the charitable food sector should be focusing its efforts on promoting economic justice, public health, and a sustainable food system. Here's what that might look like.

Implementing the Vision

First and foremost, food banks become stronger advocates for social and economic justice. This entails discarding their political neutrality in favor of taking progressive stances that reduce the incidence of poverty rather than merely treating its symptoms. It includes funding grassroots organizing to mobilize their enormous base of volunteers and clients so that they can become a force for public policy change. In terms of their relationship with their corporate donors, food banks collectively exert influence on them to take proactive steps to become more socially responsible through paying their employees living wages and benefits. The dignity of their clients and resilience of the communities they serve are core values of food banks, and growth is seen as a failure to meet the organization's poverty reduction goals. Food bank boards are required by contract with Feeding America to have at least one half of their members being the end user clients or their representatives, in an effort to shift accountability back to the food insecure.

Food banks become health-promoting institutions. They only distribute food that is of better quality and more healthful than what the average American eats. Given the vulnerability to diet-related diseases such as diabetes, the poor deserve foods that will not aggravate their existing medical predispositions. This "preference for the poor," as laid out in Judeo-Christian thinking, entails a fundamental redefining of the relationship between food banks and the food industry. The charitable food sector would no longer be downstream of industry; food waste would find a different home than in the cupboards and refrigerators of the poor.

Many food banks have already developed significant initiatives to promote local and regional food systems, such as farm stands, community gardens, and farms. These initiatives continue to grow. This food system focus is being integrated into the core operations of food banks, as they are using their purchasing power and significant infrastructure to support family-scale farmers and local food economies. This includes making their warehouses, trucking, and other resources available, as Foodlink currently does, to support food-oriented community economic development, as well as purchasing an increasing amount of food from local farmers.

These changes may seem unattainable, even utopian. For some food banks, they may even seem undesirable. This section is but a beginning sketch of what charitable food distribution could be. The charitable food system is not inevitable. It has been the direct product of policy choices and actions made by many persons. It can be transformed into a much more positive force without the collateral damage it has inflicted on society.

Recommendations

Following are some specific changes that emergency food organizations can put into place in order to move down this path.

Food banks should create a long-term strategic plan to fundamentally transform charitable food distribution. These strategic plans should include benchmarks for reducing food distribution without causing additional food insecurity, as well as for allocating at least 50 percent of organizational budgets to activities that "shorten the line" by 2027.

Food banks should modify the incentives and structural underpinnings to reflect this new direction. These changes include:

• Measuring pounds or meals distributed should be discouraged, and innovative measurements developed. Growth should be considered in a negative light, rather than desirable.

• Feeding America should forego future growth-oriented poundage goals.

• A voluntary moratorium on capital campaigns for new buildings should be implemented.

• The charitable food sector should encourage states and the federal government to reduce its support for the charitable food sector through ceasing tax breaks, reducing commodity-distribution programs, and reorienting public efforts toward changing the food environment and self-reliance for low-income communities.

Food banks must increase their advocacy on public policy to at least 10 percent of their organizational budgets by 2022. This advocacy should focus on safety-net programs but also on policies that address such issues as income inequality and poverty, such as minimum wage, affordable housing, healthcare, and labor relations, as well as fair tax and job creation-related initiatives; it should be integrated into all of the organization's activities, and at least in part be focused on building community leadership.

Food banks need to redefine their relationship with the food industry, organizing themselves so as not to be junior partners. For example, all food banks should adopt strict guidelines that prohibit them from accepting any food that is of poor quality, unhealthy, or that would harm the dignity of recipients.

Charitable food groups must foster communication about their new vision and plan. Charitable food providers need to take advantage of their opportunities to build support for a new direction. They should test educational campaigns, fundraising letters, and messaging, as well as sharing information with each other. Best practices should be identified and disseminated across the nation. Conversely, food banks should stop putting out the wrong message about the solutions to food insecurity. The single best way to do so is to phase out canned food drives, especially since they provide a very low percentage of food distributed by the charitable food system.

Summary

Charity works to the good, but charity is not a substitute for justice. The charitable food system has benefited millions by filling in the gaps of the safety net. Its practitioners should be proud of its enormous achievements in mobilizing volunteers, food, and money to feed millions of people since the early 1980s. It has been an extraordinary commitment of civil society and partnership with government and the private sector. Yet, as a society we need to recognize that the charitable food sector will not and cannot accomplish what we need it to. The weaknesses of the charitable food sector are embedded in the very structure of this highly successful system. Its entire paradigm needs a thorough transformation. It is the only humanitarian thing to do.

Food banks, pantries, and other agencies within the charitable food system must be put in service of ending hunger, not just alleviating it, through fostering economic justice, promoting healthy people and communities, and building economic and political democracy. Many food bankers recognize the weaknesses of the system in which they work, and are actively engaged in searching for and implementing solutions that will create a sea change. The seeds of change for this transformation lie within the work of these organizations and individuals. They need to be nurtured, and the barriers to change systematically addressed, if a bountiful harvest is to be reaped. As a society, we will need to overcome very real and entrenched interests that benefit from maintaining the current system. It will be a long and arduous process, requiring a generation or more to accomplish. Nonetheless, the time has come that we call out the truth to say the charitable food sector is not solving the problem of hunger. The easy solutions have been done and have only taken us a limited distance. It's time to start on the more challenging strategies.

3 The Politics of Corporate Giving

The Walmart "Fights Hunger" Pledge

Standing in the U.S. Capitol building on May 12, 2010, Walmart vice chairman Eduardo Castro Wright made a stunning announcement. He pledged that his company would donate $2 billion in food and cash over a five-year period to "fight hunger in America."[1] Against the backdrop of a dozen or so Walmart "associates" clad identically in blue uniforms, this press event featured a "who's who" of federal food and agriculture policymakers, including the co-chairs of the House Hunger Caucus, Representatives Jim McGovern (D-MA) and Joanne Emerson (R-MO); Senator Blanche Lincoln (D-AZ); and Kevin Concannon, the USDA undersecretary for food, nutrition and consumer services.

Senator Lincoln, the former chair of the Senate Agriculture Committee, acknowledged the millions of hungry children in the country; she proclaimed how this event made her realize, "We are all in this together, in fighting hunger."[2] She also commented that maintaining a strong safety net was going to be challenging in the political environment at the time. The government would need the largesse of corporations such as Walmart to meet the public's needs. Her statement symbolized a further step in the institutionalization of the nation's charitable food system.

In this ceremony, the federal government was indeed like a junior partner, lending the event a degree of political pomp and circumstance. The real power seemed to lie with Walmart, as a leader in corporate America's agenda of partially privatizing responses to social problems. This direction was hardly new. But, as with all things Walmart, the company's agenda at the event was simply bigger than everyone else's, and it milked the public relations windfall.

Perhaps even more importantly, this event demonstrated an acceptance by both Congress and anti-hunger groups that "fighting hunger" in America had been fundamentally transformed. Although many had begun to hear the phrase as a platitude, it had nevertheless retained undertones of social justice in its implication of struggle. Now such vestiges disappeared as Walmart sought to rebrand itself as a hunger fighter, running contrary to its reputation for paying rock-bottom wages and perpetuating anti-union practices.

Walmart's announcement was just one, but undeniably the largest, example of the importance of the anti-hunger field to corporate philanthropy. Corporate giving to anti-hunger groups has gone far beyond the efforts of food manufacturers and supermarkets to donate surplus products that would otherwise end up in a landfill. A wide swath of corporations such as restaurants, airlines, car manufacturers, financial institutions, and even pharmaceutical companies invest significant resources in anti-hunger initiatives. The anti-hunger sector has become central to the corporate giving portfolio. And, vice versa, corporate philanthropy has become an integral element of the anti-hunger movement's fundraising strategy, especially at the national level and within the emergency food world.

The increasing importance of corporate philanthropy to the bottom line of anti-hunger group operations comes at a price. Understanding it requires some knowledge of the history and motivation behind corporate giving. After this background, the chapter explores which companies are giving money to anti-hunger groups and, using two case studies, examine the impact of their giving on the anti-hunger cause. The chapter closes with key suggestions that will help the anti-hunger community maintain its integrity against the lure of easy but unclean funds.

Evolution of Corporate Philanthropy

In the 19th century and the first half of the 20th, corporate giving was sporadic and often limited to fundraising drives, such as those led by the Red Cross. In one well-known example, the carmaker and philanthropist Henry Ford sought to reduce dividends to shareholders so that funds could be diverted to produce more cars at lower prices, thus enabling his workers to be able to afford them. Shareholders sued him. As Jerome Himmelstein, an Amherst College professor of anthropology and sociology, and the author of *Looking Good and Doing Good: Corporate Philanthropy and Corporate Power* explains, courts ruled against him, contending that the sole purpose of a corporation was to produce wealth for its shareholders; as corporate charters broadened in the 20th century, it became increasingly acceptable for companies to donate money to causes of their choosing. It wasn't until 1952, however, that the courts settled the question of the legality of publically traded corporations being able to give away shareholder funds.[3]

Into the 1970s, corporate philanthropy remained limited and controversial. Milton Friedman, the guru of neoliberal economics, challenged the very premise of corporate philanthropy. He argued that corporations had no responsibility to society other than to create jobs and pay taxes. He contended: "Few trends could so thoroughly undermine the very foundations of our free society as the acceptance by corporate officials of a social responsibility other than to make as much money for their shareholders as possible."[4]

Harry Freeman, the CEO of Sunbeam Corporation, echoed this sentiment when he shut down Scott Paper's $3 million giving program in 1994, stating, "I don't believe in corporations giving away their money. That money is not mine to give. I have no right to give a shareholder's money."[5] However, Mr. Freeman was relatively isolated in his opinion. As of 2013, 98 out of the top 100 corporations had corporate giving programs.[6]

By the second decade of the 21st century, corporate contributions had evolved into a significant but relatively minor funding stream in the national giving picture. In 2013, corporate foundations donated an estimated $17 billion, or about 5 percent of all private giving.[7] This giving takes many forms and is often spread throughout a corporation's budget. According to the Committee to Encourage Corporate Philanthropy, only 34 percent of all corporate giving is through a company foundation, while 49 percent is cash donated through other company budgets (e.g., marketing), and 17 percent is in the form of pro bono services and product donations. Corporate dollars are being directed to a wide variety of causes with the health and social services fields capturing one-quarter of corporate funding in 2014.[8]

The evolution of corporate philanthropy has been not just a story of more companies and more donations but also a tale of changing approaches. Until the 1970s, much of corporate philanthropy remained paternalistic, grounded in the sense of duty that CEOs felt to their communities.[9] This grant making was often informed by the charitable predilections of the CEO's spouse. Over time, corporate philanthropy become professionalized and integrated in the company's core business. Typically, grant making has shifted to company foundations, whose staff members are often employed solely to this end. These professionals share information through networks such as the Association of Corporate Contribution Professionals, or their CEOs participate in the Committee Encouraging Corporate Philanthropy, and in journals such as *The Corporate Philanthropist*.

Strategic Philanthropy

Corporate perspectives on grant making continued to evolve into the 1990s. In the name of increased efficiency, companies started to deploy philanthropy as a tool to improve their financial and political standing. This approach became known as strategic philanthropy, which is defined as "the practice of targeting a company's giving efforts around a cause or issue that simultaneously provides a direct benefit for the cause and also supports the company's core business objectives."[10] Grounded in a company's values, strategic philanthropy is intended to be a win-win, benefiting the cause and the company's stock value, if not its bottom line. One advantage of this approach is that cost-conscious senior management could more easily appreciate that stock value, given its explicit links to the corporation's economic well-being.[11]

Instead of supporting a broad base of charities, a strategic giving approach funnels money from the company into a specific sector that in turn meets the company's key interests. For example, in 2015 the energy bar company Clif Bar and the organic milk cooperative Organic Valley spearheaded a $10 million donation to the University of Wisconsin to fund five endowed faculty positions in organic farming research.[12] As leaders in the organic foods industry, both of these companies stand to benefit from the research that these future faculty positions will undertake.

In a broad sense, the amount that companies donate, and to what causes, can also reflect a firm's strategic interests. According to Himmelstein, "Patterns of corporate giving reflect patterns of corporate interest." For example, corporations with large advertising budgets also tend to have large philanthropic expenditures, suggesting that their grant making is just another avenue to create markets for the company's products by way of establishing a positive public image. Companies that are labor intensive also tend to give away more money because doing so helps to attract and keep their workforce. Companies that market directly to consumers donate more than those in the business-to-business sector because of their need to keep a favorable public image. Consumer product companies tend toward human services donations because these grants provide a more visible direct impact on the consuming public.[13]

Cause Marketing

The marriage of strategic philanthropy and marketing has produced "cause marketing," also known as consumption philanthropy. Cause marketing makes the support of a charitable cause a condition of the purchase of a product or service.[14] It makes it easy for the average shopper to direct a small amount of money to their favorite causes through their everyday shopping. American Express was the first company to launch cause marketing, when in 1983 it pledged to donate one penny from every card transaction to the fund to rebuild the Statue of Liberty.[15] In the 1990s, AmEx continued with the Charge Against Hunger, which provided $21 million to Share Our Strength (SOS), based on 3 cents for every purchase made with an AmEx card.[16] Perhaps the best-known examples of cause marketing are associated with purchasing pink items to benefit breast cancer research through the Susan G. Komen Foundation, and the RED campaign which funnels a percentage of purchase of products from Apple, Starbucks, and numerous other companies to fund anti-AIDS efforts.[17]

Cause marketing has been successful in part because consumers want to support corporations that share the same values. Market research shows that 79 percent of consumers would shift to a brand because of its values.[18] Yet some observers criticize cause marketing as a superficial approach to dealing with complex problems. They see it as drawing our attention away from the societal and environmental harm that corporations cause in the first place. Angela Eikenberry, a professor of public administration at the University of Nebraska, summarizes the opposition to cause marketing: "Consumption philanthropy individualizes solutions to collective social problems distracting our attention and resources away from the neediest causes, the most effective interventions and the act of critical questioning itself. It devalues the moral core of philanthropy by making virtuous action easy and thoughtless. And it obscures the links between markets-their firms, products and services—and the negative impacts they can have on human well-being."[19]

The Motivations for Corporate Philanthropy

In the age of strategic philanthropy, corporate contributions express a company's values and sense of social responsibility, as well as benefit the firm's economic or political interests. The balance between cause and self-interest is specific to each company and to each grant, and difficult to ascertain with any certainty. For example, the cereal company Kellogg donated $1 million in 2014 to three public health and anti-hunger groups to promote school breakfast.[20] These grants could be perceived alternately as an expression of their values that every kid should eat a healthy breakfast, or as a marketing strategy to increase cereal sales in schools. Sensing this conflict of purpose, says Himmelstein, corporate giving officers often describe their work as a struggle between looking good and doing good.[21] In other words, corporate giving merits neither complete cynicism nor unquestioned gratitude, but critical analysis of the amounts, targets, and congruity between the company's giving and the degree of social responsibility embedded in its core business practices.

The Cause

A small but growing subset of firms seeks to use its role in the marketplace to leverage social change similar to nonprofits. Some have chosen to file as "B corporations," a new certification for firms wishing to use their business as a force for good.[22] In many of these instances, socially minded companies partner with their nonprofit colleagues to address a specific issue or cause. These businesses are just as mission-driven as their nonprofit colleagues, and use their unique abilities as for-profit entities to educate consumers and raise funds for a determined cause. Ben and Jerry's and Stonyfield Yogurt are two well-known examples of companies that have lent their marketing prowess and even parts of their products' packaging to specific causes they care about, such as climate change and genetically modified ingredients.[23]

These entities are quite different in their approach to philanthropy than Fortune 500 standbys such as Walmart or Bank of America. Even within large corporations, the attitude toward philanthropy can vary based on staff roles. Top-level executives in the "C suite" may be more likely to justify donations, from a utilitarian perspective, for their ability to enhance the corporate reputation or improve employee morale. Those that are directly involved with the donation process may have a closer connection to the causes and communities affected by the company's philanthropy. Their role allows them to focus on the impact of their giving. Like all philanthropists, corporate-giving professionals are committed to "doing the right thing," benefiting their communities and the broader society within determined parameters. For example, Kori Reed, the vice president of the ConAgra Foods Foundation, proudly notes that ConAgra has been funding anti-hunger causes for two decades.[24]

Access and Prestige

Corporate giving, as with nonprofit foundation philanthropy, does contribute to making the world a better place, in fields underfunded by the government, such as the arts and human services. However, that societal benefit can be muddied by the fact that corporate giving, even outside of the strategic philanthropic approach, confers numerous benefits onto the donor firm. At a basic level, it reinforces the company's standing as a civic leader and confers social status on its executives.[25]

Philanthropy can also buy access to nonprofit leaders, just as campaign contributions help companies connect with elected officials. These individuals and their organizations often have a moral authority that companies, because of their profit motive, do not enjoy. These organizations, in their role as watchdogs, policy advocates, or thought leaders, likewise can have a positive or negative impact on a company. Donations can positively influence an NGO leader's actions and speech about the donor, or, at a minimum, neutralize his or her opposition.

Reputation

Perhaps the most important benefit of corporate philanthropy is the so-called halo effect, in which companies appear angelic for their positive contributions to the community. Philanthropy helps to create a positive image and good reputation for a company, which in turn creates moral capital. The media earned by corporate donations is much more valuable than paid advertising is in bolstering a company's image. As part of a public relations effort, corporate giving lends greater credibility than does advertising.

Newspaper clips, blogs, television segments, or word of mouth are superior to a paid advertisement because, as corporate reputation experts note, "when someone says something good about you it's worth infinitely more than when you say something good about yourself."[26] Philanthropy also has the advantage of being tax deductible as compared to paid advertising or other forms of marketing.

In this fashion, philanthropy can create a kind of "moral window dressing" that can cover up the firm's other sins.[27] The value of this image boost can provide real and tangible benefits to a firm. This reputation building can, according to some corporate experts, actually bolster a firm's stock price.[28]

The retailer Target is an interesting example of this phenomenon. According to one progressive analyst: "Entry-level hourly workers in Target stores earn roughly the same pay and have more difficulty qualifying for health care coverage than their peers at Walmart. Both retailers oppose unions and have taken steps to prevent organizing efforts in stores. And both have outsourced jobs overseas to save costs. But while Walmart is perceived as a corporate giant that will do just about anything to maximize sales and profits, Target—thanks to its hip advertising campaigns and its longtime contributions to a variety of civic and cultural causes—is seen as a model corporate citizen and benevolent employer."[29]

Not only can charitable giving programs improve a company's image, but they can also provide a form of insurance against future wrongdoing. Researchers at Brigham Young University measured the impact of negative events such as the initiation of a lawsuit, or announcement of regulatory action by a government agency on company stock values. The researchers found that companies engaged in "social initiatives" preserved greater share value after these negative events occurred than those who did not participate in "social initiatives." They estimated that socially uninvolved companies lost on average $72 million per negative event as compared to $23 million for socially engaged firms.[30]

If philanthropy can protect a company against the impacts of future malfeasance, it stands to reason that it could help a company recover from wrongdoing. Two studies by business school professors, almost a decade apart, looked at this question. One examined companies with poor workplace and environmental track records and the other looked at firms with suspect accounting practices. Both studies came to similar conclusions.

Robert Williams and J. Douglas Barrett of the University of North Alabama found that charitable giving "appears to be a means by which firms may *partially* restore their good names following the commission of illegal acts." They conclude that firms do not necessarily buy their way out of trouble, but that corporate managers do make a "cost benefit analysis between charitable giving versus the economic benefits that may accrue through illegal activity."[31]

Daryl Koehn and Joe Ueng of the University of St. Thomas in Houston found that companies involved in fraudulent accounting practices were more likely than their peers to be top givers. They conclude, "It appears that firms engaged in corporate malfeasance are using corporate philanthropy either to divert attention away from their malfeasance or to restore community goodwill after a restatement (of earnings)."[32]

Business Community Interests

Finally, corporate philanthropy operates in the broader interests of the business sector. It fulfills an implicit social contract that business must behave in a responsible way. It is enlightened self-interest, suggests Himmelstein, a small price business must pay to keep conditions favorable for capitalism. It can also be seen as a "private sector alternative to socialism," in which "a network of non-profits aligned with for-profits provides human services delivered elsewhere by emerging welfare states."[33]

Corporate philanthropy lends a new dimension to the role of corporations in society. In addition to their economic functions of creating products and services, business, through its giving programs, creates for itself a new role of defining and solving societal problems. This phenomenon has political implications that reduce the role and power of the government. As Himmelstein writes: "Although corporate philanthropy presents itself as non-ideological and apolitical, it presumes a political vision, a tacit understanding about the nature of American society and the role of large corporations within it."[34] This understanding has proven itself to be at odds with addressing the root causes of food insecurity.

Giving to Anti-Hunger Groups

Corporate giving to the anti-hunger sector is widespread. Over 150 companies donate either products or cash to the top 11 national anti-hunger groups.[35] Food manufacturers, food service, and grocery stores predominate in this list, as one might expect given the moral connection between hunger and their core lines of work. But anti-hunger funding is not confined to these food and agricultural firms. It is widespread across the corporate spectrum, even among companies whose lines of work have little to do with food. Funders include financial service firms such as JP Morgan Chase, Nationwide Insurance, MetLife, and Accenture, and other Fortune 500 standbys such as Caterpillar, United, Valero, Macys, and Disney.[36]

As companies are not required to divulge details of their charitable giving except through their foundation's tax returns, it can be challenging to assess the exact amount and destination of corporate giving. Much of what companies give takes the form of in-kind products, and they donate through marketing promotions, matching employee gifts, event sponsorships, and other similar avenues. For example, the Congressional Hunger Center grossed $501,750 from its 2014 award gala, which featured sponsorships by such companies as Monsanto, Walmart, General Mills, Kellogg, Cargill, Pepsi, Kraft, Tyson, and the American Beverage Association.[37]

Through examining the available information in corporate tax returns and anti-hunger groups' annual reports, it becomes apparent that the bulk of corporate cash contributions have predominantly been directed to hunger relief groups, such as food banks and their trade association, Feeding America. In the first half of the 2010s, Feeding America has been the go-to organization for cause-related marketing.[38] When Vicki Escarra came on board in 2006 as the new CEO, after being chief marketing officer at Delta Airlines, she implemented a number of changes that allowed the organization to expand its marketing potential. The organization conducted marketing and brand identity studies, and changed its name from America's Second Harvest to Feeding America.[39] She brought in top consulting firms and new staff with experience in leading advertising agencies. The rebranding was successful and quite timely. It came at a moment when cause marketing was on the rise, and when increased attention was being paid to poverty with the economic downturn of 2008–2009.

Feeding America's "promotional partnerships" include a broad range of food products (ConAgra, General Mills, and Outshine), fast food (Panda Express), gasoline (Valero), lodging (Hilton Garden), airline miles (United Airlines), and autos (Subaru, Ford Motors).[40] One of its most long-lasting partnerships, with The Cheesecake Factory, began in 2009. The restaurant chain donates 12.5 cents per slice of a specific variety of cheesecake (which rotates on an annual basis, and whose flavor has often been derived from a big-name corporate sweet, such as Reese's, Hershey's, or Oreos).[41] As a result of these promotions, Feeding America's income from corporate promotions increased six fold from $3.5 million in 2008 to $20.6 million in 2014 (while other corporate donations went up four fold from $8.7 million to $36.2 million during the same time period).[42]

While most corporate money flows to hunger-relief groups, two organizations stand out as exceptions: Food Research and Action Center (FRAC) and Share our Strength (SOS), both of which receive millions in corporate funding annually. Although these two entities do make subgrants to grassroots groups, comparatively little corporate money flows to support state and local policy or to advocacy-oriented anti-hunger groups. For example, California Food Policy Advocates (CFPA), one of the nation's leading anti-hunger advocacy organizations, does not include a single corporate funder in its 2015 donor list.[43] CFPA and other similar organizations are in the trenches in their communities and states fighting for public policies that benefit poor people, such as affordable housing, health care, minimum wage level, welfare, and nutrition programs. This type of organization is generally a poor fit for many corporate donor programs, whose grant making tends to favor groups with a charity orientation for three basic reasons.

First, charity-based groups, such as Feeding America, are likely candidates for cause-marketing relationships because, according to Mara Einstein, companies tend to steer toward more politically neutral and more prominent organizations; Share Our Strength fits this profile as well because of its size and focus on ending childhood hunger, a very marketable cause for its emotional appeal. These organizations enjoy name recognition, attracting the greatest number of potential consumers to the product.[44]

Second, corporate-giving professionals can more easily convince upper level management to support charity-based work as a politically neutral choice unlikely to alienate consumers. Similarly, when the corporate-giving function operates from the public relations department, as it does with the food service management giant Sodexo, the grants made will tend to be those that maximize the company's PR potential. Anything that explicitly or implicitly criticizes the company, says Arlin Wasserman, the former

Sodexo vice president of Sustainability and Corporate Social Responsibility, will be avoided.[45] Hunger relief organizations provide greater opportunities for employee volunteering and public relations than advocacy-oriented groups, whose political agenda makes them a riskier choice.

Third, many corporate giving programs are not completely professionalized. Their managers may have other jobs within the company, and may not have a very sophisticated and nuanced understanding of the solutions to the problems they are addressing. Wasserman notes that Sodexo "outsourced the hard work of figuring out where to donate money" by giving a large grant to Feeding America.[46] Finally, as Himmelstein notes, making the support of charity a priority over public-policy change fits in better with the corporate sector's interests of limiting the role of government.[47]

In short, hunger relief is a highly marketable cause, because of the virtually universal repugnance to hunger. Hunger's emotional nature appeals to a wide range of people from diverse ends of the political spectrum, and the photo opportunities linked to providing bags of food to children, seniors, and families easily enhance a corporation's image as a caring entity. Hunger relief is a safe choice, one that does not threaten the business model of most companies. As we will see with Walmart, hunger relief can actually improve a company's bottom line.

Case Studies

When the purpose of corporate giving extends beyond altruism in an effort to improve the company's financial picture, it raises concerns about the complicity of the nonprofit partners that also benefit. These groups may face ethical and strategic conundrums that pit their values against their budgets. Conflicts of interest may ensue when recipient groups take money from companies using their giving to further business practices that run counter to the nonprofit mission and values. Consider the following explicit but dated example:

The Ohio Association of Second Harvest Food Banks was forced to drop its participation in a responsible lending coalition that was advocating for legislation to regulate payday loans. Rent-A-Center (a payday loan company) had pressured America's Second Harvest (the trade association for food banks, now called Feeding America) to demand that the association drop out of the lending coalition. The company was concerned that its

$500,000 donation was being used to support this legislation. A vice president of the company stated, "No business is going to support an organization whose primary purpose is to hurt its customers or put its employees in the unemployment line."[48]

The power imbalance between giver and recipient, between corporation and nonprofit group, is so great that nonprofits may be faced with unsavory compromises and collateral damage from their association with corporate philanthropists. Knowingly or unwittingly, they become pawns in corporations' grander plans, leading to ethical challenges and unintended negative consequences. The next section delves into the ethics and politics of these relationships through two case studies: of the implications of Walmart's grant making for anti-hunger work, and of a cause marketing promotion between Feeding America and Snickers.

Walmart Foundation Case Study

Walmart seems to be the biggest of everything, with big media profile to boot. It is the world's largest retailer with some 11,000 stores in 28 countries, as its website proclaims, and net sales of $482 billion in 2015. The Fortune 500 lists it as the largest US-based company in 2015. *USA Today* includes it a list of the 10 largest employers in the United States, with a domestic workforce of 1.3 million employees. As the largest supermarket chain in the United States, states *Fortune*, it controls roughly 30 percent of the domestic grocery business. The six heirs of founder Sam Walton, according to *Forbes*, are the richest family in America, worth $170 billion in 2015. Collectively, according to Americans for Tax Fairness, these individuals have more wealth than 49 million US families combined.[49]

Walmart is also known for its outsized impacts on communities, the environment, and workers. Due to Walmart's relentless pressure on its suppliers to lower their prices, 196,000 jobs in the United States were lost from 2001 to 2006 as US manufacturers moved their production to China and other low-wage countries.[50]

Walmart has been long criticized for its poor treatment of its workforce. First and foremost, its pay has lagged behind its competitors, even as it announced in 2015 an increase in wages to $9–$10 per hour.[51] Dan Schlademan, the former campaign director for the Union of Food and Commercial Workers' Walmart campaign, illustrates Walmart's hunger-level wages through the following anecdote: "Last fall [2012] we brought one hundred

workers to a meeting in Bentonville [Walmart headquarters]. The first dinner was at a restaurant that had a buffet. The people were amazed to be able
to eat as much as they could. One person told me that she hadn't eaten
meat for the past six months."[52]

Labor organizers such as Schlademan cite numerous other issues with
the company's treatment of its workers, most notoriously its scheduling
policies and its reluctance to hire workers full-time so that they can earn
benefits. Walmart is strenuously anti-union, going to great lengths to
block union organizing in its stores as a means of keeping its costs low.
For instance, it chose to go so far as closing certain stores where worker-
organizing activity was greatest under the pretext of fixing alleged
plumbing problems. Workers would then have to reapply for their jobs.[53]

Democratic staff from the US House Committee on Education and
Workforce estimates that the low wages Walmart pays its employees costs
taxpayers $6.2 billion annually in public benefits, such as reliance on SNAP,
school meals, public housing programs, and Medicaid.[54] In addition,
numerous studies, films, and articles have documented Walmart's effects
in devastating rural communities, small businesses, and in increasing
greenhouse gas emissions.

Motivation   Because of these and other practices, many of the nation's
largest cities have been able to keep Walmart out, or minimize their foot-
print within their jurisdictions. Eduardo Castro Wright, the same executive
that announced the $2 billion anti-hunger commitment, noted that the
company's limited sales in 50 of the nation's largest markets was costing the
company $80 to $100 billion annually. He indicated the company's inten-
tion to move aggressively to expand in these areas at the company's 2009
annual meeting: "So, as you can imagine, the size of the price being at that
level, with that size of opportunity, our intent and a way to go to market
in those urban locations, it's real. It's been tested. We will deploy capital in
the next few years."[55]

Walmart's former executive vice president of corporate affairs, Leslie
Dach, amplified Castro Wright's definition of capital deployment. In a
2010 meeting, he touted the value of Walmart's philanthropy to investors.
According to a transcript obtained by *The Nation*, he called "'our reputation' as 'a lever' in pursuing the company's goals, which he said include
'new markets,' among them 'urban America.'"[56]

Walmart's donations help build a positive image of the company among consumers. One way in which this image-enhancement occurs is through the use of earned media, or news articles, related to their giving programs. The 2010 launch of Walmart's anti-hunger commitment made it onto national print and electronic media. Also, their routine donations to individual organizations, such as a $100,000 grant to a local food bank, are publicized in local newspapers. Print and electronic media coverage of Walmart's anti-hunger grants undoubtedly have generated hundreds of millions of impressions over the course of the five-year grant commitment.

Links between Company Strategy and Philanthropy   With the Walmart Foundation's $183 million in donations in fiscal year 2013 (the third most of any corporate foundation in the United States), the company has substantial philanthropic resources available for deployment in its quest for expansion.[57] While on the surface Walmart's use of its charitable giving to build its reputation shares many similarities with that of other large corporations, at a closer look the company appears to have been much more explicit in the links between its giving and its profit motives. The Occidental College professor Peter Dreier perceives the company's philanthropic practices as little more than "honest graft," a term coined by the 19th-century Tammany Hall political machine. As compared to bribery and theft as dishonest forms of graft, honest graft consists of legal methods for buying influence.[58]

Dreier's wariness is due in part to the chasm between the company's labor and environmental practices and its rhetoric around its giving program. The Committee to Encourage Corporate Philanthropy, an association of corporate CEOs, comments in a recent report: "Corporate philanthropy needs to represent and be embedded in a natural extension of the company's values and operations. ... The bigger a company's reputation and the larger the gap between perception and reality, the more vulnerable the company is to reputational attacks."[59]

A legal complaint filed by 13 organizations with the Internal Revenue Service in the spring of 2015 documents this type of disconnect between the company's values and its public relations messages. It explains in detail what Leslie Dach and Eduardo Castro Wright hinted at: how Walmart has employed its philanthropic arm to further its business goals of expansion into urban markets, given flagging sales at its existing locations. This complaint requests that the IRS investigate whether Walmart Foundation misused its tax-exempt status to further its private interests, rather than the public interest for which nonprofits are chartered.[60]

The complaint contends that Walmart Foundation is not a separate entity from Walmart Inc., with the board of directors of the foundation comprising company executives, and staff salaries and all administrative expenses covered by the company. It also charges that Walmart's giving spikes in urban areas when tied to company expansion plans. This pattern is seen in Chicago, Washington, New York, Boston, and Los Angeles. For example, its donations to Los Angeles–based programs totaled only $205,000 in 2009, but increased to $1.05 million in 2010 and $1.38 million in 2011, when it filed its application for a permit for its first store in the City of Los Angeles. By 2013, giving to Los Angeles–based programs had dropped back down to $232,648.[61] These donations were accompanied by intensive PR and lobbying campaigns to build new stores in such neighborhoods as Los Angeles's Chinatown.[62]

In Boston, where Mayor Menino remained vehemently opposed to Walmart's entrance into the city, a similar pattern to the one in Los Angeles emerged. Giving spiked to $1.1 million in 2012 at the peak of the company's campaign to build in Boston, up from $125,000 in 2009. By 2013, when community opposition stopped company plans, their giving fell to just $350,000.[63]

In New York City, the retailer's philanthropic intentions were considered so manipulative that a majority of the city council members sent a cease-and-desist letter to the firm in 2014 demanding that they stop sending their "dangerous dollars" to New York City–based charities. Council speaker Melissa Mark-Viverito accused the company of waging a "cynical public-relations campaign that disguises Walmart's backwards anti-job agenda."[64]

Not only did Walmart structure the amount of its giving in accordance with its expansion plans, but it also actively and consistently used its philanthropic contributions in its public relations efforts to overcome community opposition to its expansion. According to the complaint, "When Walmart faces community opposition to new store openings, especially in urban markets, the company often launches a website aimed at garnering community support. Walmart Foundation is featured on almost every one of the (19) Walmart Community websites."[65] The company high-lights foundation contributions in the benefits that it provides.

Defending Walmart While Walmart Foundation does not require its grantees to publicly praise the retailer, it does encourage them to do so. Walmart provides its new grantees a four-page document outlining their communication expectations about the grant and the foundation. This document exceeds anything provided by the most demanding foundations. It includes the following tit-for-tat request: "When appropriate, grantees should consider the Walmart Foundation for awards that recognize corporate funders for their commitment to addressing important national or local needs/issues."[66]

Food bank leaders can be seen in videos on Walmart Inc. websites, promoting the virtues of partnering with the firm. Regarding images of food bank trucks donated by Walmart featuring their logo, Rob Johnson, the chief operating officer of the Atlanta Community Food Bank comments, "This is really a community-wide effort from individuals to volunteers to corporations. It was all about how do we bring an entire community to work on a problem together."[67] In Washington, DC, the CEO of the Capital Area Food Bank is featured in another video, around the same time that the DC City Council was considering (and passed) a measure to force Walmart to pay living wages at it DC-based stores (it was later vetoed by the mayor and the council was unable to overturn the veto).[68]

Through their words and actions, anti-hunger leaders have defended Walmart as a positive force in the anti-hunger community. For example, at the 2011 and 2012 national anti-hunger conferences, Walmart staff joined the executive directors of Feeding America and the Food Research and Action Center (FRAC) in a keynote panel, as the preeminent leaders of the anti-hunger movement.

At a national food bank conference in 2012, a staff member of WhyHunger asked the speakers whether they would request of Walmart, as their "partner," to pay their employees more as a means of reducing their food insecurity. A high-level staff member from FRAC responded that instead they ask the firm to make sure that it provides food stamp applications to their employees.[69]

At a minimum, Walmart ensures that its grantees do not publicly oppose the company. The guidelines for the Community Giving and State Giving programs, under which most grants to local organizations are made, state that opposing Walmart (the corporation, not the foundation) disqualifies a group from Walmart Foundation giving. For example, the Community Giving Program disqualifies "organizations whose programming or policies may position Walmart or the Foundation in a negative light."[70]

What Walmart Funds

Walmart Foundation's website boasts that the company has met its $2 billion goal a year early, having distributed $260 million in cash and $2.6 billion in products.[71] This comes out to roughly 1.6 billion pounds of food with a value of $1.59 per pound.[72] Its Fighting Hunger Together initiative has evolved into the Hunger Relief and Healthy Eating focus area, which has come to support parts of the food movement. The focus area's web page contains few details about their funding priorities, but instead states: "Every family should have access to affordable, nutritious, sustainably grown food. But for too many families, this simply is not reality. ... We envision a day when no individual has to wonder where his or her next meal will come from."[73]

Funding in this program area has evolved since its formal inception in 2010. In its initial stages, the Walmart Foundation's grants were more focused on support for the charitable food system. An analysis of the foundation's tax returns in the early stages of this commitment found that a predominant amount of funds were dedicated to food banks, food pantries, and other parts of the charitable food sector. While its latest returns from 2013 reveal a similar funding proclivity for supporting hundreds of food banks and pantries, it has also made important investments in supporting children's nutrition programs and related healthy eating initiatives, such as school gardens and farm-to-school programs.[74] Some examples of Walmart Foundation grant making include:

• Grants totaling $15.5 million to seven national organizations to support free meal and nutrition education programs for low-income children: the recipient organizations are not mainline anti-hunger organizations, but include such groups as 4-H, YMCA, and the National League of Cities.[75]
• The Food Pantry Holiday Makeover initiative provided donations of $20,000 each to 75 food pantries for new equipment and facilities.[76]
• The Fight Hunger, Spark Change campaign gave 50 food banks $60,000 each based on how many votes the public cast on the foundation's website for their favorite food bank.[77]

- Since 2010, the foundation has donated more than 180 trucks and refrigerated trailers to food banks and pantries nationally.[78]
- From 2010 to 2015, Walmart has awarded over $55 million to three of the nation's largest anti-hunger groups: Feeding America ($33,109,309), Share Our Strength ($9,682,000), and the FRAC ($12,525,000).[79]

Analysis These grants, among the thousands of others that Walmart Foundation has made over the course of its five-year commitment to hunger relief, undoubtedly built the capacity of the charitable food sector and a more limited number of advocacy groups. Walmart's investment in the emergency food system has made sense for the company in terms of its strategic expansion goals, but also as a way to maintain the status quo of low labor costs.

On the publicity front, hunger was a wise choice of a focus area for grant making. It resonates with Walmart's shopper base of working-class and lower-middle-class consumers, many who themselves are undoubtedly (or have been) food insecure. At the community level, the company's support for food banks and food pantries provides good photo opportunities and feel-good stories that local media like to cover. Especially in conservative small towns of the Midwest and the South, where Walmart's market share is largest, this form of corporate social responsibility is seen as a positive alternative to increasing the role of government in federal food programs or to what is perceived as anti-business minimum wage increases. This grant making is politically unassailable except by perhaps the most progressive of politicians in the most liberal communities. Yet it has the benefit of providing positive economic benefits for Walmart while burnishing its image as a caring company. It can also be seen as an attempt to inoculate the company from criticism over its low wages and labor practices.

A strong anti-hunger sector lies in the company's best economic interests. The more food banks and food stamps can provide for the needs of impoverished workers, such as those who work at Walmart, the easier it is for the company and other employers to keep their wages low. Charity and SNAP covers part of the living costs of their workers, essentially propping up Walmart's core business model of cheap labor. It is less costly to donate to nonprofit groups than to pay fair salaries, and the retailer reaps additional public relations benefits that enable it to meet its strategic expansion goals. In addition, an investment in building the advocacy capacity of the anti-hunger community to fight for the SNAP program not only subsidizes the company's labor costs, but also boosts its sales. In Oklahoma, Walmart captured 42 percent of food stamps redeemed there between 2009 and 2011, according to the *Tulsa World* newspaper. Dach, the former Walmart executive, commented that in some states Walmart redeems up to 50 percent of SNAP benefits.[80] Overall, on a national level, Walmart officials have acknowledged that they redeemed 18 percent of food stamps, or roughly $13 billion in 2014.[81]

All in all, Walmart's commitment is just the cost of doing business, a modest investment in the capacity of a core partner. Most of the $2.6 billion it claims as the value of the donation is food, which would have been thrown away if it had not been donated. By giving it away, the company saves millions in garbage disposal fees, and can claim a tax break at the midpoint between wholesale and retail value. Only $260 million, or one-tenth of the total donation value, is actually cash. And even with this cash, the company is able to take a tax deduction, most likely at around 30 percent, reducing its tax burden by $78 million.[82] Discounting inflation, reduced garbage pick-up costs, tax deductions for cash and food donations, the real cost of the Fighting Hunger Together effort is reduced by about a third to approximately $1.7 billion.[83]

Snickers Case Study

Going back a few years, in July 2010, Feeding America and Mars, Inc. announced the second phase of the Snickers Bar Hunger campaign. Their press release explained that Mars would donate a minimum of 2.5 million meals to Feeding America. If enough consumers would enter online or via text a special code found on Snickers wrappers, then Mars would donate an additional million meals (nowhere in the promotion does it translate meals into dollars, but Feeding America calculates the cost to provide one meal at 12.5 cents, or $312,500 for Mars's initial donation). To educate consumers about hunger, the actor David Arquette would be featured in a special philanthropy-themed issue of *GQ* magazine, and the NASCAR star Kyle Busch would drive a special Snickers Bar Hunger auto during a race on July 10, 2010.[84] At first glance, this campaign appeared to be a win-win-win: Feeding America would benefit from a six-figure check. Mars would get some great publicity and capture cell phone numbers or e-mail addresses from participating consumers. Consumers' awareness of hunger would be increased.

By lending its name to this promotion, and by accepting money from its sales, Feeding America provided a de facto endorsement of Snickers. It encouraged the public to purchase Snickers candy bars in order to support Feeding America's mission. Nonprofits enter these agreements because they believe that the ability of companies such as Mars to reach a large audience with their anti-hunger message can be beneficial to their cause. And they want the cash. Companies see that they can sell more products through cause marketing while building brand value and loyalty. While a direct correlation between promotions and sales has not been demonstrated, research has shown that consumers prefer to support companies and brands that engage in such philanthropic activities, and will pay more for their products.[85]

One could argue that regardless of these promotions, some individuals are going to buy a candy bar, and it might as well be one in which Feeding America gets a small cut of the profits. On the other hand, it is equally plausible to contend that Feeding America appears to have reinforced—if not increased—the sales of unhealthy foods through their partnerships with Snickers and Cheesecake Factory. In doing so, their fundraising activities have arguably contributed to the nation's diabetes epidemic.

Feeding America's mission is centered on hunger relief, but the collateral damage that this fundraising has potentially inflicted calls attention to the responsibility of the group to the public at large. It seems that it has aggravated one societal problem while raising money to address another. The ethical implications of this action remain largely unexplored in the nonprofit fundraising realm.

A second concern with this promotion is related to the use of the term "hunger." Carole Walker, the vice president of integrated marketing communications for Mars Snackfood US, commented in a press release about the 2009 version of this promotion: "The SNICKERS brand has always satisfied hunger."[86] This wordplay—alluding in the same breath to the temporary feeling that Snickers uses in its marketing campaigns, as well as to the social problem that Feeding America addresses—trivializes hunger. It is, as Mara Einstein states, "turning true human suffering into a sales pitch for a disposable consumer product."[87]

Feeding America's choice of Snickers as a nonprofit partner is typical of the corporate marketers' proclivity to fund safe, middle-of-the-road organizations that deal with symptoms (hunger relief) instead of solutions (eliminating the root causes of hunger).[88] As a result, the more politically conservative organizations gain more resources, more media attention, and increased legitimacy.

In staying away from controversy, from strategies that even remotely challenge their operating models, Mars and other cause marketers show that sales come first, the cause second. As with any marketing, it's all about perception: whatever the tactic, the one that opens consumers' wallets rules. This is not well-thought-out philanthropy, but six-and-seven figure checks piggybacked onto gut-level, tug-at-the-heartstrings marketing.

These partnerships do help feed the hungry in the short term. And yet the messages embedded in the advertising from these campaigns reinforce misconceptions about hunger among the public. These partnerships communicate that hunger is a temporary lack of food rather than a social condition of powerlessness and poverty. They decouple hunger from any historical context and from any link to corporate action or public policy. They communicate that partnerships between corporations and nonprofits can solve food insecurity rather than government action. Finally, as the medium is the message, they communicate that the public can and should express our political selves through our product purchases. Being a citizen and consumer is the same thing. There is no need to engage oneself in the political process beyond shopping.

Aggregated over time, these messages corrode our collective sense of the hunger problem and solution (not to mention our sense of citizenship). Mara Einstein sums up the net impact of this form of marketing: "We are victims of systematic misdirection. We have been taught to substitute consumption for political acts."[89]

Summary

In my former role as the executive director of the Community Food Security Coalition, I made decisions about whether to accept corporate funds. The organization accepted grants or sponsorships from Sodexo, Aetna, Organic Valley, Clif Bar, and Wells Fargo, among other companies, for our events. We didn't take a lot of money, perhaps $20,000 to $40,000 per year out of an average yearly budget of $1.3 million. More significantly, we accepted $750,000 from the UPS Foundation over a five-year period. I even wrote an article vouching for Sodexo's intentions to improve the quality of their school meals through moving to a farm to school approach.[90] I alienated some school food service professionals for accepting Sodexo's checks, especially those who were fighting against the privatization of their school meals programs.

In 2009, the fast food company Chipotle approached us to partner in a cause marketing initiative that would have landed $50,000 for our farm-to-school program. After many long and heated conversations, we decided to decline their offer. While they sourced sustainably produced produce and meat, they had refused to sign on to an agreement with the Coalition of Immokalee Workers (CIW) to pay tomato pickers in Florida an extra penny per pound. (In 2012, Chipotle did sign onto the CIW Fair Food Agreement.) We decided that a partnership with Chipotle would undermine the CIW campaign, and that we had an obligation to the broader food movement to stand up for worker rights.[91]

This anecdote indicates the complexities and challenges of organizational fundraising decisions. Every organization has to shape its own ethical boundaries and conduct a cost benefit analysis of accepting or refusing corporate funding. Money is hard to come by for most nonprofit organizations, and a corporate donation could make the difference in keeping staff employed and the lights on. Many of the fundraising issues I've mentioned are not exclusive to anti-hunger groups, but to the nonprofit movement as a whole. Yet anti-hunger work presents a special challenge because the urgency of hunger fosters a fundraising approach that seeks to raise as many resources as possible to meet the immediate need. The marketability of anti-hunger work also puts it squarely in the corporate spotlight, both to those companies seriously invested in the issue as well as to those who seek a quick boost to their corporate image.

In part because of hunger's urgency and the bottomless demand for free food, some food bankers in particular will contend that they should take the money no matter the source. They believe that they can do better with the money than the company can. Yet this fundraising strategy can result in negative implications for the broader cause of reducing food insecurity. This approach highlights a conflict that may arise between promoting the good of the organization (accepting more money allows them to serve more people and distribute more food) and achieving the broader cause of fostering healthy and hunger-free communities and individuals.

What is necessary for any nonprofit instead is a conscious and deliberate consideration of the ethical and strategic implications of accepting any funds, but especially those from the corporate sector. Such a discussion typically takes place in the process of creating a corporate donation policy. These policies take various forms, but they can be a simple sentence or two. The New York City–based international organization WhyHunger has developed an exemplary donations policy that helps the group avoid conflicts of interest. The policy is multileveled, and one essential element states that the organization will not knowingly accept funding from companies whose core business is in opposition to the organization's mission and/or undermines the efforts of their grassroots partners.[92] This has allowed the organization to maintain a progressive stance on many food system and poverty-related issues and opened dialogue with staff and board members on the complexities of working with corporations that create the problems the organization is working to solve.[93]

The examples in this chapter have shown that corporate fundraising can be problematic to the broader cause of promoting healthy and food-secure persons and communities, even while supporting organizations that are seeking to meet these goals. Part of the problem lies with the structure of nonprofit organizations incentivized to focus on their own missions and budgets and thus exclude their commitment to the broader social movements in which they operate. It becomes troublesome primarily when organizations do not consider the implications of their fundraising on the broader social movement, but instead focus solely on how corporate grants could help them fulfill their own organizational mission. A systemic failure of the nonprofit sector to train its leadership adequately in social-movement building contributes to this challenge. By and large, organizational leaders are not trained to consider the impacts or the ethics of their fundraising practices. Rather, for the most part, nonprofit support activities focus on enhancing the effectiveness and professionalism of organizational fundraising, treating organizations in isolation from one another.

Corporate philanthropy (and from the nonprofit perspective, corporate fundraising) becomes problematic when employed for purposes that are anathema to the recipient organization's mission. For example, to the extent that Walmart has used its philanthropy to enable it to continue its labor-hostile policies, underpay its workers, and to expand in new markets, its grant making arguably has a greater negative impact on the food security of its workers than the positive effects grantees are able to accomplish. While a new refrigerated truck can help a food bank deliver more fresh products to food pantries, accepting this donation creates a de facto partnership between the company and the food bank that allows the company to appropriate part of the goodwill earned by the nonprofit. In doing so, the food bank undermines the efforts of labor organizers to get Walmart to pay its workers a higher wage and better benefits. This partnership goes far beyond the acceptance of a truck. The unspoken agreement is that the food bank and Walmart are in an alliance to maintain a low-wage economy in which workers and their families depend on the services provided by the food banks as well as the federal food assistance programs for which anti-hunger groups advocate. The problem is perpetuated: Walmart saves on wages while hunger relief groups get to succeed in their narrowly phrased missions.

These partnerships also include a sometimes explicit but mostly tacit requirement that recipient groups will not act in opposition to the interests of their donors. As the Rent-a Center executive stated above, they don't want to give money to a group working against their interests. The more dependent nonprofits become upon corporations for their funding, they less likely they are to rock the boat.

The cumulative effect of this anti-hunger industrial complex is that the more moderate organizations, the ones that are more in synch with corporate philanthropy, become wealthier and squeeze out the more progressive organizations. Their approach becomes the dominant paradigm. Substantive reform becomes less likely as food banks and many national organizations have made a tacit alliance with corporate America to bite their tongues and pursue an approach that services rather than solves the hunger problem. This power imbalance similarly plays out within the anti-hunger field itself. The smaller and scrappier advocacy groups, those that often make a deeper commitment to policy change, are questioned on their very existence, and it is suggested that they would be best merged with the local food bank. For example, in Boston, Project Bread came close to being merged with the Greater Boston Food Bank in the early 2000s, while in Portland, Partners for a Hunger Free Oregon has often been questioned about the need for their group when the Oregon Food Bank is so strong.[94]

One of the challenges confronting all nonprofits dependent upon grants and other large donations is that they become more accountable to their donors than to the public they serve. To keep the funds flowing, they craft policies and programs that pander to the interests of their supporters. The long-term result is that these organizations become top-down and more focused on their own self-perpetuation than on building a vibrant and thriving social movement. This becomes especially problematic when their funders' core business practices are inimical to their missions.

Only through collaboration can anti-hunger groups begin to address the power imbalances inherent between corporate donors and nonprofit groups. Part of this collective action needs to include ways in which non-profit groups can become more conscious of the potential conflict of interests associated with corporate funding and more deliberate about their fundraising strategies, especially how they impact their organizational programming. Part also involves taking steps to build a strong social movement that prioritizes greater accountability to the people that they serve rather than to the interests of their donors.

A robust dialogue on fundraising ethics, especially as it pertains to corporate donations, has been sorely lacking in the anti-hunger field and beyond. This movement-wide dialogue on fundraising ethics, with particular emphasis on corporate fundraising, should be launched through a series of webinars, sessions at state and national conferences, position papers, reports, and town hall meetings in communities across the country.

These dialogues should lead to a statement of principles that anti-hunger groups can sign onto, one that lays out their basic precepts about their ethical and strategic responsibilities in this arena. Their responsibility should, like the Hippocratic oath, prioritize doing no harm through their fundraising practices. This statement should also call upon corporate donors to undertake business practices that minimize damage to the health and well-being of their workforces, the communities in which they are located, and their consumer base. It should also insist that companies take steps to implement social responsibility in their core business practices before anti-hunger organizations will accept their funding.

Without reversing the power imbalance with their funders, anti-hunger groups become insulated from the people they serve. They have an incredible potential to organize and build the human capital of the tens of millions of people they serve to lead a social movement for ending hunger. But they choose not to do so, in part, because it would threaten the interests of their corporate (and more conservative individual) partners. As one Oregon anti-hunger leader noted, "Feeding America could be a voice for people in poverty, but it would risk losing some of its corporate funders."[95] These sins of omission, these things that hunger relief groups don't do, or don't advocate for, are just as important in defining the anti-hunger movement as the activities they take on, or the policies they do support.

Public Health or Anti-Hunger?

Around 2010 or so, the Department of Nutrition at the Harvard School of Public Health began to produce a prodigious array of research papers that laid the groundwork for how the Supplemental Nutrition Assistance Program (SNAP) could be transformed to improve the health of its recipients. These investigations centered in large measure on the potential exclusion of unhealthy foods, such as soda, from the list of permitted products within SNAP.

To the Food Research and Action Center (FRAC), the leading lobbying force for federal food assistance programs, Harvard's research laid bare SNAP's weak flank. This cornerstone program could play a much greater role in combatting an ever-widening obesity epidemic that especially affects the low-income persons eligible for SNAP. Harvard's highly credible research couldn't be coming at a worse time. Republicans proposed to slash billions from SNAP in the Farm Bill. Even worse, Representative Paul Ryan's budget plan sought to devolve SNAP to the states, a move which would over time gut the program's effectiveness. According to SNAP defenders, the barbarians were storming the gates, with Harvard's research potentially supplying ammunition to the enemy.

This was the context when FRAC's long-time executive director, Jim Weill, requested a meeting with Walter Willett, the chair of the Department of Nutrition and the nation's most influential nutritionist. Willett has been an outspoken advocate for evidence-based policies that run counter to USDA's cozy relationship with the food industry. In the winter of 2012, Weill and FRAC's senior nutrition policy and research analyst, Heather

Hartline Grafton, traveled to Boston to meet with Willett and two other Harvard faculty members.

Weill had requested this meeting, yet its purpose remained unclear to the Harvard participants. They expected a thought-provoking conversation about the SNAP program. Instead, Weill expressed his reservations about the impact of Harvard's research on SNAP reauthorization. From his perspective, FRAC had fought for more than 40 years to protect, grow, and improve the food stamp program through multiple hostile administrations and Congresses. He commented that Harvard's research, while well intentioned, undermined the nation's social safety net, and had to be put on hold until a more politically opportune moment arrived.

Harvard's nutritionists saw this meeting as a good-faith effort by both sides to find common ground that would importantly preserve the program and secondly improve it. They staunchly opposed cutting benefits, since they all agreed that food insecurity is a massive problem in the United States, with serious health implications. Yet these two titans seemed to differ over pretty much everything else: the purpose of the SNAP program and the effects of SNAP on its participants' health.

One of the Harvard professors had done some research, and found that FRAC had accepted substantial cash donations from the food and beverage industry. Public health researchers need to follow rigorous standards on conflict of interest, with mandatory disclosures required in peer-reviewed journals. She prodded, inquiring if those contributions had not affected their position on the continued inclusion of soda in the food stamp program. Weill acknowledged that they had indeed received funding from the beverage industry, but that it did not affect their position on this topic. Unsatisfied with his answer, she insisted: would it not be possible that such funding could create a conflict of interest?

Weill, likely feeling his organization's integrity challenged, called an abrupt halt to the meeting. As of 2016, FRAC and Harvard's Public Health School have not been in touch again.[1] FRAC did not respond to multiple requests for comment.

This encounter illustrates the very real tensions between the public health and the anti-hunger communities over the purpose of the SNAP program and their respective relationships with the food industry. Anti-hunger leader Jessica Bartholow of the Western Center on Law and Poverty—and recipient of the 2013 Dr. Raymond Wheeler / Paul Wellstone

Award presented by FRAC—gave voice to these tensions: "The public health community is using poor people as pawns to get at soda companies. What they're doing is just as vicious and evil as what Paul Ryan wants to do to poor people."[2] At the heart of this conflict lies the ubiquity of sugar in the American diet and its toxic effects on our health.

Sweet on Sweets

Our brains are hardwired to crave sweet things. Michael Moss, the author of *Sugar, Salt, Fat*, notes that every single one of our 10,000 taste buds contains receptors for sweetness that connect to the brain's pleasure zones.[3] Consuming sweet foods not only provides calories to the body, but also results in the release of endorphins. As a result, kicking the sugar habit can be just as difficult as quitting smoking or other highly addictive drugs.

As our biological proclivities have contributed to the over-consumption of sugar, public health nutritionists have locked their sights on the role of added sugars in contributing to the global obesity epidemic.[4] Energy-dense, sugar fuels the body with 16 calories per teaspoon without supplying any essential nutrients.[5] Because sugary beverages do not satiate hunger, individuals typically consume them in addition to the foods in their standard diet, and the extra liquid calories result in weight gain.

From the public health perspective, manufacturers of sugar-sweetened beverages (SSBs), which include not only carbonated sodas, but also iced teas and lemonades as well as energy and sports drinks, have been fueling not just an obesity epidemic, but more pointedly a surge in diabetes. (Soda is a subset of SSBs, but throughout this chapter it will be used as shorthand for the longer and more technical SSB term.) Between 1958 and 2010, the number of people with diabetes in the United States shot up twelvefold with minority populations, such as Native Americans, Latinos, and African Americans, suffering from higher than average rates.[6] Public health researchers estimate that 50 percent of Latino and African American children born after 2000 will develop diabetes, as compared to one-third of all nonminority American-born children from that time period.[7] Total health care and estimated costs for the treatment of diabetes runs about $174 billion annually in the United States.[8]

Researchers have traced this explosion in diabetes rates to increases in sugar consumption, most of which takes the form of "added sugars," those not naturally occurring in foods such as in fruit. By the year 2000, Americans consumed 30 percent more sugar than in the 1950s.[9] Currently, Americans eat, drink, or slurp, on average, 385 calories of sugar, or roughly 23 teaspoons per day; by comparison, the American Heart Association recommends consumption of no greater than six teaspoons per day for women and nine for men.[10]

Much of this sugar is ingested in the form of SSBs. Only in Mexico, which incidentally has the dubious honor of possessing the world's highest obesity and diabetes rates, do people drink more soda than in the United States.[11] Overall, SSBs account for 48 percent of beverage purchases, with the typical American drinking about 16 ounces of soda per day.[12] Sweetened drinks remain the main delivery vehicle for sugar and the largest single source of calories in the American diet. Nearly one-third of the American sugar intake comes from these beverages.[13]

Heavy Users

Teens, especially those of color, are the heaviest users of SSBs. For example, 22 percent of Latino high school students drink three or more sodas per day.[14] Across a wide age range, African Americans consume greater quantities of SSBs than whites.[15] For example, black women ages 31–50 drink twice as many calories from sugary beverages than white women of the same age group.[16]

This excess intake of sugar also contributes to insulin resistance, which in turn fosters metabolic syndrome, a compilation of risk factors that lead to heart disease and diabetes, among other illnesses. For example, an analysis of existing studies found that for every one to two servings of sugar-sweetened beverages consumed daily (presumably a serving equals 8 ounces), the risk of diabetes increases by 30 percent.[17] One Tufts University professor estimates that SSBs contribute to 25,000 deaths per year in the U.S.[18]

Two key factors have driven the surge in consumption of sugar-sweetened beverages. First is advertising. As this wildfire of soda-induced diabetes races across the landscape of impoverished communities, soda companies pump out the advertising. In 2015, the top three SSG producers—Coke, Pepsi, and the Dr Pepper Snapple Group—blasted their message even louder and more incessantly as expanding their marketing budget to $14.5 billion, on average 13 percent of revenue.[19]

Advertising

When advertising is successful it can cause us to do strange things. As Harvard professor Frank Hu noted wryly in his presentation before the 2014 National Soda Summit, a gathering in Washington, DC, of 240 public health professionals trying to put the brakes on soda consumption: "Most sports drinks are consumed by people who don't play sports. And most energy drinks are consumed by people who have too much energy [i.e., are overweight]."[20]

Marketing explains in part the higher consumption rate among persons of color, as soda companies specifically focus their advertising at youth and communities of color. The African American Obesity Collaborative Network reports that a disproportionate amount of soda advertising through television shows, magazine ads, billboards, and other marketing campaigns targets African Americans.[21] Black children and teens view 80–90 percent more SSB-related advertising than their white peers.[22]

In addition to the marketing imbalances suffered by communities of color, the low price of soda and other unhealthy foods drive their excess consumption, especially among the poor. In a 2007 study, researchers at the University of Washington confirmed that calorie-dense foods were cheaper than nutrient-dense foods. The price of these fattening foods was also less likely to increase over time than healthier options.[23] For example, the price of soda has remained stable over the years as compared to the soaring cost of produce. With calories so cheap and nutrition so expensive, the rational choice for those on a limited budget is to rely heavily on fattening foods that contribute to chronic diseases.

The Conflict

Despite this growing body of evidence about the toxic effects of the overconsumption of sugar (and how sugar disproportionately affects the poor), anti-hunger groups such as FRAC have vigorously defended the status quo, the continued ability of SNAP recipients to use their benefits to purchase SSBs. In fact, what SNAP recipients and the poor in general consume has become a highly contested economic and political battleground. While "Big Food" companies compete for "stomach share," the anti-hunger community has aligned itself with them to protect the poor's right to choose. On the other side, the public health community and small-government advocates, both of which have, in an uncoordinated fashion and ostensibly for divergent reasons, sought to use SNAP to reshape the diets of the poor.

This conflict is about the very nature and purpose of SNAP, the cornerstone of the nation's food programs, within an evolving public health and food system context. It raises multiple questions about whether SNAP is essentially an anti-poverty program, whose electronically transmitted food benefits are primarily a form of income redistribution? Or is it, as its name states, a program that seeks to improve the nutritional status of its participants? Should health promotion be considered a primary goal of the SNAP program? Moreover, the conflict reaches beyond the impact of soda sales on the health of SNAP's 40-plus million recipients to touch upon foundational issues regarding the government's regulation of the food industry, to questions that a person's freedom of choice and personal dignity in the context of a market economy, and to address the ethical responsibility of nonprofit organizations to their constituents.

SNAP Background

These debates over the purpose and functioning of SNAP have been shaped by the changing demands on the program, and by the dynamic environment in which it has operated since 1933.

The Roosevelt administration established the food stamp program during the Great Depression to augment farmers' income by creating an additional market for their products. Initially, participants received an extra 50 cents for every dollar of stamps they bought, redeemable for fresh foods only. The program languished in the 1950s, until the Kennedy administration reinstituted it in 1961. By then, its importance in bolstering the farm economy was supplanted by an increased emphasis on its role in reducing hunger, in part due to growing pressure from the civil rights movement. Made permanent in 1964 and further modified in 1977, the food stamp program's raison d'être soon became its ability to improve the nutritional status of the food insecure.[24]

Throughout the 1960s and more recently, food stamps have continued to enjoy strong support from the agriculture industry. As retailers and processors displaced farmers in capturing an ever-greater share of the food dollar, however, their importance as stakeholders for the food stamp program grew. By 2008, the USDA estimates that the farm share was only 16 cents of every dollar spent on food.[25]

The lobbying activities of the food retail and processing industries highlight the ways in which these sectors are fully integrated as partners into the SNAP program. Manufacturers and supermarkets have evolved into more important participants in the food stamp program than farm groups, as evidenced by the amount of money they spend on lobbying. In 2013, during the height of Farm Bill negotiations, retailers and manufacturers (and their trade associations) spent about $50 lobbying on SNAP for every dollar spent lobbying by the farm sector.

Although trade associations such as the Grocery Manufacturers Association provide representation to most large food companies in the USDA and Congress, many corporations choose to do their own lobbying as well. Coke ($7.1 million), Pepsi ($4.7 million), Nestle ($3.6 million), Kraft ($2.2 million), Walmart ($2 million), and Kellogg ($1.6 million) spent the most money on lobbying on SNAP in 2013 of any food processing and retailing corporations.[26]

The support of the agriculture and food industries has fundamentally shaped the evolution of the food stamp program. The United States remains the only major nation with a program that supports the poor not through cash, but through transfers linked to its own agri-food industry. The US

Table 4.1
SNAP-Related Lobbying Activity by Food Sector in 2013

Food Sector	Dollar Value
Retailers	$10,612,000
Manufacturers/Processors	$35,570,450
Beverage Companies	$16,218,609
Farm Sector	$1,260,000
Total	$63,661,059[a, b]

a. "Lobbying Disclosure Act database," United States Senate, http://soprweb.senate.gov/index.cfm?event =selectfields.
b. I placed Pepsi under the Beverage category, though it does market a number of snack foods, including FritoLay products. I placed Kraft under the manufacturer category, although it also produces the CapriSun sugary beverage line.

government also uses this form of assistance in the international arena, tying food aid for impoverished countries to the purchase of commodities from US producers. Because food stamps have been essentially a form of tied aid, the program's structure has been downstream to the nature of the marketplace. Congress has adopted a laissez-faire approach to SNAP recipients' food choices. With the exception of minimal restrictions around hot foods, the government has allowed the purchases of the food stamp program to shift with broader societal trends. For example, if we as a society consume more processed foods and drink more sugary beverages than we did 20 years ago, then changes in the purchases made with SNAP benefits will simply reflect those trends.

Food stamps never evolved into a cash transfer program in part because the economic benefits provided to the agriculture and food industries have helped the program gain bipartisan support. While many anti-hunger advocates see such a cash transfer as more dignifying than food stamps, as it confers onto the poor the trust of knowing how to best spend their own benefits, they have not seriously pursued this path. In fact, they have strenuously opposed cashing out the program in full knowledge that cash distributions would be easier for Congress to slash in the future than food vouchers. Decoupling food stamps from its history as a food program would not only remove the impetus of the food industry to lobby for it, but also taint the program as a welfare initiative. For many anti-hunger advocates, food stamps are an income transfer program cloaked in the politically safer nutrition framework, just as anti-poverty advocates found the concept of hunger to be a moral safe harbor.

This nutrition safety zone has been largely bipartisan in nature, embodied by the historic relationship between a liberal senator, George McGovern (D-SD), and a conservative senator, Robert Dole (R-KS). The bipartisan support for food stamps began to erode in the mid-1990s when Speaker of the House Newt Gingrich proposed block granting food stamps as part of his ambitious conservative agenda called the Contract with America.[27] The erosion of Republican support for food stamps accelerated with the 1996 welfare reform, which eliminated the entitlement status of the Aid to Families with Dependent Children (AFDC) welfare program. The food stamp program came within a few votes of being block granted as well. This attack on food stamps was not successful, according to long-time advocate and law professor David Super, in part because it had less symbolic weight than AFDC.[28]

The meaning of food stamps as a nutrition program has shifted as the public health context evolved. Food stamps and other federal food programs had largely eliminated the third-world-style malnutrition that shocked the nation when highlighted in the late 1960s. Severe hunger and the illnesses that accompanied it eventually gave way to the rise of chronic diseases, such as heart disease, obesity, and diabetes. These diseases were caused by malnutrition of a different nature, more prevalent among the impoverished, but still a result of poor diet. Infectious diseases and diseases of underconsumption gave way to chronic illnesses and ailments related to overconsumption.

This "nutrition transition" opened the door for new constituencies to weigh in on the food stamp program. In particular, the public health nutrition field targeted SNAP as an important potential tool for diminishing the excess rates of diet-related diseases among the poor.[29] They challenged the anti-hunger community to reprioritize food quality over quantity, and nutrient density over energy density. They identified the food system's core competence of producing calories efficiently and cheaply as no longer a virtue, and sought to decouple the SNAP program (as well as other federal food programs) from this cheap food policy. In essence, they sought to redefine what it meant for SNAP to be a nutrition program, beyond its traditional accomplishments in reducing hunger, to one of prevention of chronic diseases. Congress embedded a symbolic yet powerful nod to the importance of nutrition to the food stamp program when it renamed it as the Supplemental Nutrition Assistance Program in the 2008 Farm Bill.

By the 2012–2014 Farm Bill cycle, however, SNAP's political cover was wearing off, and the very heart of its protective shield, its nutritional effectiveness, came under attack. Arguably, the nutrition community's critiques about the ineffectiveness of SNAP to address the burgeoning obesity and diabetes epidemics provided ammunition to the program's opponents. SNAP recipients' food choices became a rallying point around which Tea Party acolytes could converge. Conservative politicians and large sections of the public expressed moral outrage at the dietary preferences of SNAP recipients, either because they perceived them to be eating luxury foods such as crab legs, or junk food such as soda and chips. This paternalism was interwoven with the Tea Party's small-government ideology, as conservatives sought to slash SNAP by removing it from the Farm Bill for the first time in decades.

Debates over Food Choices in SNAP

The battle over the nutritional content of foods eligible for purchase in the food stamp program goes back far before the Tea Party's deployment of paternalistic outrage in service of its small government goals. It can be seen throughout the history of the program. In 1941, USDA temporarily removed soft drinks from the list of eligible foods; in 1964, Senator Paul Douglas (D-IL) sought to remove "frozen luxury foods" and soft drinks from the program, but was rebuffed in part because research showed that participants were already consuming a healthy diet.[30] In 1975, writing for the right-wing American Enterprise Institute, Kenneth Clarkson criticized the nutritional value of the food stamp program for the "little positive contribution to diet improvement and apparently worsen[ing of] the diet of some food stamp recipients."[31] In 1977, Representative Robert Michel (R-IL) introduced an amendment to exclude food items of "negligible or low nutritional value" such as ice cubes, artificial coloring, carbonated beverages, cooking wines, and chewing gum.[32] His amendment never made it out of the Agriculture Committee.

Twenty-seven years after Clarkson's report, another American Enterprise Institute–associated writer, Douglas Besharov, disparaged federal nutrition programs. He claimed that these programs made little progress in addressing the rapidly expanding obesity epidemic. He wondered why that was the case:

What, then, is preventing the modernization of federal feeding programs? Of course, various industry groups have a vested interest in the continuation and expansion of feeding programs, and they are adept at lobbying Congress. But those vested interests alone are not powerful enough to stymie reform. ... Ironically, it is liberal advocacy groups that have thwarted reform of the programs. ... But they seem to believe that admitting any weaknesses in federal feeding programs would make those programs vulnerable to budget cuts. ... Perhaps the advocates are correct to fear financial repercussions, but it makes them the main protectors of the status quo.[33]

The anti-hunger historian Janet Poppendieck laments that this, the first modern critique of the food stamp program from an anti-obesity perspective, came from the Right. She notes that this attack put anti-hunger groups on the defensive:

Looking backward, it seems unfortunate that long-term adversaries of federal assistance to the poor were the first to publicly articulate a nutrition-based critique of food stamps. Their involvement established a climate in which the anti-hunger world saw any questioning of SNAP's nutritional impact as suspect. As other constituencies—public health nutritionists and advocates of food system change—began to point to SNAP as a possible contributor to diet-related disease, a rift developed between groups that otherwise might have been natural allies.[34]

Leading anti-hunger groups were circling the wagons long before Besharov's 2002 op-ed. With their backs against the wall, threatened by Republican efforts to block grant safety net programs and end welfare as an entitlement program, mainline anti-hunger groups resisted even minor innovations with food stamp dollars, such as the passage and expansion of the Community Food Projects program (described in chapter 8) in the 1996, 2002, and 2008 Farm Bills. Just as Jim Weill sought to do at Harvard, they have tried to ignore or silence any criticism of the food stamp program's role in promoting or failing to address the burgeoning chronic disease crisis among low-income Americans.

Anti-hunger leaders appeared to have made a strategic decision that, in the words of one long-time advocate, "going into ostrich mode" was a safer political bet than engaging in a dialogue about improving the nutritional effectiveness of the food stamp program. In this calculus, advocates compared opening up SNAP to a Pandora's box that would give their right-wing opponents an entry point to cut the program and devastate the food security of tens of millions dependent on it. They essentially calculated the public health and food system advocates as less politically powerful than the Right, and able to be fended off for the time being. They made a devil's bargain, protecting the food security of tens of millions of poor persons in exchange for dropping the ball on addressing the obesity and diabetes epidemics among this same population. This choice was a no-win situation, a short-term pyrrhic victory at the long-term price of the health of their constituents.

Harvard was just one example in which FRAC had tried to shut down dialogue on ways to improve SNAP. Around the same time, senior FRAC staff members had reportedly chastised an East Coast anti-hunger group for allowing a public health researcher who favored soda restrictions to present her perspective at an anti-hunger meeting. In 2006, California Food Policy Advocates (CFPA) gained the passage of AB 2384, which created a pilot project to provide financial incentives for food stamp recipients to purchase fruits and vegetables.[35] CFPA's executive director Ken Hecht was criticized by FRAC's leadership for his organization's support of this bill.[36] In addition, anti-hunger groups had scored an agreement from key public health groups to refrain from advocating for policy changes to improve SNAP's nutrition profile during the 2012–2014 Farm Bill debates.

In October 2010, New York City mayor Michael Bloomberg dropped a bomb. His administration, in conjunction with the State of New York, requested a USDA waiver of SNAP program rules to ban soda for two years in order to assess the impact on SNAP recipients' health.[37] The waiver request drew sharp lines between opponents and proponents of the ban. It received substantial support from the public health community and beyond. Most notably, in June 2011, 17 big-city mayors joined Bloomberg in a letter to congressional leaders in support of New York City's waiver request. They argued, "It is time to test and evaluate approaches limiting SNAP's subsidization of products, such as sugar-sweetened beverages, that are contributing to obesity."[37] Cities have long been on the frontlines of America's social and health problems, with their public health departments heavily involved in obesity reduction efforts.

Ten months later, the USDA denied the waiver request. In her rejection letter, Jessica Shahin, associate administrator of the SNAP Program, enumerated the reasons for doing so. First, its size and scale was too large. The USDA preferred that a "change of this significance be tested on the smallest scale appropriate to minimize any unintended negative effects."[38] The department believed that the waiver lacked the support of the city's numerous retailers. The USDA wanted the city to do more to communicate about the new restrictions to retailers, whom they feared would be negatively impacted by the pilot. Finally they claimed that the city's proposal lacked an adequate evaluation component to determine the health impacts of such a ban.[39]

USDA's reaction was not unexpected. Implementing such a policy change and creating an effective evaluation framework in such a complex and populous place as New York City would have been ambitious to say the least. Historically, USDA has shown a marked preference for carrots over sticks, having published in 2007 a report arguing against food restrictions in the SNAP program. In this document, it contended that such restrictions would be ineffective, stigmatizing, and challenging to implement.[40] While Mayor Bloomberg may have bit off more than he could chew, the department's denial also entailed political considerations.

The former USDA deputy secretary Kathleen Merrigan believes that USDA could have worked out the kinks with New York City and approved this waiver[41] (Some anti-hunger advocates believe that USDA's leadership is not ideologically opposed to granting a waiver restricting soda, but that they have been waiting for the right circumstances to do so.) The timing of the request presented challenges, however, as it arrived amid a growing rhetoric demonizing poor people as incapable of making good food choices. Those voicing this perspective seemed to Merrigan more interested in budget cutting than in promoting the health of the poor. She and USDA secretary Tom Vilsack believed that granting the waiver might lend credence to this demonization, damaging not only the dignity of the poor, but also the integrity of the SNAP program. She writes, "So, our reluctance about the petition was more about standing up for poor people against an unflattering and untrue caricature that was being used politically to make a budget cut."[42]

As Merrigan notes, the Right had caught wind of this issue and made it its own. In at least 18 states (see table 4.2), legislators, usually Republicans, championed SNAP restrictions. Some of these were serious attempts at policymaking, while others appeared to be more in the vein of grandstanding. Many clearly used the topic to attack SNAP for its alleged waste and abuse, insinuating that recipients could not make good decisions on their own. From their perspective, food stamp recipients could only make bad choices, of either junk food or luxury items, and needed to be led down the straight and narrow nutritional path. A press release from the National Center for Public Policy Research, a free-market think tank, illuminates this moralistic bent: "When it comes to public assistance, I want people buying what they need with my money and not what they desire." It also highlighted the common belief among the Right that the poor enjoyed no right to food assistance, but it was instead "a gift from the taxpayers to the truly needy."[43] According to this line of thought, if the poor were so ungrateful or incompetent as to be buying the wrong foods with this gift, they must be corrected, or more punitively, stripped of the handout.

Congressional Republicans also jumped into the fray. In September 2013, Representative Phil Roe (R-TN) introduced "The Healthy Food Choices Act," which proposed that SNAP recipients could only purchase highly nutritious foods based on the Women Infants and Children (WIC) program guidelines.[44] (The bill never came up for a vote.) (Text cont. on p. 121.)

Table 4.2

States That Have Introduced Legislation to Restrict Foods from SNAP[a]

State	Legislative Content	Action	Date	Party of Champion
CA[b]	Requires state to request a waiver from USDA to restrict sugary beverages from SNAP	Champion removed support	2011	Democrat
DE[c]	Require state to request waiver from USDA to ban junk food from SNAP	Tabled	2014	Republican
FL[d]	Restrict use of SNAP on junk foods, ban use of SNAP at restaurants, and allow state to request waiver from USDA	Died in committee	2012	Republican
IA[e]	Requires state to request waiver to restrict purchase of junk food in SNAP	Died in committee	2011	Republican
ID[f]	Requests USDA give the state flexibility in food choices for SNAP	No action	2014	Republican
IL[g,h]	Requires state to request a waiver from USDA to ban sugary beverages from SNAP	Died in committee	2011	Democrat
IL[i]	Requires state to request a waiver from USDA to ban junk food from SNAP	Died in committee	2011	Republican
IL[j]	Requires state to request a waiver from USDA to ban junk food from SNAP	Died in Committee	2011	Republican
IN[k]	Established a pilot program for SNAP recipients to only purchase healthy foods	Passed House, Died in Senate	2014	Republican
LA[l]	Requires state to declare certain products ineligible for SNAP	Died in Committee	2010	Democrat
MI[m]	Urges Congress to improve food options in SNAP	Passed	2011	Republican
ME[cc]	Requested waiver of USDA to limit soda in SNAP	Denied by USDA	2015	Republican
ME[dd]	Requires state to request a waiver to prohibit sales of items of limited nutrition value in SNAP	Died in committee	2015	Republican
MS[n,o]	Requires state to request waiver from USDA to allow SNAP recipients to only purchase healthy foods	Died in Committee	2012	Democrat

Table 4.2 (continued)

State	Legislative Content	Action	Date	Party of Champion
NE[q]	Requires state to request waiver to allow SNAP recipients to purchase only water, juice, and milk with benefits	Died in Committee	2011	Republican
OR[r]	Requires state to ban foods with high amounts of sugar in SNAP	Died in committee	2011	Republican
OR[s]	Requires state to request a waiver from USDA to ban junk food from SNAP	Died in Committee	2011	Republican
PA[t]	Requests Congress to change SNAP to act more like WIC	Died in Committee	2011	Republican
SC[u]	Governor encouraged state to request a waiver to restrict junk food in SNAP	State changed course toward incentives	2013	Republican
TX[v]	Requires state agency to request waiver to restrict purchase of junk food in SNAP	Died in House	2011	Democrat
TX[w]	Requires state to request waiver to restrict purchase of junk food in SNAP	Died in House	2011	Republican
TX[x]	Urges Congress to amend allowable foods in SNAP to eliminate sugary drinks and junk food	Died in Committee	2011	Democrat
VT[y]	Resolution urging USDA to allow each state to develop own list of foods eligible for SNAP or to allow VT to do own demonstration project	Died in Committee	2011	Republican
WI[z]	Require the state to conduct a pilot program and request a waiver from USDA to mandate that 67% of foods purchased by SNAP be WIC-approved or be meat and fresh produce	Passed Assembly; Failed in Senate	2014	Republican
WV[aa]	Requests state to study adequacy of SNAP benefits in providing healthy diets in terms of sugary beverages	Died in Committee	2013	Democrat
WV[bb]	Urges Congress to prohibit sale of unhealthy food through SNAP	Died in Committee	2014	Democrat

Table 4.2 (continued)

a. Various articles mention that in NJ, MT, and MN similar legislation was introduced, but I have not been able to find the bills.

b. "CA SB 134, 2013-2014, Regular Session," LegiScan, http://legiscan.com/CA/bill/SB134/2013.

c. Jen Rini, "GOP's Healthy Eating Food Stamp Bill Defeated," Delaware NewsZap, June 13, 2014, http://delaware.newszap.com/centraldelaware/132760-70/gops-healthy-eating-food-stamp-bill-defeated.

d "CS/SB 1658: Underserved Communities," The Florida Senate, http://www.flsenate.gov/Session/Bill/2012/1658.

e. "Iowa House Bill 288," LegiScan, http://legiscan.com/IA/text/HF288/id/349024.

f. "ID SJM105, 2014, Regular Session," LegiScan, http://legiscan.com/ID/bill/SJM105/2014.

g. "HB 4121," 97th General Assembly State of Illinois 2011 and 2012, http://www.ilga.gov/legislation/97/HB/PDF/09700HB4121lv.pdf.

h. "Bill Status of HB 4121," Illinois General Assembly, 97th General Assembly, http://www.ilga.gov/legislation/BillStatus.asp?DocNum=4121&GAID=11&DocTypeID=HB&LegID=63404&SessionID=84&SpecSess=&Session=&GA=97#actions.

i. "Bill Status of HB 1480," Illinois General Assembly, 97th General Assembly, http://www.ilga.gov/legislation/BillStatus.asp?DocNum=1480&GAID=11&DocTypeID=HB&SessionID=84&GA=97.

j. "Bill Status of HB 1399," Illinois General Assembly, 97th General Assembly, ftp://www.ilga.gov/legislation/97/BillStatus/HTML/09700HB1399.html.

k. "Indiana House Bill 1351," LegiScan, http://legiscan.com/IN/votes/HB1351/2014.

l. "Bill Text LA HB 1152," LegiScan, http://legiscan.com/IN/votes/HB1351/2014.

m. "MI HCR 0031 2011-2012, 96th Legislature," LegiScan, http://legiscan.com/MI/bill/HCR0031/2011.

n. "Senate Bill 2293," Mississippi Legislature Regular Session 2012, http://billstatus.ls.state.ms.us/documents/2012/pdf/SB/2200-2299/SB2293IN.pdf.

o. "Senate Bill 2293," Mississippi Legislature Regular Session 2012. http://billstatus.ls.state.ms.us/2012/pdf/history/SB/SB2293.xml.

p. "Bill Would Restrict Beverage Purchases," Unicameral Update, February 11, 2011, http://update.legislature.ne.gov/?p=3263.

q. "Summary of SNAP Waivers 4.8.2011," docstoc, http://www.docstoc.com/docs/96375116/Summary-of-SNAP-Waivers-482011#. Retrieved August 8, 2014.

r. "HB 3098," Oregon State Legislature, 2011 Regular Session, https://olis.leg.state.or.us/liz/2011R1/Measures/Overview/HB3098.

s. "HB 3274." Oregon State Legislature, 2011 Regular Session, https://olis.leg.state.or.us/liz/2011R1/Measures/Overview/HB3274.

t. "House Resolution 59; Regular Session 2011-2012," Pennsylvania General Assembly. http://www.legis.state.pa.us/cfdocs/billInfo/bill_votes.cfm?syear=2011&sind=0&body=H&type=R&bn=59.

Table 4.2 (continued)

u. Joey Holleman, "In Carrot Vs. Stick Approach, Carrot Winning in SC Food Stamp Program," *The State*, May 23, 2014, http://www.thestate.com/2014/05/23/3464286/food-stamp-incentives-more-likely.html.

v. "Bill HB 1151," Texas Legislature Online, http://www.legis.state.tx.us/billlookup/Text.aspx?LegSess=82R&Bill=HB1151.

w. "Bill HB 3451," Texas Legislature Online, http://www.legis.state.tx.us/billlookup/Text.aspx?LegSess=82R&Bill=HB3451.

x. "Bill SCR 9," Texas Legislature Online, http://www.legis.state.tx.us/billlookup/text.aspx?LegSess=82R&Bill=SCR9.

y. "JRH 13: Vermont House Joint Resolution," Open:States,http://openstates.org/vt/bills/2011-2012/JRH13/#billtextRetrieved.

z. "Assembly Bill 110," Wisconsin State Legislature, https://docs.legis.wisconsin.gov/2013/proposals/ab110.

aa. "WV HCR 137 2013 Regular Session," LegiScan, http://legiscan.com/WV/bill/HCR137/2013.

bb. "WV SR 22, 2014 Regular Session," LegiScan, http://legiscan.com/WV/bill/SR22/2014.

cc. Maine Department of Health and Human Services. Press Release. "Maine Seeks to Ban Sugary Drinks and Candy From Food Supplement Program, November 23, 2015 http://www.maine.gov/tools/whatsnew/index.php?topic=DHS+Press+Releases&id=662814&v=article.

dd. 127th Maine Legislature. SP 195, http://www.mainelegislature.org/legis/bills/getPDF.asp?paper=SP0195&item=1&snum=127; Summary of LD 526 (SP 195) Maine Legislature, http://legislature.maine.gov/LawMakerWeb/summary.asp?ID=280054994.

In the Senate the archconservative Tom Coburn (R-OK) was chomping at the bit to introduce a bill that would have forced USDA to approve all waiver requests. Tom Harkin, a liberal Democrat from Iowa who supported restrictions from a public health standpoint, found Coburn's proposal unrealistic, and negotiated with him. They arrived at a compromise Farm Bill amendment, mandating that USDA allow two nutrition-oriented SNAP waiver requests.[45] Their work was for naught as Senate majority leader Harry Reid took the Farm Bill off the Senate floor before the amendment could come up for a vote. According to an anonymous congressional staffer, the beverage industry had simultaneously lobbied Reid's office not to allow a vote on this amendment.

To the public health community, the status quo made no sense and bad policy. Public health advocates often complain that the government's current SNAP policy remains inconsistent with other government initiatives, especially as 47 percent of SNAP recipients are children.[46] On one hand, the federal government funds nutrition education, dietary guidelines information, and obesity prevention efforts that discourage soda consumption. The food distributed through school lunch and WIC programs have much healthier profiles than those purchased through SNAP. Soda has even been banned from schools under new child nutrition regulations.[47] Lynn Silver, the author of the New York City SSB waiver request, notes that the entire annual allocation for disease prevention through the Affordable Care Act roughly equals the amount of food stamps estimated spent on sugary beverages every year.[48] For their part, anti-hunger groups bring up government corn subsidies (allegedly keeping high fructose corn syrup cheap), and other agricultural and non-agricultural programs as reasons for a global—and not SNAP specific approach—to addressing SSB consumption.[49]

Information Vacuum

SNAP reformers faced yet another challenge in addition to USDA's reluctance to issue a waiver and the might of the beverage and anti-hunger lobbying forces. There is no public data on how SNAP benefits are used. Without this information, the ability to assess which companies have profited from SNAP, as well as to determine what SNAP recipients purchase, is limited.

As for retailer information, USDA collects but has refused to distribute specific details in order to protect the business interests of its grocer partners; in the highly competitive grocery business, for instance, retailers claim that the release of this information would put them at a disadvantage with their competitors.[50] The *Argus Leader*, a South Dakota newspaper, sued USDA to gain release of this information, winning an initial decision by the Eighth Circuit Court of Appeals.

In 2014, USDA has issued a notice in the *Federal Register*, expressing its desire for greater transparency but also soliciting comments from 300,000 retailers on how such a release of information would affect their businesses.[51] Only 323 stores responded, with 73 percent opposed to releasing this information. Fifteen stores filed affidavits claiming that the disclosure of business data could cause them commercial harm and stigmatize SNAP retailers. A circuit court judge refused to throw out the lawsuit in September

2015.[52] In doing so, she argued, "There is a great public interest in full disclosure of the parameters of the SNAP program. When weighing the interests of retailers against the public's interest in a transparent government, the latter prevails."[53] In November 2016, the U.S. District Court in South Dakota ruled in favor of the Argus Leader in its Freedom of Information Act request, forcing USDA to release SNAP retailer data.[54]

In terms of the foods purchased by SNAP participants, such as sugar-sweetened beverages, USDA does not officially collect nor distribute this information. It did commission a study (released in November 2016) that examined SNAP purchase data from a single supermarket chain in 2011. This report found that 20 percent of SNAP purchases consisted of SSBs, candy, sugar, and salty snacks. SSBs made up 9.25 percent of all SNAP sales (which if extrapolated to all SNAP sales would total $6.6 billion in 2011), as compared to 7.1 percent for non-SNAP household expenditures.[55] This $6.6 billion figure is more than three times what Yale researchers calculated from a smaller data sample.

To rectify the information vacuum, Rep. Thomas Marino (R-PA) introduced the SNAP Transparency Act of 2013 to mandate that USDA "compile an online, searchable database of the aggregate total of each specific item purchased with SNAP benefits and the aggregate cost of those items." (This bill was not taken up by the House of Representatives nor relegated to committee.)[56] While many public health and good-governance advocates agree with Marino that SNAP should become more transparent, anti-hunger forces shrug off the need to do so. Immersed in trench warfare with the Right, anti-hunger leaders sense that the release of more information could only damage their position. As with the case of Harvard's research, they fear that it could supply ammunition to the program's enemies. They worry that the Right will make the following deviously simple argument: *SNAP recipients spend billions on junk food? Let's fix that problem by excluding junk food from the program and cutting the budget by a like amount.*

To some anti-hunger advocates, drawing the line on which information should be made available isn't so straightforward. One senior DC-based anti-hunger advocate quipped: "We don't ask how people spend their unemployment benefits. Why should food stamps be any different?" Viewing SNAP solely as an income assistance program, his comments resonate. He insinuates that as a society we demand a greater level of scrutiny on programs that benefit the poor than we do on middle class-oriented programs. FRAC's Ellen Teller, a leading anti-hunger lobbyist, echoes this sentiment: "Why are we always picking on the poor?"[57]

Anti-Hunger Response

This theme of holding the poor to a higher standard comes up frequently in conversations with anti-hunger advocates. They feel that, all too often, American society treats the poor paternalistically, because we perceive them as lazy, immoral, or just incapable of making good decisions on their own. This cultural bias carries over to the nutrition field. In supermarkets across the country, the grocery carts of the poor are scrutinized for being too junky or too extravagant. The attitude prevails among more than just nosy neighbors. Local food movement leaders, such as Michael Pollan, have been criticized for their lack of cultural sensitivity as they seek to change the food choices of low-income communities to "healthier diets."[58]

This concern about nutritional paternalism is embedded in the opposition to soda restrictions that is voiced by the vast majority of the anti-hunger community. For example, only 2 of the 17 leading anti-hunger groups on the West Coast support the exclusion of junk food from SNAP, but only within a broader context of healthy food incentives.[59] On the other side, however, the bipartisan National Commission on Hunger in its 2015 report recommends the exclusion of SSBs from SNAP, contending that, "SNAP benefits should help families meet their nutritional needs, not contribute to negative health outcomes through poor nutrition choices." The report also recommends financial incentives for SNAP recipients to purchase healthy foods.[60]

It is not that the anti-hunger community possesses any special affection for soft drinks. In fact, various food banks have taken great strides in refusing to accept or donate soft drinks, despite the fact that doing so may anger their corporate donors. Anti-hunger groups may just not perceive sugary drinks to be as serious a health risk as the public health community. But they do appreciate that food plays an important role in the lives of low-income persons (and indeed all persons) above and beyond its health impacts. The public health ethicist Anne Barnhill, author of several papers outlining the ethical case for excluding soda from SNAP, echoes this sentiment. She believes that the public health community may be too narrow in its exclusive focus on the health impacts of food. She notes that this exclusive approach on the health effects of food devalues its other functions of "sustenance, pleasure, social life, status, and giving children special treats."[61] In this context, soda plays multiple roles in the lives of the poor: the opiate of the masses, a moment of inexpensive pleasure for people unable to afford vacations, or even harm reduction for those with incredibly stressful lives. Perhaps, the poor self-medicate with SSBs. Dissecting the anti-hunger argument against SSB restrictions reveals four basic messages, each outlined below:

Not a Nutrition Program

First, anti-hunger proponents believe that advocates for exclusions are barking up the wrong tree. They see SNAP's nutrition purpose as secondary, at best, to its anti-hunger function. Others deny SNAP as a nutrition program at all. Ed Cooney, the former executive director of the Congressional Hunger Center, asserts, "There is no evidence of SNAP as a nutrition program. It was Joe Baca's idea (Baca was the chair of the Nutrition Subcommittee in the House Agriculture Committee during the 2008 Farm Bill) to change the name of the program. He didn't change the program's mission."[62] Keith Stern, a former staffer to Representative Jim McGovern (D-MA), a leading voice for anti-hunger programs, agrees: "SNAP is not a nutrition program. It isn't based on nutrition and doesn't help people eat healthfully. Its benefits are inadequate, something that (at best) restricts the ability to purchase healthy food and (at worst) promotes the purchase of unhealthy, low nutrient food."[63]

Reading between the lines, Stern is affirming a common mantra among anti-hunger advocates: "SNAP is not WIC." WIC (the Women, Infants and Children program) seeks to enhance the nutritional status of its at-risk target population of low-income pregnant women, new moms, infants, and children five years of age and younger. Families receive vouchers redeemable for specific high-protein and nutrient-dense foods, such as beans, peanut butter, milk, and produce. The WIC package is based on recommendations from the National Academy of Medicine, a congressionally chartered entity designed to provide sound scientific advice to the government. Program participants also receive nutrition education and referrals to other social services. WIC is highly regarded for saving up to $3.13 in health care costs for every program dollar.[64]

Increased Benefits Will Improve Diets

In lieu of changing which foods are eligible for purchase under SNAP, anti-hunger advocates frequently call for increasing benefits, contending that when recipients have more income, they will purchase foods with a better nutritional profile. There can be little doubt that SNAP benefits are woefully inadequate and outdated, based on a food plan that assumes households spend 2.3 hours cooking each day.[65] Nevertheless, the evidence is mixed on their claim that increased benefits directly translate into healthier diets.

Modest increases in the income of poor households do result in small changes in dietary patterns, but not always in healthful ways. Extra money typically results in more purchases of meats, sweets, and frozen foods: fruit and vegetable consumption does not increase substantially, according to one study, until a family hits 130 percent of the poverty line, and not until it reaches the $70,000 income level, according to another report.[66] In other words, there doesn't appear to exist a huge pent-up demand for healthy foods among low-income households. They prioritize their supplemental food purchases based on other factors, such as personal preference and convenience.

While increasing SNAP recipients' benefits may not translate into the desired dietary changes, a more targeted approach of reducing the price of certain foods has proven more successful. From 2011 to 2012, the USDA funded an experiment in western Massachusetts to assess if a reduction in produce prices would increase their consumption. The Healthy Incentives Pilot (HIP) reimbursed SNAP recipients 30 cents for every dollar they spent on canned, frozen, or fresh produce. They discovered that participants expanded their consumption of these products by 25 percent as a result of this intervention.[67] (This pilot program led to the creation of the Food Insecurity Nutrition Incentives program described in chapter 5.)

Although increased consumption of produce offers intrinsic health benefits, it may not be enough to diminish the incidence of obesity and diabetes. The Rand Institute experts Roland Sturm and Ruopeng An beg to differ from the healthy-food incentive model. They maintain that the low cost of food relative to income and its ubiquity fuels the obesity epidemic. Cheaper produce prices may augment consumption for the lowest income households, but without efforts to moderate the intake of calorie-dense foods, such as salty snacks and SSBs, the ability of these incentives to bring down obesity levels will be limited. "Effective policy intervention must address the need to reduce calories in the diet and replace calorie dense foods with fruits and vegetables, rather than just add fruits and vegetables to the diet," they conclude.[68]

No Link Between SNAP and Obesity

Anti-hunger groups contend that, as an income-transfer program, SNAP doesn't cause obesity, so it is "not a practical place to look to reverse the problem."[69] Ed Cooney of the Congressional Hunger Center claims that conclusive evidence does not exist to prove that SNAP either promotes or reduces obesity. Anti-hunger advocates assert that SNAP recipients eat no better or worse than other low-income Americans.[70] They hold that the nation's obesity epidemic must be dealt with systematically as it is the entire food system that ensnares SNAP recipients—and the general public—into poor food choices.[71]

While Cooney is technically correct in saying there is no conclusive evidence that SNAP promotes or causes obesity, there is a body of research that shows a correlation between SNAP and poor diets as well as the incidence of obesity (causation is notoriously difficult to prove in the public health nutrition field). For example, one study found that adult women enrolled in SNAP tend to be more overweight than similar nonparticipants; other research has discovered that the longer an adult receives SNAP benefits, the greater his or her chances of becoming obese, perhaps because the inadequacy and cyclical nature of SNAP benefits may result in obesity-causing behavior as individuals binge when their new benefit allotment arrives after a period of deprivation.[72]

In 2015 USDA released a comprehensive analysis of the dietary quality of SNAP participants, as compared to other low-income non-SNAP participants and higher income individuals, which found mixed results. SNAP participants had adequate calorie and nutrient consumption levels as compared to the other two populations, but SNAP recipients were also more likely to be obese, to drink more sugar-sweetened sodas, to have a lower healthy eating index score, and children on SNAP consumed a larger proportion of empty calories. The report concludes: "Decreased intakes of foods that contribute empty calories would improve the overall quality of the SNAP participants' diets. This is also essential for reducing the prevalence of overweight and obesity in this population."[73]

Restrictions Won't Work

Second, anti-hunger advocates assert that restrictions will simply not work. Given the complexity of the food system, with tens of thousands of products on the shelves of 200,000 SNAP-authorized retailers, making science-based decisions on which products would be excluded and then communicating those decisions would be enormously problematic. FRAC's review of its strategies states, in part: "No clear standards exist for defining individual foods as 'healthy' or 'unhealthy.'" Policymakers are susceptible to pressure from industry, and would ultimately not make sound science-based decisions. In addition, FRAC reports, these changes would put an increased burden on retailers, many of whom already struggle with existing rules. As a result, many retailers might drop out of the program, further reducing food access for the needy.[74]

Public health advocates counter that drawing the lines, at least for sugar-sweetened beverages, need not be so complicated. For example, the soda tax measure that passed in 2014 in Berkeley, California, defines SSBs as having at least two calories per fluid ounce and using added caloric sweeteners, with exceptions for milk, alcoholic beverages, meal replacements, and drinks with medical usages.[75]

Another challenge in the implementation of product exclusions from SNAP is that most food stamp recipients have additional resources with which to purchase groceries.[76] They could simply purchase soda or other unhealthy foods with their own cash, which would negate the potential health impacts of these restrictions.[77]

Restrictions Will Increase Stigma

Third, anti-hunger advocates remain deeply concerned that further food restrictions might result in individuals dropping out of the SNAP program, worsening their food security. Any practice that would identify individuals as SNAP recipients, they say, such as forcing them to separate eligible and ineligible purchases at the checkout counter, would increase the stigma associated with participating in the program. Stigma is one of the primary reasons for nonparticipation in the SNAP program, even though great progress has been made to increase user confidentiality through the conversion of benefits from paper coupons to a debit-card format in the last 15 years.[78]

Restrictions Send the Wrong Message

These arguments all seem to be secondary to the more intangible and fourth concern, that such a policy change sends the wrong message about the poor's capabilities. Anti-hunger advocates fear, as Kathleen Merrigan articulated, that junk food exclusions would cede ground in the discourse wars that frame the poor as undeserving of federal support. In essence, exclusions single out the poor for what is a society-wide problem. Such a move could undermine public support over the long-term for a strong government role in addressing hunger. Advocates maintain that soda restrictions also send a message to the poor about how society perceives their ability to manage their food choices. Restrictions violate the fundamental dignity of the poor as human beings who possess the ability to make their own decisions on a matter as basic as what they eat.[79] Ed Cooney attacks the public health community for its lack of sensitivity: "Public health sees its goals as so important that they skip over how individuals are treated."[80]

Underlying these rationales for supporting the status quo of the SNAP program is an unspoken but highly strategic motivation: that excluding SSBs and possibly other junk foods would reduce industry lobbying for the program. FRAC has deliberately built as big and broad a tent as possible for SNAP to maximize its legislative chances. They have made a strategic trade, gaining the support of industry for the program in exchange for allowing them to profit handsomely from the SNAP program. This implicit deal is grounded in the assumption that a SNAP "with warts" does more good for the poor than a smaller heath-oriented program or no program at all.

Industry: Partner or Predator?

One Wednesday in June 2014, at the Washington Hilton, the Food Research and Action Center held its 24th annual benefit dinner. There, soda companies and other food industry behemoths were honored for their contribution to reducing hunger and protecting federal food programs, from which they reap a significant portion of their sales. The dinner program reads like a "who's who" of the food industry, with half or full page ads for General Mills, Coke, Kellogg, Pepsi, the American Beverage Association, Abbott, Grocery Manufacturers Association, Safeway, Giant, Mars, Nestle, Kraft, Tyson, and the National Dairy Council.[81]

Interestingly, SSB manufacturers such as Coke, Pepsi, Dr Pepper Snapple Group, and their trade association, the American Beverage Association, do not appear on FRAC's list of funders until early 2013, presumably because of their contributions to the organization at the 2012 benefit. That was the year when Farm Bill proceedings started in earnest, and when the anti-soda in SNAP fervor was beginning to take shape in Congress. These benefit dinners have been highly valuable for FRAC. According to its tax returns, the organization grossed $288,000 in 2012 from its annual benefit dinner.[82]

The week before, two miles to the south, at the National Press Club, Gabriel Cortez electrified the National Soda Summit audience with his "Perfect Soldiers" video and spoken word performance. He recounted the story of growing up in a Panamanian American household, with a diabetic grandfather, where soda was ubiquitous. Coke occupied his family's bodies and his culture just as the American army has been an imperial force in Panama for more than a hundred years. Soda has "colonized our bodies and our taste buds." Soda cans are a cylindrical incarnation of violence, "vests of dynamite" lining his refrigerator, grenade-like containers that blow up when thrown against a wall. Cortez has learned to be a perfect soldier, doing what he is supposed to, consuming his share of the sugary elixir.[83]

These two events just a week apart lend a stark contrast in the way anti-hunger and public health groups relate to the soda and food industry. Ed Cooney summarizes this difference: "They [the public health groups] think of industry as predators. We prefer to think of them as partners."[84] To the public health community, "Big Food" fattens the American population, and especially the poor, through the manipulation of processed foods to appeal to our biological cravings for salt, sugar, and fat. Hank Herrera, a longtime community food security advocate based in Oakland, articulates this perspective succinctly: "SNAP uses poor people as a pass-through intermediary to subsidize the food manufacturers. And in the process, poor people suffer and die from the toxic foods the manufacturers produce" (Hank Herrera, e-mail communication, January 9, 2013).

The food industry reinforces their product formulation through ubiquitous advertising, often targeted at youth and persons of color, to increase consumption. For example, Kraft targets its Kool-Aid marketing at Latinos. Coke "wants to be everywhere teenagers are."[85] Public health advocates bestow the ultimate affront on soda manufacturers, when they label soda as the "next tobacco," inferring that the beverage industry has been knowingly poisoning the public in the name of corporate profits.

To many anti-hunger groups, especially the main national lobbying entities such as FRAC and Feeding America, the food and beverage industries are their friends. Industry buys tables at their galas, writes them six- and seven-figure checks from their foundations, but most importantly, according to anti-hunger leaders, plays a pivotal role in the passage of the SNAP program. Once again, Ed Cooney highlights the value of this industry alliance: "Those companies have access to members of Congress that we don't have access to, people in the Republican leadership. We find this advantageous."[86] One former food industry lobbyist—I'll call him Andrew—takes issue with this statement. To Andrew, the importance of industry support for SNAP "is a lie that they tell themselves to make themselves feel good about taking the money."

Jessica Bartholow, of the Western Center on Law and Poverty, reinforces Cooney's analysis. "It's a lonely business being an anti-poverty advocate. We take whatever friends we can use. We work by ourselves, long hours and don't have administrative staff. We don't have an army behind us. Whoever is on my side, I will work with them. When you're an anti-poverty advocate, you don't have a lot of friends."[87]

Anti-hunger groups have actively courted industry groups to protect SNAP from restrictions. Ellen Vollinger, a FRAC staff director dealing with food stamps and legal issues, led the creation of the Coalition to Preserve Food Choice in SNAP, whose members include numerous anti-hunger and farm groups as well as the main trade associations for the soda, candy, baking, snack food, dairy, supermarket, and high-fructose corn syrup industries.[88] Anti-hunger and industry groups lobby together on state and federal legislation related to protecting "freedom of choice" within the SNAP program. They have also developed common materials, including a joint "coalition statement."[89]

In addition to food manufacturers, FRAC has cultivated fast food restaurants as stakeholders in the SNAP program. For example, it supported efforts by Yum! Brands (Taco Bell, KFC, Pizza Hut) to expand a pilot project to allow homeless, disabled, and elderly SNAP participants to redeem their benefits at restaurants. FRAC staff reasoned that this program would bring the fast food industry into the fold, creating another constituency for SNAP.[90]

Ed Cooney and FRAC's Jim Weill contend that these relationships do not create a conflict of interest because industry's donations come without strings.[91] Andrew the industry lobbyist agrees that his relationship with anti-hunger groups was not transactional. "There was no explicit quid pro quo here. The money is just about making friends." A former colleague of Andrew's agrees that for a few thousand dollars he wasn't expecting to buy any influence, but that attending benefit dinners put on by FRAC or the Congressional Hunger Center is "just the right thing to do. I have a budget for it, so why not?" To Andrew, the connections between the food industry and DC-based anti-hunger staff are just a fact of life in insular Washington. "It's all about social networks. We all know each other, and see each other at the same events. My kids go to summer camp with their kids."

Yet to Jim O'Hara, the director of health promotion policy at the Center for Science in the Public Interest and the organizer of the National Soda Summit, conflict of interest may be more a sin of omission than a sin of commission. His concern isn't the donation that food companies make to anti-hunger groups, but the fact that recipient groups may censor themselves on matters related to the donor company.[92] Marion Standish, a former board member of FRAC and a leading figure in the California public health community, agrees with O'Hara. She doesn't believe that food industry donations are a conflict of interest per se, but that the behavior of groups after they receive the money is of vital interest: "If your mission is about the health and well-being of poor people, of people who are SNAP-eligible, and you refuse to allow the consideration of the implications and impacts of those products [made by companies donating money to your organization], then the question is whether you are meeting your mission."[93] In other words, when a group accepts industry's money and tries to shut down discussion about whether to allow food stamp recipients to continue to spend federal dollars on the donor's products, it is failing its own constituents.

SNAP Recipients Chime In

Ironically, the anti-hunger community has failed to demonstrate that its constituents oppose soda restrictions in SNAP, while the public health sector has conducted various studies that arrive at the opposite conclusion. This omission would seem to reinforce former food industry lobbyist

Andrew's point, that the inside-the-Beltway anti-hunger leaders are part of an elite caste that remain separated from the public. The following examples reinforce that perception.

On a segment of the MSNBC show *Up with Chris Hayes*, from 2012, the host asked his guest, a SNAP outreach volunteer and program participant named Debbie Palacios, her opinion of government restrictions on purchases with food stamps. She responded: "I don't think that would be a big problem. I think it's a good idea because it's supposed to supplement with nutritious food. ... But I do think it would benefit people to be restricted on what they could buy and should buy. ... If the government is trying to help us with the food supplements, it should be used for the right foods." When asked if her opinion was widely held among other SNAP recipients, the executive director of the NYC Coalition Against Hunger, Joel Berg, interrupted Ms. Palacios and dismissed her opinion, saying, "I know it's not [a widely held opinion among other SNAP recipients]."[94]

Examining the growing number of studies on this topic, Debbie Palacios's opinion on SNAP exclusions actually seems to be in the majority despite Joel Berg's assertions. Two peer-reviewed studies by Harvard researchers show that a majority of program recipients support excluding sugary drinks from the SNAP program. In one telephone survey, which included 418 food stamp program participants, 54 percent supported such an initiative. These figures went up to 75 percent when the restrictions were paired with healthy food incentives. In an intensive study of 107 adults in Massachusetts, of whom 64 were food stamp program participants, 59 percent of the SNAP recipients agreed that soda restrictions in SNAP would improve program participants' diets.[95] A 2011 in-person survey of 498 SNAP participants in New York City showed similar results, with 49 percent supporting the city's waiver request with only 35 percent opposing it.[96] In 2014, a statewide survey of California SNAP recipients found that 74 percent supported excluding soda from the program.[97]

To get an anecdotal sense of the perspectives of SNAP recipients and other low-income individuals, I personally interviewed 83 people at three locations: two farmers markets and a food pantry, all in Portland, Oregon, during July 2014. (The SNAP program in Oregon is called Oregon Trail.) I asked two simple questions, modified from Harvard's survey: "Would you support or oppose removing sugary drinks (such as soda) from the list of products that can be purchased using the Oregon Trail card?" and "Why or why not?"

At the two farmers market sites, Oregon Trail cardholders were inter-viewed as they came to the manager's booth to redeem their benefits for tokens usable at the market. Of 29 responses, 86 percent (25) were either in favor of removing SSBs from SNAP or on the fence, with only 14 percent (4) opposed. These numbers were not surprising, as farmers markets are known to draw a health-conscious crowd.

The food pantry at which I conducted the interviews serves a large num-ber of East Asian and Eastern European immigrants as well as US-born residents. The income guideline for food pantries is similar to that of the SNAP program. For the sake of privacy, the survey omitted a question as to whether the respondent received SNAP. Only English-language speakers participated, with a few exceptions of when a friend or child was able to translate. Over the course of four visits, 54 different adults participated. Exactly half (27) were opposed to excluding sugary drinks from SNAP, while the other half supported doing so or were undecided.

For some respondents, the question was a no-brainer, but others consid-ered it to have complex implications. Some persons answered from a per-sonal perspective, saying something like, "I don't drink soda so yes, take it off the list." Various persons didn't want to restrict other people's choices. Most knew soda consumption was unhealthy, and a few noted that they were addicted. Interestingly, diabetes came up unprompted a number of times in conversations from different perspectives. A few persons remarked that they had diabetes in their family and knew how toxic soda was to their health. On the other hand, one or two persons noted that they had diabe-tes, and needed soda as a way to boost their blood sugar quickly. Here's a sampling of some of their responses.

Against Restriction

Anonymous: "There needs to be less regulation and more freedom. People should not to be told what to eat and drink."

Anonymous: "I don't get Oregon Trail and would never buy it [soda] for my family, but am opposed to telling others what to buy."

Nafeesah: "You gotta have that sugar."

Molly: "When you're sick there's nothing better than 7 UP. When you're hot, Coke gives you energy. When you're poor, you need to get so many things done."

Anonymous: "No way, soda is good."

For Restriction

Mary: "I don't consider them [sugary beverages] food. They are the most destructive thing possible in the American diet."

Anonymous: "People should be getting nutritious food and not junk food. I would like to see a lot of junk food taken off the list."

Lidiya: "Absolutely. It's so expensive. For the same amount of money you can buy food. I come from Ukraine and try to make the best use of money to get as many nutrients as possible."

On the Fence

Kelly: "Tough question. Would it be discriminating against the poor? What if they couldn't afford any healthier drinks? The poor shouldn't be discriminated against."

Delmer: "I have been addicted to soda all my life."

Dawn: "The reality is that soda is what kids want. I would restrict it but wonder about the backlash. I used to work in a domestic violence shelter and [I've] seen what people feed their kids. Behavior change is needed. Nutrition education is needed as well."

Analysis

Both anti-hunger and public health advocates have articulated very valid claims about the pros and cons of soda exclusions from SNAP. The anti-hunger community's arguments that restrictions reinforce a history of paternalism toward the poor should not be discarded, and should lead the public health community to a deeper examination of race and class issues as they pertain to this topic. The fact that no locale has been able to implement such restrictions indicates that the anti-hunger argument is prevailing at least in the short term. The power for issuing waivers resides with USDA, and to date the department has not received a waiver request that it feels it can approve. (One suspects that USDA under the Trump administration will be more favorable to issuing waivers.)

Yet, the maintenance of the status quo should not be viewed as a reason for celebration within the anti-hunger community. Instead, it begs the question: Who wins and who loses with the current situation? For anti-hunger groups, the absence of what they perceive to be demeaning restrictions can be seen as a symbolic victory for the way America views the decision-making ability of the poor. From an economic angle, the beverage industry comes up as the big winner. No policy changes translate into their continued ability to sell billions of dollars' worth of SSBs every year through the SNAP program.

The big loser is the health of SNAP recipients, whose continued high levels of soda consumption leads them, like many other low-income Americans, toward obesity, diabetes, and other related maladies. This business as usual injures not just their bodies, but also their spirits. In the words of one Oregon health care professional, "Where's the dignity in having diabetes and being 150 pounds overweight?"[98]

Removing products from the SNAP program may indeed present practical and symbolic challenges. It might not even be effective in addressing the ever-growing health problems caused by SSBs. The anti-hunger community's argument is accurate: that systemic solutions are needed, such as a national soda tax, to reduce the harm caused by over consumption of SSBs. But the need for holistic solutions does not preclude the implementation of piecemeal measures. Doing nothing to change the status quo is morally indefensible, especially when the anti-hunger leadership has not dedicated significant effort into those systemic solutions it claims are necessary. For example, the overwhelming majority of anti-hunger groups did *not* publicly support or submit comments on the highly innovative 2015 Dietary Guidelines for Americans, which prioritizes the reduction of added sugars in Americans' diets.[99]

Dire hunger no longer stalks this country in large measure due to the food stamp program and other federal food assistance programs. This fact does not trivialize the continued existence of food insecurity or the severe health consequences, especially to children, that accompany it. Yet the poor increasingly suffer from diseases of inappropriate nutrition, such as obesity, diabetes, and metabolic syndrome. Just as the nature of malnutrition continues to evolve, SNAP must progress as well. Otherwise its effectiveness will be diminished, leaving it more politically vulnerable. Many congressional staff and DC insiders have privately predicted SNAP's demise unless changes are made to enhance its nutritional purpose.

In part, the terminology that anti-hunger and public health groups utilize in this matter marks and reinforces their differences. To proponents of SSB *exclusions*, the desired policy change represents an improvement to SNAP. As good governance, it aligns food stamp purchases with federal dietary guidelines and other nutrition programs. Opponents tend to describe the removal of soda from the SNAP eligibility list as a *restriction*, implying a punishment because participants can't make good choices. The field of behavioral economics has found that people react more viscerally and passionately to restrictions, in that they revoke an established privilege. The loss of something small currently in our possession seems worse to us than the loss of a larger potential gain.[100]

Interestingly, program participants and anti-hunger advocates frame their loss aversion in starkly different terms. SNAP recipients reacted more strongly to the potential loss of certain products that they find useful and enjoyable, while anti-hunger advocates and the beverage industry frame their opposition in abstract terms of losing the cherished value of freedom of choice, a foundational principle of our society and market economy. This perception of the freedom of choice is an illusion, however, just as the choice between Coke or Pepsi is a false choice. These options have been established for us by a food system whose structure favors the profits of the companies to the detriment of our health.

The Johns Hopkins University bioethicist Nancy Kass raises the point that we make food choices within established parameters. She notes that our consumption behavior is not free at all, but constrained by the environment in which we live. Access, location, and even our meal companions all affect our dietary choices. Similarly, the external environment through marketing (such as store-level signage and product placement) and advertising affects our ability to make healthy choices. Kass asks if the current patterns of consumption represent a freedom of choice or a social injustice, and whether government action would be interfering with personal preference or righting a wrong.[101]

In other words, the public goes grocery shopping within a food system that generates enormous amounts of collateral damage in the form of ever-increasing rates of diet-related diseases. SNAP has been designed to follow the marketplace, seeking to normalize the way in which the poor acquire food. In shifting food assistance away from commodity distributions and other stigmatizing methods, SNAP has made great strides. Yet being been downstream to a disease-producing system is no picnic either. The time has come to reconsider this fundamental arrangement with the food system.

Instead, we should be asking how the government can make use of SNAP, as well as other federal food programs with their combined $100 billion of purchasing power, to leverage broader change within the food system. Can SNAP's purchasing power be utilized to demand food manufacturers create healthier products? Perhaps, but just adding nutrients to unhealthy products is like putting lipstick on a pig (Diet Coke Plus, with vitamins B and C and anti-oxidants, has been released in the United Kingdom among other countries). Regulating foods by their nutrient content has not served the public interest well, as food manufacturers can simply skirt the regulations by adding vitamins or modestly reducing the salt or fat content. As Sue Foerster, the former head of the California Nutrition Network, says, it's like "playing whack-a-mole."[102] The problem is not so much a matter of nutrients, but our reliance on highly processed foods.

One solution might be found in Brazil, where the government is testing out nutrition guidelines based not on nutrient content but on the degree to which foods have been processed. The Brazilian government divides foods into six categories based on the degree and purpose of processing. These guidelines specifically discourage the consumption of ultra-processed ready-to-consume foods, such as instant noodles, candy bars, soft drinks, and salty snacks. These products are considered nutritionally inferior to other foods, possessing higher energy density, more sugar, and more trans fats, as well as less protein, fiber, vitamins, and minerals than other foods.[103] By their very nature, they are intended to be over-consumed and to incite compulsive over-eating, especially when they are accompanied by high levels of advertising.

The new Brazilian dietary guidelines encourage consumers to eat primarily "foods," use oils, fats, sugar, and salt moderately to convert foods into meals, limit ready-to-eat processed foods, and avoid ultraprocessed foods. Professor Carlos Monteiro of the University of Sao Paulo, a key collaborator in the formulation of these guidelines, emphasizes that just eating more healthy food is not sufficient to combat obesity and other diet-related diseases; the consumption of ultraprocessed foods must decline. He states, "Industry says everything can be part of a healthy diet. It's a lie. It's not true."[104]

Switching to this kind of dietary guidance would be hugely challenging in the United States, as can be seen by the pitched battles over reducing meat consumption and added sugars in the 2015 Dietary Guidelines. But, the country is ground zero for food companies' experimentation on the public. Americans consume the highest degree of ultraprocessed foods of any country, deriving 60 percent of our calories from them.[105] Not so coincidentally, Americans also have some of the highest rates of diabetes and obesity of any country. Nonetheless, the Brazilian model can provide us with a long-term vision for where the United States needs to go as a nation, as well as guidance for how the SNAP program can be modified to increase its nutritional effectiveness through food system change.

Summary

Historically, SNAP has been the nation's most important program for keeping food insecurity in check and protecting the health of its participants from the maladies of inadequate nutrition. Given the persistent levels of food insecurity in the United States, the nutritional safety net that it provides is sorely in need of enhancement. Yet the poor also face the additional and linked peril of illness, such as diabetes and obesity, associated with the overconsumption of added sugars and ultraprocessed foods. These health challenges frequently impoverish families and can lead to a downward economic spiral as health issues increase absenteeism and diminish work productivity. In addressing these public health matters, SNAP's impact has been far from ideal. Those who claim that SNAP does not cause obesity or foster unhealthy eating patterns have missed the point: SNAP *could and should* be doing so much more to foster positive change in this area.

The times have changed and with it SNAP must change as well. SNAP must become a different type of nutrition program, one that addresses not just the health problems associated with underconsumption, but those related to the overconsumption on inexpensive high-calorie low-nutrient foods. The status quo, in which SNAP is linked programmatically and politically to a disease-promoting food system, has created a tremendous missed opportunity to reverse the harm this system has done.

Acknowledge SNAP as a Nutrition Program

Congress should revise the authorizing language for SNAP in the next Farm Bill to clearly and unambiguously state its role as a nutrition program. Anti-hunger and public health advocates should come together to lobby for this revision, acknowledging the integral links between health and equity, and balancing healthfulness and cost concerns.

Integral to SNAP's nutrition purpose is gaining an understanding of how recipients spend their benefits. USDA should collect and release data on SNAP purchases through a searchable database, including the products purchased and the retail location, in a way that does not violate the confidentiality of SNAP recipients or the verifiable business interests of retailers. This information will be essential for researchers to better understand the impact of the SNAP program on participants' diets.

Prioritize Innovation

To fully develop SNAP's nutritional effectiveness will require innovation and evaluation at the local levels. USDA should encourage states to develop scalable pilot projects with robust evaluation mechanisms that test out restrictions, incentives, and other nonpunitive strategies that encourage the consumption of healthy foods while discouraging unhealthy food purchases. These pilot projects should also explore behavioral economic approaches that include allowing participants more control in how they interact with the program. For example, SNAP's default setting could be modified to allow participants to purchase only a limited amount of SSBs or other ultraprocessed foods in exchange for extra benefits for healthy foods. The development of an evidence base through these pilot projects should inform national-level policy through future Farm Bills.

Congress should substantially increase SNAP levels in the next Farm Bill. Benefit levels are woefully inadequate and typically last households at best three weeks of the month. At least a part of increased benefits should be tied to new program designs that prioritize the purchase of healthy foods and limit purchases of SSBs and other ultraprocessed foods.

Foster Dialogue between Stakeholders

Anti-hunger and public health disciplines see the world through very different lenses, but they share a strong bond in their concern for the well-being of the poor. This concern needs to be put in front of other divisive issues, so that the currently scrambled alliances become untangled. In doing so, they should come together and communicate forcefully and strategically that they stand opposed to those who would cut back the nutrition safety net, and to those entities that threaten the health of the poor.

Foster Systems Analysis and Change Strategies

The public interest in reducing government support for SSB consumption and its expensive public health impacts crosses the borders of the SNAP program into other parts of USDA and other agencies. The White House should establish a cross-agency policy framework that brings together stakeholders within the health care, public health, agriculture, and nutrition policy sectors to move forward with strategies that reduce federal support for SSBs.

Similarly, USDA should fund research to identify agriculture and health policy mechanisms that, when linked to federal nutrition program buying power, would invert the current market pricing, such that nutrient-dense foods become less expensive and ultraprocessed foods more expensive.

These policy changes are heavy lifts. Moving the powerful beverage industry is a huge challenge. Yet now is time for all sides to muster the courage, take their heads out of the sand, and engage in an honest dialogue, regardless of their funding sources or the political moment, about how they might collaborate for the sake of the health of the 40+ million people who receive SNAP benefits.

Shifting SNAP's annual budget of $70 billion dollars away from unhealthy ultraprocessed foods could play a pivotal role in protecting the health of the poor. Likewise, shifting even a modest percentage of these funds away from the Big Food corporations that vacuum them up could serve as a powerful investment in poverty reduction and increasing the vitality of rural communities.

5 Economic Democracy through Federal Food Programs

Food Distribution on the Indian Reservation

On Janie Hipp's first day as the senior advisor for tribal relations to USDA secretary Tom Vilsack, she met with 175 Indian leaders gathered at the White House for the 2010 Tribal Leaders Conference. Representatives from all 566 federally recognized tribal governments participated in this event; nothing comparable to it had ever been organized by an administration before President Obama took office. The tribal leaders posed their very first question to Ms. Hipp: Why did USDA remove butter from the Food Distribution Program on Indian Reservations (FDPIR) food package without tribal consultation, as required by executive order? They asked, "You have butter in your refrigerator. Why are you prohibiting it in ours?" It took Ms. Hipp a year and a half to get the USDA to reverse the decision made by the Bush administration, to remove butter from FDPIR for health reasons.[1]

As an alternative to SNAP for those persons living on or near reservations with limited access to a grocery store, FDPIR is of great importance to tribal authorities.[2] It provides one of the primary food sources for 88,600 people monthly, people who are among the poorest of the poor living in some of the most remote areas of the country.[3] The FDPIR provides households, based on size, a package of predetermined foods. These groceries are acquired by USDA's purchasing arm, USDA Foods, which procured almost $2 billion in food in 2014 for school lunches and other nutrition programs.

The decision to remove butter had indeed been made, without the required tribal consultation, by federal employees whose decisions regarding the federal food package of FDPIR can and do trump any input by tribal communities and their leaders.[4] Butter had been replaced by a "butter substitute," which arguably was not a healthier product, and the decision deeply affected families in Indian Country. Tribal leaders very clearly stated to Ms. Hipp that in the future they must be consulted before such intimate and critical decisions concerning food access and health are made.

Apart from the butter incident, USDA has, to its credit, worked long and hard with the 276 Indian nations that participate in the FDPIR program to improve the quality of the food package and to meet their desires.[5] At the local level, Indian nations manage the program implementation through the leadership of Indian Tribal Organizations (ITOs). These ITOs, along with officials from local, state, and federal governments, provide guidance to the USDA on the foods distributed through FDPIR.[6]

Not only does USDA make decisions about which foods FDPIR participants receive, but also virtually all items that USDA Foods distributes to FDPIR participants come from off-reservation. For FDPIR, a small portion of overall USDA commodity purchases, USDA has chosen to streamline its procurement in a way that generally does not differentiate this program from other initiatives that serve the broader low-income population. Despite the diversity of Native American foodways, USDA sees FDPIR as a national program, instead of a series of regional efforts tailored to meet tribal dietary preferences.

USDA has continued this streamlined approach despite the fact that Congress established the legal framework for the department to treat food access on Indian reservations differently than for the general population. By creating FDPIR in the first place, Congress clearly identified a difference in Indian country food access; it followed up the creation of the program with legislation within the 2008 and 2014 Farm Bills that established local procurement initiatives, further codifying the importance of traditional foods in FDPIR.[7] The pilot programs embedded in these pieces of legislation have been unevenly funded and implemented, but in general have failed to point a new direction for the way in which USDA sources food for FDPIR.

Now, as the director of the Indigenous Food and Agriculture Initiative at the University of Arkansas School of Law, Janie Hipp believes that despite the federal government's best intentions, FDPIR cannot fully meet the needs of Native Americans until the program is administered by tribal nations themselves.[8] She believes that tribal self-government is compromised by placing the food security of the Indian population outside its control. The political scientist David Lulka echoes this perspective, writing that the very structure of FDPIR reaffirms the dependence of Indian nations on the federal government for their livelihood.[9]

This dependence goes beyond the FDPIR's decision-making structure. FDPIR is one program among many that sets up a one-way street in which Native Americans become dependent on government handouts, instead of supporting Indian agricultural enterprises to provide food for their own people. To Hipp, it is a $100 million per-year missed opportunity to reduce poverty and build wealth in Indian country.[10]

An Accomplice to the Food Industry

FDPIR is just one small missed opportunity among many much larger USDA programs that could be doing a better job of using their economic heft for other social purposes: generating wealth in rural and urban low income communities; supporting a family farmer–based food system; treating food chain workers fairly; and protecting the environment. The $100 billion spent on federal food programs annually is not meeting its full potential, in part because the programs are grounded in the narrowest interpretation of the concept of getting a good value for the federal dollar. These expenditures are based on overriding considerations of efficiency, convenience, and low price, placing the federal government in a tightly knit partnership with a highly industrialized and economically concentrated food system. In doing so, the government bolsters a system whose negative impacts on rural communities, family farmers, workers, public health, and the environment are described in this chapter.

Our nation's food assistance programs are an accomplice in this vicious cycle, born and bred of the necessity for cheap food. They have been designed to fit into the structure of the nation's industrial food system, placing few demands on changing the way food is produced, distributed, or sold. They reinforce the ills of the marketplace rather than seek to transform them. Overall, these programs reflect a significant portion of American grocery purchases, with just WIC and SNAP combined representing more than one in every ten dollars spent on groceries.[11] Yet, until 2012 and 2013, when several writers such as Michele Simon and Krissy Clark published studies and articles on the "secret life of the food stamp," the economic heft of SNAP (as one example) rarely surfaced in public dialogues.[12]

The $100 billion spent annually on federal food programs, or even a modest portion of this sum, could go a long way to create a more sustainable and equitable food system that doesn't leave a trail of collateral damage to laborers, farmers, and communities in its wake. It could be more effectively spent, maximizing its community economic development purpose to help pull the poor out of poverty, as Janie Hipp suggests for Indian Country.

The purpose of this chapter is to stimulate a reconsideration of how these billions of taxpayer dollars could pull double duty, both to reduce food insecurity while stimulating targeted economic development to help communities pull themselves out of poverty. The first step in this journey is to understand the nature of economic concentration in the food system and how federal food programs inadvertently perpetuate injustices to workers and rural communities.

Tyson and the Chicken Industry

Federal chicken procurement provides a window into understanding the connections between food assistance programs and the effects of economic concentration in the food system. As one of the most popular items on the school menu, chicken purchases totaled almost $262 million in 2014, as one of USDA Foods' largest expenditures overall. More than two-thirds of this chicken budget in 2014, or $178 million, went to Tyson and JBS (the Brazilian conglomerate that owns Pilgrim's Pride brand), even though these companies control "only" 39 percent of the broiler industry nationwide.[13]

The chicken sector is just part of the industrial food system, controlled by a small number of powerful firms. As of 2011, the top four companies in each sector controlled 82 percent of beef slaughter, 63 percent of pork slaughter, 58 percent of turkey slaughter, 53 percent of broiler slaughter, 87 percent of wet corn milling, 85 percent of soybean processing, 52 percent of flour milling, and 44 percent of animal feed in the United States.[14] A few companies, such as Tyson, Cargill, and Archer Daniels Midland (ADM) have stakes in multiple sectors, controlling vast swaths of the food system.[15]

Not only does Tyson sell more chicken to USDA Foods than any other company, it is by far the largest vendor in the USDA Foods system, with $106 million worth of sales in 2014 (as compared to runner-up Del Monte with $77 million), capturing 7 percent of all USDA Foods procurement. Contracts with USDA Foods make up only a portion of the company's total public sector market. It also sells its meat directly to school districts and other nutrition program operators, and captures fees for processing raw commodities into finished products (see the USDA Foods section below). Federal nutrition programs likely make up a significant percentage of Tyson's food service business, which accounted for 42 percent (or $5.2 billion) of its overall chicken sales in 2013.[16]

As the 93rd-largest American company, Tyson revolutionized the chicken industry through developing a production system in which the company owns virtually all aspects of the supply chain, from chicks to feed to the processing of the finished product. As part of this system, the firm contracts with farmers to raise the animals from baby chicks until they are full grown broilers. The company controls all aspects of the operation, while offloading all of the risk onto the growers.

Most of Tyson's chicken farmers go deeply in debt to purchase high-tech chicken houses, becoming entirely dependent on the goodwill of the company to pay them a fair price and renew their contracts every few months. Farmers' profit margins are so thin that when the company provides them with a load of unhealthy chicks or bad grain, the farmers can go belly up. In *The Meat Racket*, the investigative reporter Chris Leonard blasts Tyson, noting that the firm has the power of a feudal lord, with absolute control over farmers' livelihoods. He comments, "American consumers are using their money to support a system that keeps farmers in a state of indebted servitude, living like modern-day sharecroppers on the ragged edge of bankruptcy."[17]

Leonard finds that Tyson's business is far from a boon to the economy in which it operates, but actually has been detrimental to those communities. In more than two-thirds of the 79 counties in which Tyson operates, per capita income has grown over the last 40 years more slowly than the state average in which the county is located. Tyson counties remain consistently worse off than neighboring counties. Leonard sees Tyson as a suffocating economic force on the communities in which it functions. It creates jobs, but its cost-cutting ethos restrains economic growth in rural America: "The company has expanded in economically marginal areas, and it has kept those areas economically marginal. Tyson Foods is feeding off the lowly economic position of rural America, not improving it."[18]

While the chicken industry is perhaps the most egregious example of how a highly concentrated industry can extract wealth from rural communities, leaving its residents and workers impoverished, it is far from the only industry with such a track record. An analysis of the results of 51 research studies found that industrial agriculture operations harmed the economy in four out of five communities in which they were located.[19] In another example, concentration in the grain industry has forced many farmers off the land, leading to the family farm crises of the past 30 plus years that has hollowed out huge swaths of rural America.[20]

Farmers are not the only ones being exploited at the hands of Tyson and the chicken industry. The Union of Food and Commercial Workers (UFCW) represents many workers who toil in chicken slaughterhouses. The chicken industry is far less unionized (35 percent of workers belong to a union) than the pork industry (75 percent union representation) and beef industry (65 percent union representation), in part because of its concentration in union-antagonistic states in the Deep South.[21] According to Mark Lauritsen, the international vice president of the UFCW, the poultry industry's very small profit margins and substantial fixed costs lead it to squeeze its labor costs to a minimum. As a result, it cuts corners on worker safety.

From 2007 to 2015, Tyson was cited for over 220 OSHA violations for a total of almost $7.7 million in penalties and was also responsible for the death of 11 workers in that time period.[22] In the fall of 2015, Oxfam America released a major report on labor abuses in the poultry industry. According to its president, Ray Offenheiser, "Poultry workers are among the most vulnerable and exploited workers in the United States."[23]

Rationale behind Commodity Purchasing

Historically, the original intent of commodity purchases by USDA was to stabilize agricultural markets devastated by reduced consumer demand caused by the Great Depression. The government would purchase certain foods when supply exceeded demand, and the prices being paid to producers dipped. But the chicken industry no longer needs this kind of propping up, according to one USDA policy analyst.

Instead, USDA's patronage of Big Chicken allows the federal government to utilize its massive economies of scale to purchase poultry at lower prices than individual school districts or other nutrition program operators could do on their own. Yet the low price that USDA pays does not include the externalized costs of the harm done to farmers, workers, and the environment through Big Chicken's abusive practices. Instead, taxpayers pay for these hidden costs through a wide variety of public programs, such as federal food assistance programs that are geared to help workers in these communities make ends meet. Ironically, these include the very programs for which USDA buys low-cost chicken, such as TEFAP and the school lunch program. In addition, it is into these impoverished communities that Walmart thrives, with its low budget prices and low-wage jobs for the newly desperate farm families, by redeeming in some states up to 50 percent of the SNAP benefits distributed.[24]

Leading the Way for Change

The British scholar Kevin Morgan contends that our public purchasing should be oriented toward getting "values for our money in the broadest sense and not just value for our money in the narrow sense."[25] This concept of the "power of the public plate" provides a compelling framework for how USDA could utilize its programs to lead the marketplace toward providing multiple benefits to communities, the environment, and society instead of just following and reinforcing the existing inequitable market structure. This theory is grounded in an emerging body of research showing that local economies based on small and medium-sized businesses provide numerous advantages.

The Benefits of Going Local

Going local is more than just a new food trend. The latest research has highlighted the fact that small businesses and locally owned businesses provide greater contributions to society than big business. A recent study in the *Harvard Business Review* found that investing in locally owned businesses is an ideal path for creating jobs.[26] This study contradicts the conventional wisdom in the economic development field that the best way to build a strong local economy is by attracting big business. Researchers are beginning to see that this traditional approach can be counterproductive, as larger entities are less committed to the host community, resulting in greater pollution and fewer jobs created.[27]

"Locally owned" typically serves as a proxy for small and medium-sized business. As Michael Shuman, an expert on local economy, notes, "12 percent of workers are self-employed; 10 percent work for companies with under 100 employees, and 30 percent for firms with 100 to 500 employees.

Companies with over 500 employees employ the other half of workers. Ninety nine percent of the companies in the first three categories have local ownership. The largest companies are the ones most likely to be owned outside of the community."[28]

This form of "economic gardening" not only pays off in terms of job creation, but also in multiple benefits to communities. Locally owned businesses tend to spend two to four times the money in a community than non-locally owned businesses, generating greater prosperity.[29] Scholars from Pennsylvania State University echo this finding, showing a remarkably robust "positive link between *small* firms that are locally owned and per capita income growth. Medium and larger firms appear to have the opposite effect, especially when they are not locally owned. These include big boxes as well as other chain and non-chain operations that are owned by individuals who are not also residents of the community." The scholars find that these companies may offer jobs but at the cost of reduced local economic growth.[30]

A Federal Reserve Bank of Atlanta study concluded that the percentage of people employed in locally owned businesses in a given community not only increased economic growth, but also resulted in greater county tax revenues as well as decreased poverty. Like the Penn State study, this report found that decreases in poverty rates were not correlated with the number of people employed by large and medium-sized firms. The study's author contends that, "the idea of locally owned business development is especially favorable for economically distressed rural areas when it is difficult for communities to attract outside businesses."[31]

In the food sector, various reports have examined the impact or potential impact of purchasing food from local producers. In one such study, Michael Shuman explores what would happen if just 20 percent of Michigan's food needs were produced in-state. He concludes that it would put 1 in 10 unemployed Michiganers back to work, creating 42,519 new jobs. It would provide the additional benefits of fostering an entrepreneurship revolution, reducing public assistance outlays, improving public sector fiscal health, allowing for increased investments in schools and infrastructure to attract new businesses, and stimulating rural economies.[32]

But if Michiganers grew more of their own food, they would be buying less food produced elsewhere. Similarly, if consumers were to increase their purchases of vegetables at their local farmers market instead of at the supermarket where they normally shop, the store and its distributors would bear the costs of such reduced sales. Economists call this concept "displacement," as one set of purchases displaces another. Displacement results in winners and losers: the more Michigan residents buy local apples, the fewer sales Washington State growers make. Shuman concedes that localization imposes short-term costs on some exporting food businesses, but in the long-term he contends that these changes squeeze inefficiencies—like the high costs of national food distribution—out of the system. Ultimately, he argues, localization leaves consumers with more money in their pockets, which means that they will be able to buy more local food *and* more nonfood exports from Washington State.[33]

Jeffrey O'Hara, formerly of the Union of Concerned Scientists, sees a similar overall advantage that local business provides to the economy. His research shows that even after factoring in displacement costs, there remains a modest economic advantage proffered by smaller and locally owned businesses.[34] Mary Hendrickson, of the University of Missouri, echoes this sentiment. Her research found that producers of food grown for local markets have fundamentally different purchasing patterns than industrially oriented farmers, resulting in more money being recirculated in rural communities.[35]

Much of the research of the economic advantage of local food systems looks at direct farm-to-consumer marketing. One study of West Virginia farmers' market sales discovered a net benefit to the local communities over the mainstream food system of $1.1 million annually.[36] In its comprehensive report to Congress on local food systems from 2015, USDA notes that farmers markets also result in greater tax revenues for municipalities; they build social capital and often increase sales at nearby businesses as well. Overall, direct marketing has helped to keep many farmers afloat; farms using direct marketing channels between 2007 and 2012 were more likely to stay in business than other farms not selling directly to consumers.[37]

International Food Aid

In the international development field, most other donor countries outside of the United States have long recognized the power of using their food donations as a tool for supporting the local economy of recipient nations. The American approach to international food aid is a throwback to the

1950s when food aid was designed to win the hearts, minds, and stomachs of third-world citizens in the global battle against the spread of communism.[38] Distributing American crops across the globe not only provided income to domestic agricultural interests, but also placed our country on a moral high ground with a claim that American farmers feed the world.

Food aid cultivates new markets for our products, in the same way that promotional giveaways entice brand loyalty.[39] According to an analysis of U.S. food aid, from 2010 to 2011 two-thirds of the food distributed by the U.S. government's billion dollar aid program was purchased from just three companies: Bunge, ADM, and Cargill.[40] This form of food aid is called "tied aid" because it comes with restrictions that link the assistance to products and services from the donor's economy. The vast majority of developed nations have abandoned tied aid because it results in negative impacts on the recipient country. A flood of cheap grain from abroad can distort local markets, for instance, resulting in lower prices for locally grown products, and making it hard for small farmers to make a living. This in turn can depress food production because these individuals no longer have the economic incentive to farm.[41]

While tied aid can be counterproductive in its destruction of rural livelihoods, conversely, international development practitioners have discovered that infusing local economies with cash to support local and regional food procurement (LRP) can provide a "twofer" in improving food security. This approach incentivizes increased production by farmers as well as investments by local traders in the market infrastructure. The Canadian researcher Jennifer Clapp notes: "Over the medium and long term, such incentives foster greater self-reliance in food production in regions afflicted by poverty and hunger. This type of economic stimulation for the agricultural sector has been identified as a key factor in overall development in poor countries."[42]

Writing in 1984, the political scientist Raymond Hopkins laid out the theory behind the LRP approach. He wrote that if poverty is the cause of hunger, then development—not food donations—should be the appropriate response. He notes: "Emphasizing development rather than nutrition as a principle entails looking at the investment prospects and returns from a food resource."[43] In other words, we need our food aid dollars to serve dual purposes: to feed the hungry as well as to stimulate the conditions that reduce hunger in the first place.

Twenty-plus years later, Congress decided to test out LRP under pressure from certain parts of the international development community, such as Oxfam. The 2008 Farm Bill established a five-year $60 million pilot project. Its success, along with strong support from the Obama administration, led to a permanent LRP program in the 2014 Farm Bill. Nonetheless just because the program was made permanent did not mean it was to be funded; it's all too common that many federal programs exist on the books, but Congress chooses not to fund them, or to fund them at lower levels than allowed. The LRP program was authorized at $80 million in the 2014 Farm Bill, but Congress failed to appropriate any funding for it in the 2015 cycle. The Obama administration did not include it in its 2015 budget either. In 2016, Congress did pass the Global Food Security Act (H.R. 1567), which reinvigorated the administration's investment in supporting the livelihoods of poor farmers across the globe, especially women, as a development strategy rather than a tied aid approach.

The resistance to eliminating tied aid in the international development field has marked similarities to the nature of the opposition to changes in the SNAP status quo. Just as the food manufacturers, retailers, and anti-hunger groups united to support continued soda sales in SNAP in the 2014 Farm Bill, the shipping industry, Big Ag, and international feeding groups joined forces to block growth of the LRP program.[44] Many of the international anti-hunger nonprofits have a vested interest in tied food aid as well because they sell donated food on the open market in recipient countries to fund their own initiatives. Increasing the share of food acquired through local and regional procurement threatens their funding stream. Similarly, the charitable food system (and state agencies) received $49.4 million in 2015 through the TEFAP program to move federal commodities (largely purchased from Big Food) to the poor (The Emergency Food Assistance Program"; USDA FNS June 2016).

The Power of the Public Plate
International food aid is not the only means by which governments deploy the power of food procurement to reach desired outcomes. Throughout Europe, local and national governments are using public-sector procurement as a lever to move food production and consumption toward greater environmental, social, and economic good. Officials and activists are rebranding public food procurement by leaving behind technocratic preferences for mass production and moving toward a more dynamic system, one

that can foster a civic economy grounded in sustainable production and healthy consumption patterns. In the United Kingdom and Sweden, among numerous other places, government officials are redefining what it means for the public sector to get a good value for its purchases as they seek to achieve health, economic, and environmental changes.

Redesigning Public Meals in Malmö, Sweden Malmö's foray into exercising the power of the public plate has been driven by its goal of reducing greenhouse gases and the incidence of chronic diseases among it 300,000 residents. The city's 2010 sustainable development policy targeted a 40 percent reduction (by the year 2020, based on 2002 levels) in greenhouse gas emissions resulting from the production of food it serves in schools and other institutions. By the end of 2012, the city was spending 9 million euros on organic food, or about 40 percent of its goal. Even more ambitiously, the city sought to make these changes in a cost-neutral fashion. Malmö operates on a very tight food budget of roughly one euro per person.

One strategy Malmö officials have employed to contain costs, reduce greenhouse gas emissions, and improve public health is to radically redesign their menu and shrink the amount of meat they serve—not in a way that emphasizes sacrifice, as in "Meatless Mondays," but in a positive light. One Malmö official noted, "We don't frame it in a negative way as part of a narrative of denial by denying children meat. We are giving them good food, which means meat and vegetarian food."[45] Malmö also seeks to provide seasonal menus based on locally sourced food. In addition to its cost constraints, the limited supply of organic food grown in Sweden and the lack of kitchens in many schools constitute the city's primary challenges to success.[46]

United Kingdom and Food for Life In the United Kingdom, the Food for Life "catering mark" (food service standards) has steered food service entities that provide more than one million meals every work day toward more sustainable ingredients. The Soil Association, the organic agriculture-oriented nonprofit behind the Food for Life program, certifies food service companies as meeting these marks, which are structured into Bronze, Silver, and Gold tiers. As of 2015, 25 percent of UK schools, as well as hospitals, workplaces, and universities, have signed on to these standards.[47] The Bronze-level standards stipulate cage-free eggs, humanely raised meats, no trans fats, 75 percent of all food from unprocessed ingredients, no GMO ingredients, and seasonal produce, among other criteria. Silver and Gold levels are awarded on a points system, for using higher percentages of organic, fair trade, free-range meats, and local products.[48]

According to Libby Grundy, the director of the Food for Life program, the catering marks have helped to revitalize small-scale and independent local food growers, processors. and suppliers in the United Kingdom. While there still remains a reliance on larger distributors because of the convenience that they provide, the catering marks have influenced many of these firms to buy products from smaller and local producers. She notes that there has been a social return on investment of three to one, mostly in increased opportunities for local businesses.[49]

The Evidence for Decoupling Food Aid

There is compelling evidence (and experience) to show that investing in locally and regionally oriented food systems can provide significant benefits to local economies and reduce poverty as well. The more we think about domestic and international food aid in the same conceptual framework, the more we realize that untying federal food assistance programs from Big Food and Big Ag will allow us to maximize the use of the $100 billion spent on them for improving food security. The unasked question concerning these programs is whether the current anti-hunger industrial complex is the best arena in which to use these funds to meet their intended purposes, or whether a different more targeted expenditure pattern would generate better outcomes in reducing food insecurity over the long-term.

To understand the practicalities of redirecting federal food programs toward more local and regional procurement, which are in some ways synonymous with smaller businesses, it helps to look at three different parts of the federal food assistance universe, specifically at how their expenditures might be redirected to more effectively reduce food insecurity and poverty. First, as the example with the most centralized decision-making power, is USDA Foods, which procures commodities for seven food programs. The School Lunch Program is the second example, with a focus on the impact of the farm to school movement. Although school lunch programs are run by a cadre of professional food service directors, they are highly regulated by federal, state, and local laws. The third and final example is the mammoth SNAP program, the most decentralized of the federal food programs, whose 21.3 million households (as of May 2016) choose which foods to purchase, within a skeletal framework of eligible foods.

USDA Foods

The US Department of Agriculture operates one of the largest food procurement operations in the country to support its own and the Department of Health and Human Service's extensive nutrition programs (see table 5.1). It is an extraordinarily complex operation—three agencies within USDA (one agency buys grains, another procures other foods, while a third operates the nutrition programs to which the food is destined)—are involved with USDA Foods. USDA Foods also partners with the Department of Defense's procurement arm, known as DoD Fresh, to purchase fresh produce for schools. At the state level, the distribution of foodstuffs is administered by multiple agencies, such as departments of education, agriculture, health, and general services (USDA calls these SDAs or state distributing agencies). USDA Foods works with hundreds of sovereign tribal nations, as well as purchases food for international food aid distribution. Its food reaches tens of millions of seniors, children, homeless, and other low-income persons on a daily basis.

In 2014, USDA bought $1.95 billion worth of food, through a competitive bidding process. In broad categories, it acquired $767 million of animal protein, $707 million of produce and juice, $346 million of dairy and eggs, and $127 million of grains and beans.[50] It contracts with food manufacturers to process these products into consumer-friendly form, for example turning peanuts into peanut butter. Most of its purchases are made in response to the needs of its SDA "customers" that coordinate their state's or reservation's programs on behalf of the millions of program participants.

Depending on the end-user, USDA Foods packages and prepares the foodstuffs it distributes in different ways. For example, foods destined for the TEFAP program serving low-income clients of food pantries, tend to look like products one might find in the supermarket. Those products destined for food services, such as schools, come in larger institutional packaging (nicknamed "brown box") and are often minimally processed (as in the case of a 50 lb. box of raw chicken).

Table 5.1

USDA Foods and Federal Nutrition Programs

Program Name	Purpose	Expenditures and Fiscal Year
Child Care and Adult Feeding Programs (CACFP)[a]	Meals and snacks to children in day care programs, afterschool care programs, emergency shelters, and to adults in nonresidential day care centers	FY 2015: centers are entitled to 24.75 cents of USDA commodities for each lunch or supper they serve
Commodity Supplemental Food Program[b] (CSFP)	Supplements diets of low-income elderly	FY 2015: $193,000,000
Food Distribution Program on Indian Reservations[c] (FDPIR)	In lieu of SNAP on and near some Indian reservations, where stores are sparsely located	FY 2014: $40,800,000 in cash for administrative costs; $104,400,000 in USDA commodities
National School Lunch Program[d] (NSLP)	Nutritious low-cost or free meals to schoolchildren	FY 2014: schools get 24.75 cents of USDA commodities per lunch they serve, plus bonus commodities In 2014, USDA spent $1.3 billion on 1.2 billion pounds[e]
Nutrition Services Incentive Program[f] (NSIP)	For congregate meals and meals on wheels for seniors run by DHHS	FY 2015: $2,500,000
Summer Food Service Program[g] (SFSP)	Child feeding programs when school is out of session	FY 2014: 1.5 cents per meal in USDA commodities
The Emergency Food Assistance Program[h] (TEFAP)	Provides food to low-income persons through food pantries primarily	FY 2015: $327,000,000 in food; $49,401,000 in cash; and $302,900,000 in "bonus" commodities

a. "Schools/Child Nutrition USDA Foods Programs."

b. "Cost of Food Distribution Programs," USDA Food and Nutrition Service, May 6, 2016, http://www.fns.usda.gov/sites/default/files/pd/fd$sum.pdf.

c. "Food Distribution Program on Indian Reservations Program Fact Sheet," USDA Food and Nutrition Service, July 2014, http://www.fns.usda.gov/sites/default/files/pfs-fdpir.pdf. Retrieved April 14, 2015.

d. Federal Register, V.79 No 135, July 15, 2014, http://www.fns.usda.gov/sites/default/files/Value_of_Donated_Foods_2014_2015.pdf.

Table 5.1 (continued)

e. "Schools/Child Nutrition USDA Foods Programs," USDA Food and Nutrition Service, November 2012, http://www.fns.usda.gov/sites/default/files/pfs-schcnp _final_revised-11-26-12(2).pdf. Retrieved April 14, 2015; "Nutrition Services Incentive Program: Food Program Fact Sheet," USDA Food and Nutrition Service, July 2013, http://www.fns.usda.gov/sites/default/files/pfs-nsip.pdf. Retrieved April 14, 2015.

f. "Cost of Food Distribution Programs."

g. "Schools/Child Nutrition USDA Foods Programs."

h. "The Emergency Food Assistance Program: Food Program Fact Sheet," USDA Food and Nutrition Service, June 2016. http://www.fns.usda.gov/sites/default/files/ pfs-tefap.pdf. Retrieved June 5, 2016.

About two-thirds of USDA Foods purchases are distributed to school districts for their lunch programs, complementing the federal cash reimbursement. Schools receive a credit for about a quarter's worth of commodity foods for every lunch they serve. They then use this credit to order goods from a predetermined list of products. In making their commodity choices, school food service directors, who manage extremely tight budgets, consider the price and quality of USDA items as compared to similar products available on the open market. Historically, food service directors have used their commodity allotment for "center of the plate" protein items, because these tend to be cheaper on the USDA ledger than on the open market. For example, in California in 2008, 82 percent of commodity dollars were spent on meat and cheese.[51]

Schools often find it convenient and cost-effective to pay a third party to process these basic USDA commodities into items that fit into their menu plans (this process is called "diversion" in school food jargon). In many cases, the final processed product is less healthy than the original commodity. According to a 2008 study, 50 percent of commodities selected by school districts were diverted for processing, and "have about the same nutritional value as junk foods."[52] A 2011 *New York Times* article found that this processing can also be costly. "The Michigan Department of Education, for example, gets free raw chicken worth $11.40 a case and sends it for processing into nuggets at $33.45 a case. The schools in San Bernardino, California, spend $14.75 to make French fries out of $5.95 worth of potatoes."[53]

Diversion expenditures by state vary based on culinary preferences and the location of processing plants. Table 5.2 shows the products and

Table 5.2
Commodities Diverted for Processing in Oregon (School Year 2014–15)[a]

Processing Company	Pounds Diverted	Commodity Product	Company Revenue (2014)	Notes
Tyson	1,187,665	Chicken, beef	$34 billion	Fortune 500 corporation
Jennie O Turkey	275,640	Turkey	$8 billion	Fortune 500 corp. (owned by Hormel)
JTM Provisions	273,943	Beef, pork, turkey, cheese	$150 million	Ohio-based private firm
Schwans	227,495	Cheese	$3 billion	Would be on Fortune 1000 if public
Lings	184,559	Chicken	$20–$50 million	California-based private firm
Advance Pierre Food	177,731	Beef and peanut butter	Manages $77 billion	Owned by Oaktree Capital Management
National Food Group	167,692	Apples	$60 million	Michigan-based private firm
Land O'Lakes	152,471	Cheese	$14 billion	Would be on Fortune 500 if public
Roadrunner	147,845	Cheese	$20–$50 million	Small Oregon-based firm
Pilgrim's Pride	146,136	Chicken	$43 billion	Global #637 (Owned by JBS)
Cargill Kitchen Solutions	64,932	Eggs, turkey	$136 billion	Would rank #9 on Fortune 500 if public
ConAgra	36,558	Cheese	$18 billion	Fortune 500 corporation
Trident Seafoods	25,215	Fish	$1–$2 billion	Largest seafood corporation in US
Bongards	23,000	Cheese	$78 million	Cooperative
Bosco's Pizza	20,824	Cheese	$34 billion	Owned by Tyson
SA Piazza	17,796	Cheese	N/A	Oregon based with 11–50 employees
Michael	15,544	Eggs	$3.2 billion	Owned by Post Foods
Asian Food Solutions	12,500	Chicken	N/A	Has 51–200 employees
Total	3,157,146			

a. "FDP Processor Report," Oregon Department of Education Child Nutrition Programs Food Distribution Program, School Year 2014–2015, May 1, 2014, http://www.ode.state.or.us/wma/nutrition/snp/ode_usda_fdp_processor_product_report.pdf.

companies to which Oregon schools diverted their commodity products for additional processing for school year 2014–15. Measured in pounds, the majority of these products were animal protein, with cheese the next most commonly diverted commodity. Tyson captured the lion's share of the diversion market, processing 38 percent of all diverted products in Oregon.[54] While some local Oregon companies did capture a portion of the processing market, the vast majority of the items sent out for processing went to large national or multinational firms. In fact, two-thirds of the foods diverted for processing (by pounds) were directed to large companies, those with revenues over $1 billion. Mary Stein, the former associate director of the National Farm to School Network, notes that these processors are not uniformly spread out across the country, and that the school food market could provide a stable income source for regional economic development in this sector.[55]

Improvements   Under Secretary Vilsack's leadership, USDA has been more committed to promoting diversified and local food systems than perhaps any other administration in the postwar era. Through the Know Your Farmer, Know Your Food initiative, the department has nurtured connections among the staff members of USDA's highly siloed agencies and has prioritized program implementation in numerous ways to incorporate local food systems.

Healthy Foods   In recent years, USDA has made continuous improvements to the quality of the food it provides. Years ago, the processed foods that the department ordered were well known for their poor quality and high content of salt, sugar, and fat. The USDA has dedicated extensive effort into requiring manufacturers to supply them with more healthful products. According to one knowledgeable USDA staffer, USDA commodity products can be so low in sugar and sodium that companies often must formulate products specifically for them. USDA commodities do not include "junk foods," such as sodas, candy, chips, or baked goods. While the average American diet scores 58 (out of 100 points) on the federally created Healthy Eating Index, USDA nutrition programs based on commodity foods scored significantly better. For example, in 2009, USDA Foods items delivered as part of the National School Lunch Program scored 75, while FDPIR foods scored 85.[56]

Minimally Processed Produce Pilot To encourage increased consumption of produce, especially of local origin, the 2014 Farm Bill authorized a pilot project to allow schools to acquire minimally processed fruits and vegetables (such as cut carrots and apple slices) with their commodity funds. This project would supplement the Department of Defense's produce distribution service in those states where it operates, and schools would need to go through USDA-approved vendors to purchase their produce. Schools are allowed but not required to purchase locally grown products.[57] The department selected eight states to participate, and as of April 2015 small orders totaling under $10,000 in five of the eight states have been placed. Almost all of these orders have been for in-state produce.

Small Business Targets The USDA is not obligated to purchase the absolute lowest-priced items. Federal Acquisitions Regulations, the overarching set of rules that govern all federal purchasing, do allow for preference to be given to small businesses and to minority- women- or veteran-owned firms.[58] As a result, the Farm Service Agency and the Agricultural Marketing Service have specific purchasing goals for small businesses. Sometimes these goals are met through setting aside the procurement of certain products, such as apple slices, exclusively for small businesses. Likewise, according to one USDA analyst, if there is deemed to be sufficient competition among small businesses on a certain solicitation, the USDA may break down a larger order into smaller lots to facilitate the participation of these smaller firms.

Constraints Despite USDA's newfound commitment to local foods and its admirable institutional creativity under Secretary Vilsack, USDA Foods remains a juggernaut whose tremendous inertia challenges all who would steer it in a different direction. This inertia is caused by a few different factors.

The most powerful voices outside of the department have been focused on maintaining the status quo. While some public health groups demand nutritional improvements to address burgeoning childhood and adult obesity rates, the primary forces advocating on issues related to USDA Foods has been an iron triangle of the food industry, state distribution agencies, and USDA itself. Represented by the trade association, The American Commodity Distribution Association (ACDA), the common agenda for these three sectors does converge in part with the interests of the anti-hunger community. In 2015, ACDA's Legislative Issues paper has prioritized increasing the amount of money spent on commodity purchases and their distribution to the poor, as well as increased flexibility concerning school nutrition standards. It does not include any mention of local purchasing, support for small businesses, or other sustainability criteria.[59] According to one policy advocate, anti-hunger groups and even school food authorities hold little power within ACDA.[60]

Similarly, the Food Research and Action Center typically stays focused on the resource and nutrition concerns of commodity programs, and thus avoids questions regarding the origin of commodity foods. Its neutrality allows it to capture food industry dollars. FRAC received funding from Tyson in 2011 and 2014 to conduct polls on the public's perception of hunger (Tyson has also supported Share Our Strength and Feeding America).[61] Tyson's executive vice president and FRAC's CEO issued a joint op-ed in October 2014 urging Congress to "invest what is needed in programs which are helping so many put healthy food on the table."[62]

The very purpose of USDA Foods as a supplement to underfunded nutrition programs constrains its ability to move away from the cheap food paradigm. Buying from smaller potentially more expensive sources, or building in environmental and social costs could cause the cost of USDA commodities to rise and reduce the purchasing ability of nutrition programs dependent upon USDA Foods. School food service directors depend on USDA providing a certain amount of food for their commodity quarter per meal. Not only do they need these funds to remain financially viable, school food directors also utilize them to subsidize the purchase of higher quality local and fresh foods, which may have those environmental and social values embedded in them.[63] A complex system has been built up around cheap food procurement, with the potential for changes to result in unintended consequences.

School Lunch Programs

It's not just in Europe where the school system is an arena for transforming public procurement into a vehicle for the social good. In Brazil, the federal government has directed schools to buy at least 30 percent of their food from small and local farmers. This mandate has been instrumental in supporting the family farm sector there.[64] In the United States, similar efforts have been made to bring the farm to school movement to school lunch programs. One of the best examples can be found in Southern California.

Rodney Taylor runs the Riverside Unified School District, the fifteenth-largest school district in California with 43,000 students. Located on the eastern edge of Los Angeles urban sprawl, Riverside is hot and smoggy with a population of over 300,000. Taylor came to Riverside after developing the first farm to school program on the West Coast in the late 1990s, the Santa Monica Farmers Market Salad Bar. He has committed to sourcing as much food as possible from the area, promising to buy from any farmer in Riverside County. He works closely with a farmer in nearby Redlands who coordinates deliveries from other farms to the school district. In 2013–14, the district spent $450,000 on local produce from California growers, and hopes to spend 60 percent of their $1.4 million produce budget on California-grown products in 2014–15. Taylor has accessed rice and chicken from California sources and even found a dairy in nearby San Jacinto that will provide him with milk from California cows. He prioritizes buying from small- to medium-sized farms, and will work with them on an informal bidding process whenever possible.[65]

Farm to School Background   The first farm to school programs started in the late 1990s, initiated by USDA in Florida and North Carolina, and by parents in California. Since then, the farm to school movement has grown dramatically. According to preliminary results from a USDA census carried out in 2015, 42,173 schools serving roughly 25 million schoolchildren participated in farm to school projects. Collectively, schools responding to the survey reported spending over $598 million on local foods.[66] In the 2013 census, the amount of local food purchased varied greatly state by state, ranging from a high in the 20 percent–plus range in some western states to under 5 percent in other states, especially in the South and Great Plains.[67]

The tremendous growth in farm to school projects can be traced to a number of different factors, above and beyond the growth of the local food systems movement and interest in addressing childhood obesity. First, it was a product of deliberate and capable organizing, led by the National Farm to School Network (NFSN). An initial version of the network was launched in the early 2000s and more formally established in 2005, with joint leadership between the Community Food Security Coalition (CFSC) and Occidental College's Center for Food and Justice. It has served as the focal point for farm to school organizing efforts and technical support.

Second, the CFSC and the NFSN were able to change federal procurement law to require USDA to allow school districts to express a geographic preference in their procurement. Under the George W. Bush administration, USDA had chosen to interpret conflicting congressional legislation to prohibit states from prioritizing locally grown foods. To counter this interpretation, the CFSC and the Network gained passage of legislation in the 2008 Farm Bill that expressly mandated USDA to allow school districts to give a bidding preference for minimally processed foods and fresh fruits and vegetables (e.g., cut carrots, apple slices, and in some cases specific cuts of meat, but not canned vegetables or pizza).[68]

Third, farm to school has gained key support within USDA, the White House, and Congress as an approach that all parties could support in the context of the school meals nutrition standards political battleground of the first half of the 2010s. Under Secretary Vilsack's leadership, USDA has been very supportive of farm to school as part of its broader Know Your Farmer, Know Your Food initiative. The department implemented the geographic preferences legislation appropriately, and aggressively marketed farm to school. USDA's encouragement, along with a subsequent $5 million Farm to School grants program created in the 2010 Child Nutrition Act, catalyzed substantial growth in the farm to school arena. USDA's Farm to School Program has done an apt job of coordinating efforts within the department and providing technical support to school districts in their procurement process.

As of 2015, farm to school remains universally popular in Congress among both Democrats and Republicans who might be hostile to a more regulatory approach to improving school meals. This is likely the case because of the voluntary, community-based nature of farm to school, and the positive public relations opportunities that it lends schools and congressional members.

Farm to School Data Limitations Understanding the nature of procurement under the farm to school moniker can be challenging. According to

Mary Stein of the National Farm to School Network, farm to school is characterized by three components: local food procurement, school gardens, and agricultural education. "A school with any one of these three components is a manner of farm to school, while a school with all three components has a robust program."[69] These multiple components can mean that some schools self-report as having a farm to school program without changing their food procurement. The inexact nature of farm to school can be seen in the biennial Farm to School census.

One of the key matters of confusion in analyzing that census data is an inconsistent definition of "local." Congress and USDA have chosen not to wade into this issue, leaving it to each individual school district to make its own definition. This topic has been highly contentious in discussions among sustainable food system advocates across the country. In the wide-open spaces of the West, "local" might apply to a much larger distance than in the tight confines of New England. Defining "local" as coming from within political boundaries, such as state borders, ignores the realities that for places such as New York City, the farms of New Jersey and Connecticut are geographically closer than those in the northern reaches of New York State. According to the school food services that took the time to respond to the 2013 farm to school census, there was a wide diversity of meanings of local. Twenty six percent replied that local meant within the state; 21 percent within 50 miles, 13 percent within 100 miles; 10 percent within the region; 6 percent from within 200 miles; 2 percent within a day's drive; and 5 percent had other definitions.[70]

The image that local food evokes can conflict with the reality of its production. While local food often means family-owned farms or businesses, this is not always the case. In one telling example, USDA's blog touted chicken processed in a South Carolina factory owned by the multinational JBS (operating under the Pilgrim's Pride brand) and served to South Carolina schoolchildren as being farm to school.[71]

Sustainable Procurement   The Riverside, California, school district may be smaller in size than districts in New York City or Los Angeles, but with the sheer scale of its operations Riverside faces unique but comparable challenges in connecting the dots between values and practicalities. School districts only have so much capacity to handle multiple deliveries and manage multiple contracts with smaller vendors. Larger urban districts have found it necessary to establish clear standards about their food sourcing, as the direct farm to table deliveries that many smaller schools can accept simply will not work for these enormous operations.

Los Angeles Good Food Purchasing Policy Recognizing that the region's large institutions could have a transformative impact on the food system, in 2011 the Los Angeles Food Policy Council embarked on an exhaustive 18-month process to establish procurement standards, similar to the Food for Life standards in the United Kingdom.[72] By 2012, the council, a nonprofit group housed within city government, had developed the Good Food Purchasing Policy (GFPP). That fall, both the City of Los Angeles and the LA Unified School District, which serves 650,000 daily meals, signed on to the policy.[73]

The Good Food Purchasing Policy creates a structured, tiered framework grounded in realistic expectations to help institutions achieve continuous improvement for their food procurement. It establishes a purchasing commitment plan, with five levels designated by stars. To earn stars, the institution must gain points (e.g., 10–14 points to get 2 stars; 20–24 points for 4 stars) by meeting standards in each of five different categories: local economies, environmental sustainability, valued workforce, animal welfare, and nutrition. The standards build on existing certifications when possible, such as USDA Organic or Non-GMO Project Verified. The "local economies" purchasing goals, for example, establish three levels, based not just on distance but also on the scale of the farming operation. For example, to gain one point in this category, an institution could purchase 15 percent of its annual average purchases from either a large-scale farm within 200 miles, or outside of California but from a small-scale operation.[74]

The most ambitious element of the GFPP, and what arguably makes it unique, is its thoughtful labor standards. Their standards apply not just to the institution but also to its vendors and suppliers along the supply chain, from producer to processor to distributor. Their inclusion in the GFPP is a testament to the importance of having labor representatives at the table in drafting the standards. Joann Lo of the Food Chain Workers Alliance played a key role in the Food Policy Council and in drafting these standards.

At the initial level of the GFPP, institutions must verify that their suppliers and vendors have made a written commitment to comply with domestic labor laws and allow the right to collective bargaining, among other guarantees. To earn an additional point, the institution and its suppliers must also have a social responsibility policy, which includes paying nonpoverty-level wages, health care benefits, paid sick leave, and profit sharing. Alternately, they could be fair-trade certified. At the third level, the vendors and suppliers must have a union contract with their employees, be a worker-owned cooperative, be certified by a food justice initiative, or have signed on to the Coalition of Immokalee Workers Fair Food Code of Conduct (see chapter 8).[75]

The GFPP is gaining momentum as the Food Policy Council spins off a new entity, the Center for Good Food Purchasing, to manage its expansion into other communities. School districts in Oakland, Chicago, and New York City have approached the LA Food Policy Council about adopting the GFPP to the specific contexts of their communities.[76]

Program Constraints   The ability of schools to serve food with values has been limited by the politics of austerity. Shrinking tax bases at the state and local levels have put pressure on school food services to generate revenue or at least be revenue neutral. Many schools have turned to private food service companies, such as Sodexo or Aramark, to run their cafeterias as a way of lowering costs. This privatization, occurring in roughly one-fourth of schools, has often been to the detriment of worker pay and the quality of school food, as these companies frequently take the low road to profitability.[77] A scandal in New York revealed that food service companies rely on large food manufacturers not just for cheap food, but also for rebates that enhance their profitability.[78] These incentives, just like the economies of scale that allow companies like Tyson to underbid its competitors, reinforce the corporate school food industry.

Rock bottom federal reimbursement rates have reinforced this cheap food industry and the forced cost-containment measures that have led to the deskilling of school food service labor. With labor one of the highest cost centers in the food service budget, schools have turned to serving highly processed heat-and-serve foods that can be prepared by lower-cost, less-skilled labor. When schools decide that they want to serve healthier foods that require more on-site preparation, one common barrier they find is that their workforce does not possess the skills to prepare the desired foods. Likewise, they typically find that many schools lack functional kitchen facilities. For this reason, the Obama administration has awarded $185 million from 2009 to 2015 to schools to pay for new kitchen facilities.[79]

The need for cheap food—throughout the entire procurement, delivery, and preparation processes—is not the only structural factor constraining schools from exercising the power of the public plate to purchase food with values. The school food austerity paradigm also is intricately interwoven with a common perception that children's taste preferences tend exclusively toward the highly processed and familiar. For example, Rodney Taylor spoke about initially being very skeptical that children in Santa Monica would partake of the salad bar sourced from local farmers. He was stunned when a high percentage of kids chose the salad bar over the hot meal in the schools in which the program was piloted. Taylor, like other food service directors, wanted to make sure that the food he was serving was being eaten and not thrown in the garbage. His concerns underscore the tension between the more passive client-service model (give them what they want) and the nutrition mission (teach the kids to eat better) found in the school food service profession.[80]

The School Nutrition Association's (SNA) attempts in recent years to reverse school lunch standards that mandated decreased sodium levels and increased purchases of produce and whole grains can be seen as an expression of this tension. SNA's agenda has been backed by those companies in the school food industry that stand to lose most from improved nutrition standards, such as Schwan's Pizza, the supplier of 70 percent of the nation's school pizza.[81]

From a different perspective, the nature of the food supply in many regions has exerted equal if not greater constraints on schools that purchase these foods. In many northern locations, the primary agricultural season does not match the school year, limiting the availability of products in winter months. The shrinking local agricultural infrastructure, such as slaughterhouses and packinghouses, has impeded small- to medium-scale production and coincided with the loss of farms and ranches focused on regional markets. Food hubs, locally oriented businesses that seek to help producers get their products to market, in a small but important way, have stepped in to fill the hole left by a supply chain more focused on national than local distribution. The relative lack of supply of local food with respect to demand has kept local food prices relatively high.[82]

SNAP

For all of its challenges, bringing local foods to school lunch is a picnic compared to transforming household purchasing patterns in the SNAP program. Yet the rewards for redirecting even a modest percentage of SNAP's $70 billion budget through its 21.3 million households to support food produced locally or by small businesses could have a significant impact on the way food is retailed and produced in the United States.[83] If only 10 cents of the food stamp dollar were spent on locally grown foods, it would more than double the sales of locally produced food in the US.[84]

Like USDA Foods, the SNAP program is grounded in the existence of an industrialized food system that markets cheap food, while externalizing environmental, health, and societal costs.[85] SNAP benefit levels are set at a bare minimum level, based on unrealistic expectations that households spend three times as much time on food preparation than they actually do (and have the requisite skill set to do so).[86] Given SNAP's low benefit levels, low-income shoppers are forced to search for the best value their benefits can buy.

Incentive programs, which encourage program participants to purchase healthy foods, have been a popular way to address this cost differential. The WIC Farmers Market Nutrition Program (FMNP) and its spin-off, the Senior Farmers Market Nutrition Program (SFMNP), have provided nutritionally vulnerable populations with $20 to $40 worth of coupons for local produce since the 1980s. The FMNPs have been a win-win-win, increasing participants' produce consumption while increasing access to healthy food in underserved communities and supporting family-scale farming to the combined tune of about $40 million (for the year 2015).[87]

While one branch of the Food and Nutrition Service (FNS) at USDA was operating these small programs encouraging low-income shoppers to frequent farmers markets, another branch of FNS had severed the ability of food stamp recipients to use their benefits at farmers markets. In the 1996 Farm Bill, Congress mandated that the food stamp program go from paper coupons to a debit card format as part of an effort to reduce fraud and stigma in the program. Processing the electronic benefit transfers (EBTs), however, required access to a landline telephone and modem. Congress promised free terminals to stores with a landline and electric power source, but mobile shopkeepers or farmers markets, being in a parking lot or city street, didn't have easy access to either of those things. The high costs of cell phone calls and spotty cell coverage proved to be significant barriers for farmers markets to continue accepting food stamps in the late 1990s and first few years of the 2000s. As a result, food stamp redemption at farmers markets dropped off a cliff, from $82 million in 1989 to $1.6 million in 2007.[88]

In allowing farmers markets to fall out of the picture as a venue for food stamp redemption, USDA discounted their relative importance to the program. Farmers markets were small potatoes. The department simply chose not to invest in finding technological solutions to this issue. Yet, as the local food movement boomed, it became increasingly evident through the advocacy of such groups as the Farmers Market Coalition that this technological barrier was deepening an existing trench between the food system for the well-off and the food system for the poor. If farmers market produce was truly superior, as public perception increasingly held, then it was doubly unfair that SNAP recipients as the poorest of the poor not only faced economic and logistical barriers, but also technological obstacles to accessing healthy foods. The symbolic importance of this technological disconnect was becoming too much for USDA to manage.

Two factors intervened to force USDA to reverse course. First, the rapid evolution of telecommunications was making cell phone reception more ubiquitous and calls cheaper to make. No longer did it cost 30 cents to process a dollar transaction.[89] As a result, more farmers markets were experimenting with taking SNAP, and putting increased pressure on the department to facilitate their acceptance. Second, under the leadership of Secretary Vilsack and Deputy Secretary Kathleen Merrigan, USDA prioritized local and regional food systems as a policy focus for the department. SNAP redemption at farmers markets gained the positive attention of legislators, some who represented direct marketing farmers. Facilitating SNAP redemption at farmers markets became a bipartisan win-win approach that promoted healthy eating and the possibility of increased revenue for small farmers. As a result, USDA encouraged farmers markets and state departments of agriculture to accept SNAP. Since fiscal year 2012, it has been receiving an appropriation of $4 million to cover the costs associated with this service, including providing free wireless terminals and funds to cover transaction costs.[90]

These changes laid the groundwork for public and nonprofit initiatives that connected farmers markets with SNAP recipients. Around the same time, federal anti-obesity funding through the Centers for Disease Control and Prevention, DHHS, and the SNAP Nutrition Education program invested resources into supporting direct marketing to low-income consumers.

Simultaneous to the development of technological solutions to the redemption of food stamps, farmers markets across the nation were also experimenting with offering incentives to SNAP recipients to increase their produce purchases.[91] New York City launched the Health Bucks program in 2006, supplying a $2 voucher for every $5 produce purchase at farmers markets.[92] In 2008, Paul Newman's former chef, Michel Nischan, and ex-USDA undersecretary Gus Schumacher had established the nonprofit group Wholesome Wave, which funded produce incentive programs in numerous farmers markets across the country. Utilizing a variety of catchy names, such as Market Match, Boston Bounty Bucks, or Fresh Bucks, these programs have grown exponentially since their inception.

As a result of these policy and programmatic initiatives, SNAP redemption at farmers markets grew substantially, as seen by percentage, but was still small in total dollars. By 2014, the total dollar value of SNAP benefits cashed in at farmers markets and other direct-marketing operations had increased to $18.8 million.[93]

The basic premise behind these incentives is that by improving access to healthy food combined with increasing benefits specifically for fruits and vegetables, low-income families will increase their consumption of produce. Advocates hypothesize that these additional resources, often very modest in nature, will sway some SNAP households to patronize farmers markets to take advantage of the extra funding. Farmers markets create an environment that promotes healthy lifestyles, with offerings that largely consist of produce and moderately processed foods, such as cheeses and breads. Cooking demonstrations and interactions with growers also facilitate an interactive form of nutrition education that is largely lacking from supermarkets.

By the latter part of the 2000s, USDA became an important ally in facilitating SNAP incentive programs (although advocates do note that FNS continues to throw up administrative barriers). It changed its policy to encourage farmers market SNAP incentive programs by exempting them from regulations mandating equal treatment for SNAP customers, specifying that "no retail food store may single out coupon users for special treatment in any way," even if that treatment might be preferential.[94] SNAP incentives fit in well with FNS deputy secretary Kevin Concannon's desire to see SNAP become more health promoting. Concannon points toward these incentives and the field of behavioral economics in general as an area ripe for transforming consumer behavior.[95]

Food Insecurity Nutrition Initiatives (FINI) For those not familiar with Michigan, it can be surprising to learn that it has the second most diverse agriculture of any state in the nation, just behind California. It is a major producer of berries, tree fruits, vegetables, dairy, as well as the livestock, corn and soy produced by its Midwestern neighbors.[96] Senator Debbie Stabenow has been a leading voice for policies that support local and regional agriculture as well as "specialty crops" (USDA-speak for fruits, vegetables, and nuts). As chair of the Senate Agriculture Committee during the 2014 Farm Bill process, Stabenow prioritized gaining inclusion of legislation in the Nutrition Title of the Farm Bill that would create the groundbreaking Food Insecurity Nutrition Incentives program (FINI). Another Michigan entity, the Fair Food Network, coordinated the effort to gain passage of this program. Led by a former Kellogg Foundation program officer, Oran Hesterman, Fair Food Network had rapidly grown the "Double Up Bucks" brand of SNAP incentives across the state, moving beyond farmers markets into grocery stores. An organized collaboration of groups in the public health, anti-hunger, and sustainable agriculture fields also provided key leadership and grassroots support to gain passage of this provision in the Farm Bill.

FINI provides $90 million (plus another $10 million for evaluation) over its five-year lifespan to communities for incentivizing, at the point of sale, fruits and vegetable purchased by SNAP recipients. Applicants compete for the grants, and must match the federal grant amount dollar for dollar. While the program is part of the Nutrition Title in the Farm Bill, its funding is in addition to and separate from core SNAP funds. Still in its infancy, FINI's story is instructive to understanding the opportunities and barriers for more SNAP dollars finding their ways into the pockets of locally or regionally owned and oriented farmers.

One key tension floats to the surface in examining the legislative process and the first round of competitive grants made in 2015 (USDA funded 31 projects from a pool of 86 applicants for $31.5 million).[97] The legislation does not specify the geographic origin of the products to be incentivized. Any produce is eligible. Kate Fitzgerald, a long-time community food advocate from Texas and the main lobbyist for the program, explains: "It [FINI] is paid for with federal nutrition dollars and the principal goal is to improve SNAP participant consumption of produce for improved health. Congress and USDA intend this program to be a deeper foray into the policy world of supporting healthy eating for low-income consumers."[98]

Nevertheless, the legislative language and subsequent Request for Applications issued by USDA do give priority to direct farm-to-consumer marketing, to the use of locally and regionally produced foods, and to those groups that have a track record of linking low-income consumers and agricultural producers.[99] According to Kate Fitzgerald, this reflects "a belief that there is merit in the idea that this connection provides multiple benefits to SNAP consumers and their communities."[100]

In the first round of grants, this prioritization generally had its desired impact. The vast majority of the proposals funded focused on incentivizing local and regional produce, with the exception of a handful of the largest projects in Washington State, Michigan, and a handful of southern states. In these cases, supermarkets such as Safeway and Kroger chose to participate in these projects, without a specific requirement that the produce be regionally grown.[101]

The desire to move SNAP incentives into grocery stores has been controversial in the farmers market community. As employees of the Ecology Center in Berkeley, Carle Brinkman and Ben Feldman run Market Match, California's primary SNAP incentive program with 230 implementation sites. They see ample opportunity for SNAP incentives to grow through the state's extensive network of year-round direct marketing venues, such as farmers markets. While they support taking incentives to where the customers are, such as grocery stores, they fear that FINI could stop giving preferential treatment for locally grown produce and direct marketing, such that farmers markets would need to compete with the much more convenient and ubiquitous supermarkets.[102]

One of the great challenges of farmers market–based incentive programs has been luring SNAP cardholders to the markets. Limited hours, cultural differences, perception of higher prices, and limited product offerings can all act as barriers for low-income individuals to shop at farmers markets. To reach a larger population year-round, especially in states without a twelve- month growing season, it is more efficient to go to where SNAP recipients already shop than to get them to patronize farmers markets.

Store-based SNAP incentives can benefit a related but different set of farmers than farmers market–based programs. In Michigan, for example, Fair Food Network's program requires participants to buy local or regional produce before getting credit for produce of any origin. However, those growers selling to supermarkets tend to be of a larger scale than ones selling directly to consumers. These medium-sized farms, affectionately called "Ag in the Middle," have been in decline in recent decades. Many find themselves unable to compete with ever-larger and corporate-owned farms, with their guaranteed markets and economies of scale. And they generally produce too much to make direct farm to consumer marketing cost effective. Fitzgerald notes that the importance of these farmers in rebuilding regional food systems beyond boutique-scale sales is of paramount importance: "The latest Ag Census shows an increase in small farmers (direct marketers) but a continued decline in the Ag of the Middle producers. These are the farmers/ranchers we need for farm to school, farm to hospital, real regional supplies for grocery, etc."[103]

Making FINI incentives available in grocery stores can be a double-edged sword. On one hand, doing so enables the program to reach many more people who don't shop at farmers markets. It also provides key markets for regionally oriented midsized producers. Store-based sales also help the FINI program meet its legislative goal of increasing the produce consumption of SNAP recipients.

Yet this expansion into the grocery store sector comes at a cost, foregoing the opportunity to encourage greater patronage of farmers markets. Richard McCarthy, the executive director of Slow Food USA, started one of the first SNAP incentive programs at farmers markets in New Orleans. He contends that the move toward greater efficiency in delivering SNAP incentives through supermarkets is at odds with the great accomplishments of the food movement and farmers markets in educating people about their food. "Farmers markets provide a high-touch environment that help people navigate their food choices. They help create a larger cultural shift in how people think about their food. Supermarkets will deliver a milder or diluted version of what you get through farmers market SNAP incentives."[104]

Fitzgerald argues, on the other hand, that a hybrid approach combining the hands-on experiences from farmers markets with the accessibility provided by grocery stores is ideal. She notes that experience in Detroit shows many shoppers learning about the SNAP incentive program at farmers markets, but utilizing these incentives in grocery stores.[105]

Brinkman would still like to see some preferential treatment provided to farmers markets. She prognosticates that future evaluations will show farmers market–based incentive programs to deliver superior results than grocery store–based programs. In that case, she argues that FINI should be set up to provide additional benefits through direct marketing venues, such as SNAP recipients receiving twice as much bonus produce at farmers markets than at grocery stores.[106]

McCarthy's comments hint at the dilemma advocates faced when trying to gain federal funding for what have been largely private initiatives. The potential upside is enormous, as SNAP incentives could grow over the course of a decade or two to reshape the entire SNAP program. Yet federal policy inevitably involves compromises and definitional problems that don't exist at the local level. For example, if FINI only allowed local or regional food, Congress would have to define these terms, which to date have had widely divergent meanings due in part to the massive difference in geographic scale across the country (similar in nature to the challenges for the farm to school arena).

While FINI increases the amount of SNAP incentives available by $18 million annually (not including the matching funds that the program catalyzes), advocates such as Fitzgerald, Oran Hesterman, and Wholesome Wave's Gus Schumacher (who played a key role in establishing the FMNP and SFMNP), have grander plans for its future. They would ultimately like to grow the program to $100 million or even billions per year. The larger the program becomes, the more challenging it will be for Congress to allocate "new money" (or additional funds) to FINI. At some point, FINI would likely need to become incorporated into the core SNAP program, as a revision of the rules and regulations that govern that program. This would mean that FINI would not be an optional program that some SNAP recipients choose to participate in, but instead a fundamental revision of the SNAP program itself to incentivize increased consumption of regionally grown produce. Brinkman and Feldman support putting SNAP incentives on the same debit card as SNAP itself, noting the tremendous inefficiencies that the creation of SNAP incentives has caused, in tracking and handling an alternative currency.

Whether FINI grows to this level will depend in part on the reaction of SNAP's gatekeepers, the powerful anti-hunger groups that lead the lobbying and communications efforts for the program.

Anti-Hunger Community Response to Incentives The anti-hunger community has been a Johnny-come-lately to the incentive bandwagon, in part because of its long history of not wanting to differentiate between "good food" and "bad food" for fear that such a distinction would lead to restrictions on unhealthy foods. Recently, FRAC and other groups have come to embrace incentives in the face of an avalanche of state and federal attempts to legislate restrictions in the SNAP program (described in chapter 4). These groups have realized that incentives provide them with a preferable alternative to these restrictions and demonstrate their commitment to fostering healthy diets among SNAP recipients. They have also seen that SNAP incentives used at farmers markets have generated a groundswell of positive publicity for the SNAP program, casting an aura of homespun bipartisan goodness around the food stamp program that is often missing from other media coverage. Brinkman and Feldman note that in California, some of the larger food banks have come to embrace SNAP incentives as part of a broader effort to promote access to healthy foods within the anti-hunger movement. Their perception is that anti-hunger groups remain skeptical about promoting locally grown foods, instead focusing on the cost of the food rather than its origin. They choose *value* over *values*.[107]

By 2012–2013, FRAC, for example, had become a modest champion for FINI and SNAP incentives. To Fitzgerald, the fact that national anti-hunger groups such as FRAC signed onto supporting the passage of FINI in the 2014 Farm Bill was a clear expression of how the anti-hunger movement has changed course on this issue. "It was/is a crucial step for the hunger community to publically support a program that explicitly links SNAP benefits to healthier food choices and has the potential to inform future SNAP food policy."[108]

Behind their modest embrace of SNAP incentives, many anti-hunger advocates privately hold doubts about the viability of a local food mandate within this program. They perceive farmers markets as a boutique strategy limited to the committed few who will take the time and trouble to shop there, not a viable approach that could be scaled up to meet the needs of a larger percentage of the 22.7 million households that receive SNAP benefits. David Lee, a former policy advocate for Feeding America and now executive director of Feeding Wisconsin, comments, "Shopping at farmer markets and food co-ops is generally not a very welcoming experience to people on SNAP."[109] Especially at the national level, many anti-hunger advocates remain far from convinced that the geographic origin of products should be at the center of any SNAP incentive policymaking.

Just as many hunger advocates remain skeptical about the importance of local produce (over industrially farmed fruits and veggies), their support for FINI was conditioned on it bringing additional funding into the SNAP program. FINI's $100 million budget didn't come off the top of the SNAP budget, but was "new money," extra dollars that came from reductions in conservation and commodity programs.[110] Given the $8 billion in cutbacks that the SNAP program suffered in the 2014 Farm Bill, the importance of these new dollars cannot be underestimated. Anti-hunger advocates remain vehemently opposed to the SNAP budget being utilized for other purposes, even ones that they support. David Lee euphemistically remarks, "We would need to have another discussion," if advocates were to propose integrating FINI as a mandatory element of SNAP and its core budget.[111]

FINI's Future Possibilities In addition to the political support of anti-hunger groups, the future of FINI depends largely upon its performance in fostering increased produce consumption by participating SNAP recipients. The program's evaluation will need to show that the millions invested in this program have a direct and sizable impact on participants' produce-purchasing patterns and deserves to be increased in scale to reach more persons. Assuming the evaluation demonstrates such a success and Congress chooses to invest substantially more resources into the program in the 2018 Farm Bill, advocates may face an ever-increasing challenge to maintain the local food and direct-marketing preference in the program, unless the evaluation shows that incentives at farmers markets have a greater impact than those implemented through grocery stores. Similarly, as long as FINI requires a dollar-for-dollar match, the growth of the program will be limited by the ability of communities to leverage philanthropic and business contributions to this cause.

The potential growth of FINI raises questions about the ability of local and regional food systems to meet demand. Malini Ram Moraghan, the former managing director of Wholesome Wave Investments, contends that current demand for local food far outstrips supply. "In certain cities, there are times when chefs can't get the produce they want in the quantity and variety they want. Groceries and other institutions want to stock a lot more local produce than is available. And even when product is available, these larger buyers face supply chain challenges to actually getting local produce into larger markets. Given shopper preferences for local, and using a variety of inputs from consumer surveys, syndicated research, and market consultants, we estimate there is about $25 billion worth of unmet demand for local food currently. That demand will only get met by strengthening supply chains for local food and supporting farmers as they add capacity."[112]

This inadequacy of supply points to the need for Congress to couple SNAP incentives with a new, strategic, and regional food system initiative. This initiative would need to increase the scale of existing programs that help keep farmland in production; encourage access for a new generation of farmers to land, credit, and markets; and rebuild the necessary infrastructure, such as packing houses, canneries, and food hubs to enable them to efficiently get their products to market. It would need to change existing policies to help produce growers get affordable crop insurance, as well as encourage grain growers to transition to fruit and vegetable production. It may also need to include new programs that foster local and regional food systems, especially in the context of climate change.

States and cities may play an increasing role in SNAP incentives. Some, such as Seattle and New York City, are already funding incentive programs, in part because they see them as generating health benefits for their most vulnerable residents. Municipal and state contributions can ease the matching requirement for nonfederal funds required by FINI, one of the biggest challenges that nonprofit incentive operators face.

Summary

The food movement has been successful in introducing into the mainstream the idea that food should not be an undifferentiated commodity. According to one of the leading consumer market research groups, The

Hartman Group, transparency has become a cutting-edge issue for food shoppers in 2015. In their study tailored for the food retail and processing industry, the authors assert: "Consumers are more concerned about transparency in the products and foods they consume than ever before. They are concerned about maintaining a right to know how their food is grown and handled, echoing a continued trend toward fresh, real, and less-processed food."[113] Consumers want to influence social change with their purchases, and need adequate information to shape their decisions. Transparency is a prerequisite for a new moral or civic food system, in which the production methods, labor practices, community responsibility, ownership structure, and environmental stewardship are essential elements. These are the basis of getting values for our money, as Kevin Morgan intones, not just a good value for our buck.

Federal food programs embody the very notion of opacity. At a basic level, information about how the $100 billion of federal food program dollars is spent, with the notable exception of the $2 billion in USDA Foods purchases, remains confidential and/or not readily available to the public. This lack of information is not coincidental. It is the natural consequence of a historical lack of questioning about the food in these programs. As a result, the government remains almost entirely unaccountable for the choices being made, sometimes by consumers, sometimes by public officials, for the food being purchased with taxpayer dollars. This general lack of transparency is why farm to school programs, which often tie a specific food item on a menu to a specific producer, have been such a breath of fresh air in the school lunch program. In addition to the quality and economic development benefits farm to school provides, they create a model for accountability and transparency that is largely missing from a system grounded in industrial production.

The lack of transparency in federal food programs underscores the government's approach that these programs exist to support the industrial food system. With a few notable examples described above, USDA and Congress have defined the function of the nutrition programs, by and large, as reinforcing the marketplace rather than seeking to reform it. By and large, they have not been defined as levers of change in the food system. To the extent that USDA has used the power of the public plate, it has overwhelmingly been to reinforce corporate control of the marketplace.[114]

It may indeed be unrealistic to expect USDA and the federal government to be proactive in this regard. Institutions (and politicians) are notoriously risk-averse. Even those nutrition programs that have promoted value chains, such as the Farmers Market Nutrition Programs and FINI, have done so only in response to successful models outside the Beltway. There will likely be lag time between what happens in the grassroots and federal policy. Even the advent of the farmers market nutrition programs and FINI were reactive as responses to successful initiatives at the grassroots level. From that perspective, the work of groups such as the LA Food Policy Council's Good Food Purchasing Policy provides crucial organizing opportunities to scale up state and local efforts into federal policy.

The central question of this chapter has been how to redeploy the combined $100 billion of taxpayer dollars spent on federal food programs to accelerate a food system that is not only embedded in values of democratic ownership, environmental sustainability, and fair treatment of workers, but also superior at poverty reduction and job generation. Doing so will require making transparent the economic development function of these programs, so the public can better understand the choices that are being made and act to reshape the expenditures in a way that supports our collective values.

Similar to the consensus for local and regional procurement in the international food aid arena, other programs such as food stamps, USDA Foods, and school lunch should have a much more explicit grassroots *development* purpose in addition to their *food aid* or *feeding* mission. In surfacing the development nature of these programs, our society will be able to make clearer and more conscious decisions about the type of food system we want our federal tax dollars to support. Domestic food programs should move away from tying aid to Big Ag and Big Food, toward, as Raymond Hopkins suggests, a development focus that best serves the needs of the poor and of rural communities. In making this shift, in removing the link between the public plate and the cheap food orientation of industrial agriculture, numerous questions will arise. For example, program advocates and their government counterparts should be asking how FDPIR could reinforce tribal food sovereignty. How can federal food assistance programs best support rural communities' business development opportunities such that their residents don't need to be program recipients? How can these programs move away from a hunger relief paradigm to a community economic development model? Who should benefit at the "back end" of these programs?

These changes could not and should not happen if they come at the cost of sacrificing the immediate food needs of the nation's poor. As the New Dealer Harry Hopkins pointed out, people need to eat today. Various programs such as FINI and farm to school are demonstrating that there need not be a trade-off between meeting today's needs and longer-term economic development and sustainability targets. In fact, food with values is not always more expensive than the industrial food being distributed through schools and supermarkets. A growing body of evidence drawn from conversations with school food service directors and surveys of farmers market shoppers is showing that the prices of sustainable produced food can be lower than conventionally produced foods. In addition, a full cost accounting of this food shows it to be less costly in the long run when health, environmental, and societal costs are included.

This paradigm shift will be challenging to achieve. It may be best thought of as a strategic plan for federal food programs over the medium and long term. Powerful enemies in the food industry would constrain these changes. Yet just as importantly, a lack of imagination limits our ability to redeploy these $100 billion in more innovative fashion that meets multiple purposes.

The anti-hunger community, at least at the federal level, has felt hemmed in by a persistent right-wing challenge to the very purpose of nutrition programs, especially SNAP. Instead of embracing innovation, especially around the nutrition purpose of SNAP, it has circled the wagons under the rallying cry of "do no harm." This defensive posture has unfortunately impeded its ability to embrace innovation, something that has been sorely lacking from federal food programs since the 1960s. The activist and author Mark Winne notes: "A program now more than 50 years old remains largely unchanged even though the nation that it helps feed has changed in myriad ways. Imagine a corporation or major private institution that did not conduct research and development, kept the same product line for generations, and never engaged in strategic thinking. That enterprise would be out of business (or subsidized by the federal government)."[115]

The food programs and their staunchest defenders are indeed products of the 1960s and 1970s, trapped in a time warp of a specific model of social programs. Moving into the future will require courage, innovation, dialogue, and new partners. Some of these transformations have begun to occur as the foundation community has used its financial prowess to seed change. For example, The Healthy Eating Active Living Convergence Partnership, comprising some of the nation's largest health-oriented foundations, has funded the seeds of these new partnerships by providing six-figure grants to FRAC, PolicyLink, the National Sustainable Agriculture Coalition, and the Fair Food Network. In part, FRAC's support for FINI has reportedly been strengthened by the relationships built through this process.

Opening space for new partnerships and a new vision for federal food programs does entail a reconfiguration of the anti-hunger community's relationship with the food and agriculture industry. Yet the type of innovation that the sustainable procurement represented by FINI, farm to school, and the Center for Good Food Purchasing points to the need not only for new policy, but also for a new *kind* of policy. In their *Washington Post* article, four of the most prominent leaders in the food movement, including the writers Michael Pollan and Mark Bittman, argue that the nation needs a comprehensive food and farm policy, joining agriculture production to nutrition and environmental protection. They assert that the nation's agricultural and nutrition policies are often at odds with each other.[116] This piece underlines the necessity to implement policies in the agricultural sphere if nutrition programs are to rely more on local and regional foods. Rebuilding the supply of local food and the infrastructure to distribute it efficiently will be essential, and entail policy remedies to ease access to capital, mitigate risks, and incentivize new farmers.

This level of comprehensive policy framework, or even just a smaller subset of it to link regional food system rebuilding with federal food program reform, would require the active support of a broad coalition of all in and around the hunger, health, environment, and food movements. These groups would need to come together to counter the power of special interests vested in maintaining the status quo and to combat the "incalculable damage to the health of our people, and our land, water, and air" caused by the food system.[117] It would require anti-hunger groups, as the gatekeepers of federal food programs, to fully embrace the community-oriented goals of the food movement, not just as boutique strategies that garner good press and benefit small numbers of their constituents, but as tangible goals that should be embedded in the crown jewels of the federal food program collection. Doing so would require them to rethink their partnerships that have helped them gain sufficient political power to maintain the impressive array of programs that are their legacy over the past 50 if not 80 years. The writing is on the wall. We need a new vision and new coalitions to remove federal food programs from supporting special interests and resituate them fully in the public interest. These programs must be modernized or they will face the twin peril of declining effectiveness and contradictory impacts.

6   Who's at the Table Shapes What's on the Agenda

Income Inequality and Persistent Poverty

"We are the 99 percent!" Who is the 1 percent? Forty-seven percent of Americans pay no income tax. Slogans and declarations like these have become iconic symbols of America's ever-widening economic inequality gulf. Book after book, blog after blog, and report after report have documented the nation's entrenched poverty, shrinking middle class, and concentration of wealth. Economic inequality in the United States today, exceeds that of any other major industrialized nation except Singapore, has grown to its greatest point since 1928.[1] One indicator of this ever-widening gap is the amount of money paid to CEOs. According to an AFL-CIO study of 350 companies in the Standard & Poor's 500, in 1983 CEOs earned 46 times the wages of the average worker. This amount skyrocketed to 331 times average worker pay, as CEOs in 2013 earned on average $11.7 million.[2]

The harmful effects of economic inequality on our society have been well documented. Richard Wilkinson and Kate Pickett, the authors of *The Spirit Level: Why Greater Equality Makes Societies Stronger*, contend that US citizens suffer from some of the highest rates among developed countries of violence, teenage births, obesity, and numerous other social problems because of it.[3] Other researchers have chronicled its negative impact on democracy, especially in light of the Citizens United decision that opened the floodgates for electoral expenditures from the wealthy.

The causes of economic inequality have also been well documented. The 1980s saw the business community abandoning its postwar social contract to generate shared prosperity. Offshore manufacturing wreaked havoc on industrial cities, such as Youngstown, eliminating a key source of well-paying factory jobs. Policy changes unfavorable to labor impeded union organizing, diminishing their bargaining ability. According to the Economic Policy Institute, if the minimum wage had grown at the same rate as productivity, it would be at $18.30 in 2015.[4] The ascent of neoliberal ideology led to tax cuts, such as those during the Reagan and George W. Bush administrations, concentrating wealth at the top. It also led to the elimination of welfare as an entitlement program, placing a greater burden on such noncash nutrition programs as school meals and SNAP.

The links between wages and poverty are direct and well documented. This chapter focuses on one of the solutions that vast swaths of the business community have long opposed: an increase in the minimum wage. According to Peter Edelman, a key figure in the anti-poverty struggle from the time he worked for Robert F. Kennedy in the late 1960s, America has become a low-wage nation, in which half of the jobs pay less than $34,000 per year, and one-quarter less than $22,000 per year, a level at which a family of three would be eligible for food stamps.[5]

Compared to the 1960s, fewer people now live in poverty and the depths of their poverty have been rendered less severe. This progress is not due to an increase in real wages, given the steep erosion of the value of the minimum wage since the 1960s. (This erosion has been so steep and prolonged that it has led to the development of initiatives across the country to gain passage of a *living* wage, especially within the public sector, or in economic arenas that the public sector has substantial control over, such as the tourism industry near airports.) The minimum wage's diminished purchasing power has contributed to heightened economic inequality, accounting for roughly two-thirds of the growing gap between low- and middle-wage workers. (Weakened unions explain a fifth to a third of the entire rise of wage inequality.)[6] Instead, this positive change can be attributed exclusively to an improved social safety net.[7]

As wages and related benefits still make up the vast majority (about 70 percent) of the income of the poorest fifth of nonelderly Americans, any poverty reduction strategy must seek to increase their paychecks.[8] Staff from the liberal think tank, the Economic Policy Institute, acknowledges the importance of this dual strategy, in part because of these basic statistics and in part due to a political calculus:

We need both tracks. While we support deepening the tax-and-transfer system that boosts incomes for low- and moderate-income Americans whenever feasible, if nothing is done to change the policies that have led to increasing wage inequality, it seems certain that income inequality will continue rising. This logically flows from the fact that if increased inequality continues to suppress hourly wage growth for the low-wage workforce, then we would find ourselves in the untenable position of needing more tax credits and more transfers each year to simply keep after-tax income inequality stable, let alone somewhat reversing recent decades' upward income and wage redistribution.[9]

This conclusion is echoed by a September 2016 study, in which William Rodgers III, a Rutgers University professor, predicts through economic modeling that a rise in the minimum wage correlates to reduced food insecurity. His calculations indicate that a rise in the minimum wage to $15 per hour by 2023 would result in 1.2 million households becoming more food secure. He contends that federal food programs "can only ameliorate hunger, not eliminate it, even in the best of economies."[10] A *New York Times* article from September 2016 amplifies on Professor Rodgers study and the Economic Policy Institute's analysis. In assessing a 1.2-percent drop in the poverty rate in 2015, the largest decline since 1999, it concludes that the main drivers of this good news were not federal programs, but rather the creation of new jobs, higher wages, and an increase in the number of hours low-wage workers are employed.[11]

Disconnect between Analysis and Action

Almost all anti-hunger leaders would agree with the importance of increasing wages and creating well-paying jobs in order to reduce food insecurity, especially since more than 80 percent of SNAP recipients live in households with at least one working individual.[12] For example, the Blueprint to End Hunger, endorsed in 2008 by all of the major anti-hunger groups, states: "The root cause of hunger is a lack of adequate purchasing power in millions of households. ... As a nation, we must encourage work and ensure that all who work that the results of their labor will be sufficient to provide for the basic needs of their families."[13]

Despite this awareness, the anti-hunger movement has focused almost exclusively on the responsibility of the public sector to fund nutrition assistance programs. It has been averse to dedicate time and resources to labor-related advocacy. Most of their visioning documents do not contain a wage-increase or job-creation platform. For example, the Blueprint to End Hunger does not include a single recommendation to increase the minimum wage or create new jobs. In fact, its section on "labor and industry" doesn't recommend policies or practices that could strengthen labor unions. Instead, it calls for workplace giving campaigns to hunger charities and ways in which companies can connect more of their low wage employees with federal benefits, such as food stamps. McDonald's and Walmart, among other employers, have implemented this recommendation, actively encouraging their employees to sign up for SNAP and other public benefits.

More recently, Feeding America's 2014 Map the Meal Gap follows the same pattern. It identifies low wages and high unemployment as key drivers behind the increase in poverty (of which hunger is a symptom), but does not follow up with further recommendations or even an analysis of how food banks and pantries are tackling this issue.[14]

The National Commission on Hunger's 2015 report, the product of numerous field hearings, site visits, and the testimony of dozens of leaders, eloquently acknowledges how globalization and deindustrialization have negatively impacted the food security of many families. It states, "Having sufficient earnings is the best defense against hunger and reduces the need for nutrition assistance." Yet, not a single one of its 20 recommendations to Congress and USDA addresses issues related to wages (outside of tweaks to SNAP), employment, or working conditions, much less policies to incentivize well-paying jobs. To the contrary, its only private sector–oriented recommendations calls for tax breaks and other incentives to involve the business community in anti-hunger efforts.[15] According to one participant in the process, this omission was a result of a failure to reach consensus on these matters by the more conservative and liberal members of the commission.

This disconnect between analysis and action can be seen not just in their written documents, but in the fact that most anti-hunger groups have refrained from supporting campaigns to raise the minimum wage. Following are a few examples of these missed opportunities:

• From 2012 to 2015, thousands of fast food workers have walked off their jobs and held protests in over 160 cities in support of a $15 minimum wage, but only a handful of anti-hunger groups have supported them in meaningful ways.[16]

• When the city council of Washington, DC, passed an ordinance in 2013 to mandate that big box retailers pay their employees a minimum of $12.50

per hour, none of the local or national DC-based anti-hunger groups, most of whom receive large grants from Walmart, supported the legislation.

• In Los Angeles, only the tiny Hunger Action Los Angeles (HALA) supported Mayor Garcetti's early proposal to increase the minimum wage to $13.25 per hour, although the much larger LA Regional Food Bank remained silent.[17] The situation in Illinois mirrors Los Angeles, where the HALA-like Illinois Hunger Coalition was the only anti-hunger group of many much powerful entities to support a non-binding resolution to increase the minimum wage.[18]

• During the 2014 election, ballot initiatives in Arkansas, South Dakota, Nebraska, and Alaska to raise the minimum wage won passage. Despite the fact that these were hardly fringe campaigns, only in Nebraska and Arkansas did a major anti-hunger group support the proposed legislation. Feeding South Dakota's (FSD) Fall 2014 newsletter exemplifies how many food banks prefer to remain politically neutral. It does not mention the ballot initiative at all, but instead, the lead article exhorts readers to wear orange clothes to raise awareness of hunger. The executive director's column contains slogans such as "Our motto is 'I am Feeding South Dakota,'" and 'We are Feeding South Dakota' because when we work together, we can solve hunger.'"[19]

A survey of 88 anti-hunger groups illustrates this relative lack of involvement on wage-related issues.[20] Completed in the fall of 2014 with the help of WhyHunger and the Oregon Food Bank, this informal electronic survey discovered that 61 (69 percent) of the 88 respondents reported undertaking some form of policy advocacy activity. Yet, only 13 (15 percent) reported having advocated for "wage-related public policy such as minimum wages or living wages campaigns." Of those 13 organizations, only three reported spending more than 10 percent of their organizational (and/or policy program) budget on wage-related policy. While this represents a small sampling of the anti-hunger movement, it does underscore the fact that only a small minority of groups engages in such upstream advocacy.

Most organizations fail to weigh in on these matters, and for those that do, they typically spend very little financial and political capital. Even some of the more progressive groups do not engage publically on these controversial matters, but instead invest their limited energies in coalitions or state food bank associations.[21] By doing so, they can still be at the table while reducing their public visibility, which otherwise might alienate their donors or board members. (The downside of this risk-reduction strategy is that the organization misses the opportunity to educate its donor and stakeholder base about the importance of working on anti-poverty measures.) In all but a few cases, these groups perceive this economic justice work as being peripheral to their federal food program–based policy agenda. They do so even though they understand the link between low wages and food insecurity. They know a single parent with a child working full-time at the federal minimum wage of $7.25 per hour will still make less than the poverty line. Even a single adult working at that same wage will qualify for food stamps.

The Advocate's Dilemma   The sociologist Janet Poppendieck labels this conundrum "the advocate's dilemma." She hypothesizes that advocates have seen their efforts on federal food programs successfully mitigating food insecurity. They possess the expertise, connections, and knowledge to have an impact in this area, but they also appreciate that their efforts will not resolve the hunger problem and may even result in a backlash if public expenditures on nutrition programs increase unduly. They understand that strategies like improving wages, creating jobs, and increasing affordable housing are indispensable to addressing the root causes of hunger. But their ability to be successful advocates in these areas pales in comparison to their capacity to make changes in the food assistance realm. In addition, these more politicized strategies can result in a loss of funding as well as the fracturing of their bipartisan coalitions.[22]

Ken Regal, the executive director of the Pittsburgh-based Just Harvest, confirms Poppendieck's hypothesis: "Part of the answer [about why groups don't lobby more on increasing wages] is about practical day to day life and less about ideology. We make a lot of tactical decisions on what to lobby on. With a Republican governor and Republican-controlled state legislature, it's a waste to put a lot of our time into increasing the minimum wage. I want to get stuff done, and not just protest very bad things. You get very marginalized after doing that for a long time."[23]

Advocates like Regal lobby on federal food programs because they represent the largest public investment in food security. It's not just the money that makes them fruitful areas for lobbying, but also the policy infrastructure and political consensus that has been built up around them for the past few generations.

For example, school districts have long complained about burdensome income verification and reporting requirements in the school lunch and breakfast programs. This paperwork can be quite costly, threatening the financial viability of the school meals programs. In response, advocates convinced Congress to establish a "community eligibility" provision in the 2010 Child Nutrition Act, in which schools with a high percentage of low-income students would be able to offer free meals to all students and forego the usual paperwork, thereby allowing schools to improve the quality of their food while increasing the number of students who receive free meals. In the three states that piloted community eligibility, breakfast consumption increased by 25 percent and lunch by 13 percent.[24] It is a win-win initiative that benefits school districts and student food security, and it lays the groundwork for advocates' long-held dream of universal free school meals for all children regardless of income.

Advocates gained passage of community eligibility because they had the right experience and connections to create innovative policy. They had gained the trust of the school nutrition community from years of collaboration on previous legislative and administrative advocacy. They understood how cumbersome the paperwork requirements were to schools. They enjoyed positive working relationships with USDA, whose support would be key to the implementation of this provision. They had built up a political base inside the Senate Agriculture Committee and the House Education and Workforce Committee, and connections to staff and congressional members on both sides of the aisle. They had allies outside of the Beltway whom they were able to mobilize to contact their congressional members. Community eligibility fit in a safe space, within the ideological constraints of their supporters, many of whom would have labeled them as "socialists" had they chosen a target that addressed the more structural causes of poverty.[25] And they had funders who were willing to support them in this kind of initiative, which offers evidence-based, incremental, and measurable improvements to long-established programs.

Theirs has been the consummate insider approach. DC-based lead groups, such as the Center on Budget and Policy Priorities (CBPP), Feeding America (though based in Chicago, it has a substantial DC presence), and the Food Research and Action Center (FRAC), provide the leadership in developing initiatives or identifying promising policy changes from the states. They set a national agenda for each legislative cycle and formulate strategy for gaining its passage. They disseminate their analysis to local groups, such as Just Harvest, through targeted research, conference calls, workshops, and action alerts. Each of these local groups, many of whom provide similar leadership within their own states, in turn mobilizes their own constituents to action.

Weaknesses in the Model This pyramid structure began to show stress fractures, as some of the more experienced local groups demanded a larger role in the agenda- and strategy-setting functions. Their concerns were voiced in a paper written by Joel Berg of the New York City Coalition Against Hunger (which has since morphed into Hunger Free America), and again in a meeting of a small group of long-time regional leaders in Los Angeles in 2012. Calling themselves the Demeter Network, after the Greek goddess of the harvest, these individuals sought to flatten the hierarchical structure of the anti-hunger advocacy community by gaining a greater place at the table for themselves and their grassroots constituents. Some minor but important changes came about because of their advocacy: state leaders played a larger role in setting the agenda for the annual FRAC-led Hunger Leaders meeting, and FRAC was able to fund the expansion of the communications capacity of some groups in the field.[26] Little if anything was agreed upon to further involve low-income individuals as partners in the advocacy process.

The emergence of the Demeter Network matters not so much for what it achieved, which amounted to some minor accommodations. Instead, its significance lies in the idea behind its founding: that the hunger movement could be more powerful if it drew from the insights of local anti-hunger leaders and ultimately the grassroots themselves.

Anti-hunger groups have been largely effective at their core strategy of shepherding federal food programs. Against the backdrop of the House of Representatives removing the food stamp program from the Farm Bill for the first time since 1973 and a possible $40 billion cut, hunger advocates and their allies in the Senate were able to pare that cut to a more modest $8 billion reduction.[27] Depending on one's perspective, this bill demonstrated either the power of the anti-hunger constituency in Congress to conduct damage control, or the beginning of more serious challenges to SNAP.[28]

Limiting the effectiveness of many anti-hunger groups has been their inability to tap into the full potential of the vast numbers of people they touch. One story exemplifies this missed opportunity. At the September 2013 Closing the Hunger Gap conference in Tucson, Matt Knott, the chief operating officer of Feeding America, boasted that during a critical moment in the Farm Bill his organization had leveraged 5,000 phone calls to Congress.[29] Upon further examination this apparently huge number of calls seems tiny when compared to their network's size. Those 5,000 calls break down to only 8 percent of the roughly 60,000 soup kitchens and pantries in the Feeding America network making one call. Using an alternate calculation, that means the network's 200 food banks leveraged only 25 calls each. Or that a miniscule fraction of the millions of donors and volunteers—not to mention the 46 million clients—bothered to contact their congress members. By way of comparison, the highly organized but smaller Bread for the World mobilizes 100,000 persons annually through its network of churches to make contact with their congressional representatives.[30]

A Safety Net–Only Approach   The hunger movement's relative success in protecting federal food programs, together with food banks' limited investment in mobilization, casts doubts on the movement's interest and ability to take on the challenge of a broader policy agenda, and in some cases suggests such an agenda might even be counterproductive. A longtime Capitol Hill agriculture reporter, Jerry Hagstrom, believes that if leading anti-hunger lobbying groups such as FRAC took up the minimum wage issue it would distract and even reduce their ability to hold onto safety net gains, potentially by fracturing their bipartisan coalition.[31]

On the other hand, the participation of anti-hunger groups on wage-related matters could be a powerful force. Joann Lo of the Food Chain Workers Alliance notes, "Anti-hunger groups could play a major role in supporting workers' struggles and economic justice issues. They have direct contact and relationships with millions of poor people in this country. If they not only provided services to these people, but also organized them in alliance with unions and workers centers, the potential collective power to win social change would be incredible."[32]

The advocate's dilemma puts them between a rock (the knowledge that their strategies are incomplete to resolve the hunger problem) and a hard place (the nation's political realities). No immediate exit to this uncomfortable position exists, so the hunger movement remains in a holding pattern waiting for the political winds to change direction. This limbo results in, as

Joann Lo points, a huge missed opportunity to address income inequality and poverty in a more systematic fashion. It also leads to an overemphasis on safety net programs, which by itself leaves the anti-hunger movement vulnerable to charges of fostering dependency.

Safety net programs are enormously valuable in reducing food insecurity but insufficient. As the Economic Policy Institute points out, it is not politically viable to expect them to grow big enough to solve the food insecurity problem. In *All You Can Eat*, Joel Berg describes a different vision, claiming that a 41 percent increase in safety net program expenditures would end food insecurity in America. In 2014 that figure would have been an additional $40 billion or more per year. He contends that the country needs to shift its priorities in order to reallocate its resources.[33] Countless anti-hunger leaders echo this statement, claiming that hunger is easily solvable, if only we had the political will.

Even if the anti-hunger movement could pull off this coup of increasing food programs by almost half, this approach would leave in place the structural problems that drive poverty and food insecurity today, especially among the growing number of waged workers. On its own, increasing the amount of money the poor receive from the government to compensate for the way employers exploit them through low wages, no benefits, or part-time employment does not make the poor economically secure in the long run. As Sharon Thornberry of the Oregon Food Bank points out, "SNAP does not help people build the wealth and skills they need to become more self-reliant, so that they don't have to rely on government assistance in the first place. Yet, recent and proposed cuts to the program combined with no adjustment for the rising cost of food erode the program's effectiveness as the Nation's food security safety net."[34]

Nonetheless, SNAP has shown great value in lifting households out of poverty and food insecurity, while mitigating the severity of food insecurity among those who are more in dire straits. A 2015 White House report found that in households that received SNAP food insecurity was 30 percent lower than it would be otherwise. Census Bureau research shows that SNAP has lifted 4.7 million people out of poverty in 2014, and cut in half the number of households living on less than $2 per person per day.[35]

Some households find themselves recurring to SNAP on a periodic basis, when for example a family member loses a job. A USDA study confirmed the periodic nature of SNAP participation, finding that many households remain on SNAP for modest periods of time, with the median timeframe in 2008 being 12 months.[36] While safety net programs can act as a periodic stopgap to help households overcome either these temporary situations, they are not designed to address the root causes of what has become an entrenched problem of income inequality and persistent poverty.

SNAP recipients need help finding the exit ramp off the federal benefits freeway. A former USDA administrator, James Arena-DeRosa, contends that it is unrealistic to expect anti-hunger groups to find those exits, but they should be willing to talk about them.[37] In other words, we should not expect anti-hunger groups to become experts in job creation and labor law strategy, but they should be willing to educate themselves and their constituents, as well as engage in coalitions with those that do have this expertise.

Interestingly, the 2014 Farm Bill may help recipients find those exit ramps in a proactive fashion. It included a $200 million grants program that would fund 10 states to develop pilot projects to help SNAP recipients find good jobs so that they could transition off food stamps.[38] This program evolved from the failed amendment by Representative Steve Sutherland (R-FL) to incentivize states to reduce the number of SNAP recipients on the program. It was largely a creation of the Republican majority in the House of Representatives, which sought to use employment and training programs (E&T) as a tool for reducing the total cost of the program. While anti-hunger groups vigorously opposed the initial Sutherland amendment as punitive, the expansion of E&T was not on their policy agenda.

E&T programs are not new to SNAP, but their efficacy in helping recipients gain employment has not been well documented.[39] To set the context, federal regulations mandate that able-bodied adults without dependents (ABAWDs) can only receive food stamps for three months out of every three years if they aren't employed or in a workfare program for at least 20 hours per week.[40] Yet in 2014, 70 percent of SNAP recipients lived in locales that waived this requirement, in part because of the high unemployment rates in their states. As the economy improves, it is expected that by 2016, only 25–30 percent of SNAP recipients will be in states that waive this ABAWD requirement.[41] Each state has flexibility in operating its E&T program. Some use the programs to help recipients gain skills and education needed for better paying employment, while others merely test the willingness of ABAWDs to work through requiring perfunctory job searches.[42]

Part of the Right's antagonism to SNAP lies in their belief that it fosters dependency on the government, discouraging employment. A basic fact informs this opposition. SNAP rolls grew by roughly 70 percent from the beginning of the Great Recession.[43] One cause of this rapid expansion was increased outreach and flexibility on the part of states to allow a greater percentage of eligible households to receive SNAP benefits.[44] Eighty-five percent of eligible individuals received SNAP benefits in 2013 as compared to 69 percent in 2007.[45] Another cause can be traced to macroeconomic factors such as the increase in unemployment to over 10 percent in 2008, and the rise of low-wage and part-time employment. Yet even when unemployment dropped to below 5 percent by June 2016, SNAP participation has remained relatively level, at 43.4 million persons, down from a high of 47 million in 2011.[46]

While many anti-hunger advocates would consider it an unqualified success that a greater percentage of eligible households are receiving benefits, this persistent caseload does pose a fundamental threat to the anti-hunger model. The focus on federal benefits as the main poverty-reduction tool shifts the burden for hunger reduction from employers onto taxpayers. It relieves the business sector of its responsibility to pay employees a living wage. While the Right has not embraced a higher minimum wage, the lack of a strategy on the part of anti-hunger advocates to reduce the number of households eligible in the first place for SNAP makes them vulnerable to charges of fostering excessive reliance on the public nickel. It places the program more directly in the crosshairs of its antagonists.

Anti-hunger groups have not been defusing the suicide bomb of high caseloads, given their lack of advocacy to get people off the dole and into jobs.[47] In the words of J. C. Dwyer of Feeding Texas, advocates "don't have an answer to the jobs question."[48] This blind spot leaves them vulnerable to charges of treating SNAP as the primary rather than the backup solution to poverty reduction.

Perhaps the most insidious problem with this singular focus is that it undermines the credibility of the anti-hunger sector. Survey after survey and focus group after focus group reveal that, more than anything else, the poor want living-wage jobs. Even going back as far as the 1980s, this has been the case. For example, an undated booklet from the 1980s put out by the Coalition on Human Needs, titled "How the Poor would Remedy Poverty," highlights this perspective. The authors interviewed numerous poor people about what the government should do to help them get out of poverty. The single largest answer was to manage the economy so that they could find jobs. The second answer was to provide education and training.[49]

Despite the reduction in checkout-counter stigma by swapping paper food stamps with a debit card format, for many Americans the program still carries the same perception of dependency. While Americans are conditioned to be self-reliant, strongly favoring a job over the dole, the anti-hunger community has done little to ensure that the jobs being offered to them pay a living wage.

Barriers to Working on Wages

Anti-hunger advocates' focus on safety net programs presents a double-edged sword. They have become very effective at protecting these programs and in doing so containing hunger. But, their virtually exclusive focus on these programs leaves them vulnerable. Various barriers block advocates from expanding their policy agenda to lobby on labor-related issues.

Relationship with Labor

Few anti-hunger groups regularly partner with labor unions, whose anti-poverty interests overlap with their own. Although the labor movement has been in sharp decline since the 1980s, it still remains one of the best-organized and most dominant forces in progressive politics. Unions support SNAP and other federal food programs because they know that their workers and the poor depend on them. Despite this support, many union advocates perceive the anti-hunger sector as irrelevant to their struggles. For example, they see food banks as social service agencies rather than social change agents. Unions perceive anti-hunger groups as not directly involved in their struggles, and conflicts between these two sectors have emerged as well. This conflict can take place in the following arenas.

Philanthropy   Some labor activists perceive the amount of corporate dollars flowing into the coffers of the anti-hunger community as impeding their support for living-wage campaigns. They know that many groups accept Walmart Foundation grants and thus fail to support ongoing protests to improve working conditions and wages at Walmart stores. They lament the fact that many food banks take enormous amounts of money and in-kind donations from the restaurant industry, but did not endorse the Restaurant Opportunities Center's efforts to increase the tipped minimum wage for restaurant workers. They know that the national organization Share our Strength (SOS), whose singular focus is to end childhood hunger, has chosen not to collaborate with fast food workers in their campaigns to gain a $15 minimum wage. Instead they have accepted millions from Arby's and affiliated themselves with the National Restaurant Association, a ferocious opponent of raising the minimum wage (especially for tipped workers).[50]

Wage Subsidies   When full-time workers earn so little that they qualify for federal benefits such as SNAP, these programs in essence subsidize low-wage employment. These benefits allow employers to push off part of the cost of employment onto taxpayers, while they capture the profits from their employees' labor. According to the National Employment Law Project, a leader in fighting for workers' rights, "Low wages and lack of benefits at the 10 largest fast-food companies in the United States cost taxpayers an estimated $3.8 billion per year. McDonald's alone costs taxpayers an estimated $1.2 billion each year."[51] Raising the minimum wage to $10.10 from $7.25 as proposed by President Obama would decrease expenditures in the SNAP program by $4.6 billion, according to Senator Bob Casey Jr. (D-PA).[52]

Researchers have found that the Earned Income Tax Credit (EITC), a favorite of anti-hunger groups, actually drives down wages. The EITC rewards earned wages through a tax refund, which in many cases can be a refund of all taxes paid plus an additional amount. As an incentive for persons to enter the work force, the EITC increases the labor supply. In doing so, it enables employers to offer a lower wage. One economist calculates that employers capture 27 cents of every dollar distributed through the EITC by paying lower wages.[53] This phenomenon is one reason why right-wing economists and pundits prefer the EITC to a minimum wage increase.[54]

While unions typically support these programs as tools to help working families make ends meet, they enter into conflict with anti-hunger groups over a combination of factors. When labor sees corporate-funded anti-hunger groups supporting measures that allow these companies to externalize their costs onto taxpayers, and then refraining from the difficult battles to increase wages for the same people who rely on food banks or food stamps, labor organizers question on whose side anti-hunger advocates stand.

In addition, by subsidizing low wages and penalizing unemployment (as ABAWDs must be employed to receive food stamps), the SNAP program fosters the expansion of a supply of workers willing to toil for low wages. In essence, SNAP has become a powerful ally of the business community, serving as a structural impediment to raising wages. Maggie Dickinson of SUNY New Paltz writes: "Food stamps and other work supports, then, are an essential feature of a regime of economic inequality, precarity, and increased polarization."[55]

Privatization

As part of the 2008 Farm Bill, the American Federation of State, County, and Municipal Employees (AFSCME) sought to reverse a trend of placing the administration of the food stamp program in the hands of private firms. It proposed passage of an amendment that would preempt the ability of states to privatize SNAP administration.

Anti-hunger groups differed in perspective on the AFSCME-led amendment. The Center on Budget and Policy Priorities played a key role in authoring the amendment, because staff believed doing so would ensure the integrity of the food stamp program. Feeding America allegedly opposed it because many of their food banks had entered into contracts with states to provide SNAP program outreach and support. FRAC tried to broker negotiations between AFSCME and Feeding America, but the discussions soon turned difficult. Ultimately, FRAC withdrew its support for AFSCME's amendment. Despite having passed in the House's version of the Farm Bill, the amendment was omitted from the final version sent to President Bush. AFSCME leadership felt sufficiently burned by this turn of events that its representative on FRAC's board left.[56] FRAC has not responded to multiple requests for comment.

Funding

In the food-banking sector, policy advocacy remains a relatively new phenomenon. Most groups carry less than a decade of experience under their belts.[57] Many food banks think of their budget in zero sum terms: a dollar spent on advocacy is a dollar not spent on food for a hungry person. This approach lends itself to minimal and understaffed policy departments. Results of the fall 2014 survey in which 88 anti-hunger groups participated (the same survey mentioned in "Disconnect between Analysis and Action," above), confirm that the lack of funding and staffing is the core barrier for these groups to be more active in policy advocacy and especially wage-related advocacy.

Finding targeted grants for policy advocacy can be very challenging as well. The foundation community has been reluctant to fund policy advocacy in general, much less social-justice organizing. Their hesitation can be traced back to multiple factors. Many foundations fear that they could lose their nonprofit status if they fund lobbying activities. The Internal Revenue Service's guidance is less than clear as to what constitutes lobbying, so many foundations, especially smaller ones without dedicated legal counsel, steer clear from supporting any policy advocacy entirely. Public policy advocacy also presents challenges for foundations in measuring success, often more than a simple matter of whether a group gained passage of a bill. Instead, public policy advocacy can be a long arduous process of building relationships with policymakers, other NGOs, and the media. Finally, advocacy can be controversial, dragging the foundation into murky waters that its trustees might prefer to avoid.

Silos   Funding also reinforces the existing silos in which social problems have been organized. These silos, or distinct sectors, in which the nonprofit community and government are organized, keep nonprofit employees focused on the nitty-gritty of their field. Foundations tend to provide grants in specific program areas in which their staff and board have expertise, further defining the silos and impeding cross-sectoral work. The complexity of the problems and of the responses to them likewise forces specialization.[58] J. C. Dwyer remarks, "The minimum wage is a huge and polarizing issue. Food banks don't feel comfortable that they know what they're talking about [when they wade into this topic]. It's a nebulous issue outside their core expertise."[59]

Political Challenges of Mission Creep   While silos keep employees zeroed in on their area of specialization, mission statements keep organizations similarly focused. When a group goes beyond its own narrowly defined area, it risks mission creep, with the possibility of spreading its resources too thinly. In anti-hunger groups, this expansion beyond the "nutrition safety zone" that frames their missions can land them in trouble with their conservative boards and donors. One food banker notes that the lack of focus on poverty and wage issues comes from a place of fear that it might compromise resources from corporate donors and wealthy individuals. Susannah Morgan of the Oregon Food Bank (OFB) reports that she got an earful from the city council of a conservative Portland suburb about OFB's endorsement of a referendum to increase the minimum wage a decade ago. Similarly, Safeway temporarily withheld its support from OFB for this same decision.[60] One in four respondents to the fall 2014 survey acknowledged that the reticence of board members or donors presented a barrier to their organization taking on wage and labor advocacy.

Low Pay

Although no comprehensive data is available, many food bankers will acknowledge that their own organizations do not pay their employees a living wage. As a result, the leaders of these groups may feel inhibited from pushing for a higher minimum wage when it would negatively impact their own operations by reducing funds available for purchasing food. Similarly, Saru Jayaraman of the Restaurant Opportunities Center notes that in her conversations with large anti-poverty organizations they were explicitly reluctant to endorse the Harkin-Miller minimum wage bill because they believed it would cause them an economic burden.[61]

Who's at the Table?

Joel Berg has argued passionately and repeatedly that the anti-hunger movement, in order to achieve its aims, needs to include "the significant involvement and leadership of low-income Americans." In an article published on the blog Talkpoverty.org, he chastises the movement for believing that it could be successful by merely putting a face on hunger, through telling the stories of struggling individuals, without authentically engaging them in leadership positions. He cites the experiences of other social movements, such as the civil rights and women's suffragette movements, which had blacks and women, respectively, at the forefront.[62]

Berg hits the bullseye with his analysis that the anti-hunger movement lacks the leadership of the hungry or even the previously hungry. A minority of anti-hunger groups are membership organizations that involve their constituents in decision making or in board elections. The fall 2014 survey found that less than 40 percent of respondents affirmed that their groups were membership based. Of these 34 groups, only one replied that the members were the program participants, that is, low-income persons. The boards of directors of food banks similarly tend to comprise business and civic leaders, while the major national groups feature prominent individuals in these positions. Few if any incorporate poor people. In other words, there are few accountability structures in place to ensure that these groups do indeed represent the interests of the poor.

It's not just that poor people aren't calling the shots. It's also that the movement has been historically led by white males. While communities of color suffer from disproportionate rates of poverty and food insecurity, very few of the mid- and upper-level staff in anti-hunger groups are persons of color. This whiteness has been on display (although in recent years things have changed somewhat) in the annual anti-hunger policy conference sponsored by Feeding America and FRAC. Like so much of the nonprofit sector in which women represent the bulk of employees, the larger the organization, the more likely it is to have male leadership.[63] For example, the executive directors and CEOs of major anti-hunger groups as late as 2015 were all male.[64] This stands in distinct contrast to the fact that the single women with children are among the most food insecure in the country. As Penny Van Esterik of the University of Toronto notes, "Women are least likely to be shaping the policies that determine the food system they must access."[65] For this reason, the role of the grassroots Witnesses to Hunger (described in its own section below) in bringing to the forefront their leadership is very exciting.

Mariana Chilton, the founder of Witnesses to Hunger, notes that when she started going to the FRAC-led National Anti Hunger Policy conference she was "really alarmed at the way the conference was run and who was in the room."[66] (Over the course of my own career, I have attended about half a dozen of these events myself, and I was similarly disturbed by the absence of SNAP recipients and food pantry clients).

Despite the accuracy of Berg's observation, his comments suffer from a degree of oversimplification. The women who headed the suffragette movement were not from poor families, and the poorest of the poor did not lead the civil rights movement. An untold number of barriers impede the working class from fully participating in political activities, not the least of which are a lack of time, transportation, translation, and child care.

To Berg's credit, he does try to walk his talk in this area. NY City Coalition Against Hunger has implemented its Customer Advisory Board to involve low-income persons in providing their input on food and welfare related services and programs.[67] Other groups have mobilized in similar fashions. Oregon Food Bank hired five new organizers in rural parts of the state to mobilize community residents to take action at the local level. The Hunger Task Force of Milwaukee's Voices Against Hunger program supports the hungry with data and education, so that they can become effective advocates for state and federal policies. Feeding Texas, the state food bank association, provides 21 Vista volunteers to their members who recruit low-income individuals in a "story-banking" initiative, so that their perspectives are heard. The Hunger Action Network of New York State is extremely active in involving its members in progressive causes, including the Occupy Wall Street protests and fast food workers strikes.

Despite these innovative efforts, Berg seems to be on target with his analysis of the client engagement activities of his peers. In the fall 2014 survey, 22 of 52 respondents said that, in their policy advocacy activities, the greatest level of engagement with the plight of the food insecure occurred when their organization shared stories of the poor. In only 12 groups did the poor tell their own stories to the media, however, and similarly 10 participated in lobbying visits to their elected representatives; 7 provided input on policy goals, while only in 3 of the 52 groups did the food insecure select which issues the group worked on through an advisory committee.

A former FRAC employee gives an example of how this concentration of power in the hands of a professional class, most who did not come from the ranks of the poor, shapes decision making in her former organization. She once requested that FRAC sign onto a union campaign to support workers and improve the quality of food in DC-area universities. Her supervisor's first question was whether it had anything to do with Walmart (presumably because Walmart is one of the largest donors to FRAC). She replied in the negative, but never did receive permission to sign on to the campaign. She attributes the organization's unrelenting emphasis on federal food programs and corresponding reluctance to support labor initiatives as a product of the leadership's middle-class upbringing. As someone who grew up poor, she experienced the stigma associated with being a recipient of these programs. She believes that if the leadership had the same experiences, they would be more hesitant to back federal food programs as exclusively as they do.

Were the Poor Always Missing from the Table?

The War on Poverty launched in 1964 by President Johnson created a forward-thinking mandate for the participation of the poor in poverty-related ventures. It established a framework for "community action," the underlying premise of which was based in part on the community organizing work of Saul Alinsky. It handed over control of the programmatic agendas to the local level, with a mandate to involve the "maximum feasible participation of the poor" in the running of Community Action Agencies (CAAs).[68] That participation was built formally into the running of these organizations, which today focus on such programs as charitable food distribution, energy and heating assistance, head start programs, domestic violence prevention, homeless shelters, job training, and other services. The composition of the board of directors was to be divided into thirds among public officials, the private sector, and low-income individuals.[69]

According to Mike Bonertz, the executive director of ADVOCAP, a multilocation community action program in Wisconsin, the participation of low-income individuals has been fundamental to the operation of their organization. Their board president has been poor, and his presence has radically changed the conversation about their services. Mike finds that having low-income persons on the boards has improved the agency's sensitivity and understanding of its interactions with its low-income clients.[70]

While community action agencies do not currently sit at the center of the anti-hunger movement, those organizations that were at the hub back in the 1970s and 1980s—Community Nutrition Institute, FRAC, and the Children's Defense Fund—did substantially involve low-income persons in their operations.[71] FRAC partnered with the National Anti-Hunger Coalition (NAHC). Each state elected two NAHC delegates, with one person from an advocacy group and the other a low-income person. The ten largest metropolitan areas sent additional delegates, most of whom were low-income individuals. FRAC raised money, including from the Catholic

Church's Campaign for Human Development, to fund NAHC. These grants brought them together for quarterly meetings (as well as for other purposes) and paid for their related child care expenses. The now-defunct Community Food and Nutrition Program and the Office of Economic Opportunity, established as part of the War on Poverty, also provided funding for groups in each state.

According to Nancy Amidei, the executive director of FRAC during the early 1980s, the low-income participants were primarily women, welfare recipients, and powerful organizers. They played an instrumental role in setting FRAC's policy agenda: "If NAHC didn't agree, FRAC wouldn't work on it."[72] Ed Cooney, a FRAC employee who staffed NAHC, recollects that when the NAHC worked "with anti-hunger advocates at the local, state, regional, and national level, legislative platforms were debated and decided and then presented to Congress by low-income people and anti-hunger advocates."[73]

Amidei emphasizes that the situation of three decades ago differed greatly from today's context. In the 1980s, the infrastructure existed to support this kind of coalition. Many participants came from and were trained by welfare rights organizations, which have largely disappeared. Faith groups were much larger back then and had the resources to support programming. At the university level, social work programs incorporated community participation more so than they do today. Foundations used to support community organizing to a greater degree. And the War on Poverty's mandate to engage the poor in policy matters related to their own well-being stood front and center in the thinking of the day.[74] Unfortunately, by the end of the 1980s, NAHC ran out of funding and disbanded.[75]

In the 1990s and 2000s, the operating methods of anti-hunger groups began to evolve. The entire nonprofit community was becoming more professionalized, as management gurus such as Peter Drucker helped transfer lessons from the business community to NGOs. Foundations became more focused on assessing their return on investment, with the success of long-term community organizing being notoriously challenging to evaluate. Federal programs matured and grew in complexity. Food banking was turning into an established feature of the movement's landscape. Increasingly being cast in a social services model, the field, under the leadership of Second Harvest (now rebranded as Feeding America) became increasingly focused on improving its efficiency, developing new sources of food, and enhancing its food safety practices. Advocacy groups such as FRAC were maturing and institutionalizing, which meant less tolerance for the messy and labor-intensive aspects of community organizing. Professionalism and results trumped social movement building. And maybe community engagement wasn't all that it was cracked up to be. According to Ken Regal of Just Harvest, who cut his teeth in the well-known anti-poverty group ACORN (Association of Community Organizations for Reform Now) in the 1980s, the appearance of community control over the group's agenda was in reality superseded by national staff's directives.[76]

The professionalization of the hunger movement was not, however, a fait accompli. Anti-hunger dissident Robert Egger, founder of the DC Central Kitchen, notes that things could have gone down a different path in the late 1990s. Egger was part of a committee representing the network of prepared food recovery sites, Foodchain, in its merger with Second Harvest. On the table was a proposal to decentralize the combined organization such that the rank and file—the food pantries, soup kitchens and other thousands of agencies that interacted with poor people every day—would have equal power as the 200-odd food banks. A number of the "old guard" vehemently opposed this proposal, instead preferring to keep the focus of the new organization on food banking. Egger believes that this decision resulted in a huge missed political opportunity to build the movement. Had it refocused on the grassroots level, on the food pantries and soup kitchens, it would have been much more politically engaged and more in touch with the poor. Instead, the merged entity remained focused on the politically sanitized matters of food distribution and logistics, allowing it in turn to further become in synch with its corporate donors.[77]

What Limits the Participation of the Poor?

By bringing people on the front lines to the front of the conversation about ending hunger and poverty, we stand to gain insights from their experiences, enabling us to craft more nuanced and effective solutions. Of equal importance, these individuals learn leadership skills as they stand up for themselves. They begin to see themselves as actors in their own lives rather than being acted upon. While society and these individuals have much to gain from fostering their leadership within the anti-hunger movement, it can be very challenging to engage them successfully.

For starters, the poor aren't always invited to the table. The money to recruit them, to pay for their travel and child care expenses can be difficult to find. Joel Berg acknowledges that the process of recruiting people to participate in NY City Coalition Against Hunger's Customer Advisory Board is the hardest part of the organization to fund. "Very few people fund organizing, as it's hard to see the metrics. You have to be intentional about this work: put it into your strategic plan, be intentional, and bust your butt."[78]

The lack of money isn't the only challenge. Organizing is time-consuming work with payback far off on the horizon. Organizers have to invest in relationships. Things go sideways. People's lives can be very messy. Advocates must surrender a degree of control if they are to successfully involve the community. "The egos at the heads of anti-hunger organizations don't want to step back and allow other people to lead," comments Jessica Powers, formerly of WhyHunger.[79]

Organizing can take different forms. In a community organizing model, an organizer listens to an individual's or a neighborhood's concerns and helps facilitate action on that issue. Most anti-hunger groups employ a more targeted approach to organizing. They set the goals and the strategy and mobilize people toward those goals. The Hunger Task Force of Milwaukee (HTFM) and the Alameda County Community Food Bank (ACCFB) ran into a situation in which their clients asked them to advocate on a nonfood related public policy matter, and reacted very differently.[80] When members of ACCFB's Community Advocates Against Hunger committee, comprising roughly 100 food bank clients, identified a bus-pass price increase as threatening their food security, food bank staff recognized that their clients "have only one wallet" with which to pay all their expenses. They collaborated with them to roll back the price increase.[81]

In Milwaukee, the Hunger Task Force, a no less progressive entity than its Oakland counterpart, was presented with exactly the same issue. It took a different path, choosing not to advocate on transportation policy. Sherrie Tussler, the Task Force's executive director comments, "Our area of expertise is hunger and how people get food. We are single mindedly focused on food programs. It dilutes what you are to work on nonfood programs. It becomes mission creep."[82]

Neither approach is right or wrong, but just a different way of setting organizational boundaries and strategy. Alameda County's experience may be more unusual for an organization of its size, but the Bay Area is a uniquely challenging place to work, where well-seasoned activists bristle at top-down hierarchy, especially when found within the nonprofit community.

Reluctance to Participate

Even when invited to participate, many low-income persons hesitate to come to the "anti-hunger table." Many factors intervene to keep them away. They may not feel comfortable at meetings, because of class and race barriers. They may not see others who look like them. The meeting expectations may be foreign to them, or the language used too technical. There may not be child care or translation.

As Janet Poppendieck mentions with regard to the NYC Child Nutrition reauthorization planning meeting, the policy issues being discussed can be so arcane and laden with acronyms that the layperson, even a very educated one, has trouble following them. It takes concerted effort and a long time to come up to speed to be able to effectively contribute on these matters. The poor have so many stressors in their lives that expecting them to find time to participate in social justice activities can be a stretch. Working multiple jobs, often with child-care and transportation challenges, they frequently have insufficient time to spend with their own families or take care of basic household duties. They may be homeless, or face the threat of domestic violence, or even low level of post-traumatic stress disorder from the constant struggles that they face on a daily basis to survive. Poppendieck notes, "You can't expect people to show up without some compensation, something to benefit their lives."[83]

So much shame exists in being poor and receiving food stamps that most people don't want to identify themselves as such. The Children's Alliance in Washington State has invested a significant amount of staff and financial resources into mobilizing the poor, because they believe that process to be essential. But they have no illusions about the challenges they face. Linda Stone, a long-time anti-hunger activist with the alliance, remarks, "The reason why low-income folks don't come to the table to advocate is because they are embarrassed as hell to be using food stamps."[84] Tianna Gaines, a participant in the Philadelphia-based Witnesses to Hunger states, "It's not an easy thing to say I don't have enough money to feed my kids. People are scared that their kids will get taken away from them or they will be harassed."[85]

With the poor taking shame in their economic status, it becomes quite challenging to organize them around issues of hunger and poverty. Susannah Morgan, herself a lesbian, sees parallels with the marriage equality movement. She believes that the poor should be encouraged to come out of the poverty closet: "There will be more acceptance of poverty when everyone knows someone who is poor."[86] Joel Berg acknowledges a similar difficulty: "Another challenge is that Americans who are low-income and food insecure don't want to think of themselves as poor and hungry. In contrast, top goals of other movements were to make African Americans, women, and LGBT people proud of their identity. Yet the greatest goal of low-income and hungry people is usually to escape their condition. It's darn hard to organize among individuals whose top goal is to no longer be a part of the group being organized."[87]

It's also darn hard to organize people when they don't buy into the solutions that you're proposing. One food banker from a western state notes that the group has had a lot of trouble organizing in the region, primarily because the target audience of low-income persons does not feel passionately about federal food programs. They're not buying what the food bank is selling.[88]

All too often, the anti-hunger movement seeks to advocate *for* the poor instead of *with* them. There should be no doubt that federal nutrition programs are key tools for reducing food insecurity. Yet doing things for people instead of with them is never a long-term solution. Like so much of what the hunger movement does, its successes of today don't solve the problem for tomorrow, and they even impede long-term solutions.

Finding Hope

When pressed for signs of hope that the anti-hunger movement will move toward a greater focus on economic justice, many advocates point to a generational transition in the movement's leaderships. In 2013–2014, 58 new executive directors were hired to run food banks.[89] The leaders who started their careers in the 1970s and 1980s are retiring. Some of these are the old guard that blocked Second Harvest from shifting its focus from food banks to grassroots agencies. Younger staffers tend to be more progressive, wanting their groups to embrace a political agenda that addresses the root causes of poverty, but the organizational balance of power has not yet shifted their way. For example, one staff member of Feeding America noted that the organization had a raging debate about the inclusion of economic justice–oriented analyses and solutions within a recent goal-setting document. That debate might not have happened 10 years ago. Other food bankers mention a latent interest in better engaging their low-income clients, but are searching for successful models that they can replicate. Some of the best models for leadership development and for establishing a broad and progressive policy agenda can be found in two organizations, Witnesses to Hunger and Bread for the World.

Mariana Chilton, an ethnographer and public health professor at Drexel University in Philadelphia, launched Witnesses to Hunger in 2008. A researcher who studied the impact of hunger on children's health, she was frustrated when USDA discarded the term "hunger" in favor of "food insecurity." She decided to fund a "photovoice" project with low-income women in the Philadelphia area to personalize the public debate about hunger. This effort blossomed, turning into a full-fledged leadership development initiative, with chapters in nearby Camden, New Jersey, as well as in Boston, Baltimore, New Haven, and Washington, DC.[90]

Tianna Gaines, one of the original Witnesses, explains that her participation has enabled her to "shine a huge light on a conversation that doesn't get talked about. We want the same things as others, but have to work harder to get it. They make us seem weak and lazy. I'm a mythbuster."[91] One way in which Tianna and other Witnesses bust these myths is by maintaining a high profile in the media, having done over 200 interviews, as well as presenting photo exhibits of their stories to Congress. The Witnesses have become in some cases national figures in the anti-hunger sector. Tianna, for example, has testified before Congress. Barbie Izquierdo, another Witness, was featured in the 2013 documentary, *A Place at the Table*, and has since gone on to speak at numerous conferences across the country.

The impact of Witnesses to Hunger has been profound and exciting. It has led to important policy victories, such as the when the Governor of Pennsylvania increased the low-income heating program so that residents could avoid a cut in SNAP benefits.[92] It has also transformed the agenda and programming of major national anti-hunger groups, such as FRAC and Share Our Strength, encouraging greater participation of the food insecure in their conferences and events, for example. The organization has even held its own conference in 2012; one-third of the attendees had personally experienced food insecurity.[93]

Bread for the World has an extensive network of people who, according to its long-time director, Reverend David Beckmann, "make the connection between Jesus and justice." The organization reaches 5,000 Christian congregations, with 100,000 members and leaders in 80 congressional districts. Beckmann contends that as a faith-based organization, Bread for the World has the ability, unlike many secular organizations, to make connections between hunger and poverty through the concept of "manna." Receiving 60,000 sources of funding every year, Bread is not beholden to big corporate interests like many of its fellow organizations. As a result, it is often the only national anti-hunger organization (except for WhyHunger) that participates in actions to support minimum wage increases.[94]

These two groups, and others previously mentioned, have some characteristics in common. They take risks outside of the nutrition safety zone to address the root causes of hunger. They even define the problem as broader than hunger and take action to develop appropriate strategies. They structure their work so that the people they serve lead them, involving them in providing meaningful direction to their organizations. They work in coalitions and seek to break down barriers between fields. They believe in building the capacity of their grassroots partners in order to foster their collective strength.

Summary

Increasingly, the system is stacked against the poor. Living-wage employment with opportunities for advancement has been on the decline for a long time. Job security seems to be a thing of the past. The real value of the poor's wages has stagnated in comparison to the growing wealth of the rich. Their labor is being increasingly exploited, as advances in their productivity do not accrue to them, but to their employers. Even the government programs designed to help the poor are siphoned off by corporate America, or used to tamp down their wages. Their advocates in state capitols and the halls of Congress don't invite them to the table to exercise their leadership as much as they ought to. In short, the poor do not have a seat at the table, nor are they setting the agenda.

Advocates for the poor have been successful in protecting a social safety net that has remained a driving force behind reducing food insecurity over the past 40-plus years. Toward this end, the anti-hunger community has sealed pacts with the business community and their elected representatives. In exchange for tax deductible donations and their lobbying might, anti-hunger groups have burnished corporate reputations while refraining from joining in campaigns that would harm their partners' bottom line.

The anti-hunger community's political pragmatism has no doubt exacted its costs. Its laser focus on food programs to the exclusion of other broader anti-poverty strategies has done little in the way of building the wealth, skills, and leadership capacity of the impoverished. It has allowed the business community to deny its responsibility for having to share the wealth more equitably, placing the onus back on the government. In doing so, it has turned a successful solution for the short-term into a long-term liability, rendering SNAP in particular ever more vulnerable to attack as an outdated means of fostering government dependency.

A singular focus on federal food programs as the exclusive answer to addressing what the British call "food poverty" remains problematic. The 2014 Farm Bill, in which SNAP was cut by $8 billion, could prove to be a harbinger of further more dramatic cuts, depending on which way the political winds shift. The size of the income inequality gulf caused by stagnating wages will not be—and perhaps should not be—reversed by an expansion in federal assistance. The social compact must be reforged to gain the full support of the corporate sector if economic inequality is to be reversed.

Still remaining is the question of whose job it is to move the needle on wage issues, especially in an era of a declining labor movement. Given how the political system rewards specialization and professionalization, conventional wisdom on one level has led the anti-hunger groups to say, "The minimum wage is not my department. That's the responsibility of labor unions." Perhaps expecting anti-hunger groups to work on a broader set of issues beyond their core competence of federal food programs would be to invite mission creep and to, as Jerry Hagstrom stated, doom their current achievements.

The logic of this issue specialization is undermined by the problematic composition of the anti-hunger movement's leadership. The lack of accountability on the part of the movement's professional and middle-class leadership to the poor has shaped their policy agenda. More grassroots participation would likely lead to very different priorities and strategies, especially if they were supported by organizational structures that fostered membership control. The advocate's dilemma might be resolved if the beneficiaries of anti-poverty and anti-hunger policy were more engaged in formulating such policy.

Those different structures might evolve into something very different and be called by a different name than "anti-hunger movement." It might become a more broad-based, anti-poverty or "pro-income mobility movement," a term that, according to the former Atlanta food banker Bill Bolling, resonates better in more conservative regions. It would fit in well with the expanded definition of anti-hunger work described in chapter 1. Moving in this direction will require a concerted effort, building from the experiences of individuals like Bolling, such as Ellen Parker, Mariana Chilton, Joel Berg, Suzan Bateson, Diane Doherty, Frank Tamborello, Sherrie Tussler, and David Beckmann. Following are some recommendations that might help redirect the anti-hunger movement in the direction of getting the poor a seat at the table.

• National and other prominent anti-hunger groups should exercise their leadership by dedicating staff time and resources not only to working on wage and broad anti-poverty issues, but also to actively encouraging their members and partners to do the same. They should also create accountability structures to bring in the voices of the poor such that they have influence on the policy agenda of the organization. Anti-hunger groups at all levels should expand their efforts in these directions, seeking to invest a minimum of one-third of their policy budgets into these long-term solutions.

• Anti-hunger funders should redirect grants and donations toward supporting more grassroots leadership development, community organizing, public policy advocacy on controversial topics such as the minimum wage, and coalition building between labor, anti-poverty, and hunger groups. These funders should make a precondition of granting that organizations have representation of the poor on their boards or create other accountability structures.

• Labor and anti-hunger groups urgently need to build relationships with each other to identify possible areas for collaboration. Two possible areas of cooperation include getting school food services to include labor standards in their bid solicitations and minimum wage campaigns, and to engage in capacity building and grassroots leadership development.

• Anti-hunger groups should focus on identifying and disseminating information about best practices related to grassroots leadership development and engagement on economic justice issues. The Closing the Hunger Gap biannual conference and WhyHunger's Food Security Learning Center present opportunities to share information and build peer-to-peer learning experiences.

• Hunger groups at all levels should make a concerted attempt to educate their funders, members, clients, volunteers and other stakeholders about the need to complement federal food program advocacy with increasing wages. Project Bread in Boston has done an exemplary job of creating such educational materials.

• Vista and AmeriCorps programs such as FoodCorps and the Anti-Hunger and Opportunity Corps should expand their efforts to support nonprofits in their efforts to build broad-based anti-poverty coalitions and organize low-income communities to shape community-based initiatives.

• Anti-hunger groups should set an example and make a public commitment to paying their employees a living wage, based on the local cost of living.

It is not a matter of asking anti-hunger groups to do more, to take on another set of issues on top of their already overflowing plates. Many anti-hunger staffers know what needs to be done. They know they must change direction, shift their models, reallocate resources gradually, experiment and innovate, and support each other in their evolution. All too often, they just don't know how to get there given their current set of resources and the political climate in which they operate. Frankly, what they need to fulfill their moral and pragmatic responsibility is leadership. Where that leadership will come from remains to be seen.

7 Innovation within the Anti-Hunger Movement

Closing the Hunger Gap

During the keynote session at the second Closing the Hunger Gap conference, held in September 2015, the Canadian Nick Saul (see "The Stop" case study below) urged the audience to put a cap on the amount of charitable food they distributed: "If you don't put a lid on it, it will drown you. ... To be able to say yes to some things, you have to say no to others."[1]

The initial Closing the Hunger Gap event, which had been held in Tucson in 2013, came into being as a result of many discussions among progressive anti-hunger leaders in hotel bars and coffee shops at anti-hunger conferences over the years. They were tired of the failure of these conferences to stimulate dialogues on the difficult issues that the anti-hunger movement faced. The conference organizers realized that existing anti-hunger conferences generally do not have an open call for proposals, closing themselves off to new ideas and allies, and that corporate funders for these events were possibly holding back broader discussions. So they created a new event that wasn't funded by corporate behemoths.[2] Held in Portland, Oregon, under the aegis of the Oregon Food Bank, the 2015 event brought together almost 500 persons from 41 states. They represented food banks, pantries, other anti-hunger groups as well as a wide array of other health, labor, and food groups.

Between the 2013 and 2015 events, the tenor of discussions had changed substantially. For example, labor issues were better represented than before through a workshop, plenary speakers, and a field trip. The activists packing the room discussed institutional racism in the emergency food sector, and conveyed a statement to a plenary with suggestions on how to overcome white privilege and racism in the field. The hallways buzzed with discussions about support for minimum wage increases and ways to change charitable food distribution that would foster relationship building between pantries and the impoverished instead of just facilitating a food transaction.

It is clear from these events that change is afoot in the anti-hunger field. A growing number of advocacy groups and food banks are rethinking not only *what* they do, but also *how* they operate. Some of them are expanding into new areas. Many are paying much more attention to the quality of the food they distribute. A few are pushing the policy envelope to prevent hunger rather than just managing it through boxes of food from food banks or federal food programs. Others are involving community members as full partners in their programs, rather than treating them as clients or as the "needy." And a few are rethinking the structure of their organizations so they can better fulfill their missions. Collectively, these entities are reshaping what it means to be an anti-hunger organization.

These changes have been influenced by a number of factors that have created new expectations and established new norms for anti-hunger groups. The advent of the community food security movement in the 1990s created a rationale and an identity through which anti-hunger groups could participate more fully in self-reliance and food system–oriented initiatives. The obesity epidemic, especially as it disproportionately affects the poor and persons of color, has heightened awareness of the connections between diet and health, increasing pressure on anti-hunger groups to improve the nutritional quality of emergency and school food. Similarly, growing attention to the problem of how the poor gain access to food has created new revenue streams and roles for anti-hunger groups, and reframed their responsibilities to include reforming the conventional food system within marginalized communities.

Some food banks report losing donors, as individuals tire of hearing the same lament of increased demand and empty shelves. More sophisticated givers, such as foundations, are putting food banks under greater scrutiny, demanding to see results. They're also insisting that food banks distribute healthier food. Food bankers are realizing that after 30 years of emergency food distribution, they have little to show for their efforts. They have been running on an endless treadmill just trying to meet immediate needs. It has become increasingly apparent that they needed to look for fresh approaches and new strategies to meet their goals.

Central to this search for new models has been the New York City–based group, WhyHunger. Founded in 1975 by the folk singer Harry Chapin and a former priest, Bill Ayres, WhyHunger (once known as World Hunger Year) plays a pivotal and multifaceted role in identifying and supporting innovation in the grassroots anti-hunger field, both domestically and internationally, by fostering a strong movement for food, economic, and racial justice. It helps groups to build their capacity for implementing projects that create food sovereignty and community resilience through providing resources, connecting them with their peers, fostering networks, and encouraging dialogues on the difficult questions. It sees itself as an "ally to organizations, alliances and campaigns that are calling for a minimum wage hike." With a long-term goal of facilitating emergency food programs to organize around issues of economic justice, WhyHunger is building alliances with various organizations and initiatives.[3] Part of its accountability can be traced to its donation policy, which keeps it from accepting financial contributions from organizations that adversely impact the food system.

The group also played a central role in fostering dialogue to raise challenging issues within the Closing the Hunger Gap conference, and has committed resources to help the group of leaders involved in this event to become a more cohesive and organized force for transforming the nature of the charitable food system.

WhyHunger and the emerging Closing the Hunger Gap network have a strong base of support within the food banking community, but they have a long way to go before affecting real change. The growing consensus in food banking is that one-third of groups are conservative, focused only on moving food. Another third is thought to be on the opposite end of the spectrum, deeply involved in experimentation in redefining the role of food banking. The middle third is on the fence, waiting and watching to see in which direction to go. In recent years, this pool of experimenters and innovators has grown substantially from a handful of early adapters to a burgeoning cohort.

Efforts by Anti-Hunger Groups

The sections that follow include a discussion of a number of anti-hunger groups that are implementing innovative programs in the areas of public policy, farming and gardening, race and class awareness, food access, economic development, job training, and nutrition education. These examples were chosen (by no means an exhaustive sampling), as well as the subsequent six in-depth case studies, not because these groups have figured out how to deliver emergency food better than their peers or to advocate more effectively for federal food programs. Instead, they are the ones that shine a light on how the anti-hunger movement can redirect its work toward creating a more just, healthy, and equitable society through improving individuals' health, bettering their economic conditions, catalyzing their participation in shaping their own destinies, and fostering a more just and democratic food system. These are groups that are moving beyond charity into a more holistic vision of what anti-hunger work should be.

Public Policy

Public policy is divisive, messy, and time consuming, and it yields an uncertain payoff. Despite these challenges, there are few, if any, more powerful ways than public policy to affect food security—either in a negative or positive fashion. The typical anti-hunger policy agenda focuses on protecting and expanding safety net programs such as SNAP, school meals, and WIC. Most food banks also advocate for policies that strengthen the emergency food system through providing tax breaks to businesses for food donations, and increasing funding for programs that provide commodity food and cash allotments to food banks. This section examines some of the most forward-thinking anti-hunger groups—those that advocate for more fundamental social and economic change, and those that organize and engage low-income community members to be effective spokespersons.

Hunger Action Network of New York State (HANNYS) seeks to reduce hunger today (e.g., increase funding for emergency food, stronger food stamp programs, more community gardens) while finding long-term solutions such as universal health care, living wage jobs, and affordable housing. HANNYS hosts the Empire State Economic Security Campaign (ES2), which promotes an array of policy changes to increase the living standards of the working poor: a higher state minimum wage, affordable housing, health care, creation of living-wage jobs, accessible child care, and expanded public assistance benefits. The group helped to gain an increase in the minimum wage in New York State, and collaborated with other groups in a campaign to increase personal income tax rates on the wealthiest New Yorkers. When most food banks and anti-hunger groups were distancing themselves from the Occupy campaigns of 2011, HANNYS staff members were heavily involved in the Wall Street protests.[4]

In Oakland, California, the clients of the Alameda County Community Food Bank have organized themselves into a community-based advisory committee that shapes the food bank's policy agenda. The committee advocates on anything that affects the bottom line of low-income persons in the county, such as minimum wage, housing subsidies, childcare, even the cost of bus passes. The food bank also enters into the electoral fray, to the extent that a nonprofit can engage in officeholder campaigns by hosting candidate forums on poverty-related issues.[5]

Hunger Free Colorado has established a Colorado Food Pantry Network in part to leverage the collective power of food pantries in the state as an advocate for public policies.[6] The main food bank in the Denver area, the Food Bank of the Rockies does not have a public policy presence.[7]

Race and Class Awareness

Racism is a contributing factor to the disproportionate rates of poverty and food insecurity among persons of color. Most anti-hunger groups, especially those that are better resourced, tend to be led by white staff and board members. Unfortunately, very few anti-hunger organizations are tackling this exceedingly challenging topic head-on. Solid Ground in Seattle, Washington, is the rare exception. This organization operates a suite of programs—including shelters, community farms, job training, nutrition education, cooking classes, and support to local emergency food providers—designed to reduce homelessness and hunger. They target internal challenges first, by educating staff about institutional racism and the ways to undo it. They seek to increase the representation of people of color on staff and board, and critically evaluate the cultural competency of their services. Second, on an external level, they educate the broader community through anti-racism events and by promoting anti-racism work with other area nonprofit organizations.[8]

Farming and Gardening

Many food banks have chosen to operate or support gardening and farming operations. These initiatives combine efforts to increase food security with community building, healthy food access, job training, and support for local food systems. Groups such as the Atlanta Community Food Bank

(Georgia) and the Community Food Bank of Southern Arizona operate community gardening initiatives. Community gardening appeals to food banks because it helps them meet their community building and food security goals.

Numerous food banks operate their own farms, often to increase the amount of fresh produce going into their own donation stream. Some groups, such as the Capital Area Food Bank (DC) and the Western Massachusetts Food Bank, cover part of the costs of the farming operation through operating a community-supported agriculture program (CSA), selling a portion of the farm's production to consumers. Some employ innovative sources of labor, such as the Food Bank of Iowa, which partners with a correctional facility. Others recognize that the farm can provide many benefits beyond food production. While the Hunger Task Force of Milwaukee's (Wisconsin) 150-acre farm supplies 300,000 pounds of produce for the food bank, it also includes a youth environmental education component as well as a job-training program. It even has a fish hatchery that stocks Milwaukee lagoons with 48,000 fish for youth fishing opportunities.[9]

Other organizations host an integrated set of production, education, and marketing programs that bolster the local food system. The Community Food Bank of Southern Arizona operates a 2.5-acre production and youth education farm, a demonstration garden, assistance to home gardeners with information and resources, and various farmers markets. The Interfaith Food Shuttle (Raleigh, North Carolina) runs an amazingly comprehensive set of programs that includes hiring youth from low-income neighborhoods to work on local farms and gardens, supporting local community gardens, providing educational workshops combined with farm tours, and hosting an alliance of farmers in the Piedmont region of the state.[10]

Food Access

Recognizing that many hungry persons live in food deserts, some food banks have sought to improve the offerings in these underserved areas. These efforts represent an important new direction for food banks as they seek to reform the conventional food system through which even the poorest of the poor obtain the vast majority of their food. It is an example of how food banks' roles are shifting to promote health and food security beyond established emergency food system channels.

Access to healthy affordable food can be challenging in Pittsburgh, Pennsylvania, as the city's hilly terrain and three rivers create a patchwork of isolated neighborhoods. In response, the Greater Pittsburgh Community Food Bank has operated farm stands in underserved communities since 1993. The food bank purchases products from local farmers, partnering with community groups in each neighborhood and employing local residents to staff the stands. Cooking demonstrations and recipes are offered as well, to encourage purchases.

Economic Development

Some food banks are supporting economic development activities in their regions, as a tool for "shortening the line" and generating community wealth. They're largely focused on supporting local food and farming businesses. South Carolina's Lowcountry Food Bank runs the Growing Food Locally program. Funded in part by the Community Food Project program (see chapter 9), it helps "small-scale farming enterprises become profitable through professional training, free consultations, small pay advances, and a guaranteed safety net purchase of pre-selected crops."[11] Since 2007, the Food Bank has bought more than a half-million pounds from participating farmers for distribution through its emergency food channels. In Huntsville, Alabama, the Food Bank of North Alabama has established a revolving loan fund for local farmers, ranchers, and others who need capital to run their small businesses. It is establishing itself as a community-developed financial institute to facilitate providing access to credit for local producers.[12] In Detroit, Gleaners Community Food Bank of Southeastern Michigan offers fresh produce boxes to community agencies, the contents of which are purchased from regional farmers. Some 75 to 100 percent of the produce is Michigan grown, depending on the season.[13]

Job Skills and Employment Opportunities

Similarly, many food banks are recognizing that a portion of their clients need extra help in entering the workforce or in taking charge of their lives. In response to this need, these groups are providing job-readiness training, helping individuals build their skills in a certain field, and supporting their transition out of poverty. Many of these programs are oriented toward youth or individuals considered to be at-risk, perhaps because they are homeless, have little formal education, or have been in correctional facilities.

Perhaps the best known and most emulated of these is the DC Central Kitchen (DCCK), which has spawned similar efforts in numerous organizations across the country. DCCK whose motto is "combatting hunger, creating opportunity," trains unemployed persons, the homeless and formerly incarcerated persons for jobs in the foodservice industry. In addition to building skills in specific restaurant fields, the employees also take classes to foster their personal growth. The group runs a catering business, prepares 5,000 school meals daily for low-income kids in DC, and buys much of its produce from regional farms.[14]

In the panhandle of Texas, the South Plains Food Bank operates the Growing Recruits for Urban Business (GRUB) program to "teach young adults, ages 14 to 21, life and job skills using our farm and community gardens as a backdrop to this education."[15]

While most food banks try to help as many people as possible through providing food donations, the Food Bank of Northern Nevada in Reno also employs a "high touch" approach to help individuals find their way out of poverty. Using the "bridges out of poverty" model, it runs a 16-week group training program to help participants "learn how to set future goals to move towards prosperity through coaching and facilitation led by Food Bank staff members."[16]

Nutrition Education

An increasing number of anti-hunger organizations are starting to reframe the opposite of being "hungry," and thus describe it not as being fed but as being healthy. In this context, they seek to equip their clients with the food and skills to improve their health. These efforts can be challenging, as cooking skills have been vanishing for decades. Home economics is no longer taught in schools. Public expenditures on nutrition education are a pittance compared to what industry spends on advertising unhealthy foods. The budget for the nation's largest nutrition education program, SNAP-Ed is $408 million in fiscal year 2016.[17] By way of comparison, the food industry spent $4.2 billion on advertising fast food in 2010.[18]

Food banks are trying to fill a huge hole caused by our societal inattention to this matter. Erik Talkin, the executive director of the Foodbank of Santa Barbara County (California) says, "One of the most powerful things a food bank can do is to work to assist the ability of the millions of people we work with to improve their own ability to look after their nutritional health, by improving their food literacy. This is not window dressing, it truly helps people take control of their own situation and health."[19] Many food banks are filling this gap with Share Our Strength's (SOS) Cooking Matters program, a six-week course in planning, purchasing, and preparing healthy food.[20]

In New York City, Just Food assists food pantries to acquire farm-fresh locally grown foods, while providing hands-on education opportunities through farm visits. In addition, they also train community members of diverse backgrounds to become "community chefs," who present cooking demonstrations at farmers markets, community gardens, food pantries, and community events.[21]

Putting It All Together

Under executive director Ellen Parker's leadership, Boston's Project Bread has arguably become one of the most forward-looking anti-hunger groups in the nation. Its comprehensive framework links food security to efforts to promote public health, food systems, and economic justice through policy, programs, and coalition building across Boston and Massachusetts. At the policy level, it has gained numerous victories over the years, such as a bill in 2010 that limited the sale of unhealthy food in schools. Its leadership in creating the Massachusetts Food Policy Council has led to a landmark effort to create a food systems plan for the commonwealth, one of the few states to undertake such an effort. It still advocates on federal food programs, but does so with an emphasis on promoting public health, economic justice, and local food systems.[22]

Project Bread also hosts the Massachusetts Farm to School Project, linking over 100 farms and 200 school districts to advocate for healthy local food in the commonwealth's schools and preschools. This initiative is part of a broader effort to not only increase access to school meals for low-income children, but also to dramatically improve their quality. To this end, Project Bread works in partnership with school districts to identify procurement, meal planning, and training resources that they can employ.

Project Bread is very active in programmatic work in communities across the state, connecting SNAP recipients with community-supported agriculture farms and teaching cooking classes at the Boston Public Market. The organization also plays an active role in educating the public about the importance of raising the minimum wage in addressing hunger. What fuels all of these programs is the Walk for Hunger, which, as described in chapter 1, raises a few million dollars annually from tens of thousands of individuals while strengthening the region's sense of community.[23]

The rest of this chapter examines the work of six organizations from across North America that are transforming the way anti-hunger work is done. In the Pacific Northwest, the Oregon Food Bank is catalyzing community organizing in rural parts of the state to help build self-reliance and improve access to healthy food. Five hundred miles south along the Pacific Coast, the Second Harvest Food Bank of Santa Cruz County is among a growing number of food banks that are switching their focus to creating health rather than fighting hunger, while building community leadership in the process. In Toronto, The Stop, once an emergency food program, has spawned a national network of community food centers to help residents grow, cook, and gain access to healthy affordable food. Also in Toronto, the Freedom 90 Union of food bank and emergency food volunteers is petitioning the provincial government to make food banks obsolete. Just Harvest, in Pittsburgh, is focused on creating economic justice through broad-based policy change.

Oregon Food Bank: Eliminating Hunger and Its Root Causes

Separating the fertile farmlands of Oregon's Willamette Valley from the Pacific Ocean, the Coast Range comprises low-slung mountains reaching 4,000 feet at their highest, These verdant rolling hills are far less grandiose than the volcanic snow-capped peaks of the Cascades that border the eastern side of the valley. Small towns dot the Coast Range, one of which is Alsea (pronounced All-see). Located 25 miles southwest of the college town of Corvallis, and 45 miles east from the coast, Alsea is a damp hamlet, with an annual rainfall of 92 inches. Its population of 160, with another thousand or so in the environs, has been declining for many years, due to the downturn of the logging industry across the state, and more specifically to the shuttering of a nearby US Forest Service station.

On one Saturday in April, Alsea is the site of a FEAST (Food Education Agriculture Solutions Together) community meeting, sponsored by the Oregon Food Bank (OFB) and the Ten Rivers Food Web. This gathering brings 30 people into the multipurpose room of a local church for two hours of discussion about the local food system. Seated in hard plastic chairs at long folding tables covered in plaid plastic tablecloths, the attendees include local farmers and ranchers, the church pastor, the town librarian, and other concerned community members. Before the meeting gets started, they nibble on sandwiches and pasta salad prepared by local high school students, and chit-chat in the casual manner of small town residents who have known each other for decades. Despite the friendly banter, an air of concern hangs over the room.

The meeting starts with members marking on a map their community's food assets, such as farms, grocery stores, and gardens. It continues with a discussion of the challenges in the community's food system. Alsea's physical isolation results in residents traveling long distances for grocery shopping, burning expensive fuel to do so. The local store offers some groceries, but like most small stores it tends to be costly. A mudslide would render Highway 34 impassable, cutting the town off from food deliveries. Many residents don't have stocked pantries or extensive knowledge about food preservation.

Moving on to a discussion of their priorities for improving the food system, the participants brainstorm that they would like to develop cooking classes, set up a buying club, support local farms through selling shares of their produce in a community supported agriculture (CSA) arrangement, and inventory local knowledge and resources. The discussions flow smoothly and conclude with the attendees agreeing to hold a daylong meeting to help them plan for the implementation of these ideas.

Key to the success of this event is the presence and expert facilitation of Sharon Thornberry, OFB's community food systems program manager. Sharon is at ease with the community, having worked in Alsea off and on since the late 1980s. She lives in the next town over, and is even what she describes as "shirt tail" relatives with one of the couples. The existence of the FEAST program and the organization's increasing attention to community food security has been because of Sharon's consummate networking skills, vision, and tireless advocacy.

Part Cherokee, Sharon grew up on a small family farm in Iowa. After her family lost the farm, they moved to North Carolina, where she spent the rest of her childhood. With only a high school education, she found herself a young mom with two small children living in Houston when her husband left. Forced to turn to food stamps, she struggled to come out of poverty, and moved to Oregon in the mid-1980s, where she landed a job promoting gleaning—a method of recovering crops from field and factory for redistribution among populations in need—through the local food bank. Constantly driving from one end of the state to the other in her red Jetta, Sharon has a pulse on the needs and opportunities of rural communities across Oregon. Similarly, she is able to bring lessons learned from the national context to rural communities, having served as president of the board of the Community Food Security Coalition, and as a member of the board of the faith-based anti-hunger group Bread for the World. Having won Oregon Public Health Institute's Public Health Genius Award in 2009, she is highly respected for her work trying to improve access to healthy food and support local growers across Oregon.

The Alsea event was the 51st FEAST gathering OFB had organized, most of which have taken place in rural areas. The goals of the FEAST program are as much to build community as they are to reduce hunger and support local agriculture. Meetings in other locales have led to the expansion of farm to school programs, the creation of community gardens and farmers markets, and the formation of regional action networks.[24]

The FEAST program has gained a lot of interest, with it now being used in 13 states.[25] Similarly, in 2013, a panel of peers chose the FEAST program for Feeding America's first Innovation Award in the "Lead" category. FEAST is an important but not the only initiative under OFB's Community Food Security umbrella. This program area has helped a dozen rural communities produce comprehensive food assessments as a first step toward taking action to improving their food system.[26] In the coastal town of Astoria, FEAST's assessment led to the creation of a radio talk show, nutrition classes, four school gardens, and various public education events.[27] Likewise, Ameri-Corps volunteers through the Food Bank have helped six communities produce local food guides to help residents purchase locally grown food in their counties.[28]

Oregon Food Bank's role as a national leader transcends the fantastic work of Sharon Thornberry and the Community Food Security program.

The group's commitment to end hunger through fostering self-reliance and community economic development is much more than an offshoot of OFB's efforts. It is at the heart of what the food bank does. The forward-looking vision of OFB, as an organization that not only distributes emergency food but also seeks to reduce demand on food banks, is their mission statement: "To eliminate hunger and its root causes ... *because no one should be hungry.*" Revised in the 1990s by the former board president and associate editor of the *Oregonian* newspaper, Jerry Tippens, this one sentence has served as the driving force behind the organization's embrace of Sharon's efforts its own initiative to enact some of the most progressive policy advocacy of any food bank.

Thanks to the vision of its long-time executive director Rachel Bristol, OFB created one of the first public policy departments of any food bank anywhere back in the 1990s. In the late 1990s and into the 2000s, OFB took stances on public policy issues above and beyond support for federal food programs or expanding TEFAP. According to Kim Thomas, the former director of the public policy department, "During that time we supported minimum wage increases and held fast even when some of our food donors strongly disagreed with us. We pushed for limits on payday loans and reframed hunger as an income issue versus a charity issue."[29] Today, OFB has one of the largest if not the largest public policy departments of any food bank in the country, with eight full-time staff members, four who do direct lobbying, and four who do community organizing.

In 2010, OFB's public policy stances took a turn toward the center when the board chose not to follow the staff's and its own Policy Advocacy Committee's recommendations to endorse Oregon Ballot Measures 66 and 67. These were controversial initiatives designed to improve the state's fiscal situation through progressive taxation on corporations and high-wealth individuals (both measures passed). In hindsight, policy staff has speculated that the reasons for the board's decision may have rested with its reluctance to offend high-wealth donors and corporate partners and its concern about mission creep. The fallout from this turn of events tarnished the OFB's sterling liberal credentials, but clarified the limits of the organization's policy stances. But by 2015 the food bank had returned to its more progressive policy stances, advocating for a phased-in minimum wage of $13, indexed to inflation.[30] It also established a wage floor of $14 per hour for its own employees.[31]

As much as any food bank in the nation, OFB is poised to lead the way toward a new model of food banking. Its success will be shaped by the leadership of its current executive director Susannah Morgan (as of 2016) to ensure that the organization can maintain a balance between meeting today's needs while catalyzing long-term change to ensure that all Oregonians have the right to healthy and affordable food.

Second Harvest Food Bank of Santa Cruz County: Community Empowerment for Health

Willy Elliott-McCrea has been the executive director of the Second Harvest Food Bank of Santa Cruz County for a quarter century. He possesses a calm demeanor and quiet presence until you get him going, and then he rattles off his analysis of the current state of food banking: "The world has fundamentally changed since I started food banking in the 1970s. Calories are cheap. Inequality is rising. The middle class is on the decline. The underclass is growing. It's not a matter of short-term clients anymore. We can't use the same strategies in the face of chronic need."[32]

As one of the more visionary food bankers, Elliot-McCrea draws from a wide range of topics in conversation. He moves easily between lamenting the "rise in the Gini co-efficient" (a measurement of a nation's income inequality), lambasting the toxicity of soda ("Sugar is the enemy," he says), and laying out his vision for food banking ("Food banks have to come out of their caves. They need to be networked with social services more"). Having worked at the food bank for 35 years, Elliott-McCrea's trajectory and the food bank's story are in many ways intertwined. He started as a driver, warehouse worker, and purchasing agent in 1978, after studying community development at University of California, Santa Cruz. In 1988, he became the food bank's executive director. Sadly, a year later the Loma Prieta earthquake devastated Watsonville, the town in which the food bank was located; 900 homes were destroyed and 25,000 people were forced to live in the parks. The quake transformed the organization. It went from serving 15,000 to 100,000 persons overnight, an especially daunting challenge for a declining institution with a shrinking donor base. Nonetheless, the food bank received an infusion of resources that Elliott-McCrea was able to parlay into new initiatives and a more robust organization. As it adapted to its first real exposure to the larger community, the food bank changed its name to Second Harvest Food Bank.

Sixteen years later, in 2005, Elliott-McCrea was diagnosed with colon cancer and underwent surgery. The six-week recovery period transformed his life, and consequently reshaped the organization's focus. To understand the Second Harvest Food Bank's transformation, it is helpful to know a bit more about Santa Cruz County, the community the food bank serves. Located on the central coast of California between Monterey and San Francisco, Santa Cruz County typically conjures visions of redwood forests, surfers, organic food, and hippies. Santa Cruz County and surrounding areas also have some of the most productive farmlands in the nation, yielding much of the country's lettuce, broccoli, artichoke, garlic, strawberry, and raspberry production. Farms in the area employ tens of thousands of farmworkers, 25,000 of which live in the town of Watsonville.

The demographics of Watsonville are startling. In 2009, unemployment reached 27 percent and has dropped to 8.8 percent by May 2015, still above the state rate of 6.5 percent.[33] According to Elliott-McCrea, child obesity rates in Watsonville are double that of Santa Cruz. The median household income from 2009 to 2013 in Watsonville was $43,905 annually, about 70 percent of the state average of $61,094.[34] In Watsonville 87 percent of residents are Latino as compared to 37 percent of California residents overall.[35] Watsonville is "like a third-world country, a place where a lot of people begin their American journey, Elliott-McCrea says."[36] While parts of the County, such as Watsonville, are quite destitute, the place is awash in produce.

Elliott-McCrea's recovery period made him realize the importance of cleaning up his own diet. He had been what he calls a "Mikey food banker," willing to take in and distribute any type of food. He notes, "For 25 years I had rationalized that giving out so many snacks, sweets, and sodas was fine, since all kids deserved special treats." He realized that in doing so he was harming the very people he was trying to help. He found that there was no shortage of poor quality food in impoverished communities, but what residents really needed—and wanted—was healthy fresh foods.[37]

Once he got back to work, Elliott-McCrea set about changing the food bank's direction toward "nutrition banking," in which the goal of the organization wasn't just to increase the pounds of food it distributed. Instead, Second Harvest focused on helping people to eat better and become healthier. Doing so required that clients be given more healthful food encouraged to actually consume it. It also meant catalyzing a fundamental shift in the way many emergency food recipients viewed themselves, from being a victim to taking charge of their own lives.

In 2010 the organization became one of the first food banks to stop distributing soda and energy drinks. Many food bankers, while ambivalent about distributing unhealthy products such as soft drinks, have continued this policy. Elliott-McCrea came to believe that by distributing soda the food bank was harming the very people it was supposed to be helping. He was quick to recognize that he held the upper hand in this matter. He inverted the power relations between donor and recipient, and using his moral authority, simply decided that the food bank would no longer accept these donations. While this decision did slightly reduce the weight of the food they were distributing, it also boosted employee morale dramatically. Second Harvest employees tend to be "health nuts," and this simple decision made them much more proud to work there.

Not only did the food bank stop giving out unhealthy foods, such as soda, it also dramatically increased its distribution of healthy foods, especially California-grown fruits and vegetables. In 2015, five million of a total eight million pounds of food distributed is produce.[38] Most of it came from the California Association of Food Banks' Farm to Family program, with a smaller but significant share from local farms.

Recognizing that dietary habits can be difficult to change, food bank staffers didn't just hand out bags of fresh fruits and vegetables. They acknowledged that their clients would need some extra help in knowing what to do with fresh foods that often were outside their cultural norms. To address this gap, they created the Passion for Produce program. In this initiative, participants attend a series of classes designed to help them improve their health. The classes focus on nutrition education, cooking demonstrations, and physical activity. Participants take home fresh produce bags weighing about 25 pounds and receive on-going peer support to help them stick to their resolution to lead healthier lives. The classes are led by trained community members known as *embajadores* (nutrition ambassadors), and tend to be discussion-oriented, allowing individuals the opportunity to reach their own, and more powerful, conclusions about the connections between diet and health. To date, over 3,900 unduplicated persons have attended the classes.[39] The results of the program are impressive, according to a survey of participants. Seventy eight percent have lost weight. Ninety one percent have decreased the amount of soda they drink. Ninety six percent of respondents report increasing their consumption of fresh fruit and vegetables.[40]

In addition to the benefits it provides to participants, the Passion for Produce program has fostered community-based leadership in the county, having established a cadre of more than 300 individuals as nutrition ambassadors. These individuals, many of whom have never been asked to be community leaders before, go through a six-week training course. This program is based upon an asset-based community development approach, which holds that communities and individuals have the resources at their disposal to resolve their own problems. This approach maintains that well-intentioned middle-class outsiders, such as food bankers, can play a meaningful role in helping, but ultimately cannot solve poor people's problems for them.

Part of Second Harvest's rationale for its focus on providing healthy food is the recognition that poor health can be a driver of poverty. A diet based on cheap foods of low nutritional value often leads to disease, which can reduce earnings through diminished productivity and increased absenteeism. Similarly, steep medical expenses can drive a working-class family into poverty and aggravate food insecurity. This becomes a vicious cycle. As medical expenses consume more of a family's limited budget, less money becomes available for groceries. As a result, the family resorts to purchasing cheaper, more filling food, forgoing more expensive and healthier options, further aggravating the spiral into poor health.

When combined with a community development approach, Second Harvest's health focus takes a new twist. It becomes about helping people to take charge of their lives through improving their own health. It is the opposite of a charity model in which a poor person is a recipient, his or her powerlessness reinforced by the top-down nature of the transaction with the food pantry. Instead, Second Harvest provides people with the tools to better understand the implications of their food and exercise choices and how to navigate a food system that is stacked against them.

As much as the food bank helps individuals to become healthier, it also fosters healthier communities through developing a new set of leaders. The actions of the *embajadores* not only strengthen the social networks and ties between neighbors in the county's low-income communities, but also empower these individuals to work on behalf of their neighborhoods on matters of concern to them, such as education. Many of these individuals will likely carry the experience of the Passion for Produce program with them throughout their entire lives, preparing them for greater success and service. The increased community resilience created by such a program is no small task in towns such as Watsonville, with a high degree of poverty and transience.

There are many pathways Second Harvest could have taken to accomplish its core goal of building community and family self-reliance. Staffers acknowledge that they have a core asset of inexpensive, amazingly fresh produce that can not only provide people with top-shelf nourishment, but also create an entry point for providing other benefits to society, such as fostering leadership development. They also recognize the constraints under which the food bank operates. It is a coalition of sorts that conservatives and liberals alike support. (Although Santa Cruz is a very liberal county, Elliott-McCrea contends that liberals are not known for their generosity.) A focus on public health doesn't threaten this big tent approach, in the same way that a more overtly political emphasis would. The food bank refrains from wading into contentious policy change, such as tax policy or the minimum wage, which might fracture the coalition. Instead it chooses to focus on public policy on which there is general consensus, such as the SNAP program.

Perhaps Second Harvest's greatest contribution is a sense of perspective about its purpose. Elliott-McCrea speaks often about the importance of "shortening the line," for instance by reducing demand for the food bank's services, as compared to merely "feeding the need," or distributing food. He sums up his philosophy: "Too many food bankers get hung up on trucks, docks, and warehouses, and they forget that their real goal is to get families on their feet."[41]

The Stop: Solidarity Not Charity

It's almost lunchtime at the drop-in room at The Stop, a multifaceted community food center in Toronto. All of the hard blue plastic chairs at the 10 round tables are filled, as folks wait quietly or chat with their neighbor. Pop music fills the air, and volunteers buzz about in the kitchen making preparations for the midday meal.

Nick Saul, The Stop's former executive director, hasn't been here for a few months, so there are a lot of staffers, volunteers, and community members to catch up with. Extraordinarily gregarious, he starts chatting with a man at the next table. Dave, who is wearing a black cowboy hat, sleeveless t-shirt, and glasses, receives welfare and lives in the cheapest apartment building in town: $569 per month rent, utilities included, for a 9 foot × 20 foot bachelor flat. His asthma is aggravated by the cockroach infestation in his place. To pass the time, he walks 10 miles a day.

Rewind back to 1998, when Saul was hired to run The Stop, a food pantry in a diverse low-income neighborhood of Toronto. As chronicled in *The Stop: How the Fight for Good Food Transformed a Community and Inspired a Movement*, a book co-written with his wife, Andrea Curtis, The Stop was a fairly typical food pantry, rundown and on the edge, with little that was innovative or dignified about it.

What ensued was a fascinating 15-year journey toward a new model of an anti-hunger organization that strives to "increase access to healthy food in a manner that increases dignity, builds community and challenges inequality."[42] The journey started with Saul and his colleagues asking themselves and their community some very basic questions: Is handing out food a pathway out of poverty? Is providing charity a dignified way of addressing the community's food needs? Is there a better way to run The Stop?

Soon after taking the helm, Saul insisted that the organization honor the dignity of the recipients. They started referring to the recipients as members rather than clients. They made changes to the physical space, and improved the quality of the food they offered. He insisted that they would no longer accept dead bananas or limp carrots, and they rejected industrial food experiments. He believed that these cast-offs only made recipients feel like second-class citizens. Nick believed that the members of The Stop should not have to check their humanity at the door, just because they are poor. These changes rubbed some people the wrong way. Richard, one of the key volunteers in charge of procuring the leftovers from neighborhood grocery stores, didn't appreciate the change in policy and quit. He believed that any food is better than nothing when one is broke and hungry.

Seeing that the food pantry experience provided limited value as a tool for social change, and that it caused a "slow painful death of the spirit," Saul and his staff realized that they would need to limit the energy they put into the emergency food parts of the organization. "[We] held firm to our conviction that we need to place limits on the resources we put toward the food bank or it would consume us entirely."[43] They were changing the way they think of themselves, from a service delivery organization to a social change organization that delivers good services.[44]

Step by step, The Stop started to add programs, becoming a more comprehensive and integrated community food center. The center added a gardening program and a farm stand to build community and bring healthy foods into their underserved neighborhood. It led a multiyear, multimillion-dollar initiative to transform part of an abandoned streetcar repair facility in a wealthy part of town into what is now known as The Green Barn, a gorgeously remodeled facility hosting a weekly farmers market, greenhouse, gardens, bake oven, and commercial kitchen. The Stop started to partner with a local farm, to help market its produce in local stores with a percentage of profits going back to fund The Stop's programs. In turn, The Stop became the farm's biggest customer, using its produce in programs and meals. It created a catering business that funds some of its core operating expenses and increases the visibility of its organization among the city's well-to-do population.

Given that 77 percent of the center's members receive some form of government assistance, The Stop staffers decided that it was important to advocate for expanded government benefits. They sponsored two aptly named campaigns to draw attention to the inadequacy of public safety-net programs. The Do the Math campaign asked Ontario residents to calculate via a web-based survey how much money a frugal person would need to spend on basics. On average, participants calculated that a single person would require $1,500 per month to get by, two and a half times the average welfare payment of $600 per month. This campaign asked participants to communicate to their elected officials about the need to fully fund safety-net programs.

The second campaign, titled "Eat the Math," provided well-known Toronto residents with a typical box of food from a food pantry and asked them to try to live on it for as long as possible. The participants then communicated publicly about their experiences. The purpose of the initiative was not to denigrate the food handed out by the emergency food system, but to indict the inadequacies of the welfare system that force so many people to rely on handouts for survival. Unlike food stamp challenges in the United States, this campaign was guided by community members, who have self-organized into the Bread and Bricks Davenport West Social Justice Group. They set the ground rules for the initiative based on their real-life experiences, seeking to replicate the isolation and limited choices that people living in poverty face.[45]

These two advocacy efforts illustrate the way in which Nick and the staff at The Stop think about the organization's role in fighting poverty. First, they see the role of the middle class and wealthy as not just check writers, assuaging their guilt, but as fundamental allies in the cause. They see multiclass organizing and programs that are universal in nature, rather than solely targeted to the poor, as the most durable and impactful. Similarly, The Stop's relationship with its members goes beyond the transactional nature of a food pantry or food program. By engaging and empowering the members, the center seeks to create fundamental social change. A simplified version of its mission statement might read, "Solidarity, not charity."

Popular demand for creating hometown versions of The Stop has led Nick Saul and his colleagues to create a new organization, Community Food Centres Canada. CFCC has raised $15 million to create new community food centers across the country. As of fall 2015, they have launched two pilot sites in Ontario, as well as centers in Toronto, Halifax, and Winnipeg, with two more under development in Calgary and Hamilton.[46] These centers will combine dignified food programs and services for low-income people with advocacy support and food system transformation projects. Saul describes these centers as "combining the energy and passion of the consumer side of the good food revolution with a justice perspective and an eye to social, political, and economic policy that benefits everyone."[47]

Integrating multiple programs under one roof, a characteristic model of The Stop and future Community Food Centres, adds a value beyond convenience or potential synergies. It is a model that chooses not to marginalize the poor under the rubric of charity, but to foster alliances across social classes and ethnicities. By including charity as part of a broader strategy, secondary to social change, it inverts how the emergency food system typically functions. Finally, The Stop shows that the way in which we provide for the food needs of society's most vulnerable is an indicator of how democratic our society is. Either they can be passive consumers of corporate leftovers or full participants—members, in The Stop's parlance. It's our choice.

Freedom 90: The Church Ladies Rebel against Perpetual Charity

What if the little old ladies who run the neighborhood church food pantry rebelled? What if they said, "We're 70 years old, we've been feeding people for 20 years, and hell if we want to do it for another 20"? What if they demanded that the government reduce the incidence of poverty so that food pantries don't need to exist in the first place?

Hard to imagine? Well, that's exactly what has happened in the Canadian province of Ontario. With the support of an experienced community organizer, emergency meal program, and food bank (what we call a food pantry in most of the United States) volunteers have decided to form a "union." They're calling it Freedom 90, a spoof on the "Freedom 55" financial planning advertisements that promise the good life to Canadians who work hard and invest their savings wisely, so they can retire by 55. Tongue in cheek yet deadly serious, these volunteers want to "retire" by the time they hit 90. They are tired of the perpetual emergency, of providing free food boxes every week for the past two decades, but compelled to continue because of the need they see in their communities.

They believe that "poverty is being 're-branded' as 'hunger' to mask its cause: inadequate incomes, which are due to low wages, precarious work, and social assistance levels too low to provide adequate housing and food." They hold that every resident of the province has "the right to health and dignity, including enough income to pay the rent and buy food." A "separate and segregated food system for people with low incomes" is undignified, humiliating, unsustainable, and inefficient in their opinion.[48] Clarifying their position on the emergency food system, they add:

We're not advocating the closing of food banks, rather we want to make food banks obsolete—unnecessary. ... Food banks are not bad, but charity has real limitations. Food Banks are addressing a gap in society and it is the gap that we need to close to remove the need for people to rely on food banks in the first place. ... And the other obvious question here is—why should anyone have to rely on left-over food in the first place? ... In no way is it legitimate to keep food banks open and keep people in poverty so we have something to do with the leftover food that we as consumers are responsible for.[49]

The idea for the union came out of a five-year-old campaign to reduce poverty in Ontario, the Put Food in the Budget campaign. The primary goal of the campaign was to gain an immediate $100 per month increase in social assistance checks, both to reduce hunger and as a down payment toward poverty reduction. The Put the Food in the Budget campaign held a meeting in June 2011 with the volunteer church ladies, and the idea for the union came organically out of "really good organizing and popular education."[50] The union launched in May 2012 on a wing and a prayer, and has since enrolled one hundred members. Knowing that humor can be a very effective organizing tool, they have made three demands:

1. *Lay us off!* The Government of Ontario must ensure that social assistance and minimum wage levels are sufficient for everyone to have adequate housing and to buy their own food.

2. *Mandatory retirement by the age of 90!* Many of us have been volunteering for twenty years and there is no end in sight. The Freedom 90 Union demands the Government of Ontario take urgent action to end poverty and make food banks and emergency meal programs unnecessary.

3. *Freeze our wages! Or double them!* It doesn't matter because we are unpaid volunteers.[51]

Continuing this exploration with the civic engagement of the food pantry volunteers, Mike Balkwill, the veteran campaign organizer from Put Food in the Budget, pulled together a meeting in the city of Newmarket, 30 miles north of Toronto, to explore what (if anything) the volunteers and the food pantry recipients shared in common. Talking together for the first time, these individuals identified the same list of things they liked and disliked about the food pantry. When he asked if they could imagine being involved with the food pantry in the future—either as a volunteer or as a recipient of free food—for as many years as they had already been participating (e.g., another 10 years of volunteering if they had already been helping out for 10 years), it was "like the ceiling fell in. It was like this horrible terrible feeling of oh my god could that really happen?" Finally, he asked about what gave them hope. As Mike notes, "They got political like that (snaps his fingers)."[52]

It is commonly believed that charity separates the giver from the recipient. Yet, in this case, both food pantry volunteers and recipients share the same recognition that the charitable food system is unsustainable and undignified, and that the only exit is through the government taking a larger role in ensuring the public's right to an adequate living. Both

volunteer and recipient know that the charitable food system enables corporations to keep wages low and profits high. They both know that the
charitable food system enables the government to tamp down its expenditures on safety net programs, thus minimizing taxes on the middle class
and wealthy. This same system has failed both volunteers and recipients,
yet it continues to grow, in part perpetuated by these entrenched interests,
and in part because it preys upon the volunteers' compassion and the recipients' desperation.

Just Harvest: The Solution to Hunger Is Justice, Not Food.

Ken Regal is not your usual anti-hunger activist. The 55-year-old executive
director of Just Harvest in Pittsburgh, Regal has political views that many
would consider socialist. With a great sense of humor, he delights in
recounting the foibles and corruption of Pittsburgh's political elites. Until
her retirement in 2010, he had co-directed Just Harvest with Joni Rabinow-
itz, a fiery leftist with roots in the politics of the 1960s. She is, according to
Ken, "the best organizer in town."[53]

Just Harvest was created in 1986 when it spun off from the Hunger
Action Center (HAC). HAC had been a progressive organization, created in
the previous decade by local peace and justice activists, but split in two
parts. The Urban League picked up HAC's human services programs, while
Just Harvest was created to take over its policy advocacy functions. The
mid-1980s were a tough time to be in the anti-hunger business. Pittsburgh
was coming off a series of steel mill closures, its economy and social fabric
devastated. Once a thriving industrial hub, Pittsburgh was in plain decline,
rapidly turning into the epitome of the rust belt city. Pittsburgh had long
been a union stronghold, the site of the famous 1892 Homestead strikes
and the headquarters of the powerful United Steelworkers Union. Out of
this era, Just Harvest developed tight ties with labor unions and a focus on
economic justice as the solution to hunger. Their analysis of the causes of
hunger and solutions are as progressive as any in the movement. On their
website, they argue that:

The persistence of poverty and hunger in America is a political choice: the fruit of
our political, economic and social systems. We have the power to change these systems, end poverty and abolish hunger, but it will take more than charity to do this.
Fundamental change requires political and economic reform. ...

Hunger is not just about food, it is about justice and power, and together we have the power to do something about it.[54]

Currently Just Harvest separates its work into three buckets: education, advocacy, and service provision. Its policy efforts focus on supporting the passage of federal legislation to bolster food and nutrition programs, as well as shaping the implementation of those programs at the state and county levels. The organization provides free tax preparation services to thousands of clients, filing more than 23,000 federal tax returns and gaining $41 million in refunds over the past 13 years. They've also helped families file for SNAP benefits, with more than 8,600 applications submitted from 2007 to 2015. Just Harvest plays a vital public education role in keeping the public informed about hunger through reports, media outreach, and public speaking. According to Regal, all of Just Harvest's work is designed to break down the false distinction between the "deserving" and "undeserving" poor.[55]

Perhaps because of its understanding about the role of economic concentration in shaping hunger, Just Harvest was one of the first anti-hunger groups to work on changing the broader food system as it affects low-income residents of southwestern Pennsylvania. Since the 1980s, the group has been a leader in food system activities throughout the Pittsburgh region. It catalyzed the creation of an official City of Pittsburgh Food Policy Commission in the late 1980s, to address the problem of supermarket redlining. It has helped to organize an alliance of farmers markets. It participates in the Pittsburgh Food Policy Council. Just Harvest's "Fresh Access" now facilitates SNAP recipients to use their benefits at 15 farmers markets in the region. It is also launching a healthy corner store initiative to improve access to healthy food in underserved communities in 2016.[56] Participation in these efforts also helps the group to communicate the analysis that the solution to hunger is more than just "food in, food out."[57]

Part of what makes Just Harvest such a successful advocate is that it operates two nonprofit organizations. Just Harvest Education Fund, authorized under the tax code's 501(c)(3) section, is able to offer a tax deduction for contributions but possesses limited ability to lobby. Just Harvest: A Center for Action Against Hunger operates under the IRS section 501(c)(4) as a social welfare organization. Donations to it are not tax deductible, but there are no restrictions on its lobbying activities. This designation allows the two organizations to dedicate a substantial portion of their resources into grassroots and direct lobbying on issues related to hunger and economic injustice.[58] The Center for Action has a much smaller budget, about $100,000 versus $600,000 for the Education Fund. The center is funded by donations from attorneys, individuals, and two big events, whereas the Education Fund receives numerous grants from foundations and government agencies.

This dual structure is only a small piece of the organization's multiple identities. Ken Regal suggests that the organization is different things to different people, depending upon how they interact with it. "The people who have their tax refunds done here, see us as a free H&R Block. To the people getting food stamps or welfare, we are like a friendly version of the welfare department. Aging hippies see us as the Hunger Action Coalition in 1982. To the United Way, which funds us, we are a United Way agency. And the people who attend our empty bowls dinner see us as the Pottery Barn."[59]

Regardless of public perception, a few common themes run through Just Harvest's work. The organization possesses a strong commitment to social and economic justice. It believes that all persons, regardless of whether they are eligible for public assistance programs, deserve to be treated with dignity. Finally, it holds that reforms to the food system are needed to improve access to healthy food for low-income persons and increase the income of family farmers. It is this mix of pragmatism, idealism and sense of alliance building that makes Just Harvest a model for other organizations around the country.

Summary

Some of the innovation and experimentation within the anti-hunger field described in this chapter is focused on transforming the way in which organizations approach their missions. In other cases, it is about modifying the very purpose of organizations. In both cases, these practices transcend minor tweaks to organizational programming. They are not about ways in which food banks improve their distribution of free food, or how advocacy groups have improved the operations of a federal food program. Their omission in this chapter does not mean to trivialize these constant tinkerings and honings. Instead, these examples encourage a basic questioning of the purpose and activities of anti-hunger groups. They point at two

fundamental questions. What does it mean to be an anti-hunger organization? What should the core practices of such an organization be?

All of the innovations examined in this chapter can and should be made
more central to the definition of what it means to be an anti-hunger organization. They can be broken down into two broad themes and various
subthemes.

First, they explore transforming the way in which anti-hunger groups
operate. As Nick Saul comments, food pantries can be like death by a thousand cuts to one's dignity. Both Just Harvest and The Stop make a strong
case that the poor don't have to lose their humanity when they walk in
the door of a social service agency or emergency food site. They can and
should be treated with dignity. While many food banks are trying to
improve the quality of their offerings, especially in term of fresh produce,
the food banks of Santa Cruz County and Santa Barbara County in California have gone further than most in reframing their work as "nutrition
banking." Their leadership sees the core purpose of their organizations not
as feeding people but as fostering healthy people. These food banks, as
well as numerous other profiled organizations seek to better engage the
participation of the grassroots in their programs. Some do it through soliciting direction in organizational programs from "clients," such as The Stop
in Toronto and the Alameda County [CA] Community Food Bank's community advisory board, while others try to catalyze leadership from below
through training (Oregon Food Bank and the Food Bank of Santa Cruz
County).

In the second theme, groups are recognizing the inherent limits of charity to solve the hunger problem. Some entities are helping low-income individuals to become more self-reliant through training them for employment
or gaining the necessary life skills to become employable. Other initiatives
are addressing the root causes of hunger through a more comprehensive
analysis and policy advocacy. Oregon Food Bank, Just Harvest (Pittsburgh),
HANNYS (New York State), and the Freedom 90 union in Ontario have all
embraced this approach. Some groups, such as Oregon Food Bank, Just Harvest, Foodlink in Rochester, New York, and the Interfaith Food Shuttle in
North Carolina, are implementing strategies to reform the food system
through connecting local farmers and consumers, improving access to
healthy food in underserved communities, or creating economic development opportunities. Finally, The Stop shows that charity is not the pathway

to eliminating hunger or poverty, and models how charity should play a secondary role to broader social change initiatives within an anti-hunger organization.

Collectively, these examples demonstrate how the anti-hunger movement is moving forward to redefine itself, albeit in a piecemeal fashion and generally without the support of leading national organizations. Inspiration does not come exclusively from within the movement, but also from the work of entities to the anti-hunger framework, which can provide key lessons for anti-hunger groups.

8   Innovative Models from Outside the Anti-Hunger Field

Important Lessons for the Movement

As anti-hunger groups begin to remake themselves, they often look for inspiration from other fields: community development, public health, planning, labor, and food systems, among others. This chapter examines four initiatives well-known among food and anti-hunger advocates. These organizations and funding streams hold important lessons for the anti-hunger movement. They provide models for how the anti-hunger field can do a better job of bringing poor people to the table, of how they can prioritize innovation and robust evaluation to guide their activities. They show how substantial impacts can be accomplished without compromising a group's integrity. And they show how working beyond boundaries of charity and food programs can lead to real change in improving the food security of low-income individuals.

The Coalition of Immokalee Workers leverages pressure on major food companies to improve the living standards and working conditions for farmworkers in Florida's tomato industry. The group called OUR Walmart seeks to improve the working conditions and wages for over one million Walmart employees, so that they don't have to rely on emergency food or receive federal food assistance. The Food Trust of Philadelphia reduces childhood obesity through improving access to healthy foods and nutrition education. The USDA-administered Community Food Projects grants program funds innovative systemic initiatives, using food as a tool to build communities and support local agriculture.

Coalition of Immokalee Workers: Transforming an Industry

The lot looked like any other in this poverty-stricken town of Immokalee, Florida, epicenter of the country's winter tomato industry. A ramshackle house sat next door, a ditch full of weeds, an expanse of untended grass, a rather large deciduous tree, and litter on the street. In other words, nothing to distinguish this parcel, only a few blocks from downtown, as the site of a nefarious crime. Surely, that was the way their captors had wanted it: nothing to alert the authorities that a dozen persons were living and sleeping in a truck, locked in at night, their wages stolen through debt bondage. Eventually one person escaped, informed the authorities, and the others were liberated. The captors, the Navarrete brothers, were convicted and sentenced to 12 years in prison. Amazingly, this took place in 2007.

Just like the existence of indentured servitude in the richest nation in history, south Florida is a land of extreme contrasts. Immokalee lies on the northern edge of the Everglades, a natural wilderness treasure populated by great flocks of water birds, alligators, and invasive African pythons. These thousands of square miles of largely untouched subtropical prairie and swamp abut the artificial landscape of the tomato fields, with their laser-leveled, fertilizer-laden sandy soils, covered with colored plastic sheeting and bearing identical green orbs.

Toiling in these fields are thousands of Latino and Caribbean migrants, whose precarious economic and often legal situation makes them ripe for economic exploitation, such as by the Navarrete brothers. This exploitation often comes in very mundane fashion, such as the Manhattan-level rents that lead to a dozen or more persons sharing a single-wide trailer just to make it affordable.

Addressing this workplace and community exploitation is the Coalition of Immokalee Workers (CIW). A nonprofit organization, the CIW has transformed the Florida tomato industry by gaining the agreement of 11 of the largest corporate tomato purchasers to pay workers an extra "penny per pound" premium and to support the improvement of their working conditions. The CIW started in 1993 when eight farmworkers came together to change their working conditions. One of their first actions was spurred by the beating of a 16-year-old Guatemalan boy who had taken a break from tomato picking to get a drink of water. The nascent CIW used the worker's bloody shirt as a flag around which the workers protested in front of the labor contractor's house. They held hunger strikes, some for as long as 30 days, just to get a dialogue with the farm owners about how their working conditions could be improved. The growers refused. One farmer, revealing his belief that farmworkers were subhuman, commented, "The tractor doesn't tell the farmer how to run the farm."

The CIW held community-wide work stoppages, and in 2000 undertook a 234-mile march to highlight their plight. They educated their fellow workers about their labor rights. They uncovered, investigated, and helped prosecute modern-day slavery cases and even trained law enforcement about how to identify slavery. Nevertheless, while the CIW had stopped the further slide in workers' piece-rate wages—wages that had been stagnant since 1980—it met with grower intransigence when attempting to increase tomato harvesters' wages across the board.[1]

By 2001, the CIW realized that large purchasers, such as supermarkets, fast food restaurants, and food service companies were leveraging their vast purchasing power to pressure suppliers to lower the cost of tomatoes, thus keeping wages low. It also realized that these companies were more vulnerable to public pressure than the growers, as their brands' reputations were integrally linked to the companies' stock values. The CIW decided to launch a national boycott of Taco Bell to force the company to provide increased pay (again, in the form of a "penny per pound" premium paid by the fast-food chain) and improved working conditions for the Florida tomato pickers through a supplier Code of Conduct. Campus and interfaith groups provided enormous support to this effort, and four years later Taco Bell's parent corporation Yum Brands signed onto the Fair Food Agreement. By 2015, 14 companies had also signed on, including most major fast-food restaurants, food service companies, and a handful of retail chains, including Walmart.[2] In 2015, the CIW has expanded its scope to six additional states up the Eastern seaboard and into the bell pepper and strawberry sector as well.[3]

In the Florida tomato industry, workers generally earn a piece rate, with the minimum wage providing the floor for a pay period's earnings. For round tomatoes, this rate varies depending on supply and demand for farm labor, but averages around 50 cents per bucket. A bucket holds about 32 pounds of tomatoes. The math works out as follows: Let's assume the piece rate is 50 cents per bucket and the minimum wage is $8.02 per hour, as it is in Florida in 2015. A farmworker would have to harvest about 16 buckets per hour ($16 \times \$.50 = \$8.00$) before he would pick enough tomatoes to earn above minimum wage for his services. Sixteen buckets equals 512 pounds of tomatoes. If he picked fewer than 16 buckets per hour, he would still be guaranteed the minimum wage for his services.

Since their wages are frequently based on the number of buckets they pick, the extra penny per pound would apply to all of the tomatoes the farmworker gathers. Assuming the worker picks 512 pounds of tomatoes per hour, this extra penny per pound would translate into a raise of about $5 per hour, or about 64 percent over his or her current salary. The pennies clearly add up.

The calculations get a bit more complicated, however. Since some of a farm's tomatoes go to companies outside of the Fair Food Program, the farmworker doesn't get paid the extra penny for every pound he picks. Instead, he gets the extra cent for a portion of the tomatoes that he picks based on the percentage of the farm's output that goes to Fair Food Program participating purchasers, e.g., Taco Bell. For example, Pacific Tomato Growers estimates that 35–40 percent of their sales go to participating buyers, so a worker would get a variable bonus depending on the amount he picked and the amount the grower has sold to participating buyers. The bonus is paid as a separate line item on the worker's paycheck.

In addition to improving workers' living standards, the Fair Food Program has also enabled a series of changes to their working conditions that lend an atmosphere of respect. These changes include zero tolerance for forced labor and systemic child labor; workers rights education sessions on company time; worker triggered complaint resolution mechanisms; a system of health and safety volunteers on each farm; changes in harvesting operations, such as access to shade, water breaks, and the use of time clocks; and auditing procedures to ensure that growers and purchasers are in compliance.

The outcomes of these agreements have been immediate and substantial. Workers are reporting less wage theft, fewer instances of sexual harassment, and real improvements in workplace safety and quality of life. Prior to the agreements, workers were routinely required to overfill the bucket with tomatoes above the rim of the container. After the agreements, workers just had to fill the bucket up to the brim. This small change provided them with a 10 percent wage increase.

The keystone to these agreements has been the creation of an independent entity to verify their fair implementation. The Fair Food Standards Council (FFSC) is headed by Laura Safer Espinoza, a retired New York State Supreme Court judge, and employs a staff of 8 to 10 investigators, accountants, and field auditors. The FFSC staffs a 24-hour hotline for worker complaints, checks the books of participating tomato growers to see that wages are properly paid and that the extra "penny per pound" premium is making it into workers' paychecks, and interviews farmworkers about their working conditions. An essential precondition of the verification process is that growers must put all the workers on payroll rather than having them be employees of labor subcontractors. In doing so, the growers are not able to pass the buck on the treatment of the workers, as typically happens in many farm labor situations. From the farmer perspective, doing so can be a huge administrative burden, according to Beau McHan, the harvesting manager of Pacific Tomato Growers, which on the day I visited had 400 workers in the fields.[4] Safer Espinoza notes that enforcement is a "work in progress," with most complaints about compensation, worker safety, and sanitation.[5]

In part, growers abide by the Code of Conduct because it is in their economic interest to do so. Those that are found in compliance are able to sell their crops to participating buyers. Those out of compliance lose their ability to sell. It is, in the words of one Fair Food Standards Council employee, "the carrot and stick that makes the whole thing work."[6]

To ensure that a greater share of the state's tomato production comes under the Fair Food Program, the CIW, with the support of its ally groups—Just Harvest USA, Student Farmworker Alliance, and Interfaith Action of Southwest Florida—continues to expand its organizing focus. In 2015 it sought to convince the fast-food chain Wendy's and the supermarket chain Publix to sign onto the Fair Food Code of Conduct. Publix, in particular, has been intransigent in its refusal to do so, despite having been targeted by the CIW for numerous years. For its part, a Publix spokesperson notes that the corporation is trying to hold down supplier costs, perhaps because of the direct competition from Walmart on consumer prices: "We position ourselves as customer advocates by challenging cost increases from suppliers and making sure such increases are justified. We have been successful in delaying cost increases, reducing the amounts of some increases."[7]

The CIW also has a very vital presence in the lives of farmworkers in Immokalee, beyond their work in organizing the Fair Food Program. From its modest headquarters across the street from the main parking lot where old school buses turned into farmworker transportation pick up laborers, the CIW operates a series of programs. It runs a radio station, Radio Conciencia (Radio Awareness), broadcasting Mexican pop music and community news in Spanish. When farmworkers complained about the price gouging taking place at local stores, the CIW opened a small grocery and household goods co-op within the CIW building. Because of this competition, local stores dropped their prices. Since the town doesn't have a movie theater, the CIW also offers free movies in Spanish and popcorn on Saturday nights.

Perez, a diminutive Guatemalan farmworker turned organizer in her 20s, highlights the CIW's ambitious intentions in a very casual way: "What we're trying to do here is change an entire industry."[8] That such an ambitious undertaking could be stated in such a matter of fact manner, by a woman with little formal education who doesn't speak much English, and who represents the most powerless group of individuals in the United States, speaks to the transformative power of the CIW's organizing. Even more amazing is the fact that the CIW has actually been quite successful at this transformation.

The transformation led by the CIW includes some impressive accomplishments. They've changed the nature of power relations in an industry rife with human rights abuses such that the farmworkers are being treated with increasing dignity. Not only are the cases of modern-day slavery and beatings finally coming to an end, hopefully for good, but also the daily indignities of sexual harassment, wage theft, and disrespect are on the wane. Workers are learning their rights, becoming empowered to seek recourse, and learning the value of working together. Millions of extra dollars are flowing into the pockets of some of the nation's most destitute individuals, improving their food security.

Key to their success has been an intentional focus on capacity building and leadership development among farmworkers. The CIW has prioritized building grassroots leadership to set the direction of the CIW's campaigns. This approach is in marked difference to most anti-hunger groups, which have been based on a nonprofit model grounded in the leadership of a professional class of employees and board members. The CIW's story holds many lessons for the anti-hunger sector, beyond their grassroots empowerment activities. Perhaps the most obvious lesson is the need for anti-hunger groups to reconsider their partnership with major food corporations, instead to hold them accountable for their actions that imperil the food security of workers in the food supply chain.

OUR Walmart

For almost two decades, the Union of Food and Commercial Workers (UFCW), the primary labor union representing workers in the supermarket industry, had been stymied in their efforts to gain union recognition in Walmart. Not until 2012, until they changed their tactics, did their organizing come together so well.

Leading to this reversal of fortune was a change of tactics, as the UFCW encouraged Walmart workers to take more leadership in the struggle, with the support of the UFCW. They created the Organization United for Respect at Walmart (OUR Walmart), which spearheaded these strikes and protests. Walmart employees make up the membership and leadership of this new group, and are committed to gaining improvements in their working conditions. Launched in June 2011, this group has 700 chapters in 46 states with 4,000 members.[9]

OUR Walmart is not a labor union seeking to represent Walmart employees. Instead, it's an association of Walmart employees exercising their right to free speech and free assembly outside of collective bargaining regulations. They have come together to make Walmart a better place to work and shop, with a 12-point "Declaration of Respect" that calls on the company to, among other things: pay a minimum of $15 per hour and expand the number of workers with full-time hours; provide affordable healthcare; create dependable and predictable work schedules; and respect workers as human beings.[10]

Respect is an important goal of Walmart workers. They feel abused and lied to, and they believe the company has trampled on their rights. An internal memo from a Walmart executive to the board of directors spelled out the Walmart approach: hold down spending on health care and other benefits, cap employee pay, discourage unhealthy people from applying, and disparage people with seniority who make more money but are no more productive.[11] The website www.walmartat50.org documented employees' alienation from their workplace through a photo collage and brief stories. For example, Michelle Dunivan of Virginia writes of how she was sexually harassed by a manager and then terminated for reporting the incident. Jessica Lail of Texas writes about the company forcing employees to take two- or three-hour lunches or clock in late so they don't earn overtime. Kenny James says that when he was promoted to management, he was told not to treat workers with respect, as it would empower them.[12]

Back in 2012, the UFCW rejiggered its strategy to assist the workers in their new organization. As Dan Schlademan, the former campaign director for Making Change at Walmart, notes: "We're not going to wait around for the government or Walmart to tell us that we have a right to exist. We're going ahead and supporting Walmart workers in their new organization."[13] He brought in ASGK Public Strategies, a media and branding firm started by David Axelrod, President Obama's chief political strategist. ASGK conducted opinion research among Walmart employees, helped name the OUR Walmart organization, and craft a logo, which looks like the hand sign meaning OK.[14] This end run around labor laws, harkening back to the early days of the labor movement when workers were more likely to be organized in mutual aid societies or brotherhoods than unions, is proving to be a brilliant move. According to Robert Bruno, the director of the Labor Education Program at the University of Illinois-Chicago: "What this Wal-Mart group has found, is there may be a way to essentially change Wal-Mart's behavior legally without having to actually organize 51 percent of the workers. While I'm sure that [union organizing] is still the objective, in the meantime they can create a lot of rights using less workers and without having to represent them."[15] A decision by the National Labor Relations Board (NLRB) in 2015 may wind up facilitating the unionization of Walmart, which subcontracts out its warehouse work. The NLRB ruled that companies that hire workers through another firm are liable for workplace violations and could be required to bargain with unions.[16]

One highly successful element of their campaign has been to engage community partners in supporting workers on strike on Black Friday, the biggest shopping day of the year. By 2014, protests took place in some 1,600 stores in 49 states. These events have garnered significant national press over the years.

The pressure being put on the company by OUR Walmart has resulted in major victories for Walmart workers, perhaps because it comes at a time when the company is already vulnerable. Its reputation had taken a beating in recent years, as measured by a leading corporate reputation index.[17] In January 2013 the company announced significant changes designed to boost its image. These changes included hiring veterans, increasing their purchasing of American-made goods, and developing a transparent scheduling policy (one of OUR Walmart's goals).[18]

In April 2015 the company announced that it would raise its minimum pay for 500,000 workers to $9 per hour in 2015 and $10 per hour in 2016. The cost of this move was estimated at one billion dollars.[19] Schlademan notes the link between the workers' efforts and Walmart's wage hike: "Walmart's basic business model has always been 'we're the lowest payer, we're the cheapest,' and the fact that they have been forced to change that speaks volumes about the power of the organization and what the organization's been able to accomplish."[20] These changes reflect what Julius Getman, a labor law professor at the University of Texas, calls "a battle for the soul of Walmart's workforce."[21]

Despite these positive changes, Walmart still has a long way to go in meeting worker demands. The company still resists providing full-time employment for much of its work force, cutting some workers hours to cut costs.[22] It remains vehemently anti-union. OUR Walmart continues to pressure the company to pay its workers a minimum of $15 per hour, which would cost the employer less than five billion dollars per year. In 2015, it posted a profit of $14.7 billion.[23]

OUR Walmart offers some key lessons to the anti-hunger sector above and beyond the simple fact that it takes on such a large funder to anti-hunger groups, and one whose wage practices have been widely criticized for aggravating food insecurity. It provides an answer to the jobs question that J. C. Dwyer spoke about in chapter 6, in a strategy that puts fairly compensated employment over reliance on government benefits. One of the key planks of OUR Walmart's Declaration of Respect reads, "Far too many of us have to rely on government assistance for our basic needs. Walmart should publicly commit to providing wages and benefits that ensure that no Associate has to rely on government assistance."[24]

This direction comes from solid organizing, from listening to the priorities of the workers themselves. OUR Walmart workers do not demand that their employer educate them about SNAP or help them access food pantries to supplement their inadequate wages. Nor do they advocate for increased philanthropy to food banks. Instead, they are demanding dignity and respect, values often missing from the experiences that the charitable food sector provides.

The Food Trust: Improving Access to Healthy Foods in the City of Brotherly Love

Philadelphia has a reputation for being a tough place. After all, it *is* home to Rocky Balboa and Mayor Frank Rizzo (infamous for bombing an entire city block to oust a handful of revolutionaries). While a Democrat strong-hold, it is not a liberal bubble like Berkeley, Madison, or Boulder. It is a big city with entrenched poverty and real problems. That is what makes the work of a group like The Food Trust all the more important and exciting.

The Food Trust was launched in 1992 by Duane Perry, who was at the time the executive director of the Reading Terminal Market, Philadelphia's iconic public market. Perry saw the need for the market's fresh produce to reach the city's diverse neighborhoods, where access to healthy foods was often quite limited. He created a new organization, initially called The Farmers Market Trust, establishing a farm stand in South Philly. Soon there-after, the organization started providing nutrition education classes to schoolchildren.[25] It has since evolved into one of the most complex and successful community food security organizations in the country, with 110 staff and a budget of $10 million.[26] It is one of the first organizations of its kind to make a significant difference in the food system in a municipality as large as Philadelphia, and then to implement the lessons learned across the state and nation.

Arguably, The Food Trust's most well-known work has been not in farm-ers markets or in schools, but in reshaping the landscape of food retail in underserved communities. This focus came out of a national study that showed Philadelphia to have the second-lowest number of supermarkets per capita of any major metropolitan area.[27] Residents of neighborhoods with few supermarkets also were more likely to suffer from diet-related dis-eases, such as obesity and diabetes.[28] The Food Trust worked with local gov-ernment officials to identify solutions to this problem. The program that they developed would soon be replicated across the country.

The Pennsylvania Fresh Food Financing Initiative (FFFI) championed by Representative Dwight Evans was passed by the state legislature in 2004. It established a program to provide loans and grants for the establishment of food retail outlets in underserved communities. The program, which would eventually grow to $85 million, was designed to be a unique partnership between the state and nonprofit organizations. The Food Trust would conduct outreach to potential grocery store operators and interested communities. The Reinvestment Fund, a community development organization with expertise in overseeing socially responsible projects in the mid-Atlantic region, would review applications and manage the loans and grants.[29] The state would provide the funding.

As a result of this initiative, 88 new fresh food retail outlets (supermarkets, grocery stores, and farmers markets) have opened in the Commonwealth of Pennsylvania, creating 5,023 jobs and helping 400,000 people gain improved access to healthy foods.[30] The beneficiaries are not big box retail stores, like Walmart, or other major chain supermarkets. These chains don't need the financing offered by the FFFI, as they have access to capital independently. Instead the program funds community-based ventures, co-ops, or stores owned by local entrepreneurs.

Within a few years of its establishment, the Pennsylvania Fresh Food Financing Initiative soon gathered accolades from prestigious institutions. Harvard University called it one of the nation's most innovative government programs. The Centers for Disease Control and Prevention gave it a Pioneering Innovation Award for its efforts to prevent obesity.[31] The Robert Wood Johnson Foundation, one of the nation's largest public health foundations, gave The Food Trust funding to replicate the FFFI in Illinois and in New Orleans. Subsequently, the trust began a new initiative in New York as well. Because of The Food Trust's technical assistance and organizing, similar programs are taking place in eight additional states and four cities.[32]

In 2010, The Food Trust in partnership with The Reinvestment Fund and the national equity-oriented think tank PolicyLink, started a campaign to establish a national FFFI. While their legislative goals were not met, they were able to gain the support of the Obama administration to establish the Healthy Food Financing Initiative. A partnership between the Departments of the Treasury, Agriculture, and Health and Human Services, the HFFI provides financing for food retail outlets in underserved communities. As of September 2015, $145 million has been provided to community development and finance organizations across the country.[33]

In the absence of supermarkets in underserved neighborhoods, residents often revert to shopping at mom-and-pop stores, typically peddlers of tobacco, alcohol, soda, chips, and other high-margin, low-nutrition foods. This issue of the quality of food sold in corner stores dropped into The Food Trust's lap through their efforts to eliminate soda in public schools. In 2003, when the School District of Philadelphia sought to sign a contract with a major soda company for exclusive rights to sell soft drinks in school vending machines, The Food Trust organized the Philadelphia Coalition for Healthy Children to ban sugar-sweetened beverages from school campuses. They succeeded, and in 2004, the school district banned the sale of all drinks from campuses except water, juice, and milk. Yet, soon after, they found out from various teachers that students were frequenting corner stores to buy soda and snacks on their way to and from school. Subsequent research has corroborated the contribution of corner stores to childhood obesity. One study found kids purchase foods with more than 350 calories at every visit.[34] Food Trust staffers started talking with the grocery owners, who seemed interested in the welfare of the children. But they were locked into a low-risk, low-return business model predicated on gaining high profit margins from junk food. The owners were often recent immigrants, who worked long hours, employed family members, and were using the stores as a stepping stone toward accumulating some savings and gaining some business skills.[35]

Food Trust staffers held focus groups with schoolchildren to find out what healthy foods they would purchase, and started to support a few corner stores to help them carry packaged cut fruit. With some marketing assistance, these products began to sell. As they do so well, Food Trust staffers took this innovation and expanded its scale to include stores across the city. By 2015, there were 660 corner stores participating in the Healthy Corner Store Initiative, and The Food Trust was expanding the program to include 105 stores throughout the state in conjunction with the PA Department of Health.[36] To participate, stores need to carry four healthy food items, such as fresh produce, whole grain products, and low fat dairy. In exchange, stores receive a $100 annual stipend, technical assistance, marketing materials on site, participation in a citywide marketing campaign, and eligibility to receive a $1,000–$3,000 mini-grant (funded by the PA Economic Development Department).

As with their grocery work, The Food Trust sought to bring this healthy corner store work to a national level. In conjunction with the Community Food Security Coalition and Public Health Law Policy (now known as ChangeLab Solutions), they created the Healthy Corner Store Network. The network has provided a vehicle for groups to communicate and problem solve through periodic webinars, conference calls, and skill-building events.

The Food Trust complements these successful community-based programs with a set of extensive school-based initiatives to encourage healthy eating. Their focus includes providing nutrition education to 65,000 students in the region, developing comprehensive food policies for the Philadelphia School District, educating preschoolers about the importance of healthy eating and physical activity, and coordinating farm to school projects for 25 schools serving 45,000 students.[37]

Their school and community initiatives are showing some significant impacts in reversing childhood obesity, especially among Philadelphia's communities of color. A report from 2015 has shown that childhood obesity has declined by 6 percent and severe obesity by 14 percent.[38] It's virtually impossible to determine the cause of a reduction in obesity rates, given the numerous factors involved. It's difficult to directly correlate The Food Trust's programs with that decline. But their programs have increased access to healthier foods. Their programs have reached hundreds of thousands of schoolchildren and their families, especially those living in low-income communities. In addition, researchers have confirmed that The Food Trust's systemic approach, through community and schools, through education, and through changes to policy and to the food environment, can have deeper impacts than one-off anti-obesity programs, such as exercise programs.[39]

The key to The Food Trust's success may lie in its organizational culture. It is a culture of contrasts: friendly yet professional, passionate but not dogmatic, pragmatic yet idealistic, ambitious but collaborative. The Food Trust believes that food is to be celebrated, but they have managed to avoid the elitism for which the Slow Food movement has been criticized. Yael Lehmann, their 47-year-old executive director, embodies the organizational ethos. She's incredibly savvy yet manages to be quite laidback, and even finds time to teach bass guitar to girls at a rock music summer camp. Perhaps the most important characteristic of the trust's organizational culture is that it is constantly seeking innovation. This drive, along with some very strategic thinking, has led it toward dedicating substantial resources to critical reflection of its successes and failures. To facilitate this organizational learning, it has created perhaps the most robust evaluation protocols of any organization in the food movement.

The Food Trust makes it a point to conduct thorough and rigorous evaluations of its initiatives, often partnering with the many universities in the region. John Weidman notes, "We do a lot of evaluation because much of our work is new and untested. We want to get feedback. We have a lot of intellectually curious staff."[40] The Food Trust's evaluations not only provide valuable information to improve its programs, but also provide documentation of the impacts of those programs. This body of evidence has proven key in the expansion of programs beyond Philadelphia, and in attracting the support of policymakers and funders. The quality of its research also stands out, including publication in peer-reviewed academic journals, in a field that dedicates too few resources to systematic evaluation.

The Food Trust is proof that groups can have a significant impact on a phenomenon as complex and entrenched as childhood obesity without compromising its values. It sees locally owned businesses as a core partner in its efforts, but does so through innovation and maintaining its integrity. Working grocery store by grocery store, farmers market by farmers market, school by school, The Food Trust has achieved impressive levels of change in Philly. It has shown that community-based programs, when combined with smart policy change and informed by top-notch evaluation, can indeed make Philadelphia, and many other places around the nation, a healthier place to live.

Community Food Projects: R&D for the Food Movement

Since its inception as part of the 1996 Farm Bill, the Community Food Projects program has been extraordinarily successful in funding community-based innovation. Despite its limited budget of at first $2.5 million per year and $9 million annually, as of 2015, it has generated more attention and more calls to Congress and the USDA than programs hundreds of times its size. It has played an important role in accelerating the formation of the good food movement.

This is the story of the Community Food Projects grant program and its impact on communities across the country. It stands out as an example of a highly innovative and successful federal program that is catalyzing modest, albeit systemic, changes to the food system in communities across the country.

Leading a newly formed coalition of anti-hunger, urban agriculture, and sustainable agriculture groups, the Community Food Security Coalition won the inclusion of the Community Food Projects (CFP) program in the 1996 Farm Bill. Its passage was a matter of the right framing to appeal to a bipartisan Congress, good organizing, and perhaps most importantly well-connected staffers in the House and Senate pushing it forward. Although the CFP was initially authorized at only $2.5 million annually, the funds were mandatory, meaning that its supporters did not need advocate in Congress every year just for the funds to be actually distributed.

Although community food projects in general often seek to improve the nutritional status of low-income households, they are not anti-hunger projects.[41] They aim to improve the food security of their participants, but within a broader context of transforming an inequitable and unsustainable food system. They typically engage individuals at a more intensive level than food pantries, but the number of people they reach is typically smaller. CFPs cannot solve the massive and entrenched problem of hunger in the United States. They can, however, provide a glimpse of a very different approach to the same problem.

Community food projects are small investments in innovation in the context of the failure of the mainstream food system to meet the needs of marginalized communities and individuals. Despite the diversity of programs funded, the CFPs are linked by the fact that they create methods of food production and distribution grounded in community needs and values. The only comprehensive analysis of these grants, conducted for projects taking place between 2005 and 2009, indicates an astonishing impact for only $25 million in federal money:[42]

• The production of 19 million pounds of food, valued at $19.7 million
• The farming or gardening of over 56,000 acres of land, including 9,100 community garden plots
• Receipt of food by 2.5 million persons through a community food project

• Implementation of 183 policies in communities, affecting 33 million Americans
• Creation of 2,300 jobs
• Creation of 1,000 new businesses and support given to 2,600 existing businesses
• Preservation of 3,000 acres of land
• Formation of 40 food policy councils

Not only have these community food projects been highly effective in achieving their legislatively mandated goal of transforming the food system, but they have also been changing their communities and participants in unforeseen ways. The following descriptions highlight some of the incidental benefits of community food projects.

At the neighborhood level, some CFPs have fostered a sense of community pride. The process of transforming a vacant lot in an underserved neighborhood into a thriving urban farm or community garden can build social capital among neighborhood residents, resulting in more resilient communities with decreased food insecurity. The City Farms Project in New York City provides a concrete example of the way in which residents of marginalized neighborhoods have reclaimed control over their space through collaborating in creating and caring for community gardens.

CFPs have helped to reinvigorate lost traditions, foster intergenerational communication, and rebuild connections between communities and their environments. Support to the Tohono O'odham Nation in southern Arizona has helped them to re-create their traditional food system by increasing the cultivation of tribal lands for such crops as drought- and insulin-resistant tepary beans. The project has also engaged the elders to revive the long-lost custom of harvesting the fruit of the tree-sized saguaro cactus, a ritual that includes the singing of songs that haven't been heard on the reservation for decades. This and many other CFPs funded on tribal lands stand out in the context of the USDA's management of the Food Distribution Program on Indian Reservations (FDPIR), in which sourcing local foods can be challenging.

Numerous projects employ an economic development approach to help community residents build pathways out of poverty. In North Minneapolis, Appetite for Change is marrying food access with job creation, connecting a food business incubator with a neighborhood café and farmers market in a single comprehensive effort.

In assessing the program at this writing, almost 20 years after the first Community Food Project grants were made, the importance of this seminal program as it relates to the anti-hunger community can be summed up in three ways. First, CFPs play a research-and-development (R&D) function for the food movement to innovate complex food systems programs with low-income communities. Increasingly, these grants have gone to projects that seek to increase the scale of their impact by bringing in more powerful partners or shaping local policy. They provide a model for the way that the USDA can support innovation through partnerships with community-based stakeholders.

Second, CFPs focus on changing the food environment at the community-level complements anti-hunger initiatives, which typically focus on reducing individual or household food insecurity. CFPs have filled in the cracks where the market has failed. They have provided access to healthy food in "food deserts" and helped small farmers stay on the land by providing them with new channels to market their products. This approach not only helps to build access to healthy food, but it also promotes social capital and healthy neighborhoods, which in turn affect individual health.

Third, CFPs challenge the basic premise of the mainstream food system: that food is a commodity. This premise holds that 10 pounds of potatoes is 10 pounds of potatoes, without regard to how those potatoes were grown, who grew them, and where they were produced. CFPs, like much of the local food movement, reject that notion, instead holding that the values embedded in food production, distribution, and retailing differentiate their products from those of the corporate-run marketplace. In other words, the process by which food is produced is of equal importance to the characteristics of the foodstuff itself.

Community food projects will never replace federal food programs. They do not eliminate the need for programs that enhance the food security of individuals through household-or individual-based transfers, such as SNAP. However, they do complement these programs, providing a framework for federal investment in community-led and community-based food economies. It provides a gateway for a more comprehensive approach to addressing the intertwined issues of health disparities, food insecurity, rural decline, and disempowered populations.

Summary

The four profiles in this chapter present themes that provide direction for anti-hunger groups. These themes can be grouped into three topics. First are those that touch upon how anti-hunger groups do their work. The CIW and OUR Walmart show the importance of empowering grassroots leadership as the catalyst for change, including the importance of workers in such leadership roles, while the Community Food Projects highlights the need to increase investments in innovation and experimentation, especially with regard to federal food programs. The Food Trust shows the importance of robust evaluation and openness to change.

The second set of themes relates to the type of work into which anti-hunger groups should consider redirecting their energies. The Food Trust highlights how an increased focus on access to healthy food throughout communities and schools can reduce the incidence of diet-related diseases. OUR Walmart points out that increasing wages and benefits for low-wage workers is essential so that they do not need to rely on emergency food or federal food programs in the first place. Similarly, the community food projects profile demonstrates the importance of supporting local food systems as a tool for building the wealth of low-income persons.

The third and last set of themes refers to the relationship between anti-hunger groups and corporations. The Food Trust shows us that it is possible to create meaningful systemic change while maintaining integrity to one's values, without relying on the market power of multinational corporations. Finally, the CIW and OUR Walmart demonstrate the importance of making claims on corporations so that they treat their workers and suppliers with respect and dignity and stop externalizing their labor costs onto the public.

Conclusion: Toward a New Vision for the Anti-Hunger Movement

The Institutionalized Emergency

Throughout the course of my career, when I have expressed dismay at the collateral damage caused by the emergency food system, the response has been swift and consistent, defending the integrity of food bank employees. My colleagues comment that food bankers are "good people trapped in a bad system." This response brings about a general nod of consensus, as we agree that food bankers are well-intentioned individuals with noble purposes. It's not that the emergency food system is bad in the moralistic sense, but instead ill-suited for the purpose to which it has been put.

Some of the deficiencies of the emergency food system come from the fact that it has grown by leaps and bounds, from a temporary response to a political and economic crisis into an entrenched element of the American response to hunger. As Robert Lupton noted in chapter 2, the persistence of a charity approach to the emergency food system, rather than the transition to a development strategy, has been what causes the system to generate toxic side effects on its participants.

The emergency food system has been like a rolling snowball, taking on proportions far beyond the intentions of its creators. As Sharon Thornberry noted in chapter 3, this system was not planned. Had anti-hunger advocates gathered in a room in the early 1980s to design a central response to hunger for the next three decades, they almost certainly would not have chosen to create a food sector based on charity—and yet the system grew day by day, year by year, place by place because, in the words of Janet Poppendieck, it met the needs of so many.

The crux of the problem lies in the paradox that the system, which should have been shuttered some time ago, has become institutionalized with bigger buildings, more trucks, strategic growth goals, and intricate ties to those firms that aggravate the hunger problem in the first place through their labor practices. While the emergency food system sprang up organically and grew because it was the right idea at the time, its existence and unfettered growth is now integrally linked to the nation's economy and political system.

Corporations are central to the growth trajectory of the emergency food system. The anti-hunger industrial complex, in which food charity remains a significant element, is the product of deep-rooted financial, political, and organizational connections between anti-hunger groups, USDA, and corporate America. The anti-hunger industrial complex, with its business-as-usual approach now manifest in much of the anti-hunger sector, is grounded in practices that perpetuate the current inadequate system, and along with it the problem of hunger itself.

Big Hunger has shed light on how the anti-hunger industrial complex's positive efforts to reduce food insecurity are offset by the collateral damage it causes to the health and dignity of the poor. The Band-Aid approach of the charitable food sector largely fails to address the root causes of hunger and thus the sector perpetuates its own continuation and growth. In its expansion, it provides a plausible but ineffective alternative to government-run nutrition programs for small government advocates. We can see how food banks are tied to capitalism's logic of inexorable growth, and how their organizational cultures mimic that of their corporate partners.

But the anti-hunger industrial complex does not exclusively reside in the emergency food system; it can also be seen in the way federal food programs are administered. In these cases, USDA's links to Big Food and Big Ag make up an integral part of this complex as well.

Within the federal food programs, the anti-hunger industrial complex shows itself in two ways. First, key national anti-hunger groups operate in close partnership with food and agriculture multinational firms. These firms contribute millions to their budgets, lobby with them, and sit on their boards of directors. The unwavering focus of these groups on nutrition programs—which prevents them from embracing or investing significant resources in broader hunger-reduction agenda, such as higher minimum wages, progressive taxation and trade policy, universal healthcare, and labor friendly legislation—keeps them within a nutrition safety zone, where their actions do not contradict the economic interests of their corporate partners.

Second, anti-hunger groups have encouraged a market-based approach to the operation of federal food programs. The result is that much of the $100 billion spent on these programs winds up in the bank accounts of Big Ag and Big Food companies such as Tyson, Conagra, Walmart, and Pepsi. To the anti-hunger field, these corporations are more than just friends in high places, or allies who share the same interests. When these relationships constrain the policies that anti-hunger organizations support and even limit dialogue about potential policy changes, as has happened in the case of SNAP and sugar-sweetened beverages, the appearance of a conflict of interest, if not an actual conflict, arises. The example of the Food Distribution Program on Indian Reservations (FDPIR) shows how federal food programs could do much more to generate wealth and promote economic democracy if anti-hunger groups would push USDA to implement the program differently.

Leadership

While bad systems may constrain the actions of good people, leaders can set the tone and the agenda for not only their own groups, but also, in some cases, the movement at-large. In the anti-hunger sector where the most powerful, best-resourced, and authoritative organizations are the ones most embedded in the anti-hunger industrial complex, the source of the leadership that will affect this change is in question.

The 80 or so participants of a seminar titled "Transforming the Emergency Food System," held at the 2015 Closing the Hunger Gap conference, examined this question of leadership in a break-out session at that event. Small workgroups discussed how to accomplish the goals that the larger group had identified, many of which are in the pages of this book. In the workgroup I participated in, two individuals, an executive from a large food bank and a board member of a major national anti-hunger group, insisted that this effort must be led by Feeding America, given its abundant organizational capacity. The other seven or eight folks, younger and junior-level staffers at food banks around the country, fell silent for a few moments until they found a gentle way to express their disagreement. No one wanted to state their belief in polite company—but they murmured it in the hallway later on—that Feeding America was a poor choice because it is a cornerstone of the very system that the seminar was seeking to change.

Most likely, structural change to the anti-hunger industrial complex will not be led by powerful national groups. Instead, the onus to create models that can inspire falls on leaders from smaller and local organizations. For example, Erik Talkin at the Food Bank of Santa Barbara County is showing how a food bank can improve the health of its clients. Alison Cohen has pushed WhyHunger's programming toward a greater focus on equity, social justice, and economic justice. Susannah Morgan is making a world of difference at Oregon Food Bank, putting resources into community organizing, policy advocacy, establishing a living wage for employees, and addressing institutional racism.

But it is just as important to cultivate new leadership from the grassroots as it is for current leaders to push the envelope. At the staff and board levels, anti-hunger groups need to be looking for ways to break the glass ceiling so that women and persons of color can take top positions. And they should be developing new entities (and strengthen existing ones) that enable the full participation of those most at risk of hunger to become a strong advocacy and educational voice. The Witnesses to Hunger are a vital example of how women (often of color) from impoverished backgrounds can capture center stage in formulating the direction for the movement. Their voices must be cultivated and their organization better funded to develop chapters in every state.

Hope

Three years after starting to write this book, after innumerable interviews and conversations with these and other individuals, I find I have a much greater sense of hope that the anti-hunger sector can be transformed in a positive fashion. A lot has changed since I started work on this project.

Organizing around income inequality has gathered steam. National Labor Relations Board decisions have made it easier for unions to organize in franchises, such as fast food restaurants. OUR Walmart has achieved salary increases for workers in Walmart stores. The fast food workers are putting continuous pressure on the industry to raise wages to $15 per hour. Since 2013, 15 states and 19 cities and counties have raised their minimum wages.[1] Bernie Sanders has coalesced tremendous forces around these issues, despite his loss in the 2016 presidential primary, potentially reshaping the Democratic Party to be more attentive to economic inequality. The anti-hunger movement is picking up on these trends.

The two Closing the Hunger Gap conferences (in 2013 and 2015) have brought together hundreds of staff, mainly from food banks, who want to do things differently. They see the collateral damage being done to the spirit of the poor, and the poor quality of the food they distribute. They know they need to shorten food pantry lines and to measure success in different measures than pounds and people. And they are searching for ways to reverse the racism embedded in the emergency food system.

At the same time, much of the old guard is aging out, with dozens of food bank CEOs having retired since 2012. This turnover gives these organizations and their new leaders an opportunity to do things differently than the way they "have always been done." Even at the stalwart organizations, such as Feeding America and FRAC, things are moving forward. Feeding America is experimenting with funding its affiliates to partner with other groups in their community to provide a suite of services to help their "clients" move out of poverty rather than just provide them with a bag of food. Diane Aviv, its new leader—for the first time in about a decade, someone not from the corporate sector—has already created for the first time ever a new senior level position of "ending hunger."

FRAC's new Plan of Action to End Hunger in America puts higher wages and reduced income inequality front and center by stating: "We must return to an economy and politics that provide for the nation's economic strength and growth be shared in an equitable way. That means restoring the value of the minimum wage, higher wages for struggling workers, enforcing wage and hour laws, more robust public and private job creation, job training that is effective and targeted for today's economy, and a rising share of the working-age population active in the labor force."[2] The organization has been dedicating a greater percentage of its communications efforts to educating its constituencies about issues that extend beyond federal food programs, such as wages.

Perhaps the lessons from Youngstown, which I first described in the introduction, are now becoming more actionable giving the changes in the political environment.

Toward a New Vision

Despite these glimmers of hope, the anti-hunger community remains separated from other social movements. All too often, the anti-hunger community fails to connect with a broader progressive agenda of community development, economic justice, public health, and food system transformation. Instead it remains almost exclusively focused on increasing access to food (through charity and voucher programs such as WIC and SNAP). This narrow focus reduces the collective ability of the progressive community (and I idealistically count anti-hunger advocates within this grouping) to gain its broader goals for social and economic justice.

There won't be real changes until the anti-hunger community adopts a new vision for its work, and that vision becomes the new normal. The time has come for a wholesale rethinking of the anti-hunger field, including the concept of hunger as a social problem, the administration of federal food programs, the nature of the charitable food system, and policy agenda of the field itself.

The concept of the right to food can play a pivotal role in informing this vision. While the terminology remains challenging in the United States, the breadth that this concept offers can create a new framework for action by anti-hunger activists. It can help move the anti-hunger field away from a needs-based and charity model toward a more comprehensive focus, connecting anti-hunger work with other social movements.

This new vision is being formulated as activists gather at conferences like Closing the Hunger Gap and in hallways at mainstream events like FRAC's National Anti-Hunger Policy Conference. It is being articulated piecemeal in the reports and newsletters of WhyHunger, Project Bread, Community Food Centres of Canada, Just Harvest, and many others profiled and not profiled in this book. It is placing the anti-hunger community more closely aligned with the progressive movement. That new vision contains the following components:

• Those most at risk of hunger, such as women and people of color, have a greater voice in setting the agenda for the anti-hunger sector.

• Food is a human right, and all initiatives to promote food security should be grounded in the dignity of the individual. It is the responsibility of the government to create the conditions for the achievement of this right, not the role of the private sector.

• Food banking is grounded in relationships, not transactions. It encompasses more than a box of groceries, and provides services and support to help individuals leave poverty behind.

• The food received through charity and federal food programs is of the highest quality and nutritional standards. Ideally, it supports an ecologically and economically sustainable food system.

• Achieving economic and social justice is a precondition of eliminating hunger in the long term. Economic inequality, sexism, and institutional racism are corrosive to our society. Anti-hunger work is defined by its holistic political framework, including attention and analysis to the numerous upstream policies that shape hunger's presence.

• The corporate sector can partner with the anti-hunger community when they exercise a high degree of social responsibility and transparency in their core business practices, and embrace a business model grounded in paying their employees a living wage.

• Charity and federal food program expenditures are reoriented to be more effective at generating wealth for low income and rural communities, while promoting a higher degree of economic democracy.

Overarching Recommendations

Reaching the goals of this vision will take a number of steps in the short, medium, and long term. Some of these are more easily accomplished in the short term, and can be done by individual organizations. Other recommendations are based on collaboration across the anti-hunger community, such as through the Feeding America food bank network. Yet others require federal policy changes, based on either USDA program implementation or congressional action. The intent is to provide a number of very specific steps the anti-hunger movement can take along with those that might seem impractical or even utopian in nature. Some may argue that the timeframe for action is too delayed, and that change is more urgently needed. Others may contend that there is no way the system can change so dramatically and so quickly.

These momentous changes will not be accomplished without clear goals and benchmarks. A marked lack of accountability in the anti-hunger movement must be reversed. Through increased participation on boards and other committees, the priorities of the poor can be better heeded. The Alameda County Community Food Bank sets an example on this approach for their policy program. At the organization level, staff must find ways to reverse the power dynamics and hold their donors accountable for their practices if they are to become partners. Food banks should hold Feeding America accountable to provide leadership on many different levels, including implementing incentives that shorten the line rather than feed the need. Collectively, they should advocate for USDA to become more transparent about federal food program expenditures, as a first step in evaluating the effectiveness of these programs to promote economic democracy.

Following are some overarching directions the anti-hunger movement should take to achieve a new vision for a more effective and dignifying approach to food security.

Increase the Budget of Federal Food Programs There is much truth in anti-hunger advocates' arguments that federal food programs are underfunded and could do much more to reduce food insecurity if adequately funded. Our nation's politics of austerity is woefully shortsighted; a recent report by Bread for the World shows that food insecurity results in $160 billion annually in health expenditures.[3] Investments in these programs must be maintained and strengthened, including boosting the WIC program to allow all eligible persons to participate; basing SNAP on the USDA's Low Cost Meal Plan with 25 percent higher benefit rates than the current allotment; and funding school meals at a rate that allows food services to provide healthy meals.[4] These budgetary increases are essential but not the only solution.

Foster Increased Dialogue across the Movement Significant change in the way the anti-hunger sector does business will require vigorous dialogue and self-reflection, with the goal of rethinking the definition of anti-hunger work. Discussion groups among board and staff at individual organizations should use this book and other texts as tools for re-envisioning their goals and methods. These dialogues should result in changes to practices—to foster innovation, develop new models and new evaluation techniques, and reshape fundraising methods. They can and should be embedded in organizational strategic-planning processes.

Likewise, these dialogues should take place sector-wide, and ultimately through town hall meetings as information-gathering and public educational tools. At a national level, these dialogues should be organized to reach a common vision for a redefined anti-hunger sector, with an overarching blueprint for how to reach that vision. Such a process could be led by the Closing the Hunger Gap leadership.

Communications In her book *Compassion Inc.*, Mara Einstein critiques cause marketing as a deliberate deception in proposing that shopping can solve the world's social and environmental problems. The public has similarly been misled by 35 years of messaging and practices that tout charity as the answer to hunger. While food bank marketing has not been deceitful (although the emphasis of some groups on sad-eyed children remains emotionally manipulative), it has generally depoliticized the causes of hunger to focus on self-serving Band-Aid-type approaches.

These practices need to be reversed. Educating the public about the need to address the underlying causes of hunger is essential to build public support and funding for anti-hunger groups to move in that direction. For example, organizations should focus on the need to support increases in minimum wages, change tax policy, or support affordable housing when appropriate rather than stick to sanitized exhortations that the public should come together to fight hunger.

And food banks must walk their talk in this area as well. They should not only change their donor appreciation letters, billboards, and social media feeds, but also eliminate food drives and other events that ask donors to bring food donations. These events mislead the public into believing that the solution to hunger is a few cans of food, and that by donating a few cans of beans they have done their part to solve the problem. The public has come to expect food banks to host food drives, and it will be challenging to stop the momentum of this runaway train.

Promote Innovation There exists a marked lack of dialogue and discussion in the anti-hunger community on the contradictions in the anti-hunger movement. This lack of opportunity for self-reflection is why the Closing the Hunger Gap conferences were created. This "circle the wagons" approach is on some levels intentional, as key national groups have actively sought to limit dissension from the party line at their events, and by stopping critical articles in the media.

As a result, the anti-hunger field can seem stodgy, grounded in dated models of social programs. The anti-hunger community should look beyond that perception and begin to embrace a culture of innovation and learning. The food-banking sector should experiment with different evaluation approaches to find ones that address hunger prevention rather than hunger treatment. In the realm of federal food programs, advocates should support innovation in the SNAP program to facilitate it playing a greater role in chronic disease prevention. USDA should fund research into public policy mechanisms that can redirect the $100 billion of federal food dollars and reshape the marketplace, so that nutrient-dense become foods cheaper, and foster as well a more democratically owned food system. A precondition to this approach is ensuring increased transparency of federal food program expenditures. Finally, policymakers should link federal food program priorities to regional and local food system rebuilding programs and policies so that they mutually reinforce each other.

Movement Building / New Alliances To spur this innovation in federal food programs and in the charitable food system, new players and funding streams will need to be brought into the anti-hunger community. The anti-hunger community needs to become more aligned with the goals of the progressive community, with clearer and more direct alliances with labor, food system, public health, and other progressive organizations. By shifting an increasing amount of their policy activity to minimum wage and related campaigns and complementing their social service model with a social change approach, they will be on the same page with economic justice–related groups. By advocating for SNAP as a nutrition program, and encouraging innovation to improve its healthfulness, they will find new allies in the public health community. And by cultivating the leadership of low-income individuals, especially women and persons of color, they will not only build a more powerful social movement but also prioritize the core interests of the poor. To support these efforts, funders will need to step up to the plate. They'll need to redirect their resources to grassroots leadership development, public policy, organizing, and labor-related policy, and insist as well on greater community representation in leadership roles.

Corporate Social Responsibility   To reach this new vision, the field of corporate philanthropy must also be transformed. It should no longer be acceptable to consumers, or to the non-profit community, that corporations conduct their business practices in a way that is antithetical to their philanthropy. Corporate social responsibility (CSR) must focus first and foremost on the company's core business practices; it should not be deemed ethical for a company to generate poverty and hunger through its business practices and then try to bolster its reputation through its foundation's checkbook.

Anti-hunger groups should organize, led by their national colleagues, to demand these changes, insisting on a corporate code of philanthropic ethics. This code should help companies evolve away from funding top-down, transaction-based charity toward supporting a broader approach to social change. It should include provisions that prioritize the social impact of their philanthropy over the publicity benefits of such giving, in essence bringing corporate philanthropy more in line with best practices in the foundation community.

At a Crossroads

Many anti-hunger advocates intuitively understand that the system in which they work is less than ideal. They know of its inadequacies. They also know that their work does a lot of good, but feel limited by the political context and scarce resources in which they operate. The immediacy of hunger demands that they be pragmatic, and seek to achieve what they can within the current situation.

Big Hunger seeks to help them, and society at large, keep sight of a different way of achieving food security: to see, as the slogan of the World Social Forum expresses it, that "another world is possible." It does this by bringing to light the problematic nature of the anti-hunger industrial complex, by identifying its contradictions, conflicts of interest, and collateral damage.

As an exposé, this book seeks to name that which must be changed in order for us to reach that other world. It describes the crossroads at which the anti-hunger movement finds itself. Down one path is the business-as-usual approach, the needs- and charity-based models that mitigate the problem but fail to address the underlying causes. It is a straight shot, a well-trod shortcut. Down the other road lies a more ambitious trip, filled with twists and turns, challenges, political pitfalls and enormous rewards. Many groups have already started to embark down this path. This road will require new partners, new funding sources, new ways of measuring success, and a more expansive set of goals. It will be a long and arduous journey. The time is ripe to choose this direction.

Postscript: December 2016

On December 7, 2016, the House Committee on Agriculture released its report on the SNAP program after holding two years of hearings. It confirmed the importance of SNAP, but also laid the groundwork for reform, including tightening work requirements and eliminating soda from the list of foods eligible for purchase. Media outlets have noted that this report sets up a potential conflict between Agriculture Committee Chair Mike Conaway (R-TX) and Speaker of the House Paul Ryan over the future of the food stamp program, given Speaker Ryan's stated priority of block-granting food stamps.

This seems to indicate that there is not a clear path forward for federal food programs in 2017 and 2018, as we move toward the next Farm Bill iteration. These programs will remain contested terrain, as the former bipartisan consensus has clearly evaporated but has not been replaced by a consensus of a different nature.

The post-election landscape will no doubt provide the anti-hunger community with a challenging framework to protect their gains. Yet, this landscape also provides anti-hunger groups, as all liberal sectors, with a renewed sense of urgency to unite around progressive causes. The Left appears to be laying the groundwork for increased cohesion in the face of the Trump administration, but only time will tell if the anti-hunger community decides to cast its lot with the Left, or to continue to pursue the anti-hunger industrial complex as an expression of hunger as the lowest common political denominator.

Appendix 1: Primary National Anti-Hunger Groups in the United States

Alliance to End Hunger: http://alliancetoendhunger.org

Bread for the World: http://www.bread.org

Center on Budget and Policy Priorities: http://www.cbpp.org

Congressional Hunger Center: http://www.hungercenter.org

End Hunger Network: http://www.endhunger.com

Feeding America: http://www.feedingamerica.org

Food Research and Action Center: http://frac.org

Hunger Free America (formerly New York City Coalition to End Hunger): http://www.hungerfreeamerica.org

Mazon: http://www.mazon.org

Meals on Wheels: http://www.mealsonwheelspeople.org

RESULTS: http://www.results.org

Share Our Strength: https://nokidhungry.org

Society of St. Andrew: http://endhunger.org

WhyHunger: http://www.whyhunger.org

Witnesses to Hunger: http://www.centerforhungerfreecommunities.org/our-projects/witnesses-hunger

Appendix 2: Trends in Prevalence Rates of Food Insecurity and Very Low Food Security in U.S. Households, 1995–2015

Year	Food insecurity (includes low and very low food security)[1]	Very low food security only[1]
	Percent of households	*Percent of households*
1995	11.94	4.14
1996	12.02	4.29
1997	10.11	3.22
1998	11.79	3.71
1999	10.06	2.97
2000	10.47	3.13
2001	10.69	3.26
2002	11.10	3.50
2003	11.21	3.49
2004	11.95	3.94
2005	11.00	3.87
2006	10.94	3.99
2007	11.11	4.06
2008	14.59	5.72
2009	14.69	5.71
2010	14.51	5.35
2011	14.94	5.72
2012	14.51	5.72
2013	14.28	5.58
2014	14.05	5.59
2015	12.66	5.04

1. Prevalence rates for 1996 and 1997 were adjusted for the estimated effects of differences in data-collection screening protocols used in those years.

Source: Calculated by ERS based on Current Population Survey Food Security Supplement data. "Key Statistics and Graphics," USDA Economic Research Service, http://www.ers.usda.gov/topics/food-nutrition-assistance/food-security-in-the-us/key-statistics-graphics.aspx#trends; http://www.ers.usda.gov/media/136921/trends_d.html.

Appendix 3: Index of Acronyms

ABAWD	Able-Bodied Adults Without Dependents
ACCFB	Alameda County Community Food Bank
ACDA	American Commodity Distribution Association
ADM	Archer Daniels Midland
AFDC	Aid to Families with Dependent Children
AFSCME	American Federation of State, County and Municipal Employees
AMS	Agricultural Marketing Service
CAFB	California Association of Food Banks
CBPP	Center on Budget and Policy Priorities
CFP	Community Food Projects
CFPA	California Food Policy Advocates
CFSC	Community Food Security Coalition
CIW	Coalition of Immokalee Workers
E&T	Employment and Training
EITC	Earned Income Tax Credit
FA	Feeding America
FDA	Food and Drug Administration
FDPIR	Food Distribution Program on Indian Reservations
FFFI	Fresh Food Financing Initiative
FINI	Food Insecurity Nutrition Incentives
FMNP	Farmers Market Nutrition Program
FRAC	Food Research and Action Center
GBFB	Greater Boston Food Bank
GFPP	Good Food Purchasing Policy
IHC	Interfaith Hunger Coalition
LFTB	Lean Finely Textured Beef
LRP	Local and Regional Procurement

NAHC	National Anti-Hunger Coalition
NAHO	National Anti-Hunger Organizations
NFSN	National Farm to School Network
NYCCAH	New York City Coalition Against Hunger
OFB	Oregon Food Bank
PHP	Presbyterian Hunger Program
SFMNP	Senior Farmers Market Nutrition Program
SNAP	Supplemental Nutrition Assistance Program
SOS	Share Our Strength
SSB	Sugar Sweetened Beverage
TEFAP	The Emergency Food Assistance Program
UDHR	Universal Declaration of Human Rights
UFCW	Union of Food and Commercial Workers
USDA	United States Department of Agriculture
WIC	Women, Infants and Children

Notes

Introduction

1. "In Youngstown, We Make Steel (1803–1977)," UrbanOhio.com, August 24, 2008, http://www.urbanohio.com/forum2/index.php?topic=17134.0.

2. "In Youngstown."

3. Robert Bruno, *Steelworker Alley: How Class Works in Youngstown* (Ithaca, NY: Cornell University Press, 1999).

4. See Janet Poppendieck, *Sweet Charity: Emergency Food and the End of Entitlement* (New York: Viking 1998).

5. Ken Regal, telephone interview, October 19, 2015.

6. Elizabeth Kneebone, Carey Nadeau, and Alan Berube, "Re-emergence of Concentrated Poverty: Metropolitan Trends in the 2000s," Metropolitan Policy Series, Washington, DC: Brookings Institute, November 2011, http://www.brookings.edu/~/media/research/files/papers/2011/11/03-poverty-kneebone-nadeau-berube/1103_poverty_kneebone_nadeau_berube.pdf.

7. Thomas Frohlich, Alexander Kent, and Mark Lieberman, "The Happiest and Most Miserable Cities in America," *MSN*, May 22, 2015, http://www.msn.com/en-us/money/markets/the-happiest-and-most-miserable-cities-in-america/ss-AAb0QdK#image=21.

8. "Quick Facts," US Census Bureau, http://quickfacts.census.gov/qfd/states/39/3988000.html, 2015.

9. "Youngstown Private Prison to Lose 185 Jobs," *WKBN 27*, March 31, 2015, http://wkbn.com/2015/03/31/youngstown-private-prison-to-lose-185-jobs.

10. "Second Harvest Food Bank 2014 Annual Report," Second Harvest Food Bank of the Mahoning Valley, http://www.mahoningvalleysecondharvest.org/images/downloads/SHFBMV%202014%20Annual%20Report.pdf.

11. Perhaps the most accessible and comprehensive source of information about the SNAP program can be found at Food Research and Action Center's website: http://frac.org/federal-foodnutrition-programs/snapfood-stamps.

12. Unemployment in Rust Belt states in 2015 is under the national average. In Youngstown, however, fracking has contributed to a boomlet, but its sustainability is questionable given low oil prices and the earthquakes it has caused.

13. "Food Security in the U.S.," USDA Economic Research Service, http://www.ers.usda.gov/topics/food-nutrition-assistance/food-security-in-the-us/key-statistics-graphics.aspx#trends.

14. "The Millennium Development Goals Report Fact Sheet," United Nations, July 6, 2015, http://www.un.org/millenniumgoals/2015_MDG_Report/pdf/MDG %202015%20PR%20Key%20Facts%20Global.pdf.

15. Dwight D. Eisenhower, Farewell Speech, January 17, 1961, audio recording, https://www.eisenhower.archives.gov/all_about_ike/speeches/wav_files/farewell_address.mp3.

16. Jon Kolko, "Wicked Problems: Problems Worth Solving," *Stanford Social Innovation Review*, March 6, 2012, http://ssir.org/articles/entry/wicked_problems _problems_worth_solving.

Chapter 1

1. John Eligon and Michael Cooper, "Blasts at Boston Marathon Kill 3 and Injure 100," *New York Times*, April 15, 2013, http://www.nytimes.com/2013/04/16/us/ explosions-reported-at-site-of-boston-marathon.html?pagewanted=all.

2. Ellen Parker, personal communication, May 4, 2013.

3. Ibid.

4. Janet Poppendieck, "Hunger in America: Typification and Response," in *Eating Agendas: Food and Nutrition as Social Problems*, ed. Donna Maurer and Jeffery Sobel (New York: Aldine de Gruyter, 1995) p. 11.

5. Keith Olbermann, "Worst Person in the World: Mark Nord," *MSNBC*, November 17, 2006, http://www.nbcnews.com/id/15765825/ns/msnbc-countdown_with_keith _olbermann/t/worst-person-world-mark-nord/#.UhJ1YXBG4bY.

6. Lisa Stark, "Hungry Americans No Long 'Hungry,'" *ABC World News*, November 16, 2006, http://abcnews.go.com/WNT/story?id=2659818.

7. Jim Weill, quoted in Stark, "Hungry Americans."

8. Deborah Leff, quoted in Stark, "Hungry Americans."

9. David Himmelgreen and Nancy Romero-Daza, "Eliminating 'Hunger' in the U.S.: Changes in Policy Regarding the Measurement of Food Security," *Food and Foodways* 18, no. 1–2 (2010): 96–113; p. 104

10. Susannah Morgan, personal communication, August 23, 2013.

11. Sharon Thornberry, personal communication, July 15, 2013.

12. The concept of food security was originally formulated in the international development context to describe whether a nation had adequate resources to feed its population through either agricultural production or currency to purchase food in the marketplace. Soon thereafter, it came to be used in the household context to evaluate the adequacy of family food resources. In 1995, USDA and the U.S. Census Bureau carried out the first food security supplemental questionnaire to measure household food needs. This questionnaire focuses on respondents' experiences and behaviors in the face of food shortages rather than on physiological criteria. It includes questions related to such matters as whether people worry about running out of food; actually run out of food; skip meals or cut the size of their meals because of a lack of money to buy food; and lose weight or feel hungry because of a lack of money for food.

13. "Food Security in the United States," USDA Economic Research Service, http://www.ers.usda.gov/data-products/food-security-in-the-united-states.aspx.

14. Marion Nestle and Sally Guttmacher, "Hunger in the United States: Policy Implications," *Nutrition Reviews* 50, no. 8 (August 1992): 242–245.

15. Himmelgreen and Romero-Daza, p. 101.

16. Himmelgreen and Romero-Daza, p. 97

17. Poppendieck, "Hunger in America."

18. Sara Miles in *Take This Bread* tells of her own personal story as an atheist converted to Christianity who finds personal fulfillment and a sense of community in a San Francisco church-based food pantry.

19. David Beckmann and Sarah Newman, "Faith and Food," in *A Place at the Table*, ed. Peter Pringle (New York: Public Affairs, 2013), p. 146.

20. Andrew Kang Bartlett, telephone communication, July 3, 2013.

21. Ibid.

22. David Beckmann, telephone communication, July 22, 2013.

23. Tom Cornell, "A Brief Introduction to the Catholic Worker Movement," *The Catholic Worker Movement*, http://www.catholicworker.org/historytext.cfm?Number=4 Retrieved August 19, 2013.

24. David Beckmann, *Exodus from Hunger: We Are Called to Change the Politics of Hunger* (Louisville, KY: Westminster John Knox Press, 2010).

25. David Lee, Feeding Wisconsin and formerly of Feeding America, e-mail communication, August 26, 2013; "Feeding America," Feeding America, http://www .feedingamerica.org/search-results.aspx?searchTerm=number%20food%20pantries.

26. Linda Jones, "Christianity and Charity," *The New Statesman*, April 27, 2009, http://www.newstatesman.com/blogs/the-faith-column/2009/04/charity-love-god -christians.

27. "Tzedekah: Charity." Judaism 101, http://www.jewfaq.org/tzedakah.htm.

28. Maimonides, "Eight Degrees of Charity: Rambam, Hilchot Mat'Not Ani'im 10:1, 7–14," trans. Jonathan Baker, 2003, http://www.panix.com/~jjbaker/rmbmzdkh .html.

29. "Islam Solves World Poverty and Hunger," Al-islami, http://www.al-islami.com/ islam/islam_solves_poverty.php. Retrieved January 3, 2014.

30. "Charity in Islam," International Islamic Web, http://www.alahazrat.net/islam/ charity-in-islam.php.

31. Himmelgreen and Romero-Daza, p. 98.

32. Eugene Lewit and Nancy Kerrebrock, "Child Indicators: Childhood Hunger," *Welfare to Work* 7, no. 1 (Spring 1997), http://futureofchildren.org/publications/ journals/article/index.xml?journalid=54&articleid=308&sectionid=2044.

33. Food Research and Action Center, *Community Childhood Hunger Identification Project: A Survey of Childhood Hunger in the United States Executive Summary* (Washington, DC: FRAC, 1991). http://www.cura.umn.edu/sites/cura.advantagelabs. com/files/publications/S9103.pdf.

34. Gooloo Wunderlick and Janet Norwood, eds., *Food Insecurity and Hunger in the United States: An Assessment of the Measure* (Washington DC: National Research Council of the National Academies, 2006), p. 48.

35. Janet Poppendieck, "The USA: Hunger in the Land of Plenty," in *First World Hunger: Food Security and Welfare Politics*, ed. Graham Riches (New York: St. Martin's Press, 1997), 134

36. Jean Dreze and Amartya Sen, *Hunger and Public Action* (Oxford: Clarendon Press, 1989), pp. 3,4,5,6,9.

37. "The Black Panthers Free Breakfast for School Children," *Radical Practices of Collective Care*, http://radicalcollectivecare.blogspot.com/2013/01/the-blackpanthers -freebreakfast-for.html.

38. Joel Berg, *"All You Can Eat: How Hungry Is America?"* (New York: Seven Stories Press, 2008), p. 238; Joel Berg, telephone communication, July 19, 2013.

39. J. C. Dwyer, telephone communication, July 11, 2013.

40. Mark Winne, telephone communication, July 17, 2013.

41. Mike Moran, telephone communication, July 22, 2013.

42. Susannah Morgan, personal communication, August 23, 2013.

43. The use of sad, hungry-looking children is so prevalent among anti-hunger charities—and so reviled by their colleagues—that some groups even have nick-names for these kinds of appeals. Julia Tedesco, co-executive director of Foodlink, calls them "sad girl."

44. Mike Moran, telephone communication, July 22, 2013.

45. Mariana Chilton, telephone communication, July 23, 2013.

46. Harry Hopkins, quoted in Janet Poppendieck, *Sweet Charity: Emergency Food and the End of Entitlement* (New York: Viking 1998), p. 309

47. Mariana Chilton and Donald Rose, "A Rights-Based Approach to Food Insecurity in the United States," *American Journal of Public Health* 99, no. 7 (July 2009), p. 1204; Frances Moore Lappe, Joseph Collins, and Peter Rosset, *World Hunger: Twelve Myths* (New York: Grove Press, 1998), pp. 3-4.

48. Amartya Sen, *Development as Freedom* (Oxford: Oxford University Press, 1999) p. 16.

49. Poppendieck, *Sweet Charity*, p. 304.

50. Robert Egger, personal communication, April 29, 2013.

51. Chilton, personal communication; Egger, personal communication; Winne, personal communication.

52. Graham Riches, "Advancing the Human Right to Food in Canada: Social Policy and the Politics of Hunger, Welfare and Food Security," *Agriculture and Human Values* 16 (1999): 203–211; p. 207

53. Fox News Reporting, "The Great Food Stamp Binge," video, August 23, 2013, http://video.foxnews.com/v/2595939475001/a-look-at-fox-news-reporting-the-great -food-stamp-binge/?#sp=show-clips.

54. "Dolphin Change Program Raises More than $10,000 to Help Santa Monica's Homeless," *Lookout News*, November 4, 2015, http://www.surfsantamonica.com/ ssm_site/the_lookout/news/News-2015/Nov-2015/11_04_2015_Dolphin_Change _Program_Raises_More_than_10000_to_Help_Santa_Monicas_Homeless.html.

55. "Dolphin Program Makes Change," *Lookout News,* December 1, 2010, http://www.surfsantamonica.com/ssm_site/the_lookout/news/News-2010/December-2010/12_01_2010_Dolphin_Program_Makes_Change.html.

56. Peter Virgadamo, "Charity for a City in Crisis: Boston, 1740 to 1775," *Historical Journal of Massachusetts,* January 1982; "The Deserving Poor in Colonial America: 1601–1775," *Facts on File: History Database Search.*

57. "Hunger and Poverty Facts and Statistics," Feeding America, http://www.feedingamerica.org/hunger-in-america/impact-of-hunger/hunger-and-poverty/hunger-and-poverty-fact-sheet.html.

58. Allan MacDonell, "'Witnesses to Hunger' Takes You to Place Where Food Is a Luxury—in the USA," Children's Healthwatch, February 27, 2013, http://www.childrenshealthwatch.org/wp-content/uploads/NCG_takepart_Feb2013.pdf.

59. Nick Kotz, "The Politics of Hunger: Meese Was a Little Bit Right, and a Lot Wrong," *New Republic,* April 30, 1984.

60. Jessica Chanay, personal communication, July 1, 2013.

61. Chuck Scofield, telephone communication, August 20, 2013.

62. Laura Golino de Lovato, personal communication, July 19, 2013.

63. Brynne Keith-Jennings, "SNAP Plays a Critical Role in Helping Children," Center for Budget and Policy Priorities, http://www.cbpp.org/cms/?fa=view&id=3805.

64. "Child Hunger Prevention," Partners for a Hunger Free Oregon, https://oregonhunger.org/child-nutrition.

65. Chilton, personal communication.

66. Sharon Kilpatrick, Lynn McIntyre, and Melissa Potestio, "Child Hunger and Long Term Adverse Consequences for Health," *Archives of Pediatric and Adolescent Medicine* 164, no. 8 (August 2010), http://www.ucalgary.ca/lmcintyre/files/lmcintyre/hunger%20consequences.pdf.

67. Sarah Jane Schwarzenberg, Alice Kuo, Julie Linton, and Patricia Flanagan, "Promoting Food Security for All Children," *Pediatrics* 136, no. 5 (November 2015), http://pediatrics.aappublications.org/content/136/5/e1431.

68. "Kids Café," Feeding America, http://www.feedingamerica.org/how-we-fight-hunger/programs-and-services/child-hunger/kids-cafe.aspx; "The School Pantry Program," Feeding America, http://www.feedingamerica.org/how-we-fight-hunger/programs-and-services/child-hunger/school-pantry-program.aspx; "Child Hunger Corps," Feeding America, http://www.feedingamerica.org/how-we-fight-hunger/programs-and-services/child-hunger/child-hunger-corps.aspx; "Backpack Program," Feeding America, http://www.feedingamerica.org/how-we-fight-hunger/programs-and-services/child-hunger/backpack-program.aspx.

69. Ken Regal, Just Harvest, personal communication, January 22, 2013.

70. Sharon Thornberry, personal communication, July 15, 2013.

71. "Walmart Foundation Kicks Off Summer by Continuing Commitment to Out-Of-School Feeding, Helping Families in 450 Communities," Walmart Foundation, http://news.walmart.com/news-archive/2013/06/20/walmart-foundation-kicks-off-summer-by-continuing-commitment-to-out-of-school-feeding-helping-families-in-450-communities; "Our Partners Dedicated to Results," ConAgra Foods, http://www.conagrafoods.com/our-commitment/child-hunger/conagra-foods-foundation/learn-about-grants.

72. Julie Gibson, speech at National Anti-Hunger Policy Conference, Washington, DC, March 3, 2013; "Kellogg Company Provides $1 Million in Grants to Support School Breakfast Programs," Kellogg Company, May 14, 2014, http://newsroom.kelloggcompany.com/2014-05-14-Kellogg-Company-Provides-1-Million-In-Grants-To-Support-School-Breakfast-Programs.

73. Keith-Jennings, "Feeding America Stresses Crucial Need for SNAP Benefits for Children" Feeding America, June 20, 2013, http://www.feedingamerica.org/press-room/press-releases/feeding-america-stresses-crucial-need-for-snap-benefits-for-children.aspx.

74. "FRAC Applauds Democratic House Members for Protecting SNAP," Food Research and Action Center, August 13, 2013, http://frac.org/frac-applauds-democratic-house-members-for-protecting-snap.

75. This research was completed during the last two weeks of August 2013.

76. Billy Shore, telephone communication, July 31, 2013.

77. Poppendieck, *Sweet Charity*, p. 294.

78. Peter Buffett, "The Charitable-Industrial Complex," *New York Times*, July 26, 2013, http://www.nytimes.com/2013/07/27/opinion/the-charitable-industrial-complex.html.

79. Andy Bellatti, "The Big Oversight in Our Obesity Conversation," *Huffington Post*, January 9, 2013, http://www.huffingtonpost.com/andy-bellatti/obesity-crisis_b_2433833.html.

80. Winne, personal communication.

81. Erik Talkin, personal communication, April 29, 2013.

82. Chilton, personal communication.

83. "The Universal Declaration of Human Rights," United Nations, http://www.un.org/en/documents/udhr/; Chilton and Rose, "A Rights-Based Approach," pp. 1206–1207.

84. Chilton and Rose, "A Rights-Based Approach," pp. 1204, 1207

85. Tiina Silvasti and Graham Riches, "Hunger and Food Charity in Rich Societies: What Hope for the Right to Food?" in *First World Hunger Revisited: Food Charity or the Right to Food*, 2nd ed., ed. Riches and Silvasti (London: Palgrave MacMillan, 2014), p. 205.

86. Jean Ziegler, "What Is the Right to Food," Right to Food, http://www.righttofood .org/work-of-jean-ziegler-at-the-un/what-is-the-right-to-food.

87. George Kent, *Freedom from Want* (Washington, DC: Georgetown University Press, 2005), pp. 104–105.

88. Chilton and Rose, "A Rights-Based Approach," pp. 1203–1204

89. United Nations Economic and Social Council, Committee on Economic Social and Cultural Rights, "Substantive Issues Arising in the Implementation of the International Covenant on Economic, Social, and Cultural Rights. General Comment 12," 1999, http://www.fao.org/fileadmin/templates/righttofood/documents/RTF _publications/EN/General_Comment_12_EN.pdf.

90. Ibid.

91. "The Right to Food as a Human Right," Right to Food, http://www.srfood.org/ en/right-to-food. Retrieved September 2, 2013.

92. Kent, *Freedom from Want*, p. 46

93. Olivier de Schutter, "Women's Rights and the Right to Food," United Nations General Assembly Human Rights Council, 22nd session, December 24, 2012, http:// www.ohchr.org/Documents/HRBodies/HRCouncil/RegularSession/Session22/ AHRC2250_English.PDF.

94. George Manalo Le Clair, telephone communication, August 1, 2013.

95. Chilton and Rose, "A Rights-Based Approach," pp. 1206–1207

96. Ibid.

97. Poppendieck, "Hunger in America," pp. 26–27

98. Ibid.

Chapter 2

1. Scott Helman, "How the Greater Boston Food Bank Is Meeting a Greater Need," *Boston Globe*. November 4, 2012, http://www.bostonglobe.com/magazine/ 2012/11/03/how-greater-boston-food-bank-growing-meet-growing-need/ 8BWiUXroYzxBR5DR02sgEL/story.html; Kendra Bird, personal communication, May 6, 2013.

2. Helman, "How the Greater Boston Food Bank."

3. "About GBFB," Greater Boston Food Bank, http://gbfb.org/our-mission/about-gbfb.php; Helman, "How the Greater Boston Food Bank"; "Fiscal Year 2015 Impact," Greater Boston Food Bank, http://gbfb.org/our-mission/yearinreview.php.

4. "About GBFB."

5. Throughout this book, I use the terms "emergency food system," "food charity," and "charitable food distribution" interchangeably. They all refer to the network of organizations that distribute surplus food to the needy, for free, through such outlets as soup kitchens and food pantries.

6. "How We Fight Hunger," Feeding America, http://www.feedingamerica.org/how-we-fight-hunger.aspx.

7. Ken Meter, presentation to Hunger Gap Conference, Tucson, Arizona, September 18, 2013.

8. "How We Work," Feeding America, http://www.feedingamerica.org/about-us/how-we-work.

9. Mark Rank, "Poverty in America is Mainstream," *New York Times*, November 2, 2013, http://opinionator.blogs.nytimes.com/2013/11/02/poverty-in-america-is-mainstream/?hp&rref=opinion&_r=1&.

10. Ellen Parker, personal communication, May 4, 2013.

11. Janet Poppendieck, *Sweet Charity: Emergency Food and the End of Entitlement* (New York: Viking, 1998).

12. Many food banks distribute food such as produce and dairy without shared maintenance fees. At Oregon Food Bank, the average shared maintenance fee is 3 cents per pound.

13. Julia Tedesco, personal communication, June 17, 2013.

14. Mike Moran, telephone communication, July 22, 2013.

15. Andrew Schiff, telephone communication, August 13, 2013.

16. Sharon Paynter, Maureen Berner, and Emily Anderson, "When Even the Dollar Value Meal Costs Too Much: Food Insecurity and Long-Term Dependence on Food Pantry Assistance," *Public Administration Quarterly* 35, no. 1 (Spring 2011): 26–58.

17. Mark Winne, *Closing the Food Gap: Resetting the Table in the Land of Plenty* (Boston: Beacon Press, 2009).

18. The name of the federal program that supplies food banks with commodities and cash was changed in 1990 from the Temporary Emergency Food Assistance Program to The Emergency Food Assistance Program (thus the acronym remains the

same) to reflect the understanding that the "emergency" being addressed was no longer considered to be temporary in nature.

19. Poppendieck, *Sweet Charity* ("undignified"); Mariana Chilton, telephone communication, July 13, 2013 ("racist," "classist"); Robert Lupton, *Toxic Charity: How Churches and Charities Hurth Those They Help* (New York: HarperCollins, 2012) ("toxic"); Graham Riches, "Food Banks and Food Security: Welfare Reform, Human Rights and Social Policy: Lessons from Canada?" in *The Welfare of Food: Rights and Responsibilities in a Changing World*, ed. Elizabeth Dowler and Catherine Jones Finer (Oxford: Blackwell, 2003) ("stigmatizing"); Patrick Butler, "Food Banks Are a 'Slow Death of the Soul,'" *Guardian*, September 24, 2013, https://www.theguardian.com/society/2013/sep/25/food-banks-slow-death-soul ("slow death").

20. Christopher Wimer, Rachel Wright, and Kelly Fong, "The Cost of Free Assistance: Studying the Non-Use of Food Assistance in San Francisco," Stanford Center on Poverty and Inequality, October 28, 2012, http://www.stanford.edu/group/scspi/_media/working_papers/wimer-wright-fong_cost-free-assist.pdf.

21. USDA rules stipulate that to receive the emergency food assistance program (TEFAP) products, an individual must not make more than 185 percent of poverty level. To make up for the food that I took out of the system, I made a modest donation to the church that runs the food pantry.

22. "Profiles of Hunger and Poverty in Oregon: 2012 Oregon Hunger Factors Assessment," Oregon Food Bank.

23. Lupton, *Toxic Charity*.

24. Sandburg, quoted in Lupton, *Toxic Charity*.

25. Lupton, *Toxic Charity*.

26. Nick Saul, personal communication, October 1, 2013.

27. Lupton, *Toxic Charity*.

28. Michele Simon, "Pink Slime: A Symptom of Industrialized Meat," May 15, 2015, Center for Food Safety, http://www.centerforfoodsafety.org.php53-2.ord1-1 .websitetestlink.com/blog/1128/pink-slime-a-symptom-of-industrialized-meat.

29. Michael Peck, telephone communication, May 6, 2013.

30. James Vaznis, "Without Paperwork, School Lunch Free in Boston," *Boston Globe*, September 3, 2013, http://www.bostonglobe.com/metro/2013/09/02/boston-public -schools-will-offer-free-lunches-all-students/2aaUy5sxJjIak9ndGDHxkJ/story.html.

31. "Massachusetts Emergency Food Assistance Program Fiscal Year 2014 Core Food Summary Report," Food Bank of Western Massachusetts; The Greater Boston Food Bank; Merrimack Valley Food Bank; and Worcester County Food Bank, http://www .mass.gov/eea/docs/agr/programs/mefap/fy14-mefap-cf-report.pdf.

32. Elizabeth Campbell, Michelle Ross, and Karen Webb, "Improving the Nutritional Quality of Emergency Food: A Study of Food Bank Organizational Culture, Capacity, and Practices," *Journal of Hunger and Environmental Nutrition* 8, no. 3 (2013): 294–309.

33. Sasha Khokha and Natasha del Toro, "Food Banks Feed the Hungry—and Face Tough Choices on Donations," *KQED*, October 9, 2013, http://blogs.kqed.org/newsfix/2013/10/08/114173/hunger-in-the-valley-and-unhealthy-food-donations.

34. "Adult Obesity Facts," Centers for Disease Control and Prevention, http://www.cdc.gov/obesity/data/adult.html; Daniel Willis, "Data Center: Obesity Rates by County in California," *San Jose Mercury News*, July 23, 2013, http://www.mercurynews.com/data/ci_23716262/data-center-obesity-rates-by-county-california.

35. Khokha and del Toro, "Food Banks."

36. Campbell et al., "Improving the Nutritional Quality."

37. Ibid.

38. "Healthy Options, Healthy Meals," Mazon, http://mazon.org/strategic-initiative/healthy-options-healthy-meals/; Thornberry, personal communication, October 1, 2013.

39. "Feeding America," Bristol Myers Squibb: Together on Diabetes, http://www.bms.com/togetherondiabetes/partners/Pages/feeding-america.aspx; "Healthy Food Bank Hub," Feeding America, http://healthyfoodbankhub.feedingamerica.org.

40. Helen Costello, telephone communication, October 23, 2013.

41. Marketing codes are designed to support farm income by keeping produce prices high through limiting the quality of product that can go on the market.

42. Campbell et al., "Improving the Nutritional Quality."

43. Bird, personal communication, May 6, 2013.

44. Thomas Ferraro, personal communication, June 16, 2013; Suzan Bateson, personal communication, February 22, 2013; Ross Fraser, e-mail communication, September 5, 2013.

45. Nick Saul and Andrea Curtis, *The Stop: How the Fight for Good Food Transformed a Community and Inspired a Movement* (Toronto: Random House Canada, 2013).

46. Debbie Field, personal communication, May 8, 2013.

47. Jon Stubenvoll, e-mail communication, June 25, 2015.

48. Bird, personal communication.

49. David Weaver, telephone communication, December 16, 2011; Lisa Hamler Fugitt, telephone communication, December 13, 2011.

50. J. C. Dwyer, telephone communication, July 11, 2013.

51. Hamler Fugitt, personal communication.

52. Jeff Kleen, e-mail communication, October 15, 2013.

53. Gloria McAdam, telephone communication, December 14, 2011.

54. "Legislative Update," Feeding America, July 11, 2013.

55. "Profiles of Hunger and Poverty in Oregon."

56. Michael Flood, telephone communication, November 2011.

57. "California Guide to Food Benefits," Legal Services of Northern California, http://foodstampguide.org/immigrant-eligibility-for-food-stamps.

58. Andrew Wainer, "Immigration Reform as a Way to Reduce Poverty," Spotlight on Poverty and Opportunity, April 8, 2013, http://spotlightonpoverty.org/spotlight -exclusives/immigration-reform-as-a-way-to-reduce-poverty.

59. Ibid.

60. Laura Golino de Lovato, personal communication, July 19, 2013.

61. This research was conducted from December 24, 2012 to February 8, 2013. The cut-off for a Fortune 1000 company was determined to be $1.6 billion in annual revenues for 2012, and was based on the Fortune 1000 listing for 2013. Wholly owned subsidiaries were counted as being part of a Fortune 1000 firm, if the parent company had revenues over the $1.6 billion cut-off. The Fortune 1000 designation was chosen primarily because of the ease of verifying whether a company is on the list. There were numerous other board members who worked for firms that were still quite massive, from $250 million to $1.6 billion in revenue.

62. Stubenvoll, personal communication, July 23, 2013.

63. Kevin Bott, telephone communication, September 15, 2013.

64. Joyce Rothermel, personal communication, February 5, 2013.

65. McAdam, telephone communication, December 14, 2011.

66. Natalie Jayroe, telephone communication, December 13, 2011.

67. Flood, telephone communication.

68. McAdam, telephone communication.

69. Kate MacKenzie, telephone communication, June 7, 2013.

70. "Form 990," Feeding America 7/2013–6/2014, http://www.guidestar.org/ FinDocuments/2014/363/673/2014-363673599-0b147531-9.pdf.

71. This informant, who prefers to remain anonymous, believes that the criteria are: total pounds per person in poverty (PPIP) in service area; percent nutritious food received; average county PPIP; total meals delivered via SNAP Outreach; local pounds solicited; food safety index; meals distributed per dollar; cost per dollar raised; program expenses percent of operating expenses; inventory turns; volunteer hours donated; number of individual donors per 1000-population; number of food drive pounds; percent of available dollars in service area raised from individuals; private support revenue raised; private support revenue percentage of total operating expenses; average individual gift size in dollars; individual support percent of total fundraising.

72. Poppendieck, *Sweet Charity*.

73. "Tax Benefits for your Company," Feeding America, http://www.feedingamerica. org/get-involved/corporate-opportunities/become-a-partner/become-a-product -partner/tax-benefits-for-your-company.aspx.

74. "An Update to the Budget and Economic Outlook: Fiscal Years 2012 to 2022," Congressional Budget Office, August 22, 2012, https://www.cbo.gov/publication/ 43539.

75. "Bill Analysis, AB 152," California Franchise Tax Board, https://www.ftb.ca .gov/law/legis/11_12bills/ab152_Final.pdf. By comparison, Canada does not offer tax incentives for charitable food donations.

76. "White Paper on the Emergency Food Assistance Program (TEFAP) Summary. USDA, Food and Nutrition Service Office of Policy Support, August 2013, http:// www.fns.usda.gov/sites/default/files/TEFAPWhitePaper_Summary.pdf; "The Emergency Food Assistance Program," Feeding America, http://www.feedingamerica.org/ how-we-fight-hunger/advocacy-public-policy/policy-center/federal-anti-hunger -programs-and-policies/the-emergency-food-assistance-program.aspx.

77. Database obtained from Feeding America's internal HungerNet website, 2009.

78. In 2013, the USDA purchased $228.5 million of bonus commodities. In 2014, TEFAP had $268.75 million appropriated for regular TEFAP purchases. Federal tax credits are estimated at $189 million based on a 10-year average. The latest data in my possession for state programs for FY 2008–2010 shows that states spent about $136 million on supporting the emergency food sector.

79. As of 2009, USDA commodities made up 26% of the Feeding America distribution stream, according to their Network Poundage Report (2009).

80. Feeding America, in its Network Poundage Report 2009, states the following breakdown for food distributed in 2009: USDA: 26%; Retail donated case 16%; Produce 16%; Purchased 15%; Manufacturer/producer donated case 11%; Other 7%; Salvage 5%; Food drives 3%; Prepared Food 1%.

81. John Burns, "Food Bank Urges Community to Beat 'Bama," Oanow, http://www.oanow.com/news/lee_county/article_e7ad7276-3aa8-11e3-8a41-001a4bcf6878.html.

82. Ibid.

83. Greater Boston Food Bank, 990 Report, 2010, http://www.guidestar.org/FinDocuments/2010/042/717/2010-042717782-0738c39d-9.pdf.

84. Judy Alley, telephone communication, July 16, 2013.

85. Robert Egger, personal communication, April 29, 2013.

86. A parallel can be drawn with environmentalist groups who experience a dramatic rise in membership during Republican administrations that threaten to undo environmental regulations, and, conversely, see a decline during more environmentally friendly periods. People react to immediate threats.

87. Terra Keller, telephone communication, October 15, 2013.

88. Thomas Ferraro, e-mail communication, October 14, 2013.

89. Catherine D'Amato, quoted in Helman, "How the Greater Boston Food Bank."

90. Sharon Thornberry, speech to Ecumenical Ministries of Oregon Food Justice Fundraiser. Portland, Oregon, October 22, 2013.

Chapter 3

1. This pledge consists of $1.1 pounds of food valued at $1.75 billion ($1.59 per pound), and $250 million in cash.

2. Walmart and the Walmart Foundation, "Fighting Hunger Together Campaign," video footage, http://news.walmart.com/news-archive/2010/05/12/walmart-commits-2-billion-to-help-end-hunger-in-the-us.

3. Jerome Himmelstein, Looking Good and Doing Good: Corporate Philanthropy and Corporate Power (Bloomington: Indiana University Press, 1997).

4. Milton Friedman, Capitalism and Freedom (Chicago: University of Chicago Press, 1962).

5. Freeman, quoted in Kathy Koch, "The New Corporate Philanthropy," CQ Researcher 27 (February, 1998).

6. Michael Stroik, e-mail communication, January 20, 2013.

7. "Giving USA Highlights 2014," Giving USA, http://givingusa.org/product/giving-usa-2014-report-highlights/; "Charitable Giving Statistics," National Philanthropic Trust, http://www.nptrust.org/philanthropic-resources/charitable-giving-statistics/.

8. "Measuring Purpose: Giving in Numbers Brief 2015," Committee to Encourage Corporate Philanthropy, http://cecp.co/pdfs/giving_in_numbers/GIN_8x11_HighRes .pdf.

9. Harry Freeman, "Corporate Strategic Philanthropy: A Million Here, a Million There, It Can Add up to Real Corporate Choices," *Vital Speeches of the Day* 58, no. 8 (February 1, 1992).

10. "What is Strategic Philanthropy?" *The Truist*, June 17, 2013. http://truist.com/ what-is-strategic-philanthropy. Retrieved July 7, 2015.

11. Ibid.

12. "Clif Bar Spearheads $10 Million Investment to Fund Five Endowed Chairs Focused on Organic Agricultural Research," Clif Bar, June 23, 2015, http://www .clifbar.com/newsroom/clif-bar-spearheads-10-million-investment-to-fund-five -endowed-chairs-focused-on-organic-agricultural-research.

13. Himmelstein, *Looking Good, Doing Good*.

14. Angela Eikenberry, "The Hidden Costs of Cause Marketing," *Stanford Social Innovation Review* (Summer 2009), http://ssir.org/articles/entry/the_hidden_costs_of _cause_marketing.

15. Mara Einstein, *Compassion, Inc.* (Berkeley: University of California Press, 2012).

16. I got my start in the food movement as a consultant paid with funds from a $10,000 Share Our Strength grant to launch what became the Community Food Security Coalition in 1994.

17. "Our Story," RED, https://www.red.org/en/about; "Susan G. Komen Passionately Pink," http://www.info-komen.org/site/PageServer?pagename=HQ_PP11_homepage &itc=ppftc2011:1.

18. Einstein, *Compassion Inc.*

19. Eikenberry, "The Hidden Costs."

20. "Kellogg Company Provides $1 Million in Grants to Support School Breakfast Programs," Kellogg Company, May 14, 2014, http://newsroom.kelloggcompany .com/2014-05-14-Kellogg-Company-Provides-1-Million-In-Grants-To-Support -School-Breakfast-Programs.

21. Himmelstein, *Looking Good, Doing Good*.

22. "What Are B Corps," Certified B Corporation, https://www.bcorporation.net/ what-are-b-corps.

23. Liza Stonyfield, "Organic and GMOs Don't Mix," Stonyfield Organic, http:// www.stonyfield.com/blog/organic-and-gmos-do-not-mix; Ben and Jerry's, http:// www.benjerry.com.

24. Kori Reed, telephone communication, November 1, 2012.

25. Ronald Levy, *Give and Take: A Candid Account of Corporate Philanthropy* (Cambridge, MA: Harvard Business School Press, 1999).

26. Fraser Seitel and John Doorley, *Rethinking Reputation: How PR Trumps Marketing and Advertising in the New Media World* (New York: Palgrave MacMillan, 2012).

27. Daryl Koehn Joe Ueng, "Is Philanthropy Being Used by Corporate Wrongdoers to Buy Good Will?" *Journal of Management and Governance* 14 (2010): 1–16; Robert Williams and J. Douglas Barrett, "Corporate Philanthropy, Criminal Activity, and Firm Reputation: Is There a Link?" *Journal of Business Ethics* 26, no. 4 (2000): 341–346.

28. Williams and Barrett, "Corporate Philanthropy."

29. Chris Serres, Chris "Target vs. Walmart: Is Target Corporation Any Better for Workers?" Reclaim Democracy, http://reclaimdemocracy.org/walmart_target_better.

30. Terence Lim, *Measuring the Value of Corporate Philanthropy: Social Impact, Business Benefits and Investor Returns* (New York: Committee Encouraging Corporate Philanthropy, 2010), http://www.corporatephilanthropy.org/pdfs/resources/MVCP_report _singles.pdf.

31. Williams and Barrett, "Corporate Philanthropy."

32. Koehn and Ueng, "Is Philanthropy Being Used."

33. Himmelstein, *Looking Good, Doing Good.*

34. Ibid.

35. These eleven groups are: Bread for the World, Center on Budget and Policy Priorities, Congressional Hunger Center, End Hunger Network, Feeding America, Food Research and Action Center, Meals on Wheels, RESULTS, Share Our Strength, Society of St. Andrew, WhyHunger.

36. "Mission Partners," Feeding America, http://www.feedingamerica.org/about -us/about-feeding-america/partners/food-and-fund-partners/mission-partners/; "Supporting Partners," Feeding America, http://www.feedingamerica.org/about-us/ about-feeding-america/partners/food-and-fund-partners/supporting-partners/; "Our Partners," No Kid Hungry, https://www.nokidhungry.org/partners.

37. "2014 Congressional Hunger Center Awards Ceremony," Congressional Hunger Center, http://hungercenter.wpengine.netdna-cdn.com/wp-content/uploads/2015/ 02/2014-Awards-Program-web.pdf; "2013 990 Form," Congressional Hunger Center, http://www.guidestar.org/FinDocuments/2014/521/842/2014-521842738-0b20444b -9.pdf.

38. Emily Bryson York, "How Feeding America Became the Go-to Cause for Marketers," *Ad & Marketing News*, May 3, 2010, http://adage.com/article/news/feeding-america-marketers/143647/.

39. Einstein, *Compassion, Inc.*

40. "Promotional Partners," Feeding America, http://www.feedingamerica.org/how-we-fight-hunger/our-partners/promotional-partners.aspx; "Current Promotions," Feeding America,http://www.feedingamerica.org/about-us/about-feeding-america/partners/current-promotions/index.jsp?mlpage=1.

41. "The Cheesecake Factory," Feeding America, http://www.feedingamerica.org/about-us/about-feeding-america/partners/current-promotions/the-cheesecake-factory.html.

42. "Bringing Hope to 46 million People, 2014 Annual Report," Feeding America, http://www.feedingamerica.org/about-us/about-feeding-america/annual-report/2014-annual-report.pdf; "2008 Annual Report," Feeding America,http://www.feedingamerica.org/about-us/about-feeding-america/annual-report/feedingamerica_2008_annual_report.pdf.

43. "Current Funders Include," California Food Policy Advocates, http://cfpa.net/our-funders.

44. Einstein, *Compassion, Inc.*

45. Arlin Wasserman, telephone communication, October 23, 2012.

46. Ibid.

47. Himmelstein, *Looking Good, Doing Good.*

48. Catherine Candisky and Jim Siegel, "Food Banks Group Bows to Donor's Pressure on Payday Lending Bill," *Columbus Dispatch*, May 1, 2008, http://www.dispatch.com/content/stories/local/2008/05/02/foodbanks.html.

49. "Our Story," Walmart, http://corporate.walmart.com/our-story/; "1.Walmart," *Fortune 500*, http://fortune.com/fortune500/walmart-1/; Aleaxander Hess, "The 10 Largest Employers in America," *USA Today*, August 22, 2013, http://www.usatoday.com/story/money/business/2013/08/22/ten-largest-employers/2680249/; Dan Mitchell, "Say Goodbye to Your Supermarket," *Fortune*, March 14, 2014, http://fortune.com/2014/03/14/say-goodbye-to-your-supermarket/; "The World's Billionaires," *Forbes*, http://www.forbes.com/billionaires/list/#version:static_search:walton; "Walmart on Tax Day," Americans for Tax Fairness, April 2014, http://www.americansfortaxfairness.org/files/Walmart-on-Tax-Day-Americans-for-Tax-Fairness-1.pdf.

50. Robert Scott, "The Walmart Effect," Economic Policy Institute, June 25, 2007, http://www.epi.org/publication/ib235.

51. Hiroko Tabuchi, "Walmart Raising Wages to at Least $9," *New York Times*, February 19, 2015, http://www.nytimes.com/2015/02/20/business/walmart-raising-wage-to-at-least-9-dollars.html.

52. Dan Schlademan, telephone communication, March 22, 2013.

53. Samantha Masunaga, "Pico Rivera Closure a Worry for City," *Los Angeles Times*, April 26, 2015, http://www.latimes.com/business/la-fi-walmart-pico-rivera-20150427-story.html.

54. "Walmart on Tax Day"; Democratic Staff, "The Low Wage Drag on our Economy," US House Committee on Education and the Workforce, May 2013, http://democrats-edworkforce.house.gov/sites/democrats.edworkforce.house.gov/files/documents/WalMartReport-May2013.pdf.

55. Walmart Stores, Inc., 16th Annual Meeting for the Investment Community, transcript of day 2, session 6, October 22, 2009.

56. Josh Eidelson and Lee Fang, "Obama's Budget Chief Nominee Led Walmart's Targeted Giving," *The Nation*, February 15, 2013, http://www.thenation.com/article/172952/obamas-top-choice-omb-led-walmart-foundations-targeted-giving.

57. "Top Funders," Foundation Center, June 27, 2015, http://foundationcenter.org/findfunders/topfunders/top50giving.html.

58. Peter Dreier and Donald Cohen, "Walmart's Honest Graft," *Dissent Magazine*ˆ, June 21, 2012, http://www.dissentmagazine.org/online_articles/Walmarts-honest-graft.

59. Lim, "Measuring the Value of Corporate Philanthropy."

60. John Koskinen, letter to IRS from Commissioner re Walmart Foundation EIN 205639919, June 15, 2015, document in author's possession.

61. Ibid.

62. Dreier and Donald Cohen, "Walmart's Honest Graft."

63. Kosikinen, letter to IRS from Commissioner; Meghan Irons and Andrew Ryan, "Walmart's Charitable Giving Soars in Boston," *Boston Globe*, August 20, 2011.

64. James Covert, "City Council Members Rip Walmart's Charity of 'Dangerous Dollars,'" *New York Post*, June 4, 2014, http://nypost.com/2014/06/04/city-council-members-rip-walmarts-charity-of-dangerous-dollars/.

65. Kosikinen, letter to IRS from Commissioner.

66. Walmart Foundation, "Recognizing the Walmart Foundation for its Good Works," n/d.

67. Walmart, "How Is Walmart Helping Atlanta Families Overcome Hunger," *Walmart Washington DC Community*, video, http://www.walmartcommunity.com/washington-dc. Retrieved July 2, 2015.

68. Kosikinen, letter to IRS from Commissioner.

69. Jessica Powers, personal communication, January 23, 2013.

70. "Community Grant Guidelines," Walmart, http://giving.walmart.com/apply -for-grants/local-giving-guidelines.

71. "Hunger Relief and Healthy Eating," Walmart, http://giving.walmart.com/our -focus/hunger.

72. This calculation is based on Walmart's statement in the 2010 announcement of the Fighting Hunger campaign that it would donate 1.1 billion pounds valued at $1.75 billion, or roughly $1.59 per pound.

73. "Hunger Relief and Healthy Eating."

74. Walmart Foundation, Form 990, Year 2010, http://www.guidestar.org/FinDocuments/2010/205/639/2010-205639919-06b19126-F.pdf; Walmart Foundation, Form 990, Year 2013, http://www.guidestar.org/FinDocuments/2014/205/639/2014-205639919-0afc279c-F.pdf.

75. "Walmart Foundation Helps Kids Gain Access to Food and Nutrition Education as Summer Months Bring Risk of Hunger," Walmart, June 22, 2015, http://news .walmart.com/news-archive/2015/06/22/walmart-foundation-helps-kids-gain -access-to-food-and-nutrition-education-as-summer-months-bring-risk-of-hunger.

76. "Food Pantry Holiday Makeover Campaign Awards $20,000 to 75 Food Pantries Across the Country," Walmart, December 15, 2014, http://news.walmart.com/news -archive/2014/12/15/communities-unite-in-the-spirit-of-giving-to-help-local-food -pantries-win-part-of-15-million-in-grants-from-walmart.

77. "Walmart Launches Fight Hunger, Spark Change Campaign," Walmart, September 15, 2014, http://news.walmart.com/news-archive/2014/09/15/walmart-launches -fight-hunger-spark-change-campaign-calling-on-customers-suppliers-and -associates-to-take-action-in-the-fight-against-hunger. This type of popularity contest is becoming increasingly common with corporate philanthropists because it drives traffic to company websites and captures e-mail addresses for future publicity. It also serves as a direct way to shape public perception of the company's image.

78. "Hunger Relief and Healthy Eating."

79. Walmart Foundation, Form 990, Year 2010; Walmart Foundation, Form 990 Year 2013; Walmart Foundation, Form 990, Year 2012, http://www.guidestar.org/FinDocuments/2012/205/639/2012-205639919-0b171603-FA.pdf; Walmart Foundation, Form 990, Year 2011, http://www.guidestar.org/FinDocuments/2011/205/639/

2011-205639919-0785d8-F.pdf; Walmart Foundation, Form 990, Year 2015, http://www.guidestar.org/FinDocuments/2015/205/639/2015-205639919-0c1020ad-F.pdf.

80. Leslie Dach, quoted in Michele Simon, "Food Stamps: Follow the Money," *Eat Drink Politics*, June 2012, http://www.eatdrinkpolitics.com/wp-content/uploads/FoodStampsFollowtheMoneySimon.pdf.

81. Shelly Banjo and Annie Gasparro, "Retailers Brace for Reductions in Food Stamps," *Wall Street Journal*, November 4, 2013, http://www.wsj.com/articles/SB10001424052702303843104579168011245171266.

82. "The President's Speech: Right about Stopping Offshore Tax Dodgers, Wrong about Cutting Taxes for Other Corporations," Citizens for Tax Justice, January 26, 2012, http://www.ctj.org/pdf/sotucorporatetaxes.pdf.

83. Walmart Foundation staff did not respond to multiple requests for an interview to address the information in this section.

84. "Snickers Brand Is Asking America to Help Bar Hunger," Feeding America, July 1, 2010, http://www.feedingamerica.org/hunger-in-america/news-and-updates/press-room/press-releases/snickers-brand-is-asking-americas-help-to-bar-hunger.html.

85. Einstein, *Compassion, Inc.*

86. "SNICKERS(R) Brand and David Arquette Make a Big Move to Help Feeding America Bar Hunger," *PR Newswire*,http://www.prnewswire.com/news-releases/snickersr-brand-and-david-arquette-make-a-big-move-to-help-feeding-america-bar-hunger-62190292.html.

87. Einstein, *Compassion, Inc.*

88. Inger Stole, "Cause-Related Marketing: Why Social Change and Corporate Profits Don't Mix," *PR Watch*, July 14, 2006, http://www.prwatch.org/news/2006/07/4965/cause-related-marketing-why-social-change-and-corporate-profits-don't-mix.

89. Einstein, *Compassion, Inc.*

90. Andy Fisher, "The Art of Planning a Food Security Conference," *Civil Eats*, November 17, 2010, http://civileats.com/2010/11/17/10168.

91. Chipotle did send us an anonymous donation of $50,000, even after we refused to partner with them. We decided to accept these funds because our objection was not to taking their money per se, but to being publicly associated with the company at the time they refused to support the tomato pickers.

92. Noreen Springstead, e-mail communication, July 15, 2015.

93. Ibid.

94. Patti Whitney Wise, telephone communication, August 20, 2014.

95. Ibid., ca. 2012.

Chapter 4

1. Walter Willett, e-mail communication. May 26, 2016.

2. Jessica Bartholow, telephone communciation, June 9, 2014

3. Michael Moss, *Salt, Sugar, Fat: How the Food Giants Hooked Us* (New York: Random House, 2013), p. 3.

4. While fruit can have a lot of sugars, it also contains nutrients and fiber that benefit the body and slow down the digestion of the sugars. Nutritionists tend to be more concerned about the role of sugar added to food products.

5. "Added Sugars Fact Sheet," Yale Rudd Center for Food Policy and Obesity, June 2014, http://www.uconnruddcenter.org/files/Pdfs/SSB_AddedSugars.pdf.

6. "The Facts About Diabetes: A Leading Cause of Death in the U.S," National Diabetes Education Program, http://ndep.nih.gov/diabetes-facts/.

7. Jim Krieger, presentation at Second National Soda Summit, Washington, DC, June 4, 2014.

8. "The Facts About Diabetes."

9. "SNAP Decisions: Health Impact Assessment. Proposed Illinois Legislation to Eliminate Sugar Sweetened Beverages from the Supplemental Nutrition Assistance Program," Illinois Public Health Institute, 2014.

10. "Sugar: Too Much of a Sweet Thing," Center for Science in the Public Interest, March 1, 2013.

11. Sarah Boseley, "Mexico Enacts Soda Tax in Effort to Combat World's Highest Obesity Rate," *The Guardian*, January 16, 2014, https://www.theguardian.com/world/2014/jan/16/mexico-soda-tax-sugar-obesity-health; Alejandro Calvillo, presentation at Second National Soda Summit, Washington, DC, June 4, 2014.

12. Claire Wang, "Why Pick on Soda: Trends and Patterns of Consumption," Power-Point presentation at Second National Soda Summit, Washington, DC, June 4, 2014; Tatiana Andreyeva, Joerg Ludicke, Kathryn Hendrickson, and Amanda Tripp, "Grocery Store Beverage Choices by Participants in Federal Food Assistance and Nutrition Programs," *American Journal of Preventive Medicine* 43, no. 4 (2012): 411–418.

13. "Added Sugars Fact Sheet"; Anne Barnhill, "Impact and Ethics of Excluding Sweetened Beverages from the SNAP Program," *American Journal of Public Health* 101, no. 11 (2011): 2037–2043.

14. Frank Chaloupka, Amelie Rodriguez, and Kipling Gallion, "Sugar Sweetened Beverage Consumption by Latino Youths and the Impact of Pricing," *Salud America,* Research Review. September 2013, p. 5, salud-america.org/sites/salud-america/files/Sugary-Drinks-research-review.pdf.

15. "Impact of Sugar-Sweetened Beverage Consumption on Black Americans' Health," *African American Collaborative Obesity Research Network,* January 2011, http://www.aacorn.org/uploads/files/AACORNSSBBrief2011.pdf.

16. Ibid.

17. Frank Hu, presentation at Second National Soda Summit, Washington, DC, June 4, 2014.

18. Darius Mozaffarian, presentation at Second National Soda Summit, Washington, DC, June 5, 2014.

19. Ovidijius Jurevicius, "Coca-Cola SWOT Analysis 2016," Strategic Management Insight, March 31, 2016, https://www.strategicmanagementinsight.com/swot-analyses/coca-cola-swot-analysis.html.

20. Hu, presentation.

21. "Impact of Sugar-Sweetened Beverage."

22. Marlene Schwartz, presentation at Second National Soda Summit, Washington, DC, June 5, 2014.

23. Pablo Monsivais and Adam Drewnowski, "The Rising Cost of Low Energy Density Foods," *Journal of the American Dietetic Association* 107, no. 12 (2007): 2071–2076.

24. Peter Eisinger, *Toward an End to Hunger in America* (Washington, DC: Brookings Institution Press, 1998), p. 43.

25. Patrick Canning, "A Revised and Expanded Food Dollar Series," USDA Economic Research Service, February 2011, http://www.ers.usda.gov/media/131096/err114_reportsummary.pdf.

26. Query the Lobbying Disclosure Act database, United States Senate, http://soprweb.senate.gov/index.cfm?event=selectfields.

27. A block grant is a sum of money provided by the federal government to states. It is seen as problematic for various reasons. It would eliminate SNAP as an entitlement program, allowing each state to establish its own program and set of rules. Hard-won federal regulations would be discarded and left up to the states, creating a patchwork of programs and rules. SNAP's ability to provide counter-cyclical support to the poor during a recession would also be eliminated, as a block grant amount would not be tied to economic indicators. Finally, it is much easier for the federal government to slowly erode the SNAP program as a block grant, simply reducing the allocation each state gets over a period of time.

28. David Super, "'The Quiet 'Welfare Revolution': Resurrecting the Food Stamp Program in the Wake of the 1996 Welfare Law," *New York University Law Review* 79, no. 4 (October 2004): 1271.

29. This is not to discount the concern of many public health professionals about the health impacts of food insecurity. Children's Health Watch, for example, has done stellar research on the impacts of hunger on children's brain development.

30. Gus Schumacher, Michel Nischan, and Daniel Bowman Simon, "Food Stamps: Once We Had It Right," in *A Place at the Table*, ed. Peter Pringle (New York: Public Affairs, 2013) pp. 81, 83, 84.

31. Kenneth Clarkson, *Food Stamps and Nutrition* (Washington, DC: American Enterprise Institute for Policy Research, 1975), http://files.eric.ed.gov/fulltext/ED124602 .pdf.

32. "HR 6499: National Food Stamp Reform Act" 95th Congress 1977–1978 Congress. gov https://www.congress.gov/bill/95th-congress/house-bill/6499.

33. Douglas Besharov, "We're Feeding the Poor as if They're Starving," *Washington Post*, December 8, 2002.

34. Janet Poppendieck, *Breadlines Knee Deep in Wheat* (San Francisco: University of California Press, 2014), p. 282 (pre-publication proof).

35. California Assembly Bill 2384, February 23, 2006, http://www.leginfo.ca.gov/ pub/05-06/bill/asm/ab_2351-2400/ab_2384_bill_20060913_chaptered.html.

36. Kenneth Hecht, personal communication, May 1, 2014.

37. Anemonia Hartocolllis, "New York Asks to Bar Use of Food Stamps to Buy Soda," *New York Times*, October 6, 2010, http://www.nytimes.com/2010/10/07/nyregion/ 07stamps.html?_r=2&hp&.

38. Jessica Shahin, associate SNAP administrator, letter to Elizabeth R. Berlin, executive deputy commissioner, New York State Office of Temporary and Disability Assistance, August 19, 2011.

39. Ibid.

40. "Implications of Restricting the Use of Food Stamp Benefits," USDA Food and Nutrition Service, March 1, 2007, http://www.fns.usda.gov/sites/default/files/arra/ FSPFoodRestrictions.pdf.

41. Kathleen Merrigan, personal communication, June 6, 2014; when asked at the 2013 Bipartisan Policy Conference whether she would have approved the waiver had it been her decision, she said that she would have done so.

42. Kathleen Merrigan, e-mail communication. July 6, 2014.

43. "Big Soda SNAPPing Up Welfare Dollars," press release, National Center for Public Policy Research, April 26, 2013, http://www.nationalcenter.org/PR-Coca-Cola_042613.html.

44. "Roe Introduces the Healthy Food Choices Act," press release, Office of US Congressman Phil Roe, M.D. September 10, 2013. http://roe.house.gov/news/documentsingle.aspx?DocumentID=348911.

45. "S.Amdt 1152 to S.954," Congress.gov., https://www.congress.gov/amendment/113th-congress/senate-amendment/1152/text.

46. Brynne Keith-Jennings, "SNAP Plays a Critical Role in Helping Children," Center for Budget and Policy Priorities, July 17, 2012, http://www.cbpp.org/cms/index.cfm?fa=view&id=3805.

47. Michelle Richinick, "Michelle Obama Wants to Cut Junk Food, Sodas from Schools," *MSNBC*, February 25, 2014, http://www.msnbc.com/msnbc/flotus-cut-sodas-schools.

48. Lynn Silver, telephone communication, July 10, 2014.

49. "Statements on SNAP Food Choice: Western Region Anti-Hunger Consortium Meeting," May 2011, unpublished document. The advocacy group Food and Water Watch issued a report in 2011 that debunked the claim that subsidy programs cause obesity, arguing instead that government deregulation has led to corn overproduction.

50. Tracie McMillan, "Are Stores Making Bank off Food Stamps?" *Mother Jones*, April 22, 2014, http://www.motherjones.com/environment/2014/04/are-stores-making-bank-food-stamps.

51. "Request for Information: Supplemental Nutrition Assistance Program (SNAP); Retailer Transaction Data," *Federal Register*, August 4, 2014, https://www.federalregister.gov/articles/2014/08/04/2014-18288/request-for-information-supplemental-nutrition-assistance-program-snap-retailer-transaction-data.

52. Jonathan Ellis, "Judge Declines to Throw Out *Argus Leader* Food Stamp Lawsuit," *Argus Leader*, September 30, 2015, http://www.argusleader.com/story/news/2015/09/30/judge-declines-throw-argus-leader-food-stamp-lawsuit/73109098. Retrieved May 31, 2016.

53. Lacey Louwagie, "Fight for Food Stamp Records Will Continue," *Courthouse News Service*, October 2, 2015, http://www.courthousenews.com/2015/10/02/fight-for-food-stamp-records-will-continue.htm.

54. Chris Morran, USDA Can No Longer Hide How Much Money Stores Make from Food Stamps, *Consumerist*, December 1, 2016, https://consumerist.com/2016/12/01/usda-can-no-longer-hide-how-much-money-stores-make-from-food-stamps.

55. Steven Garasky, Kassim Mbwana, Andres Romualdo, Alex Tenaglio, and Manan Roy, "Foods Typically Purchased by SNAP Households," November 2016, http://www.fns.usda.gov/sites/default/files/ops/SNAPFoodsTypicallyPurchased.pdf.

56. "Marino Bill to Increase SNAP Transparency, Accountability," press release, Congressman Tom Marino, April 26, 2013, http://marino.house.gov/press-release/marino-bill-increase-snap-transparency-accountability.

57. Ellen Teller, personal communication, November 4, 2013.

58. Julie Guthman, *Weighing In: Obesity, Food Justice, and the Limits of Capitalism* (San Francisco: University of California Press, 2011), pp. 157–159.

59. "Statements on SNAP Food Choice." From my conversations with multiple advocates, I surmise that a greater number of individuals within anti-hunger organizations support excluding soda from SNAP, but whose organizations have not taken a position or taken an anti-restriction stand.

60. National Commission on Hunger, "Freedom from Hunger: An Achievable Goal for the United States of America, 2015, https://www.aei.org/wp-content/uploads/2016/01/Hunger_Commission_Final_Report.pdf.

61. Anne Barnhill, telephone communication, April 10, 2014.

62. Ed Cooney, personal communication, June 2, 2014.

63. Keith Stern, personal communication, June 3, 2014.

64. "Women, Infants, and Children," USDA Food and Nutrition Service, http://www.fns.usda.gov/wic/about-wic-how-wic-helps.

65. Donald Rose, "Food Stamps, the Thrifty Food Plan, and Meal Preparation: The Importance of the Time Dimension for US Nutrition Policy," *Journal of Nutrition Education Behavior* 39 (2007): 226–232, http://prc.tulane.edu/uploads/Food%20StampsThrifty%20Food%20PlanandMeal%20Preparation.pdf; Rose makes the important conclusion that the food preparation time built into the Thrifty Food Plan contradicts US welfare policy that expects the labor force participation of low-income women.

66. Christian Gregory, Michelle VerPloeg, Margaret Andrews, and Alisha Coleman Jensen, "Supplemental Nutrition Assistance Program (SNAP) Participation Leads to Modest Changes in Diet Quality," USDA Economic Research Service, April 2013.

67. Susan Bartlett, Jacob Klerman, Parke Wilde, Lauren Olsho, Michelle Blockin, Christopher Logan, and Ayesha Enver, "Healthy Incentives Pilot Interim Report," US Department of Agriculture, Alexandria, VA, July 2013.

68. Roland Sturm and Rupoeng An, "Obesity and Economic Environments," *CA: A Cancer Journal for Clinicians*, May 22, 2014, http://onlinelibrary.wiley.com/doi/10.3322/caac.21237/full.

69. "Encouraging Healthy Food Purchases: Alternatives to Restricting Choices in SNAP," Center on Public Policy Priorities, June 1, 2012.

70. "A Review of Strategies to Bolster SNAP's Role in Improving Nutrition as well as Food Security," Food Research and Action Center, January 2013, http://frac.org/wp-content/uploads/2011/06/SNAPstrategies.pdf; "Statements on SNAP Food Choice."

71. Sonya Jones, telephone communication, April 25, 2014.

72. Cindy Leung, Walter Willett, and Eric Ding, "Low-Income Supplemental Nutrition Assistance Program Participation Is Related to Adiposity and Metabolic Risk Factors," *American Journal of Clinical Nutrition* 95 (2012):17–24.

73. "Diet Quality of Americans by SNAP Participation Status: Data from the National Health and Nutrition Examination Survey 2007–2010," USDA Food and Nutrition Service, May 2015, http://www.fns.usda.gov/sites/default/files/ops/NHANES-SNAP07-10.pdf.

74. "A Review of Strategies"; "Encouraging Healthy Food Choices."

75. "Revised Agenda Material," City of Berkeley, July 1, 2014, http://web.archive.org/web/20140815151220/http://www.ci.berkeley.ca.us/Clerk/City_Council/2014/07_Jul/Documents/2014-07-01_Item_23_Placing_a_Sugar-Sweetened_-_Rev.aspx.

76. "Encouraging Healthy Food Choices."

77. A Review of Strategies.

78. Larry Sly, "Provide Incentives, but Let Them Make Their Own Decisions," *The Reporter*, June 23, 2014, http://www.thereporter.com/columnists/ci_26021377/larry-sly-provide-incentives-but-let-them-make.

79. Ibid.

80. Cooney, personal communication. Underlying this opposition is a history of paternalism toward the poor that separates them into deserving and undeserving categories. Throughout American history, the undeserving poor have all too often been seen as the "other," of different ethnicity, religion, national origin or race. Obesity provides a new twist on who can be considered the undeserving poor, inflicting a sense of failed personal responsibility in maintaining a healthy weight.

81. Dinner program, document in Andrew Fisher's possession.

82. Form 990, Food Research and Action Center, 2012, http://www.guidestar.org/FinDocuments/2012/237/200/2012-237200739-09d4b032-9.pdf. These funds would

typically be considered unrestricted and available to be used to cover expenses for lobbying. This designation makes them especially valuable as compared to foundation grants, which generally cannot be used to lobby.

83. Gabriel Cortez, "Perfect Soldiers," video, February 2014, https://www.youtube .com/watch?v=tgh8NxNnhoI; Gabriel Cortez, presentation at the Second National Soda Summit, Washington, DC, June 4, 2014.

84. Cooney, personal communication.

85. Marlene Schwartz, presentation at Second National Soda Summit, Washington, DC, June 5, 2014.

86. Cooney, quoted in Jane Black, "SNAP Judgement," *Slate*, August 6, 2013, http:// www.slate.com/articles/business/moneybox/2013/08/food_stamp_choices_should _people_be_allowed_to_buy_junk_food_with_their.html.

87. Jessica Bartholow, telephone communication, May 9, 2014.

88. Robert Pear, "Soft Drink Industry Fights Proposed Food Stamp Ban," *New York Times*, April 29, 2011, http://www.nytimes.com/2011/04/30/us/politics/30food .html; "Coalition Statement on Preserving Food Choice in SNAP/Food Stamps," May 24, 2010, http://www.frac.org/pdf/foodchoicemay10final.pdf.

89. "Coalition Statement."

90. Christina Wong, "SNAP Restaurant Meals Program," n.d., unpublished document in Andrew Fisher's possession.

91. Black, "SNAP Judgment." I have heard Jim Weill make this point on numerous occasions in meetings and conferences.

92. Jim O'Hara, telephone communication, July 8, 2014.

93. Marion Standish, telephone communication, July 10, 2014.

94. *Up with Chris Hayes*, MSNBC video clip of television show, July 14, 2012, http:// video.msnbc.msn.com/up/48183376#48183439.

95. Cindy Leung, Sarah Cluggish, Eduardo Villamor, Paul J. Catalano, Walter C. Willett, and Eric B. Rimm, "Few Changes in Food Security and Dietary Intake from Short-Term SNAP Participation," *Journal of Nutrition Education and Behavior* 14, no. 46 (January 2014): 68–74.

96. Michael W Long, Cindy W Leung, Lilian WY Cheung, Susan J Blumenthal, and Walter C Willett. "Public support for policies to improve the nutritional impact of the Supplemental Nutrition Assistance Program (SNAP)," Public Health Nutrition 17(1): 219–224, http://www.ncbi.nlm.nih.gov/pmc/articles/PMC3775854.

97. Cindy Leung, Suzanne Ryan-Ibarra, Amanda Linares, Marta Induni, Sharon Sugarman et al., "Support for Policies to Improve the Nutritional Impact of the

Supplemental Nutrition Assistance Program in California, American Journal of Public Health 105, no. 8 (2015); 1576–1580.

98. Myong O, e-mail communication, June 2, 2015.

99. "Dietary Guidelines for Americans 2015: Public Comments," health.gov, http://www.health.gov/dietaryguidelines/dga2015/comments/Default2.aspx.

100. Richard Thaler and Cass Sunstein, *Nudge: Improving Decisions about Health, Wealth and Happiness* (New York: Penguin, 2009), pp. 33–34.

101. Nancy Kass, Kenneth Hecht; Amy Paul, and Kerry Birnbach, "Ethics and Obesity Prevention: Ethical Considerations in Three Approaches to Reducing Consumption of Sugar Sweetened Beverages," *American Journal of Public Health* 104, no. 5 (May 2014): 787–795.

102. Susan Foerster, personal communication, February 21, 2013.

103. Carlos Monteiro, Director of the Centre for Epidemiological Studies on Health and Nutrition, School of Public Health, University of São Paulo presentation at Conference sur les systemes alimentaires, Montreal, May 12, 2014, http://diffusionvideo.umontreal.ca/conferenciers/conferenciers.

104. Ibid. https://plus.google.com/u/0/_/focus/photos/public/AIbEiAIAAABDCPGq_sy325yRVSILdmNhcmRfcGhvdG8qKGFlMWM3MzgxODg3YjUwNGVjNzc2MGFiO WVlYTg4ZmYwYjFhYzNhMTQwAefDnYsvVRlGcHfzvl5HwKzQvwiy?sz=64.

105. Ibid.

Chapter 5

1. Janie Hipp, telephone communication, January 26, 2015.

2. USDA has designated much of Indian Country as a food desert.

3. "Food Distribution Programs on Indian Reservations," Food and Nutrition Service USDA, Nutrition Program Fact Sheet, March 2016, http://www.fns.usda.gov/sites/default/files/fdpir/pfs-fdpir.pdf; Hipp, telephone communication.

4. Hipp, telephone communication.

5. Ibid.

6. "Food Distribution Program on Indian Reservations: FDPIR Food Package Review Work Group," Food and Nutrition Service, USDA, http://www.fns.usda.gov/fdpir/fdpir-food-package-review-work-group.

7. Section 4211 of the 2008 Farm Bill mandates that USDA purchase locally grown and traditional foods, including bison. At least 50 percent of these purchases should come from Native producers. These purchases are subject to appropriations. In the

2014 Farm Bill, (section 4004) Congress established a demonstration project for a tribe to purchase foods produced locally by Indian producers. It authorized $2 million for this pilot, but as of 2015 Congress has not appropriated the funds.

8. Hipp, telephone communication.

9. David Lulka, "Bison and the Food Distribution Program on Indian Reservations," *Great Plains Research* 16 (Spring 2006): 74.

10. "Food Distribution Program on Indian Reservations." USDA officials contend that the program does provide economic development benefits to 100-plus Indian Tribal Organizations as they collectively receive $40 million from USDA for managing the program, creating numerous jobs in the process.

11. "Table 2: Food at Home Total Expenditures," Economic Research Service USDA, http://www.ers.usda.gov/data-products/food-expenditures.aspx#26636.

12. Michele Simon, "Food Stamps: Follow the Money," *Eat Drink Politics*, June 2012. http://www.eatdrinkpolitics.com/wp-content/uploads/FoodStampsFollowtheMoney Simon.pdf; Krissy Clark, "The Secret Life of a Food Stamp," *Slate*, April 1, 2014, http://www.slate.com/articles/business/moneybox/2014/04/big_box_stores_make_billions _off_food_stamps_often_it_s_their_own_workers.html.

13. "Tyson Fact Book," Tyson, http://ir.tyson.com/investor-relations/investor-overview/tyson-factbook/. The USDA uses guidelines established by the Department of Labor in determining what is a small business. Small businesses in the food industry are considered those to have fewer than 500 employees, with the exception of those in the produce-processing business, which can have up to 3,500 workers.

14. The sociologist Mary Hendrickson notes in an e-mail of April 9, 2015, the importance of analyzing concentration levels with four companies, "because from small group theory if you are in a group of four or less, you can often coordinate actions just by observation without any kind of collusion or discussion. If you start going to CR3 or CR2 then you don't have quite the full impact of the oligopoly." See also Doug Constance, Mary Hendrickson, Philip H. Howard, and William D. Heffernan, "Economic Concentration in the Agrifood System: Impacts on Rural Communities and Emerging Responses," in *Rural America in a Globalizing World: Problems and Prospects for the 2010s* (Morgantown: West Virginia University Press, 2014), pp. 20–21

15. Constance et al., "Economic Concentration," pp. 20–21

16. "Tyson Fact Book." In addition, food service comprises 26 percent of its beef sales and 17 percent of its pork sales. Tyson does not reveal how much of its sales come from schools and failed to respond to requests for information.

17. Chris Leonard, *The Meat Racket: The Secret Takeover of America's Food Business* (New York: Simon and Schuster, 2014), p. 3

18. Ibid, pp. 315–316.

19. William Heffernan, "Sociological Dimensions of Agricultural Structures in the United States," *Sociologia Ruralis* 12, no. 2 (1972): 481–499.

20. Daniel Imhoff, *Food Fight: The Citizen's Guide to the Next Food and Farm Bill* (Healdsburg, CA: Watershed Media 2012), pp. 47–49.

21. Mark Lauritsen, telephone communication, January 26, 2015.

22. Joann Lo, e-mail communication, August 31, 2015.

23. "New Campaign Exposes Widespread Abuses of Workers in America's Poultry Industry." Oxfam America, October 26, 2015, https://www.oxfamamerica.org/press/new-campaign-exposes-widespread-abuses-of-workers-in-americas-poultry -industry.

24. Simon, "Food Stamps."

25. Kevin Morgan, "Values for Money," *Agenda: Journal of the Institute of Welsh Affairs* 46, no. 1 (Spring 2012): 32–35.

26. Edward Glaeser and William Kerr, "The Secret to Job Growth: Think Small," *Harvard Business Review*, July 2010, https://hbr.org/2010/07/the-secret-to-job-growth -think-small.

27. Anil Rupasingha, "Locally Owned: Do Local Business Ownership and Size Matter for Local Economic Well-Being?" Federal Reserve Bank of Atlanta, Community and Economic Development Discussion Paper No 01–13, August 2013.

28. Michael Shuman, telephone communication, February 11, 2015.

29. Michael Shuman, "The 20 Percent Shift: The Economic Benefits of Food Localization for Michigan and the Capital Required to Realize Them," Fair Food Network, May 2013, http://www.fairfoodnetwork.org/sites/default/files/Michigan20PercentShift_FullReport.pdf.

30. David Fleming and Stephan Goetz, "Does Local Firm Ownership Matter?" Rural Development Paper No. 48, Northeast Regional Center for Rural Development, 2010.

31. Rupasingha, "Locally Owned."

32. Shuman, "The 20 Percent Shift."

33. Michael Shuman, e-mail communication, July 17, 2015.

34. Jeffrey O'Hara, telephone communication, February 9, 2015.

35. Mary Hendrickson, telephone communication, January 23, 2015.

36. David Hughes, Cheryl Brown, Stacy Miller, and Tom McConnell, "Evaluating the Impact of Farmers Markets Using an Opportunity Cost Framework," *Journal of Agricultural and Applied Economics* 40, no. 1 (April 2008): 253–265.

37. Sarah A. Low, Aaron Adalja, Elizabeth Beaulieu, Nigel Key, Steve Martinez, Alex Melton, Agnes Perez, et al., *Trends in US Local and Regional Food Systems*, AP-068, USDA Economic Research Service, January 2015.

38. Raymond Hopkins, "The Evolution of Food Aid: Towards a Development First Regime," *Food Policy* 9, no. 4 (November 1984): 345–362; Jennifer Clapp, *Hunger in the Balance: The New Politics of International Food Aid* (Ithaca, NY: Cornell University Press, 2012), p. 8.

39. Clapp, *Hunger in the Balance*.

40. Claire Provost and Felicity Lawrence, "US Food Aid Programme Criticized as 'Corporate Welfare' for Grain Giants," *Guardian*, July 18, 2012, https://www .theguardian.com/global-development/2012/jul/18/us-multinationals-control-food -aid.

41. Hopkins, "The Evolution of Food Aid"; Clapp, *Hunger in the Balance*.

42. Clapp, *Hunger in the Balance*, p. 3

43. Hopkins, "The Evolution of Food Aid."

44. Eric Munoz, telephone communication, January 7, 2015.

45. Quoted in Kevin Morgan, "The Politics of the Public Plate: School Food and Sustainability," in *International Journal of the Society of Agriculture and Food* 21, no. 3 (2014): 253–260, 257.

46. "Revaluing Public Sector Food Procurement in Europe: An Action Plan for Sustainability" Foodlinks, 2014, http://www.foodlinkscommunity.net/fileadmin/ documents_organicresearch/foodlinks/publications/Foodlinks_report_low.pdf; Morgan. "The Politics of the Public Plate," p. 5

47. "The Food for Life Catering Mark," Soil Association, http://www.sacert.org/ catering/whatisthecateringmark.

48. "Food for Life Catering Handbook Schools 2015," Soil Association, http://www .sacert.org/LinkClick.aspx?fileticket=BWq_nH9NCd0%3d&tabid=1764.

49. Libby Grundy, e-mail communication, January 22, 2015.

50. "Commodity Operations," USDA Farm Service Agency, http://www.fsa.usda .gov/FSA/dacoReports?area=home&subject=coop&topic=rpt-ps&reportType =Procurement-Dairy&subCategory=Bidder+List+Report+Dairy&summaryYear =2012&x=14&y=9; "Purchase Summary Report," USDA Agriculture Marketing Service, https://www.ams.usda.gov/reports/purchase-summary-report " Commodity

Operations," USDA Farm Service Agency, http://www.fsa.usda.gov/FSA/dacoReports
?area=home&topic=rpt-ps&subject=coop&subcategory=Bidder%20List%20
Report%20Domestic&category=Procurement-Domestic.

51. "The Federal Child Nutrition Commodity Program," California Food
Policy Advocates and Samuels and Associates, September 2008, http://cfpa.net/
ChildNutrition/ChildNutrition_CFPAPublications/CommoditiesSchoolMeals
-ExecutiveSummary-2008.pdf.

52. Ibid.

53. Lucy Komisar, "How the Food Industry Eats Your Kid's Lunch," *New York Times*,
http://www.nytimes.com/2011/12/04/opinion/sunday/school-lunches-and-the
-food-industry.html.

54. Note that Tyson sells raw chicken to USDA and then also profits when school
districts contract with the company to process it into chicken nuggets, tenders, pat-
ties, etc. In addition, the company sells these products and raw chicken to school
districts under their separate cash ledger.

55. Mary Stein, telephone communication, January 21, 2015.

56. "Nutrient and MyPyramid Analysis of USDA Foods in Five of its Food and
Nutrition Programs Summary," USDA Food and Nutrition Service, January 2012,
http://www.fns.usda.gov/sites/default/files/NutrientMyPyramidSummary.pdf.

57. "Pilot Project for Unprocessed Fruits and Vegetables," USDA Agricultural
Marketing Service, https://www.ams.usda.gov/AMSv1.0/ams.fetchTemplateData.do
?template=TemplateN&page=CPDPilotProjectUnprocessedFV.

58. "Federal Acquisitions Regulations Part 8 Required Sources of Supplies and
Services," http://arsite.hill.af.mil/reghtml/regs/far2afmcfars/fardfars/far/08.htm
#P275_47172. Retrieved April 16, 2015.

59. "2015 Legislative Issues Paper," American Commodity Distribution Association,
http://www.commodityfoods.org/assets/docs/acda%202015%20legislative%20
issue%20paper%20final.pdf.

60. Thomas Forster, e-mail communication, July 22, 2015.

61. "Know Hunger," Tyson, http://www.tysonhungerrelief.com/our-commitment/.

62. Sara Lilygren and Jim Weill, "Hunger: An Issue We Can Agree On," The
Hill, October 30, 2014, http://thehill.com/blogs/congress-blog/healthcare/222133
-hunger-an-issue-we-can-agree-on.

63. Forster, e-mail communication.

64. Fabiana Frayssinet, "From Brazil's Family Farm to the School Lunchroom Table," Inter Press Service News Agency, March 12, 2013, http://www.ipsnews.net/2013/03/from-brazils-family-farm-to-the-school-lunchroom-table.

65. Rodney Taylor, telephone communication, February 4, 2015.

66. "The Farm to School Census: Early Results Are In," USDA Food and Nutrition Service, https://farmtoschoolcensus.fns.usda.gov/home#find-your-school-district Retrieved November 7, 2015; The USDA does not track the amount of money spent on food. The Farm to School census had a response rate of 75 percent.

67. "The Farm to School Census: State and District," http://www.fns.usda.gov/farmtoschool/census#/map. Retrieved April 22, 2015.

68. "HR 2419," 110th Congress, Section 4302. https://agriculture.house.gov/sites/republicans.agriculture.house.gov/files/documents/2008farmbilllanguage.pdf. Retrieved August 27, 2015.

69. Stein, telephone communication, February 3, 2015.

70. "National Overview," USDA Farm to School Census, http://www.fns.usda.gov/farmtoschool/census#/. Retrieved June 11, 2015.

71. Samantha Benjamin-Kirk, "South Carolina Features Supreme Chicken Sandwich in Lunch" USDA Blog, January 13, 2015, http://blogs.usda.gov/2015/01/13/south-carolina-features-supreme-chicken-sandwich-in-school-lunch; Branden Born and Mark Purcell, "Avoiding the Local Trap: Scale in Food Systems Planning and Research," *Journal of Planning Education and Research* 26, no. 2 (2006).

72. Alexa Delwiche, personal communication, March 2, 2015. The purpose of the pledge is to "harness the purchasing power of major institutions to encourage greater production of sustainably produced food, healthy eating habits, respect for workers' rights, humane treatment of animals, and support for the local business economy by providing new opportunities for small and midsized farmers and job creation along the supply chain."

73. "Good Food Purchasing Policy," Los Angeles Food Policy Council, http://goodfoodla.org/policymaking/good-food-procurement.

74. "Good Food Purchasing Guidelines for Food Service Institutions," Los Angeles Food Policy Council, October 2012, http://www.thegreenhorns.net/wp-content/files_mf/1396804772goodfood.pdf.

75. Ibid.

76. Delwiche, personal communication.

77. Komisar, "How the Food Industry Eats Your Kids."

78. Nirvi Shah, "USDA to Probe Companies Running School Cafeterias," *Education Week*, June 14, 2011, http://www.edweek.org/ew/articles/2011/06/15/35rebates_ep .h30.html.

79. "USDA Awards Grants to Support Schools Serving Healthier Meals and Snacks," USDA, News Release No. 0058–15, March 6, 2015, http://www.usda.gov/wps/portal/ usda/usdahome?contentidonly=true&contentid=2015/03/0058.xml.

80. This tension is embodied in the fact that the school food trade association changed its name from the American School Food Service Association to the School Nutrition Association. Interestingly, the USDA has chosen to further invest in food service management training as essential to improving the quality of school meals.

81. Nicholas Confessore, "How School Lunch Became the Latest Political Battleground," *New York Times*, October 7, 2014, http://www.nytimes.com/2014/10/12/ magazine/how-school-lunch-became-the-latest-political-battleground.html.

82. Shuman, telephone communication.

83. "Supplemental Nutrition Assistance Program," USDA Food and Nutrition Service, April 10, 2015, http://www.fns.usda.gov/sites/default/files/pd/34SNAPmonthly .pdf.

84. Low et al., *Trends in US Local and Regional*, p. 9

85. Some food activists argue that we pay for food three times—at the checkout counter, at the doctor's office, and in our tax bills.

86. "Replacing the Thrifty Food Plan in Order to Provide Adequate Allotments for SNAP Beneficiaries," Food Research and Action Center, http://frac.org/pdf/thrifty _food_plan_2012.pdf.

87. "FY 2009–2015 Senior Farmers Market Nutrition Program Grant Amounts," USDA Food and Nutrition Service; "FY 2009–2015 WIC Farmers Market Nutrition Program Grant Amounts," USDA Food and Nutrition Service; http://www.fns.usda .gov/sites/default/files/fmnp/WFMNP-Grant-Amounts.pdf.

88. Suzanne Briggs, Andy Fisher, Megan Lott, Stacy Miller, and Nell Tessman, "Real Food, Real Choice," Community Food Security Coalition, June 2010, http://cclhdn. org/wp-content/uploads/2013/02/RealFoodRealChoice_SNAP_FarmersMarkets.pdf; "Review of the Use of Food Stamps in Farmers Markets," statement of Betty Jo Nelsen, Administrator Food and Nutrition Service, hearing before the Subcommittee on Domestic Marketing, Consumer Relations and Nutrition of the Committee of Agriculture, US House of Representatives. September 18, 1990 Serial No. 101-68.

89. Even today, few transactions combined with high service fees can mean that processing SNAP transactions are not always cost effective. One market in Michigan spends 66 cents of every dollar on transaction costs.

90. "USDA Announces Grants to Enable More Farmers Markets to Serve Low-Income Families," USDA Release No. 123.15, http://www.fns.usda.gov/pressrelease/2015/012315.

91. Bob Lewis of the New York State Department of Agriculture and Markets was instrumental in leading this effort in New York City.

92. "Health Bucks and EBT," GrowNYC, http://www.grownyc.org/greenmarket/ebt/healthbucks.

93. "SNAP Retailer Management: 2014 Annual Report," Food and Nutrition Service, USDA, http://www.fns.usda.gov/sites/default/files/snap/2014-SNAP-Retailer-Management-Annual-Report.pdf.

94. "EBT: Bonus Incentives," USDA Food and Nutrition Service. http://www.fns.usda.gov/ebt/bonus-incentives.

95. Kevin Concannon, telephone communication, February 19, 2015.

96. "Michigan Agriculture Facts," Michigan Farm Bureau, https://www.michfb.com/MI/Ag_Ed_and_Leadership/Ag_Facts/Michigan_Agriculture_Facts/.

97. "USDA Awards $31 Million in Grants to Help SNAP Participants Afford Healthy Foods." USDA, April 1, 2015, http://www.usda.gov/wps/portal/usda/usdahome?contentidonly=true&contentid=2015/04/0084.xml.

98. Kate Fitzgerald, e-mail communication, February 17, 2015.

99. "HR 2642: The Agricultural Act of 2014," Section 4208, Government Printing Office, https://www.gpo.gov/fdsys/pkg/BILLS-113hr2642enr/pdf/BILLS-113hr2642enr.pdf; "Food Insecurity Nutrition Incentive Grant Program," USDA National Institute of Food and Agriculture, https://nifa.usda.gov/sites/default/files/rfa/1415_FINI.pdf.

100. Fitzgerald, e-mail communication, June 26, 2015.

101. Karen Kinney, e-mail communication, May 7, 2015; "USDA Awards."

102. Ben Feldman and Carle Brinkman, telephone communication, August 29, 2015.

103. Fitzgerald, telephone communication, February 17, 2015.

104. Richard McCarthy, telephone communication, January 14, 2015.

105. Fitzgerald, telephone communication, June 26, 2015.

106. Feldman and Brinkman, telephone communication August 29, 2015.

107. Ben Feldman, telephone communication, August 27, 2015.

108. Fitzgerald, telephone communication.

109. David Lee, telephone communication, February 12, 2015.

110. Ferd Hoefner, e-mail communication, May 5, 2015.

111. Lee, telephone communication.

112. Malini Moraghan, telephone communication, February 9, 2015.

113. Transparency 2015, Hartman Group, http://www.hartman-group.com/upcoming-studies/transparency-2015.

114. Although through the Know Your Farmer program and emphasis on farm to school, the USDA has been nibbling at the edges in reshaping the marketplace.

115. Mark Winne, blog post, July 22, 2013, http://www.markwinne.com/time-to-re-think-food-stamps/. The response by Jim Weill, Executive Director of FRAC in his *AGree* blog post of August 2, 2013, arguably did little to dispel Winne's contentions, as he cited numerous, mostly technical changes to SNAP as proof of the way it has evolved.

116. Mark Bittman, Michael Pollan, Ricardo Salvador, and Olivier de Schutter, "How a National Food Policy Could Save Millions of American Lives," *Washington Post*, November 7, 2014, https://www.washingtonpost.com/opinions/how-a-national-food-policy-could-save-millions-of-american-lives/2014/11/07/89c55e16-637f-11e4-836c-83bc4f26eb67_story.html.

117. Ibid.

Chapter 6

1. Richard Wilkinson and Kate Pickett, *The Spirit Level: Why Greater Equality Makes Societies Stronger* (New York: Bloomsbury Press, 2009), p. 17; Emanuel Saenz, "Striking It Richer: The Evolution of Top Incomes in the United States," September 3, 2013, http://eml.berkeley.edu/~saez/saez-UStopincomes-2012.pdf.

2. "2013 CEO to Worker Pay Ratio," AFL-CIO Paywatch 2014,http://www.aflcio.org/Corporate-Watch/Paywatch-2014.

3. Wilkinson and Pickett, *Spirit Level*.

4. "News from EPI: The Economy Can Afford to Raise the Minimum Wage to $12.00 by 2020," Economic Policy Institute, April 30, 2015, http://www.epi.org/press/the-economy-can-afford-to-raise-the-minimum-wage-to-12-00-by-2020.

5. "Supplemental Nutrition Assistance Program Eligibility," USDA Food and Nutrition Service, http://www.fns.usda.gov/snap/eligibility; Peter Edelman, *So Rich and So Poor: Why It's Hard to End Poverty in America* (New York: The New Press, 2012).

6. Edelman, *So Rich and So Poor*.

7. Josh Bivens, Elise Gould, Lawrence Mishel, and Heidi Shierholz, "Raising America's Pay," Economic Policy Institute Briefing Paper # 378, June 4, 2014, http://www.epi.org/publication/raising-americas-pay/.

8. Elise Gould, "Raising Wages is Key to Improving Incomes of Low-Income Americans," Economic Policy Institute Economic Snapshot, June 17, 2014, http://www.epi.org/publication/raising-wages-key-improving-incomes-income.

9. Bivens et al., "Raising America's Pay."

10. William M. Rodgers III, "The Impact of a $15 Minimum Wage on Hunger in America," The Century Foundation, September 1, 2016, https://tcf.org/content/report/the-impact-of-a-15-minimum-wage-on-hunger-in-america.

11. Patricia Cohen. "With Pay Rising, Millions Climb out of Poverty," *New York Times*, September 26, 2016.

12. Center for Budget and Policy Priorities, "A Quick Guide to SNAP Eligibility and Benefits," http://www.cbpp.org/research/index.cfm?fa=topic&id=69.

13. Members of the National Anti-Hunger Organizations, "Blueprint to End Hunger: The Millennium Declaration to End Hunger in America," 2008, http://frac.org/newsite/wp-content/uploads/2010/03/blueprint2008.pdf.

14. "Hunger in America, 2014," *Feeding America*, http://help.feedingamerica.org/HungerInAmerica/hunger-in-america-2014-full-report.pdf?s_src=W14BDIRCT&s_subsrc=http%3A%2F%2Fwww.feedingamerica.org%2Fhunger-in-america%2Four-research%2Fmap-the-meal-gap%2F&_ga=1.65102894.108928344.1397153122.

15. "Freedom from Hunger: An Achievable Goal for the United States of America," National Commission on Hunger, 2015

16. Just Harvest and Illinois Hunger Coalition participate on the local steering committees for the SEIU's fast food worker campaigns. Hunger Action Network of NY State and WhyHunger also played important roles in NYC. Ken Regal, Just Harvest, telephone communication, September 29, 2014; Diane Doherty, Illinois Hunger Coalition, telephone communication, October 8, 2014; Lynette Pitcock, Service Employees International Union, telephone communication, October 1, 2014.

17. Frank Tamborello, telephone communication, November 5, 2014. In May 2015, however, the City of Los Angeles passed legislation raising the minimum wage to $15 per hour by 2020.

18. Diane Doherty, e-mail communication, November 4, 2014.

19. Feeding South Dakota, Fall 2014 newsletter, http://www.feedingsouthdakota.org/images/uploads/Fall-2014-Newsletter.PDF.

20. This survey was conducted through Survey Monkey. Outreach was completed through WhyHunger's newsletter (twice) and once through the Closing the Hunger

Gap newsletter, with 50 of the 71 respondents stating that their organization self-identified as coming from a food bank or food pantry, and the remainder from churches, community action agencies, and advocacy organizations.

21. For example, the SF Food Bank did not publically support a minimum wage increase on the ballot in 2014, but instead chose to participate in a broader coalition.

22. Janet Poppendieck, telephone communication, August 26, 2014, November 6, 2014.

23. Ken Regal, telephone communication.

24. "Community Eligibility Provision," FRAC Facts, http://frac.org/pdf/community _eligibility_amazing_new_option_schools.pdf.

25. Jeremy Everett, telephone communication, September 16, 2014.

26. Marissa Parisi, telephone communication, September 25, 2014; Jeff Kleen, personal communication, August 18, 2014.

27. Jonathan Weisman and Ron Nixon, "House Republicans Push through Farm Bill, without Food Stamps," New York Times, July 11, 2013, http://www.nytimes. com/2013/07/12/us/politics/house-bill-would-split-farm-and-food-stamp-programs .html?pagewanted=all.

28. After the 2014 election, the incoming chairs to the House and Senate Agriculture Committees were announced. Rep. Mike Conaway and Sen. Pat Roberts were considered by DC insiders to be hostile to the SNAP program.

29. Matt Knott, announcement to Closing the Hunger Gap conference, Tucson, Arizona, September 13, 2013.

30. David Beckmann, telephone communication, October 3, 2014.

31. Jerry Hagstrom, telephone communication, September 30, 2014.

32. Joann Lo, e-mail communication, September 19, 2014.

33. Joel Berg, All You Can Eat: How Hungry is America? (New York: Seven Stories Press, 2008), p. 238. To his credit, Berg is also one of the movement's most vocal supporters of raising the minimum wage. In a November 22, 2014 e-mail, he confirmed this analysis, adding that the extra income should come from safety net programs as well as earned income.

34. Sharon Thornberry, personal communication, October 21, 2014.

35. "Long Term Benefits of the Supplemental Nutrition Assistance Program," Executive Office of the President of the United States, December 2015, https://www .whitehouse.gov/sites/whitehouse.gov/files/documents/SNAP_report_final _nonembargo.pdf, p. 15.

36. Joshua Leftin, Nancy Wemmerus, James Mabli, Thomas Godfrey, and Stephen Tordella, "Dynamics of Supplemental Nutrition Assistance Program Participation from 2008 to 2012," USDA Food and Nutrition Service, December 2014, http://www.fns.usda.gov/sites/default/files/ops/Dynamics2008-2012.pdf.

37. James Arena-DeRosa, telephone communication, September 29, 2014.

38. "USDA Announces $200 Million to Promote Innovation in SNAP Employment and Training Programs," Release Number 0186.14, USDA Food and Nutrition Service, http://www.fns.usda.gov/pressrelease/2014/018614.

39. Ed Bolen (analyst for Center on Budget and Policy Priorities), telephone communication, November 14, 2014.

40. "Supplemental Nutrition Assistance Program, Able Bodied Adults without Dependents (ABAWDs)," USDA Food and Nutrition Service, http://www.fns.usda.gov/snap/able-bodied-adults-without-dependents-abawds.

41. Ed Bolen, Center on Budget and Policy Priorities Webinar, October 23, 2014.

42. Ibid.

43. "Supplemental Nutrition Assistance Program Participation and Costs," USDA Food and Nutrition Service, http://www.fns.usda.gov/sites/default/files/pd/SNAPsummary.pdf.

44. Dottie Rosenblum and Brynne Keith-Jennings, "SNAP Costs Declining, Expected to Fall Much Further," Center for Budget and Policy Priorities, February 9, 2015, http://www.cbpp.org/research/snap-costs-declining-expected-to-fall-much-further.

45. Dottie Rosenblum and Brynne Keith-Jennings, "SNAP Costs and Caseloads Declining," Center on Budget and Policy Priorities, March 8, 2016, http://www.cbpp.org/research/food-assistance/snap-costs-and-caseloads-declining.

46. News release, US Department of Labor, Bureau of Labor Statistics, "The Employment Situation-August 2016," http://www.bls.gov/news.release/pdf/empsit.pdf; USDA Food and Nutrition Service, Supplemental Nutrition Assistance Program, http://www.fns.usda.gov/pd/supplemental-nutrition-assistance-program-snap.

47. David Beckmann of Bread for the World acknowledges that the Federal Reserve Board has done an enormous amount for poor people by keeping interest rates at levels to stimulate growth.

48. J. C. Dwyer, telephone communication, September 17, 2014.

49. Coalition on Human Needs, "How the Poor Would Remedy Poverty" (Washington, DC: Coalition on Human Needs, 1989).

50. A review of the nokidhungry.org website on November 30, 2014, shows that Arby's is a "Core Partner" and the NRA a "National No Kid Hungry Partner."

51. "Low Wages at the 10 Largest Fast Food Companies Cost Taxpayers $3.8 Billion per Year," National Employment Law Project, October 15, 2013, http://www.nelp.org/page/-/rtmw/uploads/NELP-Supersizing-Public-Cost-Press-Release.pdf?nocdn =1. Retrieved November 13, 2014.

52. "Casey Calls for Increase in Minimum Wage," Robert P. Casey, Jr, December 5, 2013, https://www.casey.senate.gov/newsroom/releases/casey-calls-for-increase-in -minimum-wage.

53. Jesse Rothstein, "Is the EITC Equivalent to an NIT? Conditional Cash Transfers and Tax Incidence," National Bureau of Economic Research Working Paper No. 14966, May 2009, http://www.nber.org/papers/w14966.

54. Charles Lane, "End Food Stamps with a Caveat," *Washington Post*, July 1, 2013, https://www.washingtonpost.com/opinions/charles-lane-end-food-stamps-with-a -caveat/2013/07/01/52c42614-e256-11e2-80eb-3145e2994a55_story.html.

55. Maggie Dickinson, "Working for Food Stamps: Economic Citizenship and the Post-Fordist Welfare State in New York City," *American Ethnologist* 43, no. 2 (May 2016): 270–281.

56. Nanine Meiklejohn, telephone communication, September 2, 2014. The 990 tax forms filed by FRAC show the AFSCME representative Chuck Loveless on FRAC's board in 2008 but not in 2009, http://www.guidestar.org/FinDocuments/2008/ 237/200/2008-237200739-059aa983-9.pdf.

57. Susannah Morgan, personal communication, September 13, 2014.

58. Nancy Amadei, personal communication, October 3, 2014.

59. J. C. Dwyer, telephone communication.

60. Morgan, personal communication.

61. Saru Jayaraman, telephone communication, September 9, 2014.

62. Joel Berg, "A New Poor People's Movement Must Have Leadership from Poor People," Talkpoverty.org, May 20, 2014, https://talkpoverty.org/2014/05/20/jberg.

63. Erin Lamb, "Women in Power—Or Not so Much: Gender in the Nonprofit Sector," *Nonprofit Quarterly* Jan. 21, 2015, https://nonprofitquarterly.org/2015/01/21/ women-in-power-or-not-so-much-gender-in-the-nonprofit-sector/.

64. These include Bob Aiken of Feeding America; Billy Shore of SOS; Jim Weill of FRAC; Ed Cooney of Congressional Hunger Center; David Beckmann of Bread for the World; Tony Hall of the Alliance to End Hunger; and Bill Ayres of WhyHunger. By 2016, the leadership of three of these organizations had turned over, with white women taking over.

65. Penny Van Esterik, "Right to Food, Right to Feed, Right to Be Fed: The Intersection of Women and the Right to Food," *Agriculture and Human Values* 16 (1999): 225–232.

66. Mariana Chilton, telephone communication, September 11, 2014.

67. Joel Berg, telephone communication, September 15, 2014; Morgan, personal communication; Sherrie Tussler, telephone communication, October 20, 2014; J. C. Dwyer, telephone communication, September 17, 2014.

68. "History of Community Action," Illinois Association of Community Action Agencies, http://www.iacaanet.org/history.php.

69. "About CAAs," Community Action Partnership, http://www.communityactionpartnership.com/index.php?option=com_content&task=view&id=21&Itemid=50.

70. Jonathan Bader related this anecdote from his colleague Mike Bonertz, telephone communication, October 9, 2014.

71. Zy Weinberg, telephone communication, September 15, 2014.

72. Nancy Amidei, telephone communication, September 23, 2014.

73. Ed Cooney, e-mail communication, September 24, 2014.

74. Amidei, telephone communication.

75. Cooney, e-mail communication.

76. Ken Regal, telephone communication.

77. Robert Egger, telephone communication, September 17, 2014.

78. Joel Berg, telephone communication. Berg's NYCCAH has taken large grants from big corporations, such as ConAgra and Walmart.

79. Jessica Powers, e-mail communication, December 9, 2014.

80. Both groups complete exemplary work in recruiting their clients to participate in their organizations' policy advocacy.

81. Suzan Bateson, telephone communication, September 11, 2014.

82. Sherrie Tussler, telephone communication.

83. Poppendieck, telephone communication, August 26, 2014

84. Linda Stone, personal communication, October 3, 2014.

85. Tianna Gaines, telephone communication, October 1, 2014.

86. Morgan, personal communication.

87. Joel Berg, "A New Poor People's Movement Must Have Leadership from Poor People," Talkpoverty.org, May 20, 2014, https://talkpoverty.org/2014/05/20/jberg/.

88. Some time after this conversation my source informed me that the food bank's relationship with the community had changed dramatically toward becoming more of a partnership.

89. Bill Bolling, telephone communication, November 20, 2014.

90. Mariana Chilton, telephone communication.

91. Gaines, telephone communication.

92. Chilton, telephone communication.

93. "Conference Program: Beyond Hunger—Real People, Real Solutions," Center for Hunger Free Communities, May 2–4, 2012, http://www.centerforhungerfreecommunities .org/sites/default/files/pdfs/program%20final_final.pdf.

94. David Beckmann, telephone communication.

Chapter 7

1. Nick Saul, presentation to Closing the Hunger Gap conference, Portland, Oregon, September 15, 2015.

2. Jessica Powers, e-mail communication, September 30, 2015.

3. Alison Cohen, WhyHunger, e-mail communication, November 10, 2014.

4. "Current Campaigns," Hunger Action Network of New York State, http://www .hungeractionnys.org/?page_id=471; Mark Dunlea, Hunger Action Network of New York State, personal communication, March 4, 2013.

5. Suzan Bateson, personal communication, February 22, 2013.

6. "Colorado Food Pantry Network," Hunger Free Colorado, http://www .hungerfreecolorado.org/network.

7. "Who We Are and How We Help Our Community," Food Bank of the Rockies, http://fbr.convio.net/site/DocServer/Who-We-Are-14-15.pdf?docID=5326.

8. "Anti-Racism Initiative," Solid Ground, https://www.solid-ground.org/Programs/ Legal/AntiRacism/Pages/default.aspx.

9. "Hunger Task Force Farm and Fish Hatchery," Hunger Task Force of Milwaukee, https://www.hungertaskforce.org/the-farm.

10. "Agriculture Programs," The Inter-faith Food Shuttle, http://foodshuttle.org/ program/agprograms.

11. "Programs and Services," Lowcountry Food Bank, http://www .lowcountryfoodbank.org/programs-services.

12. Kathryn Strickland, presentation to the Closing the Hunger Gap conference, Portland Oregon, September 14, 2015.

13. Dominic Vitiello, Jeanne Anne Grisso, Rebecca Fischman, and K. Leah White-side, *Food Relief Goes Local: Gardening, Gleaning, and Farming for Food Banks in the U.S.* (Philadelphia: Penn Center for Public Health Initiatives, 2013).

14. "Healthy Futures," DC Central Kitchen, http://dccentralkitchen.org/healthyfutures/.

15. "Programs and Services," South Plains Food Bank, https://www.spfb.org/programs-services/grub.

16. "Bridges to a Thriving Nevada," Food Bank of Northern Nevada, http://fbnn .org/Howwework/BridgestoathrivingNevada.aspx Retrieved April 25, 2013.

17. "SNAP-Ed FY 2016 Program Allocation," USDA Food and Nutrition Service, June 30, 2015, http://snap.nal.usda.gov/snap/Guidance/FY2016FinalStateSNAP -EdAllocations.pdf.

18. Tom Philpott, "The Fast Food Industry's $4.2 Billion Marketing Blitz," *Grist*, November 9, 2010, http://grist.org/article/food-2010-11-09-the-fast-food-industrys -4-2-billion-marketing-blitz.

19. Erik Talkin, quoted in Tara Pascual, with Jessica Powers, "Cooking up Community: Nutrition Education in Emergency Food Programs," WhyHunger, n.d., http:// www.whyhunger.org/uploads/fileAssets/a86cb1_10a252.pdf.

20. Share Our Strength, https://www.nokidhungry.org. Interestingly, this program is funded by companies that are some of the main purveyors of overly processed unhealthy foods, such as ConAgra and Kraft. In addition, SOS receives funding from other food industry sources such as Arby's, Coca-Cola, Domino Sugar, Kraft, and Jimmy Dean.

21. Pascual, "Cooking Up Community."

22. Project Bread, http://www.projectbread.org.

23. Ibid.

24. "Community FEAST," Oregon Food Bank, http://www.oregonfoodbank.org/ Our-Work/Building-Food-Security/Community-Programs/FEAST.

25. Sharon Thornberry, e-mail communication, September 30, 2015.

26. "Community Food Assessments," Oregon Food Bank, http://www .oregonfoodbank.org/Our-Work/Building-Food-Security/Community-Programs/ Community-Food-Assesments.

27. Megan Newell Ching, Oregon Food Bank, e-mail communication, May 14, 2013.

28. "Resources," Oregon Food Bank, http://www.oregonfoodbank.org/Our-Work/ Building-Food-Security/Community-Programs/Community-Food-System-Resources.

29. Kim Thomas, e-mail communication, May 13, 2013.

30. "Position Statement: Oregon Food Bank supports an Increased Minimum Wage," Oregon Food Bank, 2015.

31. Lynn Knox, Oregon Food Bank, e-mail communication, November 11, 2015.

32. Willy Elliot-McCrea, personal communication, February 20, 2013.

33. "Unemployment Rate," Google Public Data Explorer, http://www.google.com/ publicdata/explore?ds=z1ebjpgk2654c1_&met_y=unemployment_rate&idim= city:CT069100&fdim_y=seasonality:U&dl=en&hl=en&q=watsonville%20 unemployment.

34. US Census Bureau, "State & County Quick Facts: Watsonville, California," http://quickfacts.census.gov/qfd/states/06/0683668.html.

35. US Census Bureau, "Watsonville."

36. Elliot-McCrea, personal communication.

37. Elliot-McCrea, "Evolution of the Network: Food Banking, Nutrition Banking and Beyond," notes for speech given at Feeding America conference, October 10, 2012.

38. Elliot-McCrea, e-mail communication, October 2, 2015.

39. Ibid.

40. "Passion for Produce," Second Harvest Food Bank of Santa Cruz County, internal document, n.d.; Elliot-McCrea, e-mail communication, October 2, 2015.

41. Elliot-McCrea, personal communication, February 20, 2013.

42. Nick Saul and Andrea Curtis, *The Stop: How the Fight for Good Food Transformed a Community and Inspired a Movement* (Toronto: Random House Canada, 2013).

43. Ibid.

44. Saul, personal communication, May 8, 2013.

45. Saul and Curtis, *The Stop*.

46. Kathryn Scharf, e-mail communication, October 1, 2015.

47. Saul and Curtis, *The Stop*.

48. "Freedom 90 Charter," Freedom 90, http://www.freedom90.ca/charter.html.

49. "Frequently Asked Questions," Freedom 90, http://www.freedom90.ca/about.html.

50. Mike Balkwill, Put Food in the Budget, personal communication, May 9, 2013

51. "Freedom 90: The Union of Food Bank and Emergency Meal Volunteers" Freedom 90,www.freedom.ca.

52. Balkwill, personal communication, May 9, 2013.

53. Ken Regal, personal communication, January 22, 2013.

54. "Learn More about Hunger and Poverty," Just Harvest, http://www.justharvest.org/index.php/event/learn-more-about-poverty.

55. Regal, personal communication, January 22, 2013.

56. Regal, e-mail communication, September 26, 2015.

57. Regal, personal communication, January 22, 2013.

58. "Structure and Finances," Just Harvest, http://www.justharvest.org/about-us/structurefinances.

59. Regal, personal communication, January 22, 2013.

Chapter 8

1. The Coalition of Immokalee Workers, "About the CIW," printed flyer, n.d.

2. "Campaign for Fair Food," Coalition of Immokalee Workers, http://www.ciw-online.org/campaign-for-fair-food/.

3. Sean Sellers, Fair Food Standards Council, e-mail communication, September 25, 2015.

4. Beau DeHan, personal communication, February 6, 2013.

5. Laura Espinoza and Sean Sellers, personal communication, February 6, 2013.

6. Sean Sellers, e-mail communication, April 10, 2013.

7. Kyle Kennedy, "Publix Ads Challenge Walmart, Urges Use of Coupons and Weekly Deals," *The Ledger*, March 26, 2013, http://www.theledger.com/article/20130326/NEWS/130329383?p=1&tc=pg.

8. Silvia Perez, Coalition of Immokalee Workers, personal communication, February 6, 2013.

9. Dan Schlademan, director of OUR Walmart, telephone communication, March 22, 2013; Susan Berfield, "Walmart vs. Walmart," *Bloomberg BusinessWeek*, December 17–23, 2012.

10. "The Declaration," OUR Walmart, http://forrespect.org/the-declaration/.

11. Susan Chambers, "Reviewing and Revising Wal-Mart's Benefits Strategies. Memorandum from Susan Chambers to the Board of Directors," http://www .nytimes.com/packages/pdf/business/26walmart.pdf.

12. "Walmart at 50," Walmart, www.walmartat50.org. Retrieved March 25, 2013.

13. Schlademan, telephone communication.

14. Berfield, "Walmart vs. Walmart."

15. Robert Bruno, quoted in Mark Guarino, "Black Friday: Walmart Protests Liken Back to Days before Unions," *Christian Science Monitor*, November 23, 2012, http:// www.csmonitor.com/Business/2012/1123/Black-Friday-Walmart-protests-liken-back -to-days-before-unions-video.

16. Shan Li and Chris Kirkham, "Companies Are on the Hook for Contractors' Labor Policies," *Los Angeles Times*. August 27, 2015. http://www.latimes.com/business/ la-fi-nlrb-workers-20150828-story.html.

17. "The Harris Poll 2013 RQ Summary Report," Harris Poll, http://www .harrisinteractive.com/vault/2013%20RQ%20Summary%20Report%20FINAL.pdf; http://www.rankingthebrands.com/PDF/The%20Reputations%20of%20the %20Most%20Visible%20Companies%202013,%20Harris%20Interactive.pdf. "The 2012 Harris Poll Annual RQ Public Summary Report," Harris Poll, http://www .harrisinteractive.com/vault/2012_Harris_Poll_RQ_Summary_Report.pdf;http:// www.rankingthebrands.com/PDF/The%20reputations%20of%20the%20Most%20 Visible%20Companies%202012,%20Harris%20Interactive.pdf. Its score went from 69.25 to 66.3 from 2012 to 2013. A score of 65–69 is considered "Fair" on this index.

18. "Walmart to Boost Sourcing of US Products by $50 Billion over the Next 10 Years," Walmart, http://news.walmart.com/news-archive/2013/01/15/walmart-to -boost-sourcing-of-us-products-by-50-billion-over-the-next-10-years; Schlademan, telephone communication.

19. "How Wal-Mart's CEO Came to Support a $1 Billion Wage Hike," *Bloomberg Business*, February 19, 2015, http://www.bloomberg.com/news/articles/2015-02-19/ wal-mart-s-1-billion-wage-hike-spurred-by-customer-service-woes.

20. Schlademan, quoted in Cole Stangler, "Walmart Workers Still Unsatisfied, 7 Months after Widely Celebrated Pay Raise," *International Business Times*, September 23, 2015, http://www.ibtimes.com/walmart-workers-still-unsatisfied-7 -months-after-widely-celebrated-pay-raise-2106949.

21. Julius Getman, quoted in Berfield, "Walmart vs Walmart."

22. Shannon Pettypiece, "Wal-Mart Cuts Some Workers Hours After Pay Raise Boosts Costs." *International Business Times*, August 31, 2015, http://www.bloomberg

.com/news/articles/2015-08-31/wal-mart-cuts-some-workers-hours-after-pay-raise
-boosts-costs.

23. "Wal-Mart Wage Hike to $15 an Hour Would Cost It $4.95 Billion: Study," *Reuters*. June 10, 2016, http://www.reuters.com/article/us-walmart-wages -idUSKCN0YW2EA.

24. "The Declaration."

25. "Food Matters," The Food Trust, Spring 2012, http://thefoodtrust.org/pdf/ FoodMatters_Spring2012_5.pdf.

26. John Weidman, The Food Trust deputy executive director, e-mail communication, September 11, 2015.

27. R. Cotterill and A. Franklin, "The Urban Grocery Store Gap," Food Marketing Policy Center, University of Connecticut, Food Marketing Policy Issue Paper 8 (1995).

28. "Pennsylvania Fresh Food Financing Initiative," The Food Trust, http:// thefoodtrust.org/php/programs/fffi.php.

29. Ibid.

30. Ibid.

31. Ibid.

32. Weidman, e-mail communication.

33. Ibid.

34. Sabrina Tavernise, "Obesity in Young Is Seen as Falling in Several Cities," *New York Times*, December 10, 2012, http://www.nytimes.com/2012/12/11/health/ childhood-obesity-drops-in-new-york-and-philadelphia.html.

35. Weidman, e-mail communication.

36. Ibid.

37. "Farm to School Program," The Food Trust, http://thefoodtrust.org/php/ programs/farm.to.school.php; "Preschool Initiative," The Food Trust, http:// thefoodtrust.org/php/programs/preschool.php; "Nutrition Education," The Food Trust,http://thefoodtrust.org/php/programs/nutrition.education.php.

38. Jessica Robbins, Giridhar Mallya, Amanda Wagner, and James W. Buehler, "Prevalence, Disparities and Trends in Obesity and Severe Obesity Among Students in the School District of Philadelphia, Pennsylvania 2006–2013," *Preventing Chronic Disease* 12 (August 20, 2015), http://www.cdc.gov/pcd/issues/2015/15_0185.htm.

39. Tavernise, "Obesity in Young."

40. Weidman, e-mail communication.

41. The 2014 Farm Bill merged CFP with the Hunger-Free Communities program, with an additional focus of connecting low-income communities with federal food programs. The impact of these new guidelines on the program's funding is still yet to be determined.

42. Michelle Kobayashi, Lee Tyson, and Jeanette Abi-Nader, "The Activities and Impacts of Community Food Projects, 2005–2009," *Community Food Security Coalition,* October 2010, http://foodsecurity.org/pub/CPF_Activities_Impacts_2005-09 .pdf.

Conclusion

1. "State Minimum Wages: 2015 Minimum Wage by State," National Conference of State Legislatures. November 10, 2015, http://www.ncsl.org/research/labor-and -employment/state-minimum-wage-chart.aspx; "City Minimum Wage Laws: Recent Trends and Economic Evidence," National Employment Law Project, http://www .nelp.org/content/uploads/City-Minimum-Wage-Laws-Recent-Trends-Economic -Evidence.pdf.

2. "A Plan of Action to End Hunger in America," Food Research and Action Center, October 2015, http://frac.org/pdf/plan-to-end-hunger-in-america.pdf.

3. "The Nourishing Effect: Ending Hunger, Improving Health, Reducing Inequality," 2016 Hunger Report, Bread for the World, http://hungerreport.org/2016/?_ga =1.12785783.1393181138.1448438228.

4. "A Plan of Action."

Index

Note: page numbers followed by "f," "t," and "n" refer to figures, tables, and endnotes, respectively.